JOURNALS AND LETTERS

OF

Mother Theodore Guérin

MOTHER THEODORE GUERIN
From an oil painting made in Paris in 1858 by order of Bishop de St. Palais

JOURNALS AND LETTERS

OF

Mother Theodore Guérin

FOUNDRESS
OF THE SISTERS OF PROVIDENCE
OF
SAINT MARY-OF-THE-WOODS
INDIANA

———

EDITED WITH NOTES

BY

SISTER MARY THEODOSIA MUG, B.A., B.S. MUS.

———

FOREWORD

BY

HIS EXCELLENCY
THE MOST REVEREND JOSEPH E. RITTER, D.D.
BISHOP OF INDIANAPOLIS

SAINT MARY-OF-THE-WOODS
INDIANA
2005

NIHIL OBSTAT

FINTAN WALKER, PH.D.
Censor Deputatus

IMPRIMATUR

✠ JOSEPH E. RITTER
Bishop of Indianapolis

November 25, 1936

First Printing 1937
Second Printing 1942
Third Printing 1978
Fourth Printing 2005

TO THE MEMORY

OF

MOTHER MARY CLEOPHAS FOLEY

Who as Mistress of Novices for Eighteen Years and
Superior General for Thirty-six Years Labored
Unceasingly to Perpetuate the
Teachings of

The Venerated Foundress, Mother Theodore Guerin

and

By Her Long and Arduous Efforts Obtained
The Introduction of the Cause for the
Beatification and Canonization
of
The Servant of God

FOREWORD

Nearly a hundred years have elapsed since Mother Theodore Guérin came with her small band of nuns to Indiana. Her life was filled with crosses and trials, but was correspondingly rich in blessings. Out of the years of struggle and sacrifice there was born a flourishing community which she saw firmly established before her death in 1856.

Mother Theodore was an indefatigable worker, but she still found time to impart some of her courageous spirit, as well as her deep spirituality, through her many letters to her daughters in religion. These writings deserve careful reading. They attest her solid virtue and are at the same time a notable contribution to historical knowledge.

For some years the cause of the Foundress of the Sisters of Providence has been before the Sacred Congregation of Rites, the diocesan process having been completed in 1914. The *Journals and Letters of Mother Theodore Guérin* should arouse new interest in the cause of her canonization. We welcome their publication and hope they may win advocates for her cause and hasten the day when she will be accorded the honors of the altar.

✠ JOSEPH E. RITTER
Bishop of Indianapolis

Feast of St. Catherine
November 25, 1936

INTRODUCTION

In 1840, it was the twenty-second of October, Anne-Thérèse Guérin, in religion Mother Theodore of the Sisters of Providence, with five other Sisters alighted from a stagecoach in a woodland near the banks of the Wabash and was told that this was the journey's end. The journey had begun on the twelfth of the previous July from Ruillé-sur-Loir in France where was the Motherhouse of the recently founded congregation of the Sisters of Providence. The bishop of what was then called the Diocese of Vincennes, Indiana, Bishop de la Hailandière, had appealed to them for help, and they had accepted his invitation to share his labors and his indigence. To answer such a call had required of them readiness to undergo sacrifice and privation, but even the generosity that inspired them to undertake the long journey with all its hardships and mischances must have felt some strain when they found themselves at the home prepared to welcome them—a part of a poor farmhouse in the woods.

Yet it was not without significance that they called themselves Sisters of Providence; for on this rude beginning have been erected the achievements of their first century, Providence surely disposing and providing, since of merely natural aids there was always a dearth. On the spot which marked their journey's end there stands today their Motherhouse in America and alongside of it the noble buildings of the College of Saint Mary-of-the-Woods. And more impressive than any material monument to their success under a favoring Providence is their

Congregation itself; grown now well beyond the thousand mark from that small original band of six.

Dux femina facti. Providence selects its own instruments, and of however little human worth these instruments may seem to be when they are chosen, they grow under the hand of Providence equal to the work to be done. This is why we are justified in judging the stature of the worker from the dimensions of the work, and why we are not disappointed when we expect to find great endowments of nature and grace in one who has done great things in the service of God and His glory.

The woman leader of this exploit needed no ordinary qualities to carry out the mission assigned to her. The size of the work alone is proof of that. That she must have possessed these qualities, the accomplishment of her task in so remarkable a way, and the esteem and veneration in which her Sisters and all who knew her held her, would seem to make further attempts at demonstration unnecessary.

But in this case we have other and satisfying evidence of what she was in her *Journals and Letters* now for the first time published. They are an unconscious self-portrayal of a woman of courage and foresight who in the midst of discouraging difficulties built for the years to come; of a superior, firm in government and administration; and through all, of a human personality with an understanding heart that made her tolerant of the lesser generosity of others, and still left her competent to guide the weaker zeal of the halting towards the accomplishment of the great work in hand. We see her patiently enduring the affliction of ever-increasing ill health and at the same time careful to provide, as far as the limitations of times and means would allow, for the health and comfort of others.

Towards those who by their position in the Church had the right to give her directions or commands she always

shows herself humbly submissive. Still she could not overlook the duty that lay upon her to preserve intact as she had
received them the essentials and the spirit of her Institute.
This insistence on preserving the essentials of the Institute of
the Sisters of Providence was, naturally enough, the occasions
for some misunderstandings out of which was to grow the
greatest trial of her life. But she knew how to suffer in silence
and await with patience the dispensation of Providence. Of the
greatest trial, the difficulties with Bishop de la Hailandière,
there is little to be found in the *Journals and Letters*. The
reputation of another was involved here, and she was content
to let time bring her vindication.

The first Journal tells the story of the journey from
France to Indiana and recounts the happenings of the early
days at Saint Mary-of-the-Woods, The second and third
Journals are concerned with further journeying in the interests of the new foundation. The Letters show us Mother
Theodore at work, providing for the spiritual and intellectual development of the Sisters, planning and establishing
new missions, counseling and consoling her daughters in
their trials and difficulties, rebuking the slack and strengthening the discouraged.

But the *Journals and Letters* are of importance, not
merely as a human document portraying a holy life for our
edification; they have significance also as primary sources
for the history of the Church in the Middle West. The student of foundations will not overlook them, nor the writer of
the history of Catholic education. They are a not unim-
portant contribution to the evidence in any account of the
beginnings of Catholic education in the United States. This
alone, apart from all question of the edification they might
afford, would be a sufficient reason for bringing them to
light. The likeness they may bear to accounts of similar

foundations in other parts of the country or at other times does not make them superfluous, but rather tends to emphasize what is in some danger of being slighted in such studies, the supernatural element which is never lacking in the works that are works of God. This new account will help us to understand that the enterprises, conceived and undertaken and carried to successful issues in the cause of Catholic education in the United States, have been built up for the most part from nothing and out of nothing as far as material aids were concerned. But just for that reason they have demanded a larger outlay of human worth and devotion and a fuller outpouring of divine assistance. The Catholic worker in education is called upon to get out of his poverty results equal to what others get out of their wealth of resources. On a merely natural basis his problem is insoluble.

The work of the editor has necessitated the supplying of a historical preface and many explanatory notes. This work has been diligently and conscientiously done and in no way interferes with the objectivity of the document or prevents us from hearing the voice of Mother Theodore speaking to us across the years.

JOHN F. McCORMICK, S.J.

Loyola University, Chicago
July 22, 1936

HISTORICAL SKETCH

Interest in the writings of Mother Theodore is of long standing. In 1904 Benziger Brothers of New York published the *Life and Life-Work of Mother Theodore Guérin* and reviewers of the book made special comment on the letters it contained. They expressed the hope, too, that a complete collection would soon be forthcoming.

Since that time the cause for the beatification, and canonization of the holy Foundress has been introduced at Rome and her writings have been approved by the Sacred Congregation of Rites (*Acta Apostolicae Sedis*, September, 1926). This official sanction gives new value to the letters. It also awakens new interest; hence, as the old appeal for her letters has been often renewed of late, this compilation has been made.

Newman says, "For the arriving at the inside of things, the publication of letters is the truest method. Contemporary letters are facts." To these words of his it may be added that letters not designed for publication show the writer of them in the clearest light: they are a true self-revelation. Several of the press notices expressed similar ideas. Quoting but one, *The Month* (Stonyhurst, August 1904) drew this inference: "To judge from her letters she [Mother Theodore] must have been exceptionally gifted by nature and grace."

The volume now offered constitutes a companion book to the *Life and Life-Work of Mother Theodore Guérin*, and, with the notes interspersed, explains situations not fully developed in the biography. Though written primarily for the Sisterhood, it includes material that may be of general interest. Besides Community data hitherto buried in the archives, it contains items pertaining to the ecclesiastical history of Indiana and incidents that give color to pioneer life and the struggles and successes of foundation days.

This work does not purport to be a historical treatise, though every statement can be verified. It has a plan all its own, with digressions and personal touches that aid in the understanding of the characters and circumstances mentioned. The historian might prefer more formality, but the general reader will, no doubt, be in accord with Dobson who said,

> For detail, detail, most I care,
> (Ce superflu si nécessaire!)
> I cultivate a private bent
> For episode, for incident.

Of Mother Theodore's art in giving details, rich in episode and incident, the evidence will herein appear. Nothing escaped her. Though her narrations are lengthy, it has been thought well not to curtail them.

All the journals and nearly all the letters here given are translations from the French, revised chiefly from the early translations made by Sister Mary Eudoxie Marshall with a view to publication. All the original manuscripts went through two fires. The first fire occurred in February 1889, when the Motherhouse erected by Mother Theodore in 1853 was burned to the ground; the second, two months later, when the orphanage at Highland, Vineennes, was destroyed. After the fire at Saint Mary's Sister Mary Eudoxie took the material to Highland where she would have convenience to continue her work. She had the papers spread out on her table but was not in the room when the alarm of fire in the orphanage was given. Before she could get back to secure them, they had been thrown from the window with other articles and were scattered by a high wind. Some of the papers were picked up on the highway half a mile distant. How many were lost at this time cannot be known. Several of the letters recovered have holes burned in them by falling sparks. Mother Theodore's diary bears water marks but is otherwise intact.

The unacquainted reader will probably ask, Who was Mother Theodore?

She was a native of Brittany, France, born at Etables (Côtes du Nord) October 2, 1798. Her parents were Laurent Guérin and Isabelle Lefèvre. She was the second eldest of their four children, two boys and two girls. One brother died in infancy; the other, at the age of seven years, asleep on his cot near the fireplace, was burned to death when his bed covering accidentally caught fire. Her sister lived to old age.

Mother Theodore was baptized the morning of her birth and was named Anne-Thérèse. The registration made on the same day in the city hall bears the date, according to the calendar of the First French Republic, *12th of Vendémiaire of the year VII*. She was dedicated to the Blessed Virgin by her pious parents and was early trained to self-discipline and efficiency.

Under the old régime both families had plenty of the world's comforts, but the Great Revolution reduced them to necessity. The Lefèvres were staunch royalists of the lesser nobility. There is mention of them from the sixteenth century in the titles of the Duchy of Penthiévre. Hidden away in a trunk, a little cap worn only by ladies of rank proved Madame Guérin's title. But in those days safety lay only in concealment of all rank and titles. Gentility and refinement, nevertheless, were in the blood, and these with strong faith and intellectual keenness were characteristics that Madame Guérin transmitted to her offspring.

The ancestry of the Guérin family can be traced to the ninth century, to an old family in Italy originally from Venice, which had lived for several centuries in southern France. One branch migrated to the north of France; another settled in Ireland.

Laurent Guérin was a captain in the French navy. His record of service shows him to have been a worthy seaman and a faithful adherent to Napoleon. After the Emperor's defeat in Russia in 1812, M. Guérin landed in the south of France and proceeded on his journey home. To arrive more quickly, he left his companions of travel at Ouailles and set out alone across country. He had not gone far when he was waylaid by brigands who robbed and murdered him.

News of the tragedy so prostrated Mme. Guérin that it was ten years before she completely recovered. Anne-Thérèse, only fourteen years old at the time, had to assume the care of her helpless mother, of her little eight-year-old sister, and of the home. In addition poverty was their portion. Hitherto they had had their father's support; now, a cottage by the sea and a small garden plot constituted their fortune. Anne-Thérèse, inheriting from her father a soldier's courage and a tact for business affairs, faced her task heroically, with a child's inexperience, it is true, but with a woman's thought; and the faith that had been so deeply imprinted in her soul by her devout parents sustained her and gave her a wisdom beyond her years.

As a child she was buoyant, mischievous, commanding, yet amenable to parental authority. During the hard years of her youth she was kept braced up by her lively disposition. As she developed into womanhood she manifested those rare qualities that marked her for high achievement and sanctity in later life. She had a fine appearance and an attractive personality and, as might be expected, there were many offers for her hand. She promptly declined all, but gave no intimation of the desire she had cherished during those strenuous years of consecrating herself to God as a Religious. She had, in fact, pledged herself to this life on the day of her First Communion, when she was but ten years old, by an act of consecration as solemn as her confessor would permit. Though it was not a vow, she always considered her promise binding. She had a strong attraction for the Carmelites and early began to prepare herself for the cloister by practicing the austerities of the rule of Carmel and devoting herself to prayer.

But Providence had other designs on Anne-Thérèse Guérin. Unexpectedly meeting a Sister of Providence of Ruillé-sur-Loir, she decided to apply for admission into the newly-founded community. Ruillé was a country town on a small stream called the Loir in the Diocese of Le Mans. Its parish priest was the zealous Jacques François Dujarié, who "had been ordained in a cellar and said his first Mass in a barn." In 1806 hoping to repair the ravages made by the Revolutionists he engaged two pious young women to open, a school in his parish and visit the sick of the neighborhood. These devoted women were soon joined by others. They lived under a simple rule given by Father Dujarié and wore a plain secular dress. They took no vows and were free to withdraw at the end of the year, should they so choose.

After twelve years of this Christian and social welfare work, with branch houses in several towns, the little society passed from a semi-religious body to that of an organized community, with a rule formulated by Father Dujarié aided by Father Chapelle of the Fathers of the Faith (suppressed Jesuits), and approved by the local Bishop. A habit was adopted and the vows of Poverty, Chastity, and Obedience were taken by the older members. A superior general was elected in the person of Mlle. Josephine Zoë du Roscoät, daughter of Count Casimir Holland du Roscoät, one of the distinguished *émigrés* of the Revolution. In this estimable, mature woman, though but recently admitted, Father Dujarié found a leader for his rising community. But she lived only four years. However she achieved much in the time that God left her to Ruillé, and her example and prestige drew many others to follow in her footsteps, among whom was Aimée Lecor, who became Mother Mary, the Superior General that received Anne-Thérèse into the now prospering order. The name of Mother Mary, who held the office of Superior for nearly fifty years, will appear often in the letters of this volume.

Mlle. Guérin entered the Community at Ruillé-sur-Loir, August 18, 1823, and was given the name of Sister St. Theodore. Two years later, on September 8, 1825, she took her first vows; and on the same day she was appointed superior of the establishment of Rennes, a school numbering six hundred pupils. The children had been the despair of their teachers, but they were soon brought under control by Sister Theodore. Then through the children the parents were reached. Many, depraved and forgetful of all religious responsibilities, now awakened to a sense of Christian duty and of the social proprieties. In a very short time that section of the city, shunned by all self-respecting persons, became the pride of all the inhabitants. The Bishop of Rennes and the civil authorities attributed the reformation solely to the influence of Sister Theodore.

After nine years spent at Rennes superintending the large institution, Sister Theodore was transferred to Soulaines, a small country town. Here her time was divided between teaching and visiting the sick. In order to fit herself for the latter duty, she studied medicine and pharmacy under a Dr. Lecacheur. In view of her later career this training was a valuable asset.

Several certificates of high credit had been awarded her

by the school inspectors and, finally, in May 1840, a medallion decoration was bestowed upon her by the Academy of Angers (*Université de France*). Her sixth year in Soulaines was spent in anticipation of the work awaiting her in another part of the world.

The Sisters of Providence owe their establishment at Saint Mary-of-the-Woods indirectly to the holy and illustrious Bishop Bruté, first Bishop of Vincennes, who was consecrated on October 28, 1834. At that time there was but one priest belonging to Vincennes, the Reverend Simon Petit Lalumière, though two other priests were ministering in this large diocese, which included all of Indiana and the eastern third of Illinois. These two were the Reverend Irenaeus St. Cyr, in the north around Chicago, and the Reverend Joseph Ferneding in the southeast; but they were lent for only one year by their respective Bishops, Rosati of St. Louis and Flaget of Louisville.

Unbaffled, Bishop Bruté turned his eyes to France. Thither he went in the summer of 1835, and thirteen months later returned with nineteen missionaries—priests, deacons, and students—including four Eudists to found a college at Vincennes. One of the Eudists was the Reverend Stanislaus Buteux, who eventually became the first chaplain at Saint Mary-of-the-Woods.

The population grew rapidly in Indiana and soon more priests were needed. Sisters and Brothers also were needed for the establishment of schools. To procure foundations of Religious and to increase the number of the diocesan clergy, Bishop Bruté sent his Vicar General, the Very Reverend Celestin de la Hailandière, back to France in the spring of 1839. The latter was in Paris late in July when he learned of the death of Bishop Bruté and of his own appointment to the See of Vincennes, as a Bull of Gregory XVI, dated May 17, 1839, had named him Coädjutor with the right of succession.

Bishop de la Hailandière was consecrated at Paris on August 18th. Immediately he set out in quest of Religious for his diocese. The Congregation of Holy Cross in Le Mans gave him six Brothers with their Superior, Father Sorin, who became the renowned founder of Notre Dame University. They did not arrive in Indiana, however, until the fall of 1841. From Ruillé-sur-Loir the Bishop obtained the promise, with a proviso, of a colony of Sisters of Providence. The Mother General, replying to the Bishop's request wrote (September 12, 1839): "We have only one Sister capable of making the foundation. If she consents, we shall send you Sisters next summer."

That "one Sister" was Mother Theodore. When volunteers were solicited for the Indiana mission Mother Theodore was not among the number that offered themselves. She did not object to going to a foreign land, but, with her poor health and what she called her unfitness, she shrank from the responsibility of conducting the enterprise. Only when told that the great good work would have to be abandoned unless she undertook it did she consent to assume the charge.

In forwarding to Mother Theodore her authorization as the founder of the new mission Mother Mary wrote (June 16, 1840): "Notwithstanding your representations and the fears you expressed to the Bishop, it is decided that *you* will be the Superior of the Motherhouse, and the Superior General of all the other houses that shall be established from it, until such time as the two prelates, the Bishop of Le Mans and the Bishop of Vincennes, shall otherwise ordain."

As the names of those who were associated with the Servant of God in the foundation of Saint Mary-of-the-Woods will frequently occur, a few words about each one may be of interest.

Sister St. Vincent Ferrer, Victoire Gagé, was born at Le Mans, June 15, 1800; her death occurred at Saint Mary's July 1, 1874. She had been designated Assistant to Mother Theodore by the Superior General at Ruillé-sur-Loir. She was Mistress of the boarding school at Saint Mary's from its opening, July 6, 1841, until the following spring, when she was sent to begin the first establishment, which was made at Jasper, Indiana, March 19, 1842. In October, 1843, she took over the school in Vincennes, previously conducted first by the Sisters of Charity of Nazareth, Kentucky, then by the Sisters of Charity of Emmitsburg, Maryland. Here she remained until she was chosen to open the school in Terre Haute, which began classes January 2, 1849. She was Superior of the house in Fort Wayne from 1851 to 1856, and at Evansville from 1856 to 1860, after which she remained at the Motherhouse. Her declining years were passed in prayer and retirement, and the chronicle adds, "in light, humble employments at her urgent solicitation." She was noted for her deep piety, unobtrusive manner and cultured bearing, but most particularly for her affectionate charity and peaceful courage in the trials of life.

Sister Basilide, Josephine Sénéchal, born at Chateaudun, Eure et Loire Departement, February 10, 1812, died at Saint Mary's, October 12, 1878. She had been substituted for another Sister who was prevented by illness from coming to America. Though she had not been one of the many volunteers, when asked if she would be willing to go to a foreign country she replied: "Yes, if we shall not be separated from Ruillé. Assured that such would not be the case, as far as could be foreseen, she generously aligned herself with the others that had been chosen.

Sister Basilide was one of the teachers at the opening of the Academy in 1841, meanwhile assisting in the novitiate and presiding there at the recreation periods. She was Directress of the boarding school from March 1842 until August 1848. The next eight years she was Superior of the house in Madison. At the retreat of 1856 she was elected Procuratrix, an office she held until 1877, at which time she was retired from active service.

Sister Basilide had a virile character, a lively and amiable disposition. She is mentioned by Booth Tarkington in his "The Two Van Revels" as a great favorite among the pupils at the Academy, among whom were his mother, and, later, his three cousins.

Sister Olympiade, Therese Boyer, was born at Orleans November 11, 1806. She took pride in saying she was as old as the Community (which was founded by Father Dujarié in 1806). She died at Saint Mary-of-the-Woods, January 22, 1893. From her father, a soldier in the wars of Napoleon, she inherited an indomitable will and a great power of endurance. The first year of her noviceship she had training in a hospital in Orleans; the second, she spent at Soulaines under Mother Theodore. Although she had volunteered for Indiana she was not selected by Mother Mary for the new foundation. She then appealed to the Bishop of Le Mans, who advised Mother Theodore to accept her for the services she would be able to render—she was an expert in tailoring, an excellent cook, healthy and strong, with an aptitude for taking care of the sick. Mother Theodore, appreciating her ability and feeling that more help would be needed, was glad to receive her among the little band of missionaries destined for Vincennes. She made her profession at Saint Mary-of-the-Woods the following February

(1841). Mother Theodore taught her pharmacy and associated her with herself in taking care of the sick and dispensing medicines. Sister Olympiade's skill as a nurse and her gay spirits caused her fame to extend far into the countryside. She loved the poor and was zealous to do good to souls as well as to alleviate corporal sufferings. Her beneficiaries used to enjoy relating some of her quaint dicta. Once when a poor sufferer was moaning rather loudly she soothed him thus: "My good man, you have been so wicked, you ought to be glad you have one big pain." In later years her eyesight failed her. Thus incapacitated for duty she roamed about the grounds, affording the pupils much amusement by her cheerfulness and the tales she would tell of her experiences with the students of the early days and of her many other contacts. If they remembered her advice, given in season and out of season, they also remembered her favors—cookies, apples, peaches, and goose-berries. After her death her friends in the world had one hundred Masses said for her.

Sister Mary Xavier, Francis Louise Lerée, born in Berille, Manche, March 13, 1813, died October 8, 1897. She entered at Ruillé-sur-Loir for the Indiana mission, May 1, 1840, and received the habit July 16, the day of her departure for America. Her profession of vows took place August 13, 1843. Most of her religious life was spent at the Motherhouse. Some three or four years of missionary life, however, passed at Vincennes and Fort Wayne, give the valued letters found in this volume, which show her to have been deeply pious, especially devoted to the Blessed Sacrament, and always self-sacrificing in her domestic duties. She excelled in the practice of poverty and was most assiduous in her employment as clotheskeeper. Because of a tendency to quick temper, Mother Theodore affectionately called her "Fagots." She lived to a ripe old age, and was cherished very tenderly by the younger generation of Sisters. The necrology says:

"The price of her was from afar, and from the uttermost coasts."

The last and youngest of Mother Theodore's associates was Sister Mary Liguori, Louise Tiercin, who was born at Fougères, Brittany, August 11, 1818, and died at Saint Mary-of-the-Woods, January 25, 1847. Eleven years as a boarder in a convent school gave her a good education, which was supplemented by several years' experience as secretary to her father, who was the government's notary for ecclesiastical affairs. Her beautiful penmanship and her satisfactory handling of the business brought her letters of compliment from the Sovereign Pontiff, Gregory XVI.

Inclined to deep piety and asceticism she was permitted at the age of sixteen to bind herself by the vow of virginity, which she renewed every six months. At the age of twenty-two, hearing of the contemplated Indiana foundation she repaired to Ruillé-sur-Loir to offer herself for America. Talented, educated, showing unusual administrative ability, as well as possessing a comprehensive mind and a sympathetic heart, she soon was looked upon as the one to be the successor of the holy Foundress. Letters between Mother Theodore and the Superiors at Ruillé show that she was being trained for the office. Her early death, therefore, was a distinct loss to the rising Congregation of Saint Mary-of-the-Woods.

Sister Mary Ligouri took her vows of religion on August 19, 1842. Two months later she opened a school at St. Francisville, Illinois, and in December, 1843, at St. Peter's, Montgomery, Indiana. In August, 1844, she founded the mission at Madison, Indiana, where she remained until December, 1846, when she was brought home to die.

Though scarcely seven years had been her life-span in the Community, she had achieved the solid virtues of the mature Religious. It might truly be said she loved hardships.

Pious, zealous, and generous, possessing remarkable wisdom and tact, she left a lasting impression everywhere. And she had the distinction of having suffered persecution for justice sake. "They threw stones at us," she wrote from Madison, "but God did not permit that any should strike us. Rotten eggs, however, broke upon us; but that did not hurt us." . . . "We were snow-balled on our way to church; what matter?" . . . "Shouts and threats below our windows at night frighten the other Sisters very much. I do not mind them; these things do not keep me awake"—and so forth, this brave-hearted young Sister!

Another name that must be added to the list of associate foundresses is that of Sister St. Francis Xavier, Irma le Fer de la Motte, although she did not arrive at Saint Mary-of-the-Woods until a year later than the others. Bishop de la Hailandière secured her in Brittany and sent her in November, 1839, to Mother Theodore at Soulaines, hoping he could prevail on the Sisters to start at once with him for Vincennes. But the Sisters were promised to the Bishop only for the following summer; accordingly, Mother Theodore took her first postulant to Ruillé-sur-Loir to make her novitiate. Irma's health was so delicate all the time at Ruillé that she was not permitted to set out with the little colony that left in July, 1840. She had pledged herself to Vincennes, however, and she could not be happy elsewhere. Although her health had not improved, when she consulted the Bishop of Le Mans about her vocation he replied: "I do not know that you will arrive at Vincennes, but I do know that you must start."

Humanly speaking she was a failure—no health, no aptitude for the schoolroom, no fitness, apparently, for any kind of work. In announcing her Mother Mary wrote: "You will see, my Theodore, that she is good for nothing but to love God." Fourteen years later, after Sister's death, she wrote:

"I was mistaken, I was in truth, mistaken." Although Sister St. Francis never developed domestic ability, as she tells in her letters, her career in Indiana may fittingly be termed "the triumph, of failure."

Before leaving France she was permitted to take perpetual vows and in addition, a vow of consecration to the Blessed Sacrament. She arrived at Saint Mary-of-the-Woods November 15, 1841, and that happy event was looked upon as one of the greatest favors granted to the young Community.

A life of Sister St. Francis Xavier written by her sister, Madame de la Corbinière, was published in France in 1879 under the title, *Une Femme Apôtre*. An English, translation, was brought out at Saint Mary-of-the-Woods in 1882, bearing the title *An Apostolic Woman*, or *Life and Letters of Sister St. Francis Xavier*. An enlarged and revised edition published in 1917 retained only the subtitle. A reprint of the latter edition with considerable addenda was issued in 1935.

Sister St. Francis Xavier was born at St. Servan, Brittany, April 16, 1816; she died at Saint Mary-of-the-Woods January 31, 1856. Within a week after her arrival at Saint Mary's she was teaching Latin and drawing at the boarding school and in the novitiate. She assisted Mother Theodore in the training of the postulants and novices, and at the first election held in the Community (1848) she was chosen "Second Assistant and would have charge of the novices." This office she held until her death, which occurred eight years later. Her biography, so delightfully written, is an exposition of the motto on her tombstone—*Zelus domus tuae comedit me*.

Ruillé was generous in giving these worthy and accomplished subjects for the Indiana foundation. Mother Theodore had been decorated by the *Université de France*. Sister

St. Vincent and Sister Basilide also were licensed teachers, and the three novices were capable persons giving promise of great usefulness as they matured; while Sister St. Francis Xavier was a treasure of rare ability and holiness. The Right Reverend James O'Connor, Bishop of Omaha, wrote to Saint Mary's on June 12, 1882:

> When I visited you two years ago, I was sensibly impressed by the religious atmosphere of the place. I thought I saw in many of your members evidences of a higher order of piety. I was at a loss to account for this, at the time, not knowing how they could have enjoyed any exceptional advantages of training or directors. But, now, it is all plain to me. "What a man sows that shall he reap." I saw the harvest, but until I read of Mother Theodore and Sister Xavier, and their companions, I did not know the sort of seed that had been cast into the furrow.

Mother Theodore was given only a little more than fifteen years to achieve her work in America—years of poverty, labor, hardships, sickness, trials of all kinds that surrounded her "like bees and they burned like fire among thorns" (Ps. 117:12).

Exhausted by the conflict, rather than by years, she departed this life May 14, 1856, in the fifty-eighth year of her age. The veneration in which she was held by her contemporaries may be expressed in the words of St. Augustine, speaking of his own mother:

> She was the mother of Thy Servants, O my God, and those amongst them who knew her praised Thee in her, feeling Thy presence in her heart as witnessed by the fruits of her holy life.

*   *   *   *   *

The letters of Mother Theodore contained in this volume begin with the moment when she set out from her convent in France upon her career as a foreign missionary. A detailed narration of the events that happened within the ensuing three months constitutes her first letter, or "Journal of Travel," so called to distinguish it from her ordinary correspondence. It was addressed to her Sisters in France and was intended for all who, she knew, would be interested in the little band that had left home and country forever in order to win hearts to God in regions where He was scarcely known.

THE EDITOR

CONTENTS

ILLUSTRATIONS

JOURNALS AND LETTERS

OF

MOTHER THEODORE GUÉRIN

PART I

FIRST JOURNAL OF TRAVEL

——

A la Plus Grande Gloire de Dieu

𝕭𝖗𝖆𝖚𝖎𝖑𝖑𝖆𝖓 𝖉𝖊 𝖑𝖆 𝖗𝖊𝖑𝖆𝖙𝖎𝖔𝖓 𝖉𝖊 𝖓𝖆𝖙𝖗𝖊 𝖁𝖆𝖞𝖆𝖌𝖊 𝖊𝖓 𝕬𝖒𝖊𝖗𝖎𝖖𝖚𝖊
1840

THE moment of separation and of death had come at
last. We had to leave all. After having made the most
painful sacrifices, which had cost our hearts so much,
we had to break the last ties by tearing ourselves away from
our dear "Providence" of Ruillé, that home so tenderly loved by
all the Sisters of Providence.

It was the twelfth of July. That was the last day the sun
would shine upon us in this happy abode. At nine o'clock in the
evening, the hour for all to go to rest, we were embracing our
dear Sisters for the last time. We received also the last blessing from our Lord in our small but lovely chapel; in a word, we
bade adieu to all that was dearest to us upon earth. And to add

1

still more to the bitterness of this sacrifice, the hand of a
Mother, alas! was not to be raised to bless us.[1]

At length the hour had struck. We were obliged to tear
ourselves away from this heart-rending scene. The carriage
was waiting; we entered; the door was closed upon us, and all
was at an end for us (so to speak); it was like the moment of
death.

The weather was gloomy. The silence of the tomb reigned
all around. Nothing disturbed the monotony, save the dull
sound of the carriage wheels and the broken sobs of the poor
exiles, who offered to God in silence the sorrow of their heavy
hearts. The first night of our painful journey seemed very long;
it ended, however, and at the dawn of day we found ourselves
in the city of Le Mans, which we saw without seeing. We
alighted mechanically from the carriage and went to the house
of our dear Sisters, who lavished upon us their kind attentions
with touching affection.

How much we owe to Canon Lottin [Rector of the Cathedral at Le Mans] for his incomparable goodness to us! He
was like a father and showed us the most sincere devotedness. Owing to our inexperience, we should have made many
a blunder had it not been for his wise counsels. Moreover,
we owe to his generosity several pious gifts, especially that
precious particle of the Holy Cross of our Lord Jesus Christ,
which has been, I feel, our safeguard; and it will continue to
be such in the future, I hope, through the mercy of the
Almighty.

On the sixteenth, at four o'clock in the morning, this most
estimable priest was at the Cathedral, to offer the Holy
Sacrifice of the Mass for us and to feed us with our Viaticum of
Salvation, that aid from on high might be with us in setting
out upon our perilous voyage. Fortified by the saving

[1] Mother Mary, the Superior General, had gone to Rennes, to be present at
the retreat held there for the Sisters of the establishments in Brittany.

Mysteries and by the blessing of this good priest, we got into the coach, accompanied by our faithful friends, M. and Mme. Marie, and took the road to Lisieux, thence to Havre.

On the eve of our departure I had received a big bundle of letters from Rennes, Orleans, and Soulaines. I had not had time to read them all, having been obliged to remain up packing and roping our trunks until midnight. Now in the carriage, I opened one from Sister St. Edmund;[2] enclosed in it was another from M. Legros (the agent of the ship company), in which he told me not to start until he would notify me, as the vessel on which he intended us to embark was not yet ready. What was to be done in this conjuncture? We had already met with a number of contradictions in connection with the coach. Now that we were in it, we could no longer choose, but had to continue our journey and leave to Providence to arrange matters for us: which, indeed, was admirably well done. We traveled on without any trouble whatever, M. Marie providing for all our needs like a most devoted brother.

France seemed to wish to make us regret her even more than we did, by displaying before our eyes all her loveliness, for this part of Normandy is singularly charming. The exquisite steeple of the Cathedral of Séez! One would imagine it was lace-work, so delicate is the tracery. But, though there was so much calculated to attract attention, I have retained a confused idea of it all; for, when the soul is deeply preoccupied, the eyes look but see nothing.

We arrived at Lisieux at ten o'clock at night, and left at five the next morning, reaching Honfleur about ten. When I beheld the sea I nearly fainted. My eyes were covered with a mist, and

---

[2] Sister St. Edmund was one of the Sisters at Soulaines, the town from which Mother Theodore had corresponded with the ship's agent regarding the transportation of the travelers. She is mentioned with appreciation of her efficiency in the official letter from the University of Angers (April 15, 1840) when a medallion decoration was conferred on Mother Theodore by the French Academy, Department of Education.

there was a ringing in my head. I do not know what caused me to experience this painful sensation, which preceded all reflection on my part; moreover, I had been brought up on the seashore. Little by little I recovered from this state, and after having taken a very good dinner, ordered by M. Marie, we went aboard the steamboat, and were afloat on that sea which would soon carry us much farther. During the trip from Honfleur to Havre I was slightly seasick—a forerunner of something worse.

On the boat we made the acquaintance of the Superior of the House of Mercy established at Havre, a providential circumstance, undoubtedly, for when we arrived in the city there was no one to meet us or to see to our affairs. This good Mother took us to her convent; and then, accompanied by our indefatigable friends of Soulaines, she sought the vessel on which we were to embark. While they were going one way I went another, to provide for our most urgent needs by looking up a lodging for the night. We were received, as I have already said in a previous letter, by the Ladies of St. Thomas with that tender charity which characterizes them. You know all the particulars from our letters, and from what M. and Mme. Marie have related. These good people gave, no doubt, an exact account of all that concerned us; but, I am sure, they omitted to mention the eminent service they themselves had rendered us, their kind attentions, their generous, devotedness. It is impossible to say how much we owe to them. Oh, I shall never forget that room of "Le Bras d' Or" where I received their last farewell, that sad moment when I descended the stairs! Happily, I was soon in the open air on the square which led to the hospital. I could not see. My limbs would scarcely bear me up. Sister Olympiade led me to my room. When I got there I wept freely, which relieved me. I kissed my crucifix. It would remain with me to teach me that the life of a Christian, and especially that of a Religious, must be a life of privations and sacrifices. Going to the chapel I placed this last sacrifice, with those which had preceded it, at the feet of our Lord in the tabernacle.

Poor Sister St. Vincent's foot was getting better of the bruise caused by a trunk falling on it. Almost everything was ready for our departure, which had been deferred for three days but which was to take place the next morning, Sunday, July 26th. We had opened a box sent by the kind Countess de Marescot. Like a good mother, her tender solicitude had provided dainties and medicines for the long voyage of her children.[3]

We had written all our farewell letters, settled our accounts with the dear Ladies of St. Thomas, and at five o'clock in the morning bade them a last adieu. As we walked toward the wharf through the silent streets of Havre, we met an old sailor from the hospital, who had gone an hour ahead of us and was returning to say that the vessel would not sail that day! We had to return to the hospital. But we were glad of it; for at least we could assist at Mass, though we could not go to Holy Communion, having broken our fast.

The day passed rapidly and brought us to the twenty-seventh, the beginning, in reality, of our exile. We went to the wharf without exchanging a single word with one another, offering in silence our sacrifice to God. Reaching our ship (the *Cincinnati*), we ascended with firm step the narrow plank which was to separate us from the cherished land of France. I passed over first and was immediately followed by my companions. Having seen that all our baggage was on board, and having well paid the porters, we went to our room in order to recover a little from the excitement, then went on deck to look at Havre once more. There we learned that

[3] The Countess de Marescot, a benefactor of the Motherhouse of Ruillé-sur-Loir, sent to the Sisters embarking at Havre a box containing among other things, medicinal orange flowers, with 3000 francs in gold to help pay for their passage.

attempts had been made to steal some of our belongings; but nothing appeared missing, thanks to a good Breton who seemed very devoted to us.

We learned also that we were not to have a stewardess. A young woman was offered, but as her exterior did not please us we declined taking her. We had reason afterwards to congratulate ourselves on our prudent refusal.

On the Sea

It would be difficult to describe what passed in my soul when I felt the vessel beginning to move and I realized that I was no longer in France. It seemed as if my soul were being torn from my body. Finally we left the harbor. Fort Francis First was the last object we beheld. It too disappeared, for we were already on the ocean.

We watched the sails being unfurled one after the other; we saw them swelled by the wind, hurrying us away from our beloved France. I shall not undertake to describe what was going on aboard the ship. Sad, and leaning against the cordage, I was contemplating the shore of my country, which was flying away with inconceivable rapidity and becoming smaller and smaller at every moment. All was commotion and noise on deck, but, absorbed in painful reflections, we neither saw nor heard anything. We again offered up to Heaven the sacrifice of all that we loved, and we thought of those who were weeping for us.

O my dear friends! O my Country! How much it costs to give you up! And you, my sister, the only one left of my family,[4] I did not see before my departure but you were not

---

[4] Mother Theodore's sister, Marie Jeanne Guérin, then Madame Louis Barthélemy Le Touzé, still lived at the old home in Etables, Brittany, Côtes du Nord. It was completely off the way from the port (Havre) where the Sisters were to embark, and time did not permit Mother Theodore to go to see her. Madame Le Touzé, having a young family, was not able to go to Havre to see the Sisters off; hence the mutual sacrifice. She was "the only one left" that is,

forgotten, nor will you ever be, nor will he who has been such a father to me [Monsieur de la Bertaudiere, benefactor at Soulaines].

While I was thus preoccupied, my poor companions were weeping also; nearly all had bid adieu to a tender father or beloved mother. How their hearts were bleeding at that time!

The wind continued to blow and removed us farther and farther from land, Havre seemed like a speck. I was turned toward the city when a word of adieu struck my ear and drew me from my revery. It was the perfidious passport thief, of whom I spoke in my first letter. He was with his worthy associate, the carpenter of the vessel, who speaking both French and English might have been of great assistance to us, especially as he was the only one, either among the crew or the passengers, who knew the two languages. These men leaped into a boat which awaited them, congratulating themselves, no doubt, upon having deceived and robbed the poor French Religious! [The "good Breton" had stolen a purse which contained a considerable sum of their money.]

Soon after these men had left, the rolling of the vessel made us seasick. In a few hours we were so extremely weak that it was impossible to remain up; we were forced to go down to

of the immediate family, as it may be recalled from the preface that her father, Laurent Guérin, had died in 1814, and previously, her two brothers in their early childhood. The mother passed to her reward May 12, 1839—the year before Mother Theodore came to America. There were numerous relatives on both sides of the families of the Bagot, Renaut, LeClerc, LeBreton, Juhel, Guyomard, among many others, and especially the Heurtel, descendants of the celebrated Pierre Yves Heurtel, *Chef de battalion au 6 Régiment de la Garde Royale, Chevalier de la Legion d'Honneur.* To an older generation belonged the Venerable Messire Yves François Moro, Priest, and one time Curé of Etables; and of her own generation there were cousins, also of the Guérin name as well, who had entered Religion. Madame Le Touzé had a grandson, Abbé Theodore Le Touzé, in 1930 Rector of the parish of Pordic, diocese of St. Brieuc. Marie-Jeanne Guerin Le Touzé died February 2, 1877. One of her daughters entered the convent at Ruillé-sur-Loir in 1846, and in 1854 came to Saint Mary-of-the-Woods. She bore the name Sister Mary Theodore, given her in honor of her aunt, Mother Theodore.

our little room. There we were fit for nothing but to take to our beds. Courageous Sister Basilide, after giving to the fishes the little she had on her stomach, came to ask whether we needed anything. For two days she alone was able to take care of us. All were so weak that we could not get up to the second row of berths in our little cabins; these were not used for three days. Mattresses laid on the floor served for beds for the weaker ones among us.

On the third day the weather became calmer. We were feeling better and went on deck to look again for France; but, alas! it had disappeared. There was nothing to be seen but sky and water. I forgot to say that the first night we heard a cry in the hold—"Thieves! Thieves!" These cries were followed by a fearful uproar; then all became quiet again, the noise beginning anew the next night.

All my poor companions were nearly dead. Sister Basilide alone was able to be around. She went up to get something to eat and did honor to it. In order to get what we needed we had to make very energetic signs, otherwise we could not have made ourselves understood by the captain who did not know a word, no, not a single word of French; but he was, and continued to be, full of attention and kindness, ready to do anything to make things pleasant for us.

We were all very sick. When one was feeling a little better, she went to aid another, to hold the head of one who was a little sicker than herself. You never saw such a comedy. It had, at least, a good side to it, inasmuch as it proved to us that my charitable Sisters were more concerned about others than about themselves. We were too weak to talk, however; thus we passed the first day and the two following days, scarcely exchanging a word.

On the afternoon of the third day we saw the coast of England on our right, and on the next day, the coast of Ireland. On the fourth day the sea was as calm as the river Loir; there was no wind at all. We felt better and could ap-

RUINS OF HOME OF
MOTHER THEODORE
From photograph presented
in 1921 by l'Abbé Dutertre,
Vicar of Etables, France

At Etables (Côtes du Nord) Brittany

In this church
MOTHER THEODORE
was baptized and
made her
FIRST COMMUNION

CHURCH OF ETABLES

preciate our condition, which, however, was not very brilliant. I was surprised to find the ocean so thickly inhabited. From the deck we saw a number of ships sailing, each one in its particular direction. This gave to the sea an appearance of grandeur and of life. Eighteen ships were counted that day; and, later, as many as twenty-five or thirty were in sight on the horizon. We loved to see them, especially the French vessels, but we saw few of these.

This day is a notable one in our annals, for our appetites had returned. We were obliged to go to the captain's table for our meals. It was impossible to eat in our room on account of its closeness and bad air; we therefore seated ourselves at his table, which was covered with a poor cloth all in holes. Meat was served up *so-so*. Imagine us there without table napkins or spoons, obliged to eat with the blade of our knives, and a fork. Soup was served (M. Marie had given strict orders that we should have soup every day), a sort of thick soup made of meat, rice, vermicelli, and I do not know how many other things; nevertheless, it was not too bad. The captain swallowed his in the twinkling of an eye, then began to carve the fowl and beefsteak. Having served us, he filled up his own plate with meat, an egg, some stew, toast, cooked prunes, and a large dose of mustard and pepper. I mention everything—it is the American "hodge-podge." During the first days we had an abundance served up, but this lasted only a fortnight. We always had coffee in the morning and tea at night; such is the American, custom.

As soon as the captain had dined that day he went down hurriedly into the hold. We did not know the cause of his sudden departure, but all at once we saw coming up from the hold three men with pallid and wicked countenances, trembling as though they were at the foot of the scaffold. These half-naked men were robbers who had escaped from prison and hidden themselves in our vessel, evading the researches of the police. It was they who had made all the uproar

on the previous nights. For two days such a strict guard had
been   kept   that   these   unfortunate   creatures,
pressed by hunger, were now obliged to show themselves and
to come out of their hiding places. I think the captain threatened to throw them into the sea, for they cast themselves
down at his feet with such a supplicating look that one could
not help pitying them. He did not intend injuring them,
however, as only a moment later he ordered something to
eat to be given to them. They devoured the food with such
voracity that I thought they would make themselves sick.
The captain, to pacify the passengers on the lower deck, had
to give the robbers some work to do. While they pulled ropes
with one hand, they were cramming down enormous pieces
of biscuit.

The coolness and kindness of the captain were admirable.
Not content with treating them well, two days later he paid
their passage on an English vessel which was going to Havre.
We were much pleased to see them leave, one in particular
who struck us with fear a true *sans-culotte*. He was hardly
decently covered. His black cotton trousers were tied on
with a sort of handkerchief; a tattered shirt was the only
other garment he had on. His hair was half a foot in length;
his face so dirty and repulsive, and at the same time so vil-
lainous, one could not but have a feeling of fear on beholding
him.

The following days there was a great calm, The sea was
like a vast plain covered with motionless ships which, like
our own, were awaiting the wind. They looked like houses
or trees, according to their distance from us. About thirty
were in sight. It was interesting later to watch them sail and
to compare their swiftness with that of our *Cincinnati*; indeed, it was not without a little feeling of pride that we
beheld the latter always ahead, catching up with those that
had gotten the start of it, and leaving far behind those which

had been near it. Now and then there came a little gale together with a fog (the weather changes oftener on sea than on
land). While this lasted we made good headway, but went out
of our course, the wind being contrary.

On the fifth of August the wind blew violently from the
northeast. In the morning the sea was already troubled, but
in the evening, the wind increasing constantly, the waves
rose up in a fearful manner and dashed with terrible noise
against the sides of the vessel. I cannot describe the majesty
which the sea thus raging presents to view—those walls of
waves with their foam dashing on all sides, beneath which
lies a dark bed. The poor ships, awhile ago so tranquil, were
driven about and seemed on the verge of sinking. The waves
appeared like mountains that came to bury us in the depths.
Our ship, driven by an aft wind, broke through them impetu-
ously and braved them nobly. Everyone had disappeared
from the deck but ourselves. Finally, we also left this imposing yet terrible spectacle, and went down to our room
which, considering the height of the waves, was almost entirely under water. We said our Office, but the wind so
increased the rolling of the ship that we could neither stand
nor kneel down. We became seasick again, and this brought
upon me that inflammatory fever which nearly took me to
the depths of the ocean.

We went to bed, but it was not to sleep. The hurricane
continued with the same fury in the midst of absolute darkness. The sea lashed our poor ship fearfully; at every instant
we thought it would sink. It is a horrible thing to pass the
night at the bottom of a vessel, hearing continually the dreadful creaking which makes one fear that it will split open,
and that those whose only hope is in it will be engulfed forever. During this time we prayed to Mary Immaculate; she is
the sailors' Star and their great resource. We made the sacrifice of our lives to God, should it please Him to require it.

Our room had the appearance of a tomb into which death was making terrible efforts to enter. The flickering light of a lamp hung up in the captain's cabin, dimly seen through a trap-door, rendered the illusion still more striking. At last this night, so fearfully long, passed away and brought us to the morning of the sixth of August. But the feast of the Transfiguration was not to lead us to Tabor, for the tempest continued and did not cease until evening.

It was extremely painful to be sick on an American ship which was lacking everything, even good water. These privations, however, were not what caused me the most pain, nor was it the fear of dying without the sacraments, for I had prepared myself to the best of my power before embarking. On the other hand, the sacrifice of my life cost me nothing. To what could I be attached now that all my ties were broken? But what did affect me was the deep regret my poor companions would have suffered had they been obliged to confide my mortal remains to the waves. God was satisfied with our resignation. Five days later I was better, though I was not well a single hour on sea. At length the storm ceased and the greatest calm ensued.

During the tempest we had made good headway. Thus, I thought to myself, thus it is with tribulations: they bring us nearer to Heaven, the desired end of our pilgrimage.

The days previous to this tempest, which I have just described by anticipation, we perceived a three-mast ship which was sailing toward the west, like ourselves, and about as rapidly. In the evening I saw them hoist their flag. As I watched it closely I thought I could distinguish the French flag. You know that during the days of my French life never did I like the tri-color. Well! I liked that one. It made my heart throb, and tears came to my eyes. It was a French vessel. I greeted it with all my heart. It bears away my brothers to far distant countries! Our ship also hoisted its flag, and I was sorry, because the vessel seeing that we were Americans felt no sympathy for us and sailed off at once. We never saw it again.

In the evening we remained purposely on deck to see and examine at leisure the ravishing spectacle that was presented to our view. In order to describe it properly an abler pen than mine would be needed; if, indeed, it be at all possible to describe it:—that pure sky, the majestic sun which seemed to descend so proudly into the waters; that luminous ray darting from it, reaching even to us, and gilding the waves lightly stirred by the evening breeze; large fish joyfully bounding about, racing after each other, and playing amid the waves quite close to the vessel—all this adding to the beauty of the scene already so inspiring.

Oftentimes I enjoyed this pleasure, always new to me; and, I must say, it excites a delightful feeling toward the Author of these wonders. I felt happy in belonging to Him and said within myself: What will our good God be in our True Country, since even in our exile He is so great, so powerful, so magnificent! Often, too, we beheld the moon rising at the other extremity of the heavens. It also had its particular kind of beauty, and sometimes the aurora borealis added still more to the magnificent spectacle. After contemplating these imposing scenes, we went down to our cabins to mingle our voices with Nature's majestic voice in blessing and praising its Author. Having finished our prayers, we threw ourselves on our pallets, or rather, placed ourselves in our boxes [berths]; generally, however, not to find repose. In the morning we felt more tired than we did the night before.

How can I express the sadness that filled our souls on the first Sunday that we had to pass on the ocean! Like the prodigal son we said: The servants in our Heavenly Father's house have bread in abundance, and we are dying of hunger. Retired within our room, we read the Ordinary of the Mass aloud and united our intention with that of the priests who were celebrating, and with the faithful who had the happiness of assisting at the Holy Sacrifice. Oh! with what earnestness we begged the Almighty not to abandon us, and to bestow on us a share in the fruits of the Holy Mysteries!

It seemed to me that Heaven heard our entreaties and that we were nearer to God. I was so fully persuaded of this that every day, leaning against the vessel in a little corner that I had appropriated on deck, I prayed for all our friends. I prayed for you, dear Mother, for you all, my very dear Sisters, for you, dear benefactors to whom we owe so much, and especially for you, dear friend, or rather mother [the Countess de Marescot] who, just as we were on the point of leaving France without even having the means wherewith to depart, came like a visible providence to withdraw us from this state of painful anxiety. Yes, by an unprecedented example of generosity, and that so eminently Christian, you provided for all our wants and more. Ah! With tears of gratitude we daily offer most earnestly our fervent prayers to Him who considers as done to Himself whatever is done to the least of His own. He will keep an account of your gifts. Your gold is placed at interest in His eternal treasury. If at some future time we are able to do any good in a foreign country, you will have a great share in it; for what would have become of us without you?

I owe it to the exactness of my narrative to state that I prayed most particularly for my friends at Soulaines. I am more frequently in spirit at Soulaines than anywhere else. It is in the poor barn [of a church] there that I make my visits to the Blessed Sacrament; there I hear Mass; in a word, it is there that I transport myself in spirit to pray where, so often, I was alone with my God.

Our situation did not change much from day to day. We said our prayers in common and made our spiritual reading.

Whenever I was able to be up we all passed our days on deck. The Sisters sewed, studied, walked up and down the captain's room. We were mistresses of everything around us, and, wherever we installed ourselves no one intruded.

I passed my days contemplating the sea, the clouds, the vessels, the fish. The aspect of the sky is much more diversified on sea than on land. Oftentimes the sea was calm like an immense mirror upon which was very exactly reflected the pure sky. Mist from the waves, lit up by the rays of the sun, displayed as it were thousands of pearls and all kinds of precious stones, which seemed to frolic about over a vast extent of the surface. The effect was admirable. The slight tremor of the ruffled waves, set in motion by a light breeze, is perceptible only a short distance; the waters beyond seem perfectly motionless.

What a religious pensiveness seizes the soul on beholding the sky and the ocean, which seem to the voyager as the only objects in creation! And oh! how magnificent is the setting sun, which found me every evening at the same spot like a faithful courtier! And how beautiful and majestic is its rising when, as the Prophet says, "He hath rejoiced as a giant to run his course!"

From the sixth I had been deprived of the pleasure of contemplating these beauties, but on the thirteenth my good Sisters dragged me up onto the bridge, for the air in our room had become foul. An English ship on its way to Europe passed near us; we charged it with our best compliments, but presume it failed to carry out our commission.

Once quite a novel scene attracted us from our revery: a whale of enormous size appeared. It spouted columns of water to an amazing height, and from time to time the monster came towards us; it came, in fact, within a gunshot and exhibited its massive head, which seemed as big as a house. But our proximity was not to its liking, it seemed, for it directed its course elsewhere, lashing its tail with such vigor that had a ship come in its path it would have overturned it.

Finally we came to the fifteenth of August, that day of joy and happiness for all true children of Mary. We were all somewhat depressed at being deprived of the happiness of receiving the Sacraments on that day. Instead of the ringing of the merry bells, we had the rumbling of the waves; for the chants of the Church, we heard only the rough voices of the sailors, or the cries of a dozen children in the hold of the vessel. But we made the sacrifice of everything, and again addressed our petitions to the Almighty with our wonted confidence, uniting ourselves to our brethren who, happier than we, were singing canticles to the Lord in His holy temple.

The sixteenth was remarkable for two incidents—it takes so little on shipboard to produce a sensation—: the first was a fire caused by the carelessness of a sailor who had let the contents of his pipe fall on his bed. Happily the fire was noticed before it had burnt farther than the mattress and hammock. The second event was more tragic. The billows were covered with blood, and death had captured another victim. Do not be alarmed. It was only a fish which had been caught with the harpoon, a sea hog (porpoise) so large that six of our vigorous sailors were hardly able to drag it aboard. It lashed away with its tail in a most frightful manner and its cries were a smothered sound, a sort of grunt, such as a hog that is being killed would make. It struggled so violently that no one dared approach it; but at last one sailor braver than the rest, evidently a butcher by trade, ventured, and cut its throat with a knife, thus finishing the work.

The fish resembles very much the animal mentioned above; its flesh has exactly the same taste as pork. In its snout, about ten inches long, were a number of very sharp teeth. I counted eighty-two in the upper jaw, the longest about three-fourths of an inch, all shaped like a stiletto. The flesh furnished food for all the crew during a week. We also ate of it to satiety. The comrades of the porpoise, whether through revenge or to have their share of the prey, pursued us for more than two hours. They leaped about showing their enormous, wide-open mouths. They were like a shoal of fish. This species is quite common in the ocean; we saw thousands of them in calm weather. Arranging themselves side by side, like a well-disciplined army, they move from one part of the ocean to the other. We were very much interested in these aquatic squadrons.

On the seventeenth there was rough weather again, but we were now somewhat inured and were not frightened. This storm was succeeded, as is ever the case, by a profound calm which left us in perfect solitude. We saw absolutely nothing but sky and water—no more vessels, no more French flags, and even no more fish—nothing!

Now I must make you acquainted with our traveling companions. You already know from our previous letters our little captain and his crew. You remember we told how attentive he was, never once changing his manner toward us. But I do not think I spoke of two Jews we had on board, one a venerable Rabbi, who did not think it beneath his dignity to show us a pleasant countenance. The other seemed more concerned about his traffic than his prophets. We seldom spoke to him. Notwithstanding the advances he often made, he did not succeed in gaining our favor. Our Bretons were more fortunate. We took them under our protection, especially Brassier, his wife and six children.[5]

---

[5] Thomas Brassier, with his family, was coming to seek his fortune in the United States. Mother Theodore engaged him to follow her to Indiana to work for the Community; she advised him however to remain in New York until she would notify him to come, and she even promised him the money necessary for the journey, with the understanding that he would pay it back from his wages. He arrived at Saint Mary's late in the fall of 1840. Some of his descendants are still in the neighborhood.

Among the Germans there were two or three persons in whom we took special interest because they were so miserable. One was a poor old woman over seventy years of age, who was always sick, though in appearance as strong as a person of forty. She seemed to have been well reared. Like myself, she owed her salvation only to the orange flowers given us by the good Countess de Marescot. There was another family which was quite interesting. It was composed of three brothers and three sisters, tenderly devoted to one another. They were going to settle in America.

After the tempest of the seventeenth and the calm that followed, there came a good aft wind. All our sails were out and we went at the rate of eight knots an hour. But the rolling was so great that we were thrown and bruised in our beds and were obliged to leave them and spread our little mattresses on the floor. The vessel rolled about like a nut on the sea. When it leaned to the right, it drew our beds and all that was in the room to that side; then, regaining its equilibrium, it threw us with equal violence to the left. Every-thing aboard shared the same fate. There was a terrible noise in the captain's room, and on the lower deck also; bottles, pots, kettles, plates, and dishes, were all mingled together. In our cabin there might have been seen dishes rolling from one side of the room to go and give a noisy embrace to jars of preserves on the other. The Sisters, too, might have been seen falling down as if their legs had been cut off at one stroke. Our dear plump Sister Liguori fell against me with all her weight. I thought I was killed. Fortunately I avoided the impact somewhat, but one of my legs was terribly bruised. Four times we lighted the candle, but it could not be kept in place. Never did we laugh so heartily as that evening. The next morning the sport continued, the same rolling. The Sisters went up for breakfast, climbing with hands and feet as best they could; but scarcely were they at table when suddenly the rocking became so violent that it upset the plates and dishes, and made a marmalade of everything. Poor Sister Liguori, thrown down by the shock, fell under the table. Luckily they were alone.

When a vessel is thus tossed about, it is surprising to feel one's self lifted up by the air, and then to feel an enormous weight which seems to crush one down like grapes in the wine press. The force of the air in these circumstances, and the pressure it exerts on the body, can scarcely be imagined.

This rocking and rolling had brought us to the Banks of Newfoundland, where we arrived on the twenty-second, twenty-six days after our departure from Havre. All day there was a pleasant aft wind, so that we passed the Banks in twenty-four hours. The water here is green, just like the color of our glass bottles. We saw neither fish nor bird. The next day was very calm; but on the twenty-fourth, good St. Bartholomew sent us a great storm for the anniversary of the final decision of our departure for America. Our sufferings were now greater than ever. Poor Sister St. Vincent could bear up no longer. She was quite sick during the entire passage, particularly in this last part of the voyage, but was always pious and resigned, as she is wont to be. She edified us very much by the simplicity of her faith and, indeed, by all the virtues of a good Religious. All suffered in body, heart, and mind. Everything in us seemed to change, except charity, which united us in God. All love one another tenderly, and this consolation is well calculated to support us under the pains we suffer, and also under those which await us.

For several days there were contrary winds and very dangerous currents. The sea was agitated as far as the currents reached; but on the sides, in front, and behind them, it was calm; one might have thought they were marked by a line. The bubbling of the waters was interesting to look upon, but it pleased us particularly because, in consulting the map, we found that it announced our near approach to New York. The captain made his review on this day (August 29). There were fifty-eight passengers, we being the only cabin passengers.[6]

On the thirtieth we saw three whales together. They were near enough for us to examine them. The back of a whale is of a dark brown color. When the enormous creature is without fear its movements are slow and calm. It spouts out water apparently by respiration, as its jets seem to be regular. The animals that we have noticed on the sea seem less savage than those on land; they have not so often felt the inconvenience of being in the neighborhood of man, hence they are not so mistrustful. On the same day we also saw pretty birds playing in the cordage. They let themselves be taken in hand quite easily. One of them was brought to me and I examined it closely. They are much like our swallows, but the plumage is softer. When I had looked at the dear little thing as long as I wished, I gave it its liberty, and it did not wait to be pressed.

This day was also the fifth Sunday that we passed on the ocean. The weather was serene and the sea as smooth as a mirror; thus it happened on each successive Sunday, which was quite singular. It would seem that God wished to give us a symbol of the Christian's day of rest by the calm of nature. And, what was most striking was, on Monday the wind would always begin again.

The thirty-first was a Monday. A furious storm arose. The sea was fearful. Almost all our sails were furled. One was nearly carried off, notwithstanding the efforts of the whole crew. Several were torn asunder. The masts were

---

[6] Just here in Mother Theodore's manuscript "brouillon," rough draft, she terms it—the only copy of this narrative now extant, are found the words *Ce journal est envoyé à Ruillé jusqu' à là*.

bent like reeds. I had never seen the sea so rough. It was fearfully beautiful.

The ship seemed to float amid a cloud of snow, extending all around for a distance of over sixty feet. We were all wet by a sort of a mist produced by the dashing of the waves against the vessel.

Nothing was heard on board but screams and lamentations. The captain, his officers, and all the crew were constantly at work, drenched with perspiration and salt water, not taking time either to eat or to rest. The women were crying, the children screaming.

Our good Rabbi was shedding bitter tears. When one terrific crash came he thought he heard someone say we were sinking. Giving a loud cry, and throwing his arms about a man near by, he exclaimed: "O my friend, I shall not leave you; we shall die together! Adieu, my wife and child"—and so on.

While all this was happening below, we were above on the upper deck at our usual places contemplating all that surrounded us, calm and resigned to whatever the Lord might ordain. Our Rabbi, when he had recovered a little from his fright, came up trembling and was astonished to find us so tranquil. I told him that we had asked pardon of God from the bottom of our hearts, and that we hoped to obtain it through the Precious Blood of Jesus Christ and the merits of His holy Mother. He answered not a word. Night having come on we could no longer remain on deck; we therefore went down to our prayers as usual and, having invoked Mary, Star of the Sea, we went to bed. During the whole night, and the next day, also, the storm continued.

The morning of the third day was more calm. We had left the ocean and entered upon the bay leading to New York. The weather now had become very mild. The sea was clear enough and tranquil enough to let us view a shoal of pretty fishes, bright blue in color, which followed the ship in amazingly vast numbers. We saw also some cod, but only a few. Our captain tried to fish, but as he had no bait, these little creatures seemed to enjoy making sport of him.

At three o'clock the pilot arrived. I think I have already told you of his incivility and haughty manner, and need not now repeat; for I remember having sent you a letter of appalling length while we were yet in the bay. After supper that evening we saw for the first time the sun sinking into the waves. This spectacle, as I have said before, is always admirable, but that evening it was particularly beautiful; indeed, ravishing. During the night we heard a singular noise. I got up at one o'clock to investigate. Looking through the porthole I saw we were on a rapid current over which the vessel was moving swiftly; that was what occasioned the unusual noise.

At dawn the next day the first object that met our eyes was land!

I have already described to you *de mon mieux* what went on in my heart at that moment. Today I shall spare you a repetition of my jeremiads. Having said our prayers with the greatest union of spirit, we went on deck and saw, quite distinctly, the land toward which we had been sailing for forty days.

We saw trees, gardens,—a superb view. Imagine our surprise when, thinking we should find a wild, uninhabited land, we saw houses of dazzling whiteness, with columns of charming peristyles.

The gardens are beautiful and perfectly kept. This magnificent landscape varied at every moment and seemed always to increase in loveliness. The entrance to New York is, according to general opinion, the most beautiful sight it is possible to behold. A contrary wind, scarcely perceptible, prevented us from entering the channel and forced the pilot to tack about every quarter of an hour, as though it would wish to give us more time to admire these beauties.

At two o'clock we entered the channel, at this point eight miles from the city. Here nature and art appear to vie with each other in order to embellish this delightful spot. In particular, there is a hilly plateau to the south, and a sort of little town that is called Quarantine. The houses there are all new, built in amphitheatre form, each one surpassing the other in beauty; but of the American style, which is quite pretty.

If the land offered objects for admiration, the sea presented a spectacle no less enchanting. Ships were moving all around us, some coming in, others going out. Our captain called attention to a packet coming behind us which had started from Havre before we had. This seemed to please him very much—such is the pride of the mariner. We also beheld a great many steamboats, which proudly, in spite of wind or tide, seemed to laugh at our efforts. An American frigate, also, entered ahead of us, but we did not admire its structure; it was badly built, too large and heavy. Besides, its sails were one-third too low. Advancing thus, little by little, we came to where the vessels cast anchor. This is the bay proper, and at five o'clock we were at anchor [Friday, September 4].

At New York

"At last, we have arrived," we said to one another, "the perils of the sea are passed!" We threw ourselves on our knees, and with hearts full of gratitude we offered our thanks to God for all the benefits He had bestowed upon us. We prayed to Him also for our future; we could not but feel some anxiety about it. The ship ceased to move. What joy for the Americans! They were going to see again those that were dear to them. They were expected. The telegraph, in announcing the arrival of the *Cincinnati*, had caused many a heart to throb; but not one was anxious about us, not one was throbbing for us. "Behold," we said, "houses, but not our dear Providence home. Behold people, but not our Sisters. We shall not meet with friendly faces, with devoted hearts, in this foreign land. Here we shall be looked upon with contempt, perhaps with hatred; at most, we shall meet only pity."

While these painful reflections were oppressing our hearts, the Custom House officers came to visit the ship. They were very friendly but no one was so kind as the good doctor of whom I have already written, and who came now bringing refreshments to us. In our circumstances his kindness did more good to our hearts than to our stomachs. I am happy to give you the name of this gentleman—Doctor Sidney A. Doane. Later he told the people it would bring a blessing to any one who would render us the least service. Do pray for him, for he is a Protestant. Without him, what would have become of us in New York? It was he who informed the Bishop of our arrival, because the deputy of Monseigneur de la Hailandière [the Bishop of Vincennes] had not yet arrived in the city. It was he who spoke to us the first consoling words we heard in the New World, so new to us, "Soon," he said, "you will be surrounded by numerous friends who will be happy to see you. The Bishop of New York will be much pleased to make your acquaintance. You will find in his Vicar General, Father Varela, a real father. He is a Spanish priest who speaks French, and an excellent man whose life is spent in doing good."[7]

[7] The Vicar General mentioned above, the Very Reverend Felix Varela, was according to Thomas F. Meehan (*Catholic Historical Review*, January, 1919), "a priest from the Bishop's House in New York, a Cuban driven here by political troubles in 1823. He was a solid theologian, wrote several works in his native language, which circulated extensively throughout Cuba and Spanish America. In English he contributed largely to Catholic papers and periodicals." The name of this distinguished ecclesiastic appears several times in Mother Theodore's diary in the record of her correspondence.

Doctor Doane presented us with some beautiful peaches which he himself had gathered, and the other good things he had brought. His words, and his manner of acting—a stranger, a non-Catholic, and an *American*—surprised us so much that we were almost mute. I could stammer out only a few words of thanks, and already he was far away, enjoying secretly the satisfaction of having done a good deed.

Scarcely had he vanished than we began to share his gifts with our poor traveling companions. The Rabbi had given me a fine orange when I was sick. I now gave him one in return and, for interest, added a pear of enormous size. The other Jew also received his portion, and our old lady was not forgotten. Finally, half an hour after the doctor's departure, many a heart was blessing him while partaking with a keen appetite of the provisions he had brought.

I told you before that the captain, not having been able to prevail on us to go ashore, notwithstanding the privilege granted by the Custom House officer and the doctor, left us for New York. That was before the doctor's second visit. Here again we see how Providence directed the poor exiles; for, had we landed that evening, having no recommendations, we would have been obliged to stay at a hotel. And which one should we have selected without knowing a word of English, in a city where you would have to speak to twenty persons before meeting one who could understand you? And what would have become of our baggage? Here, all this is very disconcerting; one can scarcely understand it far from the scene. However, the departure of the captain left us sad; we had lost our human support. See what frail man is! Even the later visit of the physician had not altogether reassured us. We were uneasy. Our door was fastened with more than usual care; our prayers were not said with that secure feeling we had before; and sleep did not enter our cabin that night.

As soon as day dawned we arose in the hope of getting rest on *terra firma*, and now we prayed with more confidence than on the preceding evening. On deck we could see how much nature had changed its aspect since the day before. The sea was frightful; it seemed impossible to land. To attempt such a thing would be too expose ourselves to perish in the port. The rain fell in torrents.

This too was something providential, for if we had landed then we would have disturbed the plans of Providence which afterwards proved so advantageous to us. The captain's mate went to get fresh provisions for our breakfast; we added what we had received and arranged all on the table. The milk that Dr. Doane had brought we put into the coffee, thus giving our Americans a breakfast *à la française*.

Up to three o'clock in the afternoon nothing seemed to favor our landing, and the next day would be Sunday! We had already passed five Sundays on board, besides the Assumption, hearing Mass only with the fishes. We thought that that was enough. The council opened, but the votes were divided, and we adjourned without coming to a decision.

While we were in this perplexity we saw a small row-boat coming toward us. Great was our joy on recognizing our captain. He was accompanied by two gentlemen unknown to us; one of them, dressed in black, had a venerable appearance, and I would have taken him for a priest had he worn a cassock; but he was dressed like a secular. He was, however, the Spanish priest, Father Varela, of whom Doctor Doane had spoken, sent by the coadjutor Bishop [Most Reverend John Hughes] out to the bay for us. He gave us the most gracious welcome. He said that he had come on the part of his Lordship, that we were not to be uneasy about anything, that he had found lodgings for us with a French lady where we would be perfectly well received. The captain appeared happy to see us in such good hands. He showed us a thousand courtesies and was full of attention for Father Varela. Everybody gathered around us and envied our lot, for they were still to remain on board another whole day before being permitted to land.

A pretty little green rowboat awaited us at the foot of a ladder, but the sea was frightful. No matter. We had to go. We bade farewell to our good captain, then embraced our poor old woman, who came to us weeping and threw herself into our arms. The others wept, also, and called down upon us a thousand blessings.

I whispered to the Sisters, "Come, if we have to die, let us die, but say nothing!" With these words I descended first, by the rope ladder, without experiencing the least uneasiness; the others followed, none showing fear except poor Sister Ligouri, who was pale and trembling as though she were sure of meeting death in the waters.

As soon as we had all descended, and Father Varela and the two porters had followed with our packages, which amounted to little or nothing, the necessaries for two days, the boat moved off, full as an egg. The rowers battled with the waves. The water entered in on all sides. The rain continued to fall. We were rocked as we had never been before, but I paid no attention to this, my eyes being fixed on the vessel we had just left. We exchanged farewells with our friends whom we should probably never see again but in the Great Valley. Our hearts were heavy. We were leaving those with whom we had suffered. We were leaving our poor ship which, during forty days, had been our only hope. To leave it was truly painful, so true is it that misfortune binds hearts together.

Before knowing it we were at the dock. The boat entered under a sort of porch built out over the water and stopped at the foot of a stairway, where we got out. The sea was no

longer beneath our feet, we were on the soil of America!
Impossible to describe what passed within our hearts at that
moment! As for myself, I was so affected that I could scarce
utter a word. How I longed to be alone! But, no. We had to
talk, even to be more amiable than usual, to manifest our
gratitude to our kind doctor whom we now met again, for we
had come to Quarantine where we were to take a steamer
which was due to pass there in a few minutes. Doctor Doane
took us to his own house where a good fire awaited us. We
dried our clothes a little, and ten minutes later we boarded
the waiting steamboat.

There we took leave of the doctor, and, always accompanied
by Father Varela, we went on sea again, but only for a short
time. Half an hour later we were at New York, or at least at
the wharf of that city, which we did not see, for we only passed
from one boat to another, and thence in two carriages to a
country place named Brooklyn—à une campagne nommée
Brooklyn—and which I had mistaken for the city of New York.
Hence my error in writing [Journal de Soulaines] that New
York had no streets nor public squares, etc. Be so kind as to
consider that a misstatement.

Every one who saw us seemed thunderstruck, or changed
into a statue of salt like Lot's wife, and stood still, staring at
us as if we were some extraordinary beings. But we tried not
to be put out of countenance, and neither good nor evil was
done us.

Arrived at Mrs. Parmentier's, we were received as angels
from heaven; which demonstration quite covered us with
confusion. It would be impossible to relate all the attentions,
the tender care, the kind forethought of which we were the
object during the five days that we spent in the house of
this excellent Christian. I wrote long details of all this, and
also of the generous devotedness of good Mr. Byerley, who

succeeded in getting our baggage through without Custom House inspection, at the cost of infinite trouble to himself.

I believe I also told you how much we owe to the Reverend Father Varela, not only for the kindness shown at our landing but also during the whole time that we remained in Brooklyn. This reverend gentlemen did not stop there, but carried his charitable attentions so far as to send a devout young Englishman to accompany us to Philadelphia. As the latter could not speak French, Mr. Byerley not wishing him to be our only guide gave us his head clerk as interpreter during our journey. He spoke French very well, though he was an Italian. See how many delicate attentions we received from the good friends we found in New York.

I wrote you also about the Church [St. Peter's, Barclay Street], of its elegance, of its being as light as if it had been made of crystal, of the dazzling whiteness of its walls, of the pews which were of solid mahogany, of its galleries with four rows of seats placed in tiers, which give it the appearance of a theatre. The speaker seemed to be talented, though we really understood nothing of his sermon. His audience listened attentively. The Mass and Vespers were sung to music which, however, did not particularly please me. I had a great deal more devotion in our poor barn at Soulaines. notwithstanding the lack of harmony there. The church was filled with men, there were at least as many men as women, and all comported themselves perfectly well. We did not see one woman who did not have on a bonnet. Here the shepherdesses wear bonnets and even the milkmaids while milking their cows. The milk is carried around in quite a stylish conveyance drawn by two horses at such a rate that one might think it were the president's carriage rolling along. The men who distribute the milk from door to door are dressed up as if for a wedding. It is impossible to have any idea of the extravagance of the Americans without having witnessed it.

The houses have an elegant appearance, especially those in the country. The city of New York is beautiful, but of a beauty severe and sombre—quite depressing. The houses are mostly red brick, extremely high. The streets are over thirty feet wide, with fine brick sidewalks, above which are suspended awnings to shade the numerous stores. At certain distances there are crossings paved with a stone that looks very much like our slate stone. The Americans never cross a street but at these places, which are at right angles. The other streets are badly paved. There are here, as at Paris, many fine carriages, especially a new style which is unusually elegant.

There are separate sections in the city for the different kinds of business; for example: for the sailors, for the soldiers, for the wholesale merchants, etc., etc. In the latter, and in the navy quarter, no women are to be seen; not from fear of being insulted, however, for women are much respected here, more so than in Europe. To be wanting in respect towards them would be a shameful thing, and would brand the guilty one with an indelible mark. We saw no public buildings other than the City Hall and the Post Office which, however, offered nothing remarkable. The Catholic churches are small and badly built, even the cathedral.

But there is a large number of Protestant churches which raise their pointed steeples high above the dwellings. There are churches for at least fourteen or fifteen different sects, but not one is sheltered by the saving sign of the cross. Nowhere in America does the sign of salvation appear to cheer the soul. What pained me most in traversing the city was to see churches everywhere without the cross; also many cemeteries even in the city itself, sad and cold, like the marble placed on top of the graves, as if to prevent the resurrection of the poor bodies beneath. How consoling, on the contrary, is it to see the Tree of Hope planted in the *champs des morts*. It overshadows the mortal remains of the children of the Church, and keeps them for immortality. I shall say nothing further of the city of New York, which I went to see only once, and then only to be able to tell you something about it.

I come now to what concerns us personally. On Monday we had the opportunity of going to confession, and on Tuesday, the feast of the Nativity of the Blessed Virgin, of receiving Communion. While shedding an abundance of tears, we renewed the consecration of ourselves to God for the mission to which He had deigned to call us. How sweet for us the moment when we had the happiness of uniting ourselves to Our Lord in the Holy Sacrament, after having been so long deprived of this inestimable favor.

On this happy day also at ten o'clock all our baggage arrived without going through the Custom House. This was a privilege not enjoyed even by the Princess Gallitzin, Superior of the Ladies of the Sacred Heart, who passed through New York six days before ourselves on her way to found a house at St. Louis, quite near Vincennes.

Mr. Byerley was not satisfied with getting the baggage through; he paid the drayman, the porters, etc., and, here, this is not a small matter. The driver was the bearer of a letter addressed by Mr. Byerley to Mrs. Parmentier. The literal translation is as follows: "Nothing was opened aboard the *Cincinnati*. The Custom House officers were very obliging. Captain Barston told me that Dr. Doane said he had visited the hospitals at Paris, and had there witnessed the incomparable conduct of the Sisters, and that in his opinion it would bring a blessing on any one who would render them the least service. Consequently, he would be mortified to receive any thanks for his attention." This latter phrase led me to think he had learned that I desired to know his name in order to write to him. However this may be, I thought it my duty to address a few words of thanks to him and also to Mr. Barston, our captain.

As the transportation of our baggage was impossible by the railroads and steamboats that would convey us to the West, our good Mr. Byerley took charge of getting our trunks and boxes from Mrs. Parmentier's, and of having them packed up properly and sent to Cincinnati to the address of reliable parties who would forward them promptly to Vincennes.

All our little affairs being thus arranged, and your long letter despatched, we decided to set out for Philadelphia on the tenth where we hoped to find news from Vincennes. All the Parmentier family would accompany us—Madame and Adele, and dear little Rosine who is only twelve years old. Father Varela, and Mr. Byerley and his clerk were also of the number. Our other guide was aboard the steamboat taking care of the few effects we were carrying with us for the journey.

We went through the little town of Brooklyn, which, however, has thirty-five thousand inhabitants, and also the big city of New York, which numbers four hundred thousand, and proceeded to a large river or rather arm of the sea. That is the port where the ships arrive, and so great is their number that the harbor resembles a forest in whiter. To us the sight was charming.

Here we went aboard a very splendid steamer, whose length must have measured one hundred meters. Hardly had we entered this floating mansion than we saw coming, all out of breath, our good Father Varela, who, notwithstanding his numerous occupations, wished to say his last adieu and to renew his offer of service. We thanked him and our devoted Mr. Byerley most cordially. Then they departed recommending us very specially to our two escorts. As to the dear ladies, they could not make up their minds to leave the boat; they insisted on going with us to the other side.

The machinery was set in motion and we started. We admired the port in passing along and also its surroundings. We saw again with pleasure our *Cincinnati*, but what particularly struck our eyes, and especially our hearts, was the sight of the French flag over a small ship. "Oh, adieu, dear Country!" we exclaimed, "we are going far away from thee. This is perhaps the last sign that will bring thee to our minds. But we shall not need any sign, for thou livest in our hearts." Then interiorly we said to ourselves: The true country of a Christian, but above all of a Religious, is Heaven, towards which we are tending; it is for God that we have made this sacrifice, and, I may add, He has already repaid us, for His protecting hand has assisted us in a visible manner, and we cannot but recognize the attentions of His Providence.

Finally we arrived at the other side, where the immense engine which was to take us was already smoking. More than a hundred persons were elbowing each other, each one wanting to enter first. In the midst of this commotion we received the *adieux* of those devoted friends who had treated us so hospitably. Then, preceded and followed by our attentive guides, we entered one of those large coaches where forty persons can be seated. As many as sixteen of these coaches can be drawn by the same engine. Scarcely were we seated than the whole thing started off like lightning, and we beheld unfolding before our eyes a magnificent country—verdant and fertile fields, charming villages, their frame houses painted white, with pretty green window casements and blinds of the same color. All this was new and produced a delightful effect. We went so fast that in an hour we had made twenty miles (more than eight French leagues), and always through a beautiful country.

The railroad runs at the edge of the canal, upon which were a considerable number of boats drawn by fine horses trotting along the other side of the canal. Often we came across other canals (there are a great number of them in America) which, together with the railroads and the rivers, make communication in this country very easy. At no great distance from each other there are stations, the architecture of which is quite original. The trains stop, not to feed the horses but to change passengers. Some ascend, others descend. Then we hear a little bell, which seems to have a magic power, for as soon as it greets the ear the train moves off with such rapidity that we seem to fly rather than run.

We remarked that the scenery became more delightful and more varied the nearer we approached Philadelphia. The villages were closer together. In all the towns we saw churches, but again I note that the cross does not surmount their lofty steeples. This saddens the soul. Here and there herds of cattle, flocks of sheep, of geese, etc., on the grass in the woods, lent life and variety to the scene.

Around Philadelphia and Baltimore

In a very short time we were in Philadelphia. On leaving the train we saw crowds of travelers coming down from the coaches like hail. Each one hurried to claim his baggage. They snatch the things from one another's hands. A hundred drivers, whip in hand, all rush up together to offer their self-interested services. They almost take possession of your bags whether you will it or not. Our few belongings were sent to the Bishop's residence where Father Frenaye [the Vicar General] lived. We were told it was quite near, only on the next street. We thought we would walk there, but had about half a league to go; which here is considered nothing at all.

We found Philadelphia much prettier than New York.

The streets are perfectly straight and divide the town just like a draught board. All are at least three miles in length and fifteen meters wide. The houses are of red brick, and in many of them the doorsteps, the window sills, and the six steps leading up to the door, are in beautiful white marble, which sets off handsomely the brick and the iron balustrade at each side of the doorsteps. Excepting the public monuments I do not think I have seen anything in Paris that approaches the richness and splendor of this "Queen City of America."

The Bishop received us with admirable kindness. Father Frenaye then took us to the Sisters of Charity and our two escorts bade us farewell. This Reverend gentleman informed us that the Bishop of Vincennes had not sent anyone to meet us, and that he himself had written that it was unnecessary. The brave Father told us that we could travel very well without knowing English, that it was not indispensable. However, after reflecting upon the matter, I decided not to set out alone, and the Bishop of Philadelphia approved my decision; consequently, Father Frenaye and I wrote to Bishop de la Hailandière that we would remain there until someone came for us.

We were accommodated by the Sisters of Charity, who showed us the kindest hospitality. We remarked virtues in these good Sisters which excited our admiration. They are model religious, so perfect that we cannot aspire to their virtue. The Superior has the finest religious exterior that I have ever seen. She is tall, and gifted with such a pleasing countenance that we could not help loving her. She has such a gentle appearance, such a modest carriage, yet so noble, that one might take her for a being from Paradise. Her seven Sisters are also very charming, but they have not attained the exterior perfection of their good Superior. Not one of them knows a word of French; yet they found the means of making us spend very pleasant recreations.

Not only in the Community did we find subjects of edification; the city of Philadelphia presents many others. It is a city of benediction. On Saturday afternoon we saw more than a hundred persons at confession, the good Bishop having the largest number of penitents. On Sunday he said Mass at six o'clock, and he gave Holy Communion for half an hour at the eight o'clock Mass. Even at the High Mass there were still some communicants. All comport themselves so perfectly that there is not the least noise heard.

In witnessing the faith and piety of these new Catholics, many hitherto unbelievers, a painful reflection saddened my heart. What, I said, have those days of wrath arrived when the patience of the Lord is exhausted by the culpable indifference of France? He will abandon those unfaithful nations to a reprobate state, and will choose to Himself a more faithful people. Oh! no, this thought is too painful! The mercies of the Lord can extend equally, even over our poor country, so dear to our hearts, and over this land of exile, without exhausting its treasures.

Extraordinary conversions have taken place of late in Philadelphia. We saw among others a celebrated physician who is looked upon by all as a man of surpassing merit; he has that appearance, too. And a general, converted some months previously, had given such admirable example that ten of his subalterns entered the Church. All are at present fervent Catholics.

The Cathedral, of Gothic style, would be very fine in its architecture if it were higher, but it is about twenty feet too low. This defect is so apparent that it is remarked by everyone, The interior is ornamented with taste and magnificence. The altar is very high, and is all gilt. There is a beautiful exposition, also gilt, and very fine candelabra and crucifix. On each side of the altar is a pyramid of gilded brass, which must produce a brilliant effect when all the tapers are lighted; even by themselves they are quite ornamental. The pews are finer still than those in New York, and all have cushions upholstered in green or crimson. I find that rather too much. The service is all carried on with music, as everywhere else in America. I do not fancy that. Every Sunday there are two sermons, and the congregations, so numerous, are very attentive.

During our stay in the city the good Bishop gave us constant marks of friendliness. He came frequently to see us and received us always with admirable benevolence. As soon as our arrival was known in the city, a crowd of French people came to visit us. Our costume was admired by all. And indeed ours is much superior to that of our good Sisters, who are dressed in black serge and were a little lustring cap no worth two sous. They have also a sort of bonnet made of pasteboard covered with lustring; and, truly, holy poverty loses nothing here.

We went out twice to view the surrounding country, which is indeed worth seeing. There are superb hills, on whose sloping sides are beautiful English gardens, and here and there houses of a pleasing style. But what adds most to the beauty of this part of the country is the magnificent river at the foot of the hills, gliding along so tranquilly that one would take it for a small lake rather than a river. But nothing of all this is comparable to what they call the Water Works. The plant is on a high hill which dominates the city on the west and which, by a wonderfully arranged mechanism, furnishes water to every house in this large city. By force pumps, through subterranean pipes, the water from the river is forced to the height of 120 feet; there it is received and kept in five reservoirs of an enormous size made on the hill or mound; there too it is filtered and then passes through thousands of small pipes, which resemble the arteries of the human body and distribute the water to the very extremities of the city. The pumps which supply these basins make such a deafening noise that one would truly become deaf by remaining there any length of time.

Altogether this forms a magnificent group which nature and art have combined to adorn in a special manner: on one side a mountain covered with green trees, picturesque rocks from which gush forth fountains in delightful variety, statues of women, of children, of old soldiers, but all very modest— they did not forget to dress them. On the other side are the Water Works in the center of which is a fountain that can compare well with that of the park at Versailles. There are also winding stairways to go up to the reservoirs, and at certain distance Chinese arbors where those who make this ascent can rest themselves. As one ascends, a delightful view is presented: on one side the city with its fine dwellings, its steeples towering aloft, its numerous terraces; on the other, vast hills forming an ampitheatre and covered with beautiful foliage. At the foot of the hills flaws the wide river divided into two parts, one of which supplies the Water Works; the other receives the ebb and flow of the sea, and is covered with a number of steamboats and ships with their flags of all the European nations. The whole view is truly a wonderful sight; but the heart of the Catholic is deeply afflicted on finding on all the most beautiful American monuments only the weathercock, a symbol of fickleness and inconstancy.

Returning, we saw on all the roads and in the streets innumerable railroad trains. It is impossible to have any idea of all their commotion without having seen it. Here all is movement, transportation, but transportation by steam. The very air is clouded by it. This, then, is America near the sea coast, a world of action, of opulence, of magnificence, of courtesy; but there it ends. There are other beautiful sights in America but they are a wild, uncultivated kind, beauties of a world which seems to be in its cradle. Those who have not seen that part of America have no idea of what the West is, which, as I have already said, is a new world in the New World.

Before passing on I must tell you something about Philadelphia that may seem peculiar. It is this: the houses which are not of brick or stone are sold at auction in the stores like cupboards and wardrobes. If people are not pleased with the spot they had at first chosen they call for the house-movers, who transport the house from one place to another without disturbing the furniture. Mrs. Parmentier told me she had dined in one of these houses while they were moving it, and nothing on the table was disturbed.

While we were waiting for an answer from the Bishop of Vincennes, the president of the Terre Haute Bank arrived with his wife. He was willing to take charge of us, and it was decid-ed that we should leave with him. But Providence again dis-posed otherwise, to our great advantage, and sent us a French priest from Canada, who was himself going to Vincennes, Reverend William Chartier by name. He was of the greatest assistance to us.

Our departure was settled upon for Friday, the eighteenth [of September]. During the whole time of our stay in Philadelphia we received the kindest attention from the Bishop who was like a father to us. Father Frenaye also ren-dered us every possible service; so it was with regret we left all these friends, especially the dear Sisters who had given us such good example. We had been happy in their house, had heard two Masses every day, performed all our religious exer-cises in their chapel; in fine, we were too well off there, and such was not our vocation. We had come to suffer, and to suffer in the West of America. Our good Sister St. Vincent had had the fever, but she was better now, so there was nothing to pre-vent our leaving.

On the eve of our departure, I received a letter from good

Mr. Byerley who informed us that, charged to our account, Mrs. Parmentier and himself had advanced $140.00 to Thomas Brassier, that Breton of whom I have already spoken. With this amount he was to go to Vincennes, and then return it to us when he would be able to do so. After receiving this new token of the devotedness of our friends of New York, we took leave of those of Philadelphia.

Our excellent Father Frenaye accompanied us in a carriage to the railroad station where we took the train for Baltimore, a city situated southwest of Philadelphia about one hundred and sixty miles. We made this trip in a few hours, sometimes by train, sometimes by boat, but always by steam. I cannot give you details of this portion of the country that we crossed so rapidly, for it rained so heavily that we could scarcely see anything. Moreover, a great part of the time we were on the water—Chesapeake Bay—and only now and then caught a glimpse of the coast; nevertheless, here and there we met with some scenery which was very beautiful, yet less delightful in Maryland than in Pennsylvania.

At Baltimore we went to a hotel for the first time in this country. They served us up a Friday—*maigre*—repast, perhaps the first for them, after keeping us waiting two hours. They gave us oyster soup, fish, butter, etc., and hot biscuits (this is American bread); but there were by compensation fine potatoes, finer than those we have in France. The meal was courteously served by two negroes, whose attentions were very annoying, as we understood not a word of what they said. Finally the dinner came to an end by a dessert in American style, everything on the table being changed, even the lamp. It cost us *fifty cents a piece*; the price is the same everywhere.

The good Bishop of Philadelphia had written to the Sulpicians at Baltimore recommending us to their care. They sent a priest to meet us who conducted us to the Sisters of

Charity. Our guide, Father Chartier, had a room with the Sulpicians. Not one of the Sisters knew French. The Superior seeing our weariness tried to ask in French if we wanted to go to bed. She said instead *etre cocher* (to be a coachman). I, on my part, called her a negro. I do not know what I was trying to say. See what it is to be in a country without knowing the language. It is surely disagreeable and exposes one to grave inconvenience.

The next day, after a good night's rest, we went to the cathedral where we had the happiness of receiving Holy Communion. This cathedral is, without doubt, the finest monument of architecture consecrated to Catholic worship in the United States. It appeared to me to be about two hundred-fifty feet in length by one hundred-fifty in breadth. There are twelve side altars in as many small chapels, a very rare thing in this country. But this church is much too heavy, too massive, and too low; one feels oppressed in it and, as it were, crushed under an enormous weight; one can scarcely breathe. There are two fine paintings here sent from France by Louise XVI. One represents the taking down from the Cross; the other, St. Louis accompanying one of his wounded soldiers during the war of the Crusades. So lifelike are the pictures, they seem to speak.

Baltimore is not nearly so fine a city as Philadelphia. The streets are extremely wide and the city is very extensive. The people make you take endless walks telling you all the while, "It is quite near, just on the next street." We remained there only Friday night and Saturday morning until 10 o'clock, when we started for Frederick. Before leaving we received a visit from the Vicar General (the Archbishop was absent). This reverend gentleman, who is also Superior of the Sulpicians, is French. Deluol is his name. He has a fine appearance, is brilliant and witty, and has retained all the vivacity of a Frenchman. We were delighted to meet from time to time some of our countrymen, but now we had to bid farewell to this one and go to the train which was to take us that very day to Frederick. This was the last time we were to travel on land by steam.

The country we then passed through was fine, but of a wild style of beauty. On both sides were to be seen high hills covered with trees, and between them a pretty river upon which there were many mills, the water being held by dams that, when full, let the limpid water escape in a way that is singularly pleasing. The mountains have been tunneled so that the railroad cars can run through, and in several places enormous masses of overhanging rock seem ready to crush the traveller with the locomotive that bears him along. The opening from a distance appears so narrow that one would judge it impossible for a train to pass through; yet, in the twinkling of an eye you see the engine rush in as into a box made expressly for it, but fitting so exactly that if a living creature were there, it would be crushed before having time to see what was coming. These steam engines are indeed wonderful, but very dangerous.

Frederick is rather small and built on a level. A carriage sent by the Sisters was waiting to take us to their house, as they also had been notified of our coming by the Bishop of Philadelphia. We were graciously received by Mother Rose, former Superior General of the Sisters of Charity. This good ex-Mother is a model religious, filled with the virtues of her state, especially humility and charity. All the Community regret her, but she is delighted to be relieved of the burden of the superiorship. She told us all about the beginning of her institute, which had very trying times. These good Americans had, in fact, to undergo inconceivable privations; but Heaven blessed their sacrifices, for they have now a Community that does great good. It is destined especially for the instruction of the poor and chiefly of orphans; however they have a fine Academy. They teach the various sciences scarcely known in our French schools, but they excel in music, which is an indispensable thing in this country, even for the poor. No piano, no pupils! Such is the spirit of this country—Music and Steam! At Frederick, of the five Sisters three teach piano and guitar. These Sisters have an excellent religious spirit; tender piety, great charity, regularity,—in fine, all the virtues of the true Religious. I am happy to render them this testimony.

At Frederick we saw Jesuits dressed as those good Religious were in the first days of their Institute—wide cassock belted in, crucifix, and their small four-cornered hats. That sight did me good. The Superior came to see us, showed us much kindness and escorted us through his establishment, which is all in perfect order. But most to be admired was the beautiful church built by these good Fathers, superior to anything we have seen in this country. It forms a cross perfectly regular and very large. The church is somewhat similar in the interior to our chapel at Ruillé in its beautiful ceiling and pillars. The altar is marble, finely wrought and of exquisite polish. The exposition is of agate and of surprising beauty. There are also two large vases of alabaster on the altar, wherein lights are placed when evening cornes on. This has a peculiarly beautiful effect on account of the transparency of the vases; one cannot tell whence the light proceeds. The church is surrounded by buildings all erected to the glory of God and the benefit of humanity. At the right stands the college where one hundred and twenty students are receiving gratuitously an excellent education. On the left are the orphan asylum and the Sisters' academy. Behind the church is the Jesuit novitiate, and in front, the house of the professed members. The good Superior very graciously showed us everything in detail. We remained in Frederick only Saturday evening.

Having been advised to exchange our habit for a secular dress, as there was bigotry and fanaticism in the country farther west, we made our preparations. On Sunday morning after hearing Mass we left in a conveyance they call a stage, which was to take us to Wheeling, Virginia, on the Ohio River, a city two hundred and nineteen miles distant. We had to cross the Alleghany Mountains which separate Maryland from Virginia, Pennsylvania, and Ohio.

OVER THE ALLEGHANIES BY STAGECOACH

At ten o'clock we got into the stage and began a new style of traveling, at least new for us. Our coach, like all those in western America, was enclosed only by oil-cloth curtains that could be raised when desired, for now we were on the land, and no longer flying through the air or floating on the water. We were alone with our traveling companion [Father Chartier] who had become, as it were, a member of the family.

In this part of the journey every moment unveiled new beauties. At every turn new grandeurs rose before us. Sometimes we were on heights where mountain-tops were our footstools; below were superb defiles where magnificent valleys spread their verdure; and in the distance other mountains were superposed one upon the other so as to form an amphitheatre, where the eye is lost in the ravishing spectacle, so calculated to elevate the soul towards the Author of all things.

After having laboriously climbed these tremendous heights our poor horses seemed unable to go any farther. Then to let them rest, our pitiless driver lashed them with his whip, and the poor animals descended these mountains with the rapidity of lightning. The roadway at times inspired terror also. On one side vast, jutting rocks would overhang, upon which were giant trees apparently uprooted and ready to fall at any moment; on the other hand, frightful precipices, whose depths one cannot fathom, were ready to swallow us up if our horses made the least false step. This was not the only danger. Bandits infested the mountains, and we had to travel both day and night. But the protecting hand of the Lord, which guarded us on the deep, preserved us from accident and harm on the land.

Everywhere we remarked the vast number of trees that were brought low by the axe of time. Like corpses they lay awaiting burial, and seemingly imploring a friendly hand to give them back to the earth whence they had sprung. I am convinced that the vegetative quality of the land here is due to the decomposition of the decayed trees. I cannot describe the sad feelings that take possession of the soul at the sight of this death in the midst of life.

Here and there were some log cabins. Around these huts, exposed to the rigor of all the seasons, the trees have been burned down in order to get sufficient ground to raise corn for food for the inhabitants. Cows, chickens, geese, and hogs are the sole fortune of these poor people, whom our French Republicans call "the Happy Americans."

In crossing the mountains, we experienced in a very striking manner, quite new to us, the variations of atmosphere. The evenings became cool after days of suffocating heat, and during the night we could scarcely endure the piercing cold that seized us. In the morning, we were not a little surprised to see the valleys as white as they are with us in January. Soon the sun drew up the vapors, which formed in a fog. Then the heat began again.

On the Ohio River Boat

At last we arrived at Wheeling, a town situated on the Ohio, a river that separates the state bearing that name from

Pennsylvania. Here we took a steamboat down the river to Cincinnati, a city distant three hundred and fifty-five miles. The boat, very small for this country, was crowded with passengers. Usually the river boats are divided off into two apartments, one for men, the other for women. There are beds in both; those that are well arranged have little cabins each containing two berths, the one above the other, where a person is rather comfortable. In this boat there were no cabins; simply beds, twelve in number. And eighteen women were there before us!

There was no alternative; we had to bear it. In the daytime it was well enough, for we remained outside, notwithstanding the extreme heat. But at night we had to retire. We greatly needed rest after passing two days and two nights in the stagecoach; but there were no beds. Straw ticks without sheets or pillows were spread on the floor and we were invited in mockery to lie down there. I answered that we could not do that. This amused the American passengers and increased my chagrin. All the others lay down to rest, but we, dejected, were still sitting there on our chairs. At length, overcome by fatigue and yet more by the extreme heat of this narrow room where thirty persons were shut up—six had come after us—and there was the heat of a stove besides, I decided that I ought to lie down so that my companions would do the same. Before I could make up my mind to do so, however, I went on deck and threw myself on my knees to beg of God the grace to bear this humiliation. I returned more calm and put myself on the half of one of the straw beds; my Sisters did likewise. Our yielding increased the mockery of our fellow travelers. It was the last time we lay down to rest, however, during the four long days that we spent on this horrible boat. The negro women in particular seemed to delight in passing over us and treading us under foot like straw.

To put the last touch to our misfortune, our boat was running aground half the time. We feared we should be obliged to remain in these desolate places where nothing was to be seen except, from time to time, a poor log cabin. Our situation was not a pleasant one. We had to listen to the cries of about twenty small children who were in the room or in the one adjoining. In the daytime we were obliged to stay in a small space on deck where we were alone, it is true, but where the heat was excessive, not only from the burning sun above us, but from the boiler just below us and a hot pipe nearby.

There was some compensation, however, in the beautiful scenery along the river which is called *"la belle rivière,"* beautiful above all others. And it merits the title, not only on account of the limpidity of its waters, through which the bottom of the river can be distinctly seen, but also on account of the superb hills between which it glides so gently along. How many delightful moments we had admiring those hills, whose conical shape tops were covered with trees festooned with vines. There were a few small villages, also, and our boat stopped at each of them. We passed the skeletons of several steamboats, foundered, burned, wrecked. The sight seemed to make no impression on the Americans. They are so accustomed to such accidents that the papers scarcely mention them. It is surprising that a single boat escapes when the river is low, for when a boat is grounded, so much steam is put on to release it that the danger is great.

After four long days we arrived at Cincinnati, towards four o'clock in the afternoon, on Saturday, the twenty-fourth. Father Chartier went to see the Bishop [Most Reverend J. B. Purcell] to learn where we should go. This good Bishop came himself to get us, hired carriages and took us to the Sisters of Charity, who were expecting us. A very nice room had been prepared.

And now we were on the confines of Indiana! (The Bishop of Cincinnati is the Vicar General of the Bishop of Vincennes, and reciprocally the latter is the Vicar General of the Bishop of Cincinnati.)

Dinner was served, but the need of food was not the most imperative; it was rest we needed above all; so, after saying our prayers, we hastened to our beds. It was seven days since we had undressed.

We were far from supposing that, in the midst of the city where we had been so well received, we were to find a multitude of enemies athirst for the blood of the French. Until then we had not fought unto the shedding of blood, but this was a night of slaughter. I may say without boasting too much that several of my enemies perished by my hands, but I was sorely wounded. All my Sisters, except Sister Basilide, bore the glorious scars which proved that they, too, had undergone a bloody battle with the mosquitoes.

After the seven o'clock Mass said for the Religious, we visited the Bishop, who had sent us an invitation to call on him. He was not surprised to see us covered with wounds. He told us that Father Chartier had also been attacked by a squadron of this terrible army, and, like ourselves, was in a pitiable state. There are such quantities of mosquitoes in Cincinnati that the air is darkened with them as with a cloud. After our visit with the Bishop we went to the cathedral for High Mass. I could not restrain my tears in seeing the poverty and destitution of this church. Never in all my life had I seen such a miserable one.

We left Cincinnati on the twenty-sixth and again took a steamboat, but a better one than that which had brought us there, and arrived the next morning at Madison, a town in Indiana where Bishop de la Hailandière was making his pastoral visit. This town is only about eighty-five miles from Vincennes. When we landed we learned that the Bishop had gone to another mission. We waited for him two days in an inn where we nearly died of lonesomeness.

Finally, October first, toward seven o'clock in the evening, Father Chartier entered the room followed by the Bishop and two other gentlemen, all in citizens' clothes and covered with mud up to the knees. I could scarcely recognize the Bishop in this condition. He gave us his blessing, told us we were to be settled near Terre Haute, and gave as an excuse for not sending for us that his priests were all sick. He conducted us himself to the steamboat and promised to join us at Vincennes in two weeks. It was a great comfort for us to have seen him even for so short a time, but we were quite sad to have to go to Vincennes without him. However, we had to make this sacrifice. We left him to go aboard a large boat where we had private rooms and were quite comfortable.

Continuing to descend the Ohio, we directed our course toward Louisville, Kentucky, which is forty-five miles from Madison. I wished to spend a day there in order to pay a visit to Reverend N. Perché,[8] a missionary priest whom I had known at Angers and who was then living only about three miles from Louisville.

We reached the city in a few hours. As the boat was to stop there for some time, we went ashore to see the good Angerin. We were received by the Sisters of Charity, but a different community from those we had seen in the East. These were from Nazareth, under the direction of Bishop Flaget, in whose diocese we then were. Leaving my companions with these dear Sisters, and accompanied by Father Chartier and Sister Basilide, I went to Portland, the mission of Father

---

[8] Napoleon J. Perché; later, Archbishop of New Orleans. His Excellency spent two weeks at Saint Mary-of-the-Woods, Christmas 1841, donated a set of furnishings for the chapel, and was active thereafter in procuring subjects for the Community. He died in 1883. He is named among the benefactors of the institution.

Perché. He was away from home and was not to return till the following day; so we were deprived of the pleasure of seeing him.

At our return we had the honor of meeting the greatly esteemed Father Badin, that veteran among the missionaries, who for fifty years had exercised the functions of the ministry undertaken for the love of God and the salvation of his brethren. He was the first priest ordained in this country and, though he has suffered unheard-of trials and fatiguing labors, he still retains all his French gayety and joviality, if I may thus express myself. His stories provoked hearty laughter. His countenance expressed innocence, candor, and holiness; one feels better after seeing him. He remained a long time with us at the Sisters'. His enquiries about my traveling companions led to the discovery that one of the number, Sister Olympiade, is his cousin. We felt it a great honor to be related to this holy man.

The next morning, feast of the Angels, he heard our confessions. It was a sweet consolation to address ourselves to this venerable priest. It seemed that the words of divine truth had extraordinary strength coming from those lips which had been employed so long in teaching the truth and had affected so many wonders. He has indeed suffered for the faith. He now beholds forty priests in those parts that he alone evangelized for twenty years. During one period he was twenty-one months without seeing a Catholic priest, consequently, unable to have the benefit of sacramental confession.

This holy man, having heard our confessions and encouraged us, said Mass for us. Then he came to take breakfast at the good Sisters,' who are admirable for their charity, notwithstanding their poverty which appears to me to be very great. They have nearly the same costume as the other American Sisters of Charity, except the head-dress. They wear a bonnet, if a bonnet it can be called, consisting of a piece of pasteboard of at least a foot in diameter, to which a second piece is attached to form the front. Behind, there is a curtain of lustring attached to this bonnet and which falls down the middle of the back, like that worn by our Vendéennes. Under this coarse exterior they hide very precious virtues and rare talents. The Superior possesses artistic talent in a high degree. She reproduces nature with an accuracy and a dexterity that are truly remarkable. They also teach music; without this branch, again I say, no pupils, neither rich nor poor.

These Sisters have no boarders here; they could not provide their fare. They served us boiled potatoes, dried herrings, corn bread, and old butter; we understood that the salt-fish was extra in our honor. We were amply compensated for the absence of bodily comforts, however, by the extraordinary kindness we met with.

The American Catholics here have the spirit of the Christians of the primitive Church: great charity, the love of hospitality which St. Paul recommends so strongly to the faithful of his time, an ardent zeal for the cause of the Gospel, in fine, all the virtues of the Fathers of the Faith. I met several ladies of the highest rank, who had nothing more at heart than to bring up their children for the service of the Altar and Religion.

Having spent a long time in conversation with our good countryman, Father Badin, speaking much of Orleans and all dear France, we bade farewell to this holy priest and to the good Sisters and went to our boat which was to start at 3 P.M. that day. At the dock we learned that we must wait another day. We did not leave till 10 A.M. This delay gave us the opportunity to examine the town a little. Louisville has sprung up as it were by magic, in a few years only. It is pretty, the streets are regular, and the houses (built *à la française*) are quite elegant. I have seen nothing better except Philadelphia; which, however, is far superior. The happy location, its rapid growth, its commerce, give us reason to presume that it will, before long, become one of the principal cities of America.

The following day we were again on the beautiful Ohio. Soon after leaving Louisville we came to the rapids, over which no boats can possibly pass; a canal, therefore, has been constructed with locks which hold back the water by enormous gates. When the boat is in one of these locks the water in the other can be seen more than sixteen feet below. One would imagine that there is going to be a terrible fall down, and that the boat must perish. Not at all! One side of these lower gates is opened and the water precipitates itself forcibly into the inclosure; then, when it has risen to a level with that where the boat is, the other gates are opened and we enter the lock. This operation has to be gone through six times before we come to the river again, which here has resumed its tranquil appearance, and continues to carry upon its surface a great number of boats.

After passing the dangerous rapids, the aspect of the river changes completely; the land is level and the water flows so gently that one would think it was still water. Islets also dot the river here and there, and the green trees reflected in the water produce a delightful effect; you would imagine there is another forest planted down in the waters, particularly just before we come to Evansville, a little town in Indiana, where this river, justly styled "The Beautiful," displays itself in all its beauty and magnificence.

At Evansville we saw the Ohio for the last time on Sunday evening, October fourth, at the setting of the sun. Nothing troubled the charm and silence of this solitude. Making the most serious reflections on what we beheld, and on our present position, I said to myself: Thus does life also pass away, now calm, now agitated, but at last the end is attained. Happy, ah, thrice happy they who can then look out to the never-ending future with calm and confidence, who can cast themselves on the bosom of God, the Center of our felicity. Naturally I also made reflections about ourselves. We were at the end of our journey by water. If the heavy fog which gathers there every night had not dimmed the light of the moon, we would have gone ashore; so it was only on Monday morning that we landed at Evansville. We were now only fifty-five miles from Vincennes. This was a great joy to us and filled us with gratitude to God, who had protected us in His goodness during this long and perilous voyage.

IN INDIANA

Our happy feelings soon gave place to considerable depression on account of a sight which we had believed would increase our joy. It was the condition of a missionary priest and a conversation with him. He is under the jurisdiction of the Bishop of Vincennes and has evangelized this section of the country. So extreme was his poverty and so complete his destitution, that I shall run the risk of being accused of exaggeration in describing it; yet there is nothing in my narrative but which I have seen and touched. I shall relate all.

The priest is about twenty-eight years of age. His exterior bespoke mildness and he seemed refined; but he was so poorly clothed that one would easily have offered him an alms. He had on an old torn coat, shoes in the same conditions, trousers all patched up by himself. The collar of his shirt, which was in rags (excuse the expression), hung around his neck. All this was so striking and seemed so strange that I could not forbear telling him that his housekeeper was not very tidy. In a mild tone he answered that a servant was the last thing they stood in need of in this country. "What!" said I, "You have no housekeeper? Who then does the housework, makes your beds, prepares your food?" He replied, "My companion and I eat only corn-bread, which is brought to us every day by a baker. We have only a log hut for our church, house, and school. At night we spread a mattress on a bench and there, wrapped in our coverings, we take a little rest. When we are away on missionary duties, and one or the other always is, we sleep on hay or straw or sometimes under a tree."[9]

If this narrative, given with the greatest simplicity, saddened us, our hearts were still more oppressed at the sight of the hut which served as a temple to the God of Heaven and earth and as a habitation for His ministers. With these impressions we got into the stage which was to convey us to Vincennes.

Five minutes later we entered a thick forest where we saw the most singular kind of road that could be imagined. It was formed of logs, of trees that had been felled to clear the way and then were brought together as though to form a raft [corduroy]. Where some of these logs had become rotten, there were large holes. The coach jolted so terribly as to cause large bumps on one's head. This day, indeed, we danced without a fiddle all afternoon. The road was really dreadful. Thus jumping and tossing about, we arrived at a farmhouse in the forest, where we decided to spend the night. The kind people gave up to us one room containing three beds, and they took Father Chartier, I know not where. Here we awaited the dawn of that day by whose light we would at length behold the town of Vincennes, towards which we had been journeying so long.

---

[9] This holy priest was the Reverend Anthony Deydier, one of the zealous missionaries whom Bishop Bruté brought from France in 1836.

The morning clear, the sun bright, we set out early. The road continued to be very rough, but our horses ran at full speed. About two o'clock Father Chartier, who sat with the driver, exclaimed, "Look! There is Vincennes!" I do not say that I heard the words with joy. My heart was too much oppressed to experience any other feeling than that of sad disappointment. We had yet about three miles to make. We prayed during all that time. As we were to find only our God in the desert and an unknown country, we endeavored to render Him propitious to us.

At last we had arrived at Vincennes! Vincennes!! The conveyance stopped. We were taken to the Sisters of Charity, who live near the episcopal residence, and who had been requested by the Bishop to take care of us until his return. After partaking of some food and putting on again our religious dress, we begged to be taken to the cathedral, *Ciel!* What a Cathedral! Our barn at Soulaines is better ornamented and more neatly kept. I could not resist this last shock and wept bitterly, which relieved me somewhat. I could not possibly examine this poor church on that day—the following day I did so with more calm. It is a brick building with large windows without curtains; most of the panes of glass are broken; on the roof there is something like the beginning of a steeple, which resembles rather a large chimney fallen into ruins. The interior corresponds perfectly to the exterior:—a poor wooden altar, a railing unfinished and yet seemingly decaying from age. The Bishop's seat is an old red chair which even our peasants would not have in what they consider a nice room. To conclude, I have seen nothing equal to the poverty of the cathedral of Vincennes. I can say nothing of the town except that I doubt whether it will ever grow much on account of its position—solitary, situated in an undeveloped part of the country, on the banks of a little river which is navigable only in winter; however, as I have not the gift of prophecy, I shall speak only of the present and say that it is quite gratuitously they call it a town. Only one street is paved and I really believe the others are impassable in winter. It is said there are four thousand inhabitants, but I think they would have hard work to find that number.

Here in Vincennes we met the Eudists sent by Louis de Rennes to found a college. Their house is a good one but not yet paid for. It was a real pleasure to see again these good Bretons who were my near neighbors at Rennes. Their presence helped us to bear the *ennui* we felt while waiting for the Bishop.

When the Bishop came home he explained in full all the reasons he had for locating our house in the country. Although they did not coincide with our view of the matter, after making our representations we consented to start for Terre Haute, and the departure was set for Sunday evening, the eighteenth of October. A fearful storm which did great damage here prevented our leaving that night. We learned that four postulants who were awaiting us had gone on six weeks before, and also that we had a chaplain who was seeing to the building of the house. This good priest [Father Buteux] came to Vincennes for us, and appeared worthy of the reputation he had acquired. He is a Parisian who has a very brilliant education and who has renounced all that the world offers to flatter and attract the human heart, in order to come and gain souls in this unevangelized land. Bishop Bruté brought him from St. Sulpice four years ago.

I believe I have not told you anything about the Bishop's house, and of those steps from which he fell into the snow when he was starting out on one of his first pastoral visits. We have seen those steps and have ascended them; and although there was no snow we ran the risk of imitating the good prelate, for the six steps are made of rotten wood badly joined which shake under one's feet. His house, which is small, serves as a store where his priests come and get what is indispensable to them. All that is there is the property of each one; but very often both father and children have not those things that are of the first necessity. This is the reason why his church and house are in such a poor condition; for bread must first be provided. As for pork, it cannot be dear, for there are swine by the thousands here.

Milk, too, is plentiful in summer; nearly every family has cows. Poor beasts! They give little trouble to their owners more than to milk them. At Vincennes I saw these poor creatures, covered with rain or dew, standing before the doors waiting to be relieved of their precious burden. This being done, some strokes with a stick were given to send them back to the woods; and they, without any resentment, came back the following day to return good for evil. The poor hogs have their ears or tails mutilated to distinguish them from the neighbor's hogs. Even horses are not better cared for. All the time that they are not in the service of their masters they have to provide for themselves, and the forest is their only shelter. This is the way that animals are treated in this country; it makes one feel bad, and indeed you can hear their cries from morning till night. At Vincennes, especially, one might think she was in Noah's ark. The confused noise is deafening. The two pianos that the Sisters have for twelve pupils, and which are going from the beginning of the day to the end, add to the confusion. This you will say is queer, Well, such is the village of Vincennes.

On the seventeenth of October Sister Basilide fell sick. A storm having delayed our departure two days, the attack had time to increase and an inflammatory fever set in. We decided to wait for a change for the better; but this dear Sister, as courageous as ever, wished to leave, notwithstanding her condition; so on the twentieth, at ten o'clock at night, we took the stage for the town of Terre Haute, so greatly dreaded. The night was dark, the roads were very bad. There had been a hard rain for thirty-six hours, which might have made us fear a little deluge. The river, just before almost dry, had now overflowed to such, an extent that in several places we could not pass; bridges had been swept away by the torrent; thus, it was not without danger that we were traveling, especially in the night; in fact, we had gone only six miles when the stage was upset in a deep mud hole, throwing us head foremost. When we got up on our feet again, the great trouble was how to get out; for the stages are not open either in front or in the rear, and ours was about five feet wide. Our poor sick Sister lying on the floor caused us great uneasiness. Happily she was less bruised than the rest of us, for we had wrapped her in a heavy cloak and a comfort, and given her a pillow. Bundled up in this way, she was greatly protected.

In endeavoring not to fall upon her I hurt my head, and got a large bruise on my shoulder which is not yet entirely well. Each one in extricating herself cried out, "Oh! my head!" "Oh! my arm!" Finally we became reassured, seeing we all had the use of our members, though we were battered and sore. Having extricated ourselves from the stage, we carried Sister Basilide to a little log cabin which, fortunately, was quite near. The man of the house was so kind as to go and help our driver, and we were left to groan at our ease and to warm ourselves in this narrow abode. The woman, about sixty years of age, asked us who we were. As we could not answer except in French, she continued quietly smoking her pipe. (Smoking seems customary among the women in this part of the country; even young girls smoke; this seems very strange.)

With much trouble the stage was lifted out of the mud hole and we resumed our journey; but a little distance

farther on we had to give it up. We spent the remainder of
the night in another farmhouse beside a good fire that the
family built for us. At daybreak we continued on our way
towards Terre Haute, where we arrived in the afternoon
without further accident. Terre Haute is larger and finer
than Vincennes, yet it is not pretty. Like all American cities
it is laid out on a large scale; in some places the houses are
a gunshot from each other. We passed the night there in a
hotel, and the next day heard Mass in a small Catholic church
[St. Joseph's] which has just been built. It is quite
good for this country. After Mass we returned to our poor
sick Sister, and having had breakfast, took the stage which
was finally to bring us to our destination.

The house that is being erected for us is only four miles
from Terre Haute; so, by leaving at ten o'clock in the morning, we should be at Saint Mary-of-the-Woods at noon. Well,
you will see! Having procured some provisions we went in
the stage to the river bank, for a river named Wabash separates the town from the road that leads to our habitation.
As there is no bridge, we were obliged to wait our turn to be
ferried across. We waited until three forty-five in the afternoon, that is, more than five hours and a half. At last we
crossed, but scarcely had we been on the road ten minutes
than we were again in the forest, and the ground was so
covered with water that it was like a vast pond. The plank
road having disappeared, it became dangerous to travel on
account of trees which had fallen here and there. No matter!
The horses were whipped up and they rushed into the water.
At every moment we were on the point of being overturned,
although Father Buteux went ahead with a pole to sound the
road. At length, unable to go any farther, the water being
too deep, wet to the skin he had to get up with the driver.
Once the carriage struck a stumbling horse, and a wheel
went over the trunk of a tree, and lo! the carriage was

again thrown on its side. The water entered the coach and the horses were swimming rather than walking. It was like being in the middle of a sea, but in a sea surmounted by a thick forest; for the trees are so near together that it required all the experience of American drivers to be able to get through. There was imminent danger for us, and we had two miles to cover in this way.

I may say, however, that I was not at all alarmed. When one has nothing more to lose, the heart is inaccessible to fear. The water poured in on us. We thought we were surely gone this time; but the driver without losing his American coolness managed the horses so dexterously as to set the carriage up again. We could see dry land a short distance beyond, but the water we had yet to go through was deeper than that we had already passed. The horses, however, were cheered at the sight of land, and went into a gallop, the water passing over their backs. There was water in the carriage too. No matter. Five minutes later we were rolling along on *terra firma*.

The Journey's End

I cannot tell you what passed within me during the next half hour. I do not know myself, but I was so deeply moved that I could not utter a word. We continued to advance into the thick woods till suddenly Father Buteux stopped the carriage and said, "Come down, Sisters, we have arrived." What was our astonishment to find ourselves still in the midst of the forest, no village, not even a house in sight. Our guide having given orders to the driver, led us down into a ravine, whence we beheld through the trees on the other side a frame house with a stable and some sheds. "There," he said, "is the house where the postulants have a room, and where you will lodge until your house is ready."

LOG CHAPEL AND FIRST PROVIDENCE CONVENT
SAINT MARY-OF-THE-WOODS, 1840
Drawings by Sister Mary Emanuel Rinke from water color pictures
made in 1842 by Sister St. Francis le Fer de la Motte

We had agreed among ourselves that our first visit would be made to the Blessed Sacrament, and that we would not speak to anyone before having satisfied this longing of our hearts. The priest preceded us and we followed in silence to the church. The Church!! I send you the picture!! Yes, dear friends, that is the dwelling of the God of the Universe, in comparison with which the stables wherein you shelter your cattle are palaces! There it is that every day the Lamb of God is offered up, a sacrifice for the living and the dead! There He reposes night and day in a small *custode* in which the priest can scarcely put his two fingers! No tabernacle, no altar, for can the name of altar be given to three planks forming a table forty inches long, supported by two stakes driven into the ground?—that is all, for there are no altar cards, no stand for the missal, in fine, nothing but what I have mentioned. A cotton cloth is spread over these planks; there is a small altar stone; and now you have the whole altar. Except at the time of Mass, the pyx, the chalice, and the rest are covered with a dark blue calico which seems to have been used as a bedspread by the good country people. This, then, is the church of this place, which is also our chapel. It serves moreover as the dwelling of the priest, and still it is only about thirteen feet wide and fifteen feet long. I have just measured it. The furniture consists of the altar above described, a bed covered with mere rags, two little tables, one laden with books at the foot of the bed, the other in a corner serving as a writing-desk; there are, besides, two old trunks, an old chair, and a small bench. Here it is that for four years this Parisian has dwelt, he who was brought up in one of the most luxurious cities in Europe, and who now in the flower of his age, with his brilliant education, might be prominent in ecclesiastical circles and occupy an important position. The Archbishop of Paris made him the most advantageous offers to retain him, but he refused everything to come and suffer for his God and to gain souls to Him. He boards with the farmer who lodges us. The children of the house, the farmer and his wife are the hosts; but the banquet! Generally bread and coffee, potatoes and bacon—that is all. Nevertheless, this apostolic man told me yesterday, in laughing, that he had yet to learn where the crosses and privations are. Is he the one then who is the most to be pitied? I do not think so. His flock is scattered over an area of sixty miles. He oversees the building of our house and works at it himself like a common laborer, whenever free from the duties of his ministry. He even chops our wood, buys and carries our provisions, etc.

Returning to the moment in which we entered the chapel:— having prayed, wept, and thanked Almighty God for past favors and begged his assistance for the future; having prayed for you, dear Sisters, and for you all, dear friends and benefactors in France, and having placed ourselves under the protection of the Blessed Virgin Mary, we went to embrace the postulants who were awaiting us.[10] They led us to a small room which had been given up to them by the good farmer, Joseph Thralls. This rooms serves as bakery, refectory, recreation room. It is also an infirmary, and this is the only use it serves constantly. We have also a part of the garret, where they had put eight ticks, filled with straw, on the floor. It is so crowded that we have to dress ourselves on the beds and make them up one after the other, this strange dormitory is directly under the roof which is made of shingles badly joined, thus letting in the wind and rain, making it very cold.

---

[10] The four postulants awaiting the Sisters at Saint Mary-of-the-Woods were Miss Mary Doyle, Miss Frances Theriac, and Miss Agnes Dukent, all of Vincennes, and Miss Josephine Pardeillan, who had come from Alsace to join the Indiana foundation. Miss Theriac's poor health prevented her remaining more than a month. Miss Doyle stayed a year and a half. Miss Dukent, as Sister Agnes, and Miss Pardeillan, as Sister Marie Joseph, developed into admirable subjects whose names will occur frequently in the letters of this volume.

We were obliged to bring our dear Sister Basilide down to our room, for she is still quite ill, and God only knows whether she will ever recover. Sister Mary Xavier is also ill, but she does not suffer so much and has not constant fever. We take the best care of them we can, but God has not yet blessed our efforts.

It was, then, in this poor room that we were installed, and here we continue to live in the midst of the forest far from the habitations of men. Here too, but less courageous and less mortified than Father Buteux, we have already found the cross and privations. Here too in an outside kitchen open to the winds Sister Olympiade makes us soup of bacon, and salt beef, except on fast days. Friday, also Saturday last, Vigil of All Saints, she did indeed make *maigre* soup, for she had no butter either for the pot, the sauce, or for the table.

On All Saints Day our baggage came, all in perfect condition, thanks to the precautions taken by Mr. Byerley, who had all the boxes covered with pack cloth. There was a jar of butter put in by our dear Sister St. Vincent. Imagine how delighted we were to have it for our winter provision. There was also a jar of delicious Chalais preserves. See how rich we are!

The day after our arrival we went to look at our new house, now building. Like the castles of the knights of old, it is so deeply hidden in the woods that you cannot see it until you come up to it. Do not conclude, however, that it is built on the model of Father Buteux's. No, indeed. It is a pretty two-story brick house, fifty feet wide by twenty-six feet deep. There are five large openings in front. The first stone was laid August seventeenth and it is already roofed. Today they began plastering, but there are yet neither doors nor windows; all is being done, little by little. As to our garden and yard, we have all the woods. And the wilderness is our only cloister, for our house is like an oak tree planted therein.

Here is the list of our movables: twelve folding beds, an old bureau, a small cupboard or buffet—*bois blanc*—for the dishes and bread, a dozen wooden chairs and a table for the kitchen. Our dining-room table belongs to the farmer. As to the kitchen it is only a stove placed outside. We have pots, pans, etc., also a soup tureen, two dozen plates, two dozen spoons and forks, and one dozen knives. Besides these we have the trunks and boxes in which we brought our belongings from France. Some unbleached muslin was bought for sheets. This, then, is what we have for the foundation of a house, which the Bishop foresees will one day be a flourishing institution. No doubt; but we shall have to suffer much. Many things are wanting to us, yet we dare not complain. Shall we not be, and are we not already, in our own little nook? Besides, did we not come here to suffer—we who were so well provided for in France?

The French family whom I mentioned before [Brassier] are here. The man is to clear a corner of our land where cabbage and other vegetables will be planted next spring if we do not freeze before that time; for they say that the winter here is unbearable. Every year several persons are frozen to death.

I am not sure whether I told you of the insupportable pride of the Americans, However, I shall give you a little incident which happened yesterday, and which came very near putting me in the bad graces of everybody. Well, yesterday we had our washing done, the first of this kind, probably, ever done here. I shall not relate all the trouble we had to organize things, to get a tub, etc. I leave that for you to imagine. But I shall tell you that we had employed a young woman, an orphan, wretchedly poor and miserably clad, to help us wash. I attempted to show her what to do. At first she refused to take any direction, but, by coaxing, I secured the favor of showing her.

When dinner time came, there was my washerwoman sitting down at table with us. I was so indiscreet as to say it would be better for her not to take dinner with the Community. I wish you could have seen the change in the countenances of our American postulants! I had to compromise by telling the girl she might eat with the reader at the second table. The mere name of "servant" makes them revolt, and they throw down whatever they have in their hands and start off at once. You cannot hire either a man or a girl for more than a month at a time.

Just now we are suffering from the want of *sabots*. It seems to me that if I only had the tools I could make a pair for each one of us. We shall not be able to go outside without sinking deep in the mud, except when it freezes. In the winter we shall at least be able to keep warm, for we might burn fifty cords of wood without clearing ten acres of our land.

It is astonishing that this remote solitude has been chosen for a novitiate and especially for an academy. All appearances are against it. I have given my opinion frankly to the Bishop, to Father Buteux, and, in fine, to all who have any interest in the success of our work. All have given reasons that are not entirely satisfactory; yet I dare not disregard them. The spirit of this country is so different from ours that one ought to be acquainted with it before condemning those who know more about it than we do; so I await the issue before passing judgment in a positive manner. If we cannot do any good here, you know our agreement, we will return to our own country.

Dear France! Though far away, it is she nevertheless who, like a good mother, sends help to this poor diocese. She feeds our missionaries, helps to build our churches, to adorn them, in a word she does everything. Without the aid of France, what really would become of the poor missionaries who, notwithstanding, are so miserable? What would become of us also? It was a Frenchman, Joseph Picquet of Sainte Marie, Illinois, who gave the money to build our house. Who will now support it? Oh! The Daughters of Providence must fear nothing as to their future. They must confide themselves entirely to their good Mother, The Blessed Virgin Mary.

End of the First Journal

BIOGRAPHICAL NOTES

More than passing mention is due to the estimable Brooklyn family that gave hospitality to the Sisters when they landed in America. The name Parmentier is among the most distinguished in the Catholic history of New York. Beginning with 1815, the year in which Andrew Parmentier settled in Brooklyn, it is identified for a period of eighty years with every movement in the Church, connected with benevolent and social welfare.

Andrew Parmentier was a noted horticulturist. He established not only his botanical garden in New York, but several others in adjoining states in which, particularly, the culture of the table grape was a specialty. He was an authority as a landscape gardener also, his ideas being a departure from the old formal plans and exact regular lines, in favor of nature's course; this gave him an enviable reputation at home and abroad.

Apart from his commercial and artistic achievements, he was the type of Christian gentleman, philanthropic, and zealous for the promotion of the Faith. His death in 1830 was looked upon as a public loss.

For some years his business was continued by his wife, Silvia Parmentier, assisted by her daughter Adele. Eventually the estate was sold and divided up into city lots. The homestead, however, was retained, and it was there that Mother Theodore and her companions were welcomed when they landed in America, September 5, 1840. Many a bishop, missionary priest, and religious had been sheltered there; many another would follow the Sisters of Providence and receive the same gracious attention; but it is safe to say that none were more intimately associated in friendship with this admirable family during the succeeding years than the Sisters of Saint Mary-of-the-Woods.

Mother Theodore's diary records the exchange of letters between them until her death. All the letters received from the Parmentier family are preserved, but very few of the letters of Mother Theodore to them have been recovered. They were worn out by being sent around to the different friends who had made acquaintance with the servant of God during her brief stay in Brooklyn, and who followed with interest her work in Indiana.

Mrs. Parmentier spent her life in doing good. Confraternities were promoted by her, and one in particular, the Holy Childhood, was inaugurated by her in this country through the suggestion of Mother Theodore. When Mrs. Parmentier passed away her eulogy was summed up in these words, "Her life was saintly, her works those of a saint."

Mrs. Parmentier had two daughters, Adele and Rosine. Adele, later Mrs. Bayer, attained preëminence through her work among the sailors. She was called "The Angel of the Navy." Thirty years of her life were spent in caring for the spiritual and temporal wants of the sailors at the Brooklyn Navy Yard. The seamen of the world revered her as an angel and a friend.

Besides English Mrs. Bayer spoke French, Spanish, Italian, and German. In her visits to the ships she carried with her stores of rosaries, scapulars, pictures, and pamphlets. She obtained shore leave for the Catholics, that they might perform their religious duties, or secured permits for priests to attend them in the Navy Yard. She founded club rooms for them and provided good reading matter. She induced them to deposit with her one-half of their pay, which she put in the bank for themselves or their families; she had as many as a hundred bank books at a time for those reckless men who otherwise would not have saved a penny. Her prayers, her labors, her whole life, in fact, was for the sailor. (Reverend J. Van der Hayden in *Catholic Builders of the Nation*, Vol II, p. 34.)

In October 1925 took place (quoting from the Brooklyn

Tablet) "a double celebration under the auspices of the Parmentier-Bayer Centenary Commission—the unveiling of a tablet at the entrance to the Botanical Garden near the Museum, to Andrew Parmentier, famous Belgian horticulturist, artist, and philanthropist, who founded, just one hundred years ago, the first botanical garden in Brooklyn, and a tablet in the Brooklyn Navy Yard to his daughter, Adele Bayer, styled "the Guardian Angel of the Sailors."

Miss Rosine, while not engaged in such prominent works of mercy as her sister, was also renowned for her activities in Catholic enterprises. By her will she left the old home property to the Sisters of St. Joseph, who conduct therein a commercial school. It is pleasant to note that the house which had been honored in giving hospitality to so many holy and celebrated personages, including the Founder of Notre Dame and the Foundress of Saint Mary-of-the-Woods, should be devoted to a work of religion—Catholic Education. The name of the last scion of this illustrious family is thus linked with the others in hallowed perpetuity.

———

Samuel Byerley, also mentioned in the Journal, was a wholesale grocer in New York, well known to Mrs. Parmentier who engaged him to get the Sisters' baggage from the custom-house.

He was unremitting in his courtesies and kind services to the Sisters during their stay in the city, and when they were leaving he saw them safe on the boat that took them across the Hudson, even giving them his chief clerk, who could speak French, to accompany them as far as Philadelphia. Mother Theodore's diary has frequent mention in subsequent years of provisions—a sack of coffee, a barrel of sugar, etc.—received from this good friend.

Mr. Byerley with his family embraced the Catholic faith in 1841. Some years later he moved to northern Indiana, settled near South Bend and started a large dairy. He went beyond his means in the fine buildings he erected and, the dairy not becoming a success, his project proved a failure.

In grateful remembrance of his generosity Mother Theodore had him send his two daughters to Saint Mary-of-the-Woods to be educated without expense to him. The letters written to her by Mr. and Mrs. Byerley show their admiration of her and her institute, as well as a truly Christian spirit in bearing the reverses they had encountered in the West. Another venture, now in the city of South Bend, proved more of a success, and the Byerley name still exists in that industrial city.

———

Joseph Thralls was the farmer at Saint Mary-of-the-Woods with whom the Bishop of Vincennes had made arrangements to accommodate the Sisters until their own house would be ready. In his little dwelling, comprising four rooms and the loft where the corn was stored, four young women had boarded a month awaiting the Sisters who arrived on October 22, 1840. One room, half of the corn loft, and a wood shed were allotted to the Community now numbering ten persons. They lived thus crowded together for five weeks, Mr. Thralls then sold the property—the house and about eighty acres of land—to the Bishop for eighteen hundred dollars and moved to another location in the vicinity. Although it would seem this was good compensation for the property, since the land had been bought originally by Mr. Thralls for less than three dollars an acre, it was generous in the family to leave their little home and settle elsewhere. The Sisters have always held this kindness in grateful remembrance, and "Uncle Joe" and "Aunt Sallie" are household names in the Convent.

The Bishop informed the Sisters of the purchase of their home by a letter dated November 22, 1840, saying: "You are soon going to be rich proprietors. I have bought Thralls' property and paid $200 less for having waited." Bishop de la Hailandière had promised the Bishop of Le Mans and the Superiors at Ruillé to give the Sisters their home in Indiana. This was the first step in the fulfilment of his promise.

Joseph Thralls died February 21, 1865, aged seventy-two years. His wife died October 14, 1876, aged eighty-three. An obituary in the New York *Freeman's Journal* said in part: " 'Aunt Sallie', as she was fondly called by old and young, was one of the early pioneers of Vigo County, Indiana, and the last of the noble little band that some sixty years previously had left their homes in Kentucky and come to seek new homes and fairer fortunes in the wild forests of Indiana. She and her late husband, a man whose memory is and ever will be held in benediction at Saint Mary's, were for many years the main support of the missionary priests in these parts. And, too, they were the first to receive the good Sisters of Providence on their arrival from France. 'Aunt Sallie' was more favored than most women in this world, for she lived to bless her children to the third generation. She had twelve children and thirty-five grandchildren."

Two brothers of Joseph Thralls, Jacob and Francis, held lands adjoining his. The little settlement went by the name of Thrawls Station.

In the spring of 1838 Bishop Bruté bought from Joseph Thralls for the sum of fifteen dollars a plot of ground 12 rods by 24 rods (about one and four-fifths acres) on which he built a fair-sized frame church. The Bishop called the church *Saint Mary-of-the-Woods*, and soon the station became known by the same name.

The church burned down in February 1840, eight months before the arrival of the Sisters. This misfortune accounts for the poor log chapel described by Mother Theodore. On the clearing where the church had stood was built the first academy. That hallowed spot is now the south half of the court of what was formerly known as Saint Mary's Academy, but which, since the closing of the high school department in 1931, has become a unit of the college group.

The first academy, having soon become too small, was enlarged in 1846 by a wing on each side. This in time also became too small and in 1860 a new building of large proportions was begun, surrounding the first except in front. Owing to the Civil War, which broke out the following year, and other causes of delay, it was not until 1870 that the new house was entirely occupied and the original building taken away. This new academy served without the front section until 1898, in which year the present four-story structure was completed, making an enclosed court, which, as has been said, includes the site of the first Catholic Church in Vigo County and the first Academy of Saint Mary-of-the Woods.

PART II

EARLY LETTERS
(1841-1843)

MOTHER THEODORE'S letters, as recorded in her diary, number nearly five thousand. The first from Saint Mary-of-the-Woods were naturally to the Sisters in France, to their Bishop at Le Mans, and to the Mends whose names have been mentioned in the Journal of Travel. Many of these letters have not been recovered.

The first on file is to Reverend Augustine Martin, whose interest in the rising Community of Saint Mary-of-the-Woods entitled him to be called its first benefactor. He gave the Sisters their first eight-days' retreat in the New World (November 30 to December 7, 1840), at which time he saw how they were situated and realized the difficulties that confronted them, some being of a peculiar and very trying nature. Referring to these matters he wrote (December 21, 1840), "In all this and by all this, my good Mother, may God be praised and glorified. He permits all these little miseries in the beginning to test your courage as Mother and consolidate the work. You know well, Mother, that all the works which God does by human hands must be affected by the infirmity of man and be purified and consecrated by tribulation. Have great courage. Every trial is a blessing.

The first retreat opened the way to mutual confidence. Father Martin was the instrument used by Almighty God to impart life and strength to the perplexed and suffering Mother Foundress. The second retreat, which he also gave (August 1841), cemented more firmly the bond of union between him and the Sisterhood. He was untiring in his efforts to get subjects for the order. He was the founder of the museum, by gift of his large collection of geological specimens. He gave the first physics apparatus to the newly

71

opened Academy. In circumstances of grave and vital importance to the Community, as well as to the diocese, he was the
medium of communication with the Holy See; in fact, he spon-
sored every movement for the well-being and expansion of the
institution.

Father Martin was born in 1802, at St. Servan, Brittany.
After completing the Humanities at the College of Rennes he
began his studies for the priesthood. He was a protégé of the
saintly, Abbé Jean Marie de Lamennais. According to the
Catholic Encyclopedia, "as a seminarian, he was employed at
the great Almonry of France in Paris under Cardinal Prince de
Troy and Vicar-General J. M. de Lamennais. There he came in
contact with Montalembert and other disciples of Felicité de
Lamennais, and acquired the polished manners that never left
him." He came to Indiana in 1839, having resigned his chap-
laincy in the Royal College of Rennes, in order to associate
himself as a missionary with Bishop de la Hailandière, who
made him his Vicar General. From 1839 to 1845 he was successively pastor at Vincennes, at Logansport, and director of
the Seminary at Vincennes. In 1846 failing health took him to
the South. Having detached himself from the Diocese of
Vincennes, he went to Louisiana where he was pastor, first at
Baton Rouge, then at Natchitoches. In 1852 he was appointed
Vicar General by Archbishop Blanc of New Orleans. In 1853 he
was named first Bishop of Natchitoches. He died in 1875.

TO THE VERY REVEREND AUGUSTINE MARTIN,

V.G. LOGANSPORT, INDIANA

Providence of Saint Mary's, May 1, 1841

Dear Sir and Honored Father in Our Lord,

The letter you had the kindness to write to me was
received with the postulant you sent. The young girl appears to be a very good child; perhaps we shall find her such.
Since she has been sent and recommended by you, presumption
is in her favor. She arrived without any mishap last Sunday,
the twenty-sixth of April. She now bears the name

of Sister Augustine.[1] I suspect a little devotedness towards you influenced her choice, which I certainly did not find bad.

Our little Philomene[2] is a good child who tries to correct her faults and to acquire the virtues that are wanting to her. She has already made notable progress, with several victories over her humor, and today she is to be received into the novitiate by a ceremony in the chapel consisting of the chanting of the *Veni Creator* and the *Ave Maris Stella*, and announcing the names of the candidates. Could we choose a more beautiful day to increase, in one way, the number of the children of our poor little institute who are, likewise, by so many titles children of Mary? Two other postulants will share this favor with her [Sister Stanislaus Reade and Sister Gabriella Moore]. You see the number is increasing since the retreat. Yes, Father, since last we received your blessing the number of subjects has increased; we are now sixteen persons in our House.

Pray, O pray Our Lord that they may be holy and altogether according to His Heart. Pray especially, dear Father, that my sins and infidelities, opposing the designs of Almighty God, may not draw His maledictions upon this infant Community. How many reasons I have to fear this misfortune! This fear, however, does not take away my confidence; for, in His mercy, the God of Love has deigned to send me crosses, and with this precious heavenly gift a certain strength to bear them, I may even say, a love of these crosses and a firm reliance on this way of crucifixion.

[1] Sister Augustine, Miss Mary Ann Graham of Peru, Indiana.

[2] Sister Philomene, Miss Catherine Doyle.

Sister Philomene was a sister of the Fathers William and Philip Doyle, students in the Ecclesiastical Seminary at Vincennes, and of Sister Lucy who entered the Community a year later and lived therein to advanced age. The family belonged to Logansport, Indiana, where Father Martin was pastor at that time. Sister Philomene was the first recruit received by the Sisters of Providence after the first four postulants mentioned in the preceding journal. She entered November 29, 1840, brought to Saint Mary's by Father Martin who, on that day, began the retreat to the Sisters—their first retreat in their New World home.

The holy counsels that you gave us during our retreat have greatly aided me. We say among ourselves that our good God showed you our future in order to warn us against a surprise, and to strengthen our souls for the day of tribulation.

I have followed exactly your recommendations in regard to the Bishop, and I have found them good—indeed, very good. He is an excellent father. I have never found a more compassionate heart, one more charitable, under so cold an exterior. One thing that deeply grieves my heart is the pain we give to him. So far there is nothing but complaints about us. I confide this to your paternity, lamenting it, and at the same time admiring the ways of Providence; for, most truly we are all disposed to do all we can to acquire the perfection of our state, to walk with courage in the narrow path, and to follow the Divine Spouse who has deigned to call us in preference to so many others who would be worth infinitely more than we are. This good will, of course, is not equally strong in all the Sisters; but you know, dear Father, grace is not given equally to all, nor at the same time. With a little patience, I hope all will go on well; but, in the meantime, we are under humiliation. Oh, good way for the proud, accustomed to be praised, admired, and carried along, and who now find themselves, like rejected stones, good for nothing!

As to myself in particular, I cannot cease admiring the merciful ways of God. Thank Him for us and beseech Him, let me repeat it, that we may become daughters according to His Heart. I am forgetting myself, in writing such a long letter. You will pardon me when you learn that for a long time I have yearned for this consolation, and only my illness prevented me from giving myself this satisfaction sooner.

We hope you will have the kindness to come again to give us our retreat at the end of the summer. We desire it most intensely. May you find us all belonging to God, and find us good. This is the fervent wish of her who is, with the most profound veneration, my most honored Father.

Your very humble servant,

SISTER ST. THEODORE[3]

The next priest actively engaged in behalf of the new Community at Saint Mary-of-the-Woods was the pastor at Madison, Reverend Julian Delaune. A native of Brittany, he soon developed a highly sympathetic interest in the work of another native of Brittany, the Foundress of the Sisters of Providence in Indiana, and concerned himself about procuring subjects for her, at the same time expecting to be one of the earlist beneficiaries of his own zealous efforts.

Father Delaune, a scholarly and spiritual man, was one of the missionaries brought over from France in 1836 by Bishop Bruté. His first priestly labors were in the neighborhood of Vincennes: at St. Patrick's, St. Peter's, and Saint Mary's. In 1842 he was appointed to St. Michael's Church, Madison, where he remained until June 1846. He then severed his connection with the diocese and went to take the presidency of Saint Mary's College, near Lebanon, Kentucky, (previously conducted by the Jesuits), to which Father Sorin of Notre Dame had just transferred his Brothers. Two years later, upon the Brothers' return to Notre Dame and the closing of the college in Kentucky, Father Delaune went to Rochester, in the Diocese of Buffalo, to be director of a new college established in that city. There his health failed and he returned to France. He died in Paris in 1849 at the age of thirty-seven years.

His loss to the Diocese of Vincennes was keenly felt both by the priests and people of Indiana, who esteemed him, in the words of Bishop Alerding, "a pious, active, zealous, and charitable priest, and a man of much energy of character and earnestness of purpose."[4]

---

[3] Although the word "Saint" was dropped from her name in addressing her, Mother Theodore retained it in her signature.

[4] Alerding, *A History of the Catholic Church in the Diocese of Vincennes* (1883), p. 352.

TO THE REVEREND J. DELAUNE, MADISON, INDIANA

Saint Mary's, May 31, 1841

So we shall have a postulant from Madison! I cannot sufficiently express my thankfulness, dear Reverend Father, for the
interest you take in our novitiate. Yes, we must have
subjects if we are to continue the work begun here at Saint
Mary-of-the-Woods. In the six months that have passed since
our arrival twelve have joined us. That would be very encouraging if all persevered; but, fortunately, one returned to her
family, unable to sacrifice her affections; and there are some
others whom we shall be obliged to dismiss unless a great
change takes place in their hearts. I beg your Reverence to
pray for these dear children, that they may acquire the spirit
of their holy vocation. It is difficult for many to understand
the necessity of religious obedience; especially does this seem,
to be the case in this country where the spirit of independence
is carried into everything. You understand what I mean,
Reverend Father. Be pleased then to assist me by your fervent
prayers in this great work of forming them to the religious life,
and send us all the good subjects you can.

I bless God for this increase, and also for the tidings
received today from the Bishop of Kentucky [Bishop Flaget] to
whom you had the kindness to recommend us. He expects to
send us a postulant in a few months. She is a little above the
age at which we like to receive them, but we may accept her if
everything else is satisfactory. In gratitude for your kindness
we shall all offer our Communion tomorrow for you and the
intention for which you requested our prayers. In Jesus, Mary,
and Joseph,

Yours most humbly and gratefully,

SISTER ST. THEODORE

FACSIMILE OF AN ORIGINAL LETTER OF MOTHER THEODORE
Reduced one-half

October 19, 1841

Dear Vicar General:

The little orphan girl arrived in good health. It is not necessary to say that we shall take tender care of her—I am sure that you do not doubt that. As regards her money, send it just when convenient.

I thank you for rejoicing with us in the arrival at New York of our dear Irma, and for your wishes for our happiness and prosperity. They will be realized, I hope, if you ask it of God. Oh, I entreat you, dear Father, to place on your paten at the Holy Sacrifice this poor little Community, whose needs you understand so well, and which is so severely tried in its beginning. Its crosses and trials give me confidence. But I derive my hope above all, and most especially, from our utter incapacity, for it is always upon nothingness that God is pleased to rear His works. If at any day we accomplish some good here, the glory will certainly be His alone, since He has employed for this end instruments more capable of spoiling everything than of making it succeed.

In that God, so good, I am, with sentiments of the deepest veneration, *Monsieur le Grand Vicaire,*

Your very humble servant,

SISTER ST. THEODORE

Religious of Providence

Providence of Saint Mary's, October 19, 1841

The Irma mentioned in this letter was Irma le Fer de la Motte, in religion Sister St. Francis Xavier, whose life was so closely linked with that of Mother Theodore Guérin. She had pledged herself to the Indiana foundation and had gone to Mother Theodore at Soulaines in November, 1839, with the expectation of starting at once for Vincennes, Learning that the Sisters were not to go until the summer following, she went to the Motherhouse at Ruillé-sur-Loir to make her novitiate.

But when the Sisters were chosen for this "foreign mission"
in the spring of 1840, Sister St. Francis was not among the
number. Her delicate health had decided the superiors to
retain her in France. This was a trial for both Mother
Theodore and Sister St Francis, but they parted in the hope of
soon being reunited in Indiana.

The families—Martin and Le Fer de la Motte—were neighbors at St. Servan and closely united in friendship. Father
Martin said Mass soon after his ordination in the chapel at
Lorette on the Fer de la Motte estate. This family friendship
accounts for the personal mention that frequently occurs in
these letters. To Father Martin Irma ascribes her courage to
follow her vocation as a missioner in Indiana.[5]

The next letter is to the Reverend Joseph Kundek, another
of the early friends and benefactors of the Community. Father
Kundek became the first resident pastor of Jasper in 1838,
with a congregation of fifteen families. Although an Austrian
nobleman, he had no other means than the wealth of an apostolic spirit and an untiring energy. He was a noted organizer
and builder. Besides erecting the churches at Jasper, Fulda,
and Troy, the German church at Madison, and the first German
church in New Orleans (while he was there for his health), he
built the court house in Jasper and laid out the town of
Ferdinand and built a fine stone church there. In 1842 he
established the Sisters of Providence at Jasper, and ten years
later he brought the Benedictine Fathers from Einsiedeln to
the diocese.

In 1851 he was made Vicar General by Bishop de St. Palais.
Alerding's *History of the Diocese of Vincennes* (p. 305) says of
him: "He was a most remarkable man; his herculean labors
seem almost superhuman. His memory in Jasper and the surrounding country will remain forever in benediction." He died
December 4, 1857. The high regard Mother Theodore had for
him is apparent in her letters. The two following refer to the
first mission opened by the Sisters of Providence, their first
Parish School.

---

[5] *Life and Letters of Sister St. Francis Xavier*, edition 1935. Providence
Press, Saint Mary-of-the-Woods.

TO THE REVEREND JOSEPH KUNDEK, JASPER, INDIANA

Providence of Saint Mary's, Dec. 9, 1841

Monsieur le Missionnaire:

We received very gratefully the postulant you had the kindness to send us. Accept our thanks for this, as well as for all the preparations you are making to receive our Sisters, whom we shall send to you in the month of March as you desire. But I should be much pleased if you would be so kind as to wait for the feast of St. Joseph and have the installation on that day. It would be a great consolation for us to place our first establishment under the patronage of this great Saint, who is a patron of our Congregation.

I cannot say anything yet of your good little postulant, except that she seems nice, and especially very pious. She is writing to you.

Accept the homage of profound respect and lively gratitude with which I am, Monsieur,

Your very humble servant,

SISTER ST. THEODORE.

TO THE SAME

February 14, 1842

Monsieur le Missionnaire:

I must begin by begging you to pardon my delay in answering your esteemed letter. I am truly ashamed; but I was waiting for our good Father [the Bishop], who was here, to decide which would be better: you to come for the Sisters, or they to go to Vincennes. His Lordship desires that you come with your carriage for them, if it be possible. They will be ready to start on Friday, the eleventh of next month. Should it be impossible for you to come yourself, could you send a trusty man? I shall send their baggage afterwards by a steamboat or by the stage.

In regard to the secular housekeeper, if it could be easily arranged, we prefer to do without her. Will it be too late, do you think, to decide about this when the Sisters shall have arrived at Jasper? Do what may seem best.

I hope to see you soon, to recommend in a very particular manner the dear daughters whom we confide to you. May they procure the glory of God and respond to your zeal for your dear flock! This is my most ardent wish; and for this end we spare nothing, since we give good Sister St. Vincent, who is our Assistant, to form this first establishment. The Sisters who are associated with her [Sister Marie Joseph Pardeillan and Sister Gabriella Moore] are, like herself, filled with piety and good will. Everything leads us to hope that God will bless these first fruits, even on the day chosen for their installation—Saturday, the day consecrated to the special veneration of Mary our good Mother. It is also St. Joseph's feast. What a happy coincidence!

Deign to accept the homage of respect and gratitude with which I remain, Monsieur,

Your very humble servant,

SISTER ST. THEODORE.

Now comes a letter to the Bishop of Le Mans, to whom Mother Theodore had confided all her fears and anxieties about undertaking the American mission. Inasmuch as the House in Indiana was under his protection, it was natural for her to acquaint him with every little detail concerning the foundation and to pour out her whole heart to him. The following letter begins this confidential correspondence:

TO THE MOST REVEREND J. B. BOUVIER,
BISHOP OF LE MANS

Saint Mary-of-the-Woods, August 22, 1842

My Lord and venerated Father,

Permit me to come and converse with you for some moments about your daughters of the Woods. Their sorrows and their joys are yours, since you are so kind as ever to be their father.

Some months ago a gloom was spread over our solitude on account of very sad news which had reached us. We were threatened with the loss of our father! We heard that you were going to leave Le Mans. I cannot tell you how grieved we were. We looked upon this event as a real calamity for our dear Sisters in France, but more especially for ourselves; because if our House in Indiana exists, if it has already begun to prosper, it is indeed to you, next to God that we owe it. You have been constantly for us the best of fathers and our protector. Judge, then, whether the fear of losing you must not have been painful! It was the same, too, with our Bishop. Therefore he hastened to make us share in his joy when he learned from the newspaper that Your Lordship had declined the Archbishopric of Tours. We have all returned sincere thanks to Our Lord, and we continue to thank Him every day for having preserved you, our good father, to us.

Bishop de la Hailandière is always interested in us, never ceasing to give us proofs of it. He is having considerable work done to our house, too much in fact for his resources. He exhausts himself and imposes privations upon himself for us; and yet I am not satisfied. I should like to pay our debts before doing things that are not necessary. On several other points, too, I am not always of his opinion; for instance, as to the reception of subjects, the admission to the

habit, and even to the vows, and the acceptance of establishments. I am afraid of proceeding too quickly, and the
Bishop says that in this country nothing is done slowly; however, His Lordship is satisfied with expressing his opinion
without making it a law; hence, so far, we have received only
the subjects that suit us, and he has allowed us to send away
two postulants chosen by himself before our arrival. As to
the first, he allowed us to act; but for the second he assisted
us with his authority.

Thus far we have only one establishment [Jasper], which
has cost nothing to our House and which gives out of its abundance. We should be happy if it could always go on this way,
but we fear somewhat for the future. One would require the
talent of never seeming to oppose the will or even the desires
of our Bishop, but to bring him always, by good reasons, to will
of his own accord what one desires, and to let him think it is
done as he has wished. I think, my Lord, that you understand
my thought, and that you will be so good as to interpret it
favorably.

I tell you all this only as a prelude to a favor I am going
to ask in the name of all your daughters of the Woods,
whether French or American. It is this:—That you will
never permit this poor little House of the Forest to be separated from its trunk. If you cut it off it will wither like the
branch cut from the tree which gave it life. I believe we are
even more attached to our dear Ruillé, to our good Mothers,
than when we were at a less distance from them; and this
sincere attachment is readily shared by all our Sisters of
the New World.

A good religious spirit is being established little by little
in our Community, which is always on the increase. We
are now six professed Sisters, nine novices, and eight postulants. The example of Sister St. Francis Xavier is of great
advantage in forming our young candidates to the religious

life. Having learned the fundamental, they end by practicing all the religious virtues. There are some who are admirable for courage and devotedness. How much good in germ is this little seed, which would develop of itself if it were well cultivated!

Above all, it seems to me, there is a great charity, a true affection among the Sisters; and since we are rid of that novice of whom I spoke to you before, I have neither seen nor heard anything which would show disunion. But that person indemnifies herself for no longer harming us within, by harming us without. She has taken as an associate a Catholic lady of good reputation, and they have started a school at Terre Haute in opposition to ours, and they are succeeding; we shall have very few pupils next year. We do not expect this trial to last long, as there is so much inconstancy in the Americans. It is certainly very painful for us to meet with obstacles where naturally we ought to find help.

Another contradiction was the arrival here of Mlle. Bernard without our having had the least suspicion that she was even in America. She was brought by the Bishop who, without telling us we *must* receive her into the novitiate, wished it very much. Notwithstanding, I said I would not receive her, and the poor thing was to return to Vincennes, when Sisters St. Francis and Basilide, overcome by her entreaties and nice appearance, begged me to allow that Ruillé might be consulted about her. I reluctantly consented, and she awaits the answer here.

We have just had our retreat; it closed on the fifteenth of this month. Four postulants received the habit. Sister M. Liguori took her vows. The ceremonies are very touching here in the midst of the forest. The retreat was very edifying because of the recollection of the Sisters. Not a word was spoken, even during the periods of relaxation, except for very necessary things. One could not help feeling a holy emotion in beholding these good Americans so occupied with the affairs of their souls, with the desire of pleasing God, of making sacrifices to Him. Please pray for them.

I have just received a kind letter from our dear Sisters St. Charles and Eudoxie. The former tells me that our good Mother is willing to forgive and forget my faults. I hope God will render to her a hundred-fold for the good this favor does me. Deign to strengthen the bonds which unite me to this dear Mother, and to give your paternal blessing to all your daughters of Indiana, especially to the one who has the honor to be, my Lord.

The very humble servant of Your Lordship,

SISTER ST. THEODORE.

What the faults were to which Mother Theodore alludes in this letter is not known; but some instances in which she incurred her Superior's displeasure may he cited, as gathered from her contemporaries. When the Sisters were selected for Vincennes, and Sister St. Francis Xavier (Irma le Fer de la Motte) was not among the number, Mother Theodore urged strongly that Sister had pledged herself to Bishop de la Hailandière and that she had gone to Ruillé only to prepare herself for the Indiana foundation. Mother Theodore might also have been too insistent when she found that among her associates for Vincennes there was no one who could teach music (the Bishop of Vincennes had requested a music teacher for his mission); in fact, she was reprehended for her want of submission, as Mother Mary termed it. Further, on the advice of the Bishop of Le Mans, Mother Theodore had accepted a novice who had appealed to him for the privilege of joining her little band. Mother Mary had said that she would say neither Yes nor No, that Sister Theodore might do as she pleased about it; yet, when Mother Theodore accepted the novice, Mother Mary was disappointed. Another cause of her disapproval was that, later, Mother Theodore gave to the Bishop of Vincennes two hundred dollars to complete the purchase of the Thralls' property at Saint Mary-of-the-Woods, money that Mother Mary had given "for the needs of the Sisters."

God's ways are inscrutable. Mother Mary was a fine, good Mother Superior, remarkable in administration and greatly admired by her Community, as may be inferred from the fact that she was retained in office nearly fifty years. Yet there were times when the conflict of views between her and Mother Theodore was the occasion of sharp suffering to the latter. It was the means, no doubt, employed by Divine Wisdom to bring the holy Foundress up to that perfection which would make her worthy of the sublime mission for which she was destined. Deprived of the greatest of human comforts—the support of her Mother General—she necessarily had to rely completely on Divine help and consolation.

TO THE VERY REVEREND A. MARTIN, LOGANSPORT

September 6, 1842

Dear Vicar General:

Your praises of the young person you have the kindness to offer us cause us to accept her willingly and with gratitude. You have replied in advance to the objections we might have made, particularly as to the trial it might be for her to see her sister say the Office, teach, and, perhaps, later on, advance while she would have to remain in an inferior rank. But your wisdom has foreseen all this, and you have assured yourself of her dispositions relative to the situation.

This dear child may come, then, whenever you wish to send her; or, which would be more pleasing to us, bring her yourself. That would give great pleasure to every one here, but to none more than to her who remains with deepest veneration

Your very humble servant,

SISTER ST. THEODORE.

September 8, 1842

Monsieur et cher Compatriote,

You could give us no better proof of your interest in our
work than your efforts to send us subjects. If God wants us in
the diocese, as you seem to think, we have a great work before
us, a work that requires brave and self-sacrificing hearts.
Engage your brother priests to encourage vocations; no doubt
in their missionary travel well-disposed young people will be
found. If these are in good health and otherwise desirable for a
religious body, they will be useful even without the qualifications for teachers. By their humility, obedience, and piety, they
will draw down God's blessing upon us, while fulfilling the
domestic duties of the convent.

We will accept good subjects for both kinds of duty, and
endeavor by our prayers to make return to those who aid us and
are truly our benefactors. What would the material part be without the spiritual? We are pleased with the postulant you have
sent us. You know our needs, you know what kind of subjects we
want. I feel confident that any you send will be desirable. What a
sweet providence it is to find friends thus willing to assist us.

Accept the profound gratitude of my poor little Community,
and be pleased also to aid us with your prayers. If you can put
me in communication with other ecclesiastics who might be
able to send us subjects, the favor will be gratefully acknowledged by her who has the honor to remain

Your humble servant,

SISTER ST. THEODORE.

Saint Mary's, September 27, 1842

Monsieur le Missionnaire,

Sister St. Vincent Ferrer writes me that a music teacher

is again asked for at your mission. It is absolutely impossible to give one at present. We are obliged then to ask you to wait some time longer. Several of our novices are taking lessons of the Music Master. Some among them are fairly well advanced and give us hope that in a few months we shall be of more assistance to you. And I will tell you in confidence, I have not one now who would be able to fulfil your hopes. It is necessary that all should spend some time here in order to be instructed, not only in the sciences but also to be formed to virtue. The great misfortune of communities is the placing of their subjects too soon on the missions. As for ourselves, who are foreigners, having little knowledge of the language, you understand that more time is required to prepare our novices, and that the first year of their novitiate was almost lost.

Pray, then, have a little patience with us. Be firmly convinced that the glory of God, the salvation of souls and, very especially, the good of your establishment, induce us to defer the change of Sister Gabriella[6] to which at first I agreed, overcome by your entreaties, but which, truly, was not the most advantageous thing for your house; so God did not permit that our good father [the Bishop] should approve of this change for the present. Let us submit, all of us, on both sides, and let us do what depends on us to advance the glory of our dear Jesus, the Spouse of our souls and of His Holy Church. After that, let us remain in peace; for we are not called upon to do all the good possible, but only that which we can do.

I should be happy to see you. If Heaven grants me this favor I shall return thanks from the bottom of my heart. I commend to you very particularly all my dear Sisters. Aid

---

[6] Father Kundek had suggested that Sister Gabriella be replaced by a music teacher.

them to acquire the spirit of sacrifice and of death to self. Pray for them, pray for all the Daughters of Providence, and most particularly for the pressing needs of the one who is, in our Divine Saviour,

Your devoted servant,

SISTER ST. THEODORE.

TO THE SAME

Saint Mary-of-the-Woods, Indiana (No date)

Monsieur le Missionnaire:

I have received your two most gracious letters and I thank you for them very cordially. I learn with pain of the illness of Sister St. Vincent. It is surprising that, being sick, she went out Friday in such cold weather. I do not approve of that kind of fervor; it is not fervor at all, but real imprudence. Scold her, I beg of you, for she well deserves it.

I know also that this dear Sister, though full of good will, is sometimes too severe with her Sisters, and that she causes authority to be too much felt. I am sure she does not perceive this fault. Often I have spoken to her about it, and recently I have written to her on the subject; but I doubt whether that will correct her. It seems to me that you, her confessor, in whom she has much confidence, can do more than anyone else. This is for the glory of God, therefore do I propose it to your zeal. I feel that it would be superfluous to recommend to you the health of these dear Sisters, especially of the one who is now sick. So sure am I of your charity that I should consider it a fault to doubt it an instant.

If we had only to wish it, we would send you immediately a Sister to teach music, but the will can do nothing against the impossibility of complying with your request. I think I have already told you that we have no musicians among our Sisters. A master gives lessons here to the pupils and to the postulants. It is equally impossible to fix the time when we shall be able to give you one. This pains me, for there is nothing that I am not disposed to do for the house which you honor with your protection, and of which you are the father.

You are also a benefactor of our entire little Congregation. I therefore take the liberty to beg of you to think of our Institute when you can send some of your parishioners away to a boarding school. I dare assure you that nowhere can they receive a better education than in our school. I recommend this matter to you as to our true friend. I beg of you also to accept the homage of the profound veneration with which I am

Your very humble and obedient servant,
SISTER ST. THEODORE.

Trial came early to the little colony in the Woods. On October 2, 1842, fire destroyed the barns and granary. A plentiful harvest had just been gathered in. The buildings contained feed for the stock, the winter supply of flour and other provisions, and all the farm implements. Now all was gone.

To add to the distress of the Sisters the merchants of Terre Haute refused them further credit. The Bishop then sent three barrels of flour from Vincennes, and later a Mr. Sanford, who had a mill about four miles west of Saint Mary's, let them have what they needed, payment at their convenience. The Sisters always remembered with deep gratitude this kind consideration of Mr. Sanford.

The ensuing letter is to thank for a gift of a thousand francs sent by the Bishop of Le Mans and the Motherhouse of Ruillé upon learning of the calamity that had befallen the Sisters in Indiana.

TO THE MOST REVEREND J. BOUVIER, BISHOP OF LE MANS

Saint Mary-of-the-Woods, Indiana, Feb. 23, 1843

My Lord and Father:

With feelings of the most sincere gratitude I come to thank you for the very paternal letter which Your Lordship has deigned to write to us, and which did us so much good; as also did that of our beloved Mother, which shows so well her good heart. You also suffer on our account with our dear Superiors. Our afflictions are yours—we have never doubted it; and yet to read it in your dear letters increases our joy, without however increasing the filial love and respectful attachment which we entertain for you; for these sentiments cannot be greater than they are.

My Lord, truly we have much to suffer in our deep forest, surrounded by enemies, having no other support, no other consoler than God alone. I in particular have trials which are personal, were it only that of having charge, almost alone, of a Congregation already numerous, to whom I have not always bread to give; and often I do not know where to procure what is absolutely necessary for the morrow, not counting the many contradictions which happen daily, and the fear of being burned down by our enemies. How often in looking at my dear Sisters leaving the chapel after night prayers have I not said to myself: It is perhaps the last time that we shall meet together at the feet of Our Lord. How often this winter have I not started out of my sleep, thinking that I heard the noise of the flames and saw their terrible light!

I believe our situation here is not well understood. Despite these sufferings (I tell you this, Father, very simply), I have generally preserved peace of heart, and even my natural gaiety. Sometimes I have even felt full of love and gratitude towards God who has deigned, in spite of my sins, to grant me the grace of suffering for Him; which favor appears to me greater than all the other gifts of heaven. This habitual state of calm, it is true, has from time to time its tempests. I am sometimes so depressed, so disheartened that I feel inclined to excessive sadness. In these moments I have often felt that I should be glad to die; but immediately thinking of my Sisters, I have been ashamed of my cowardice and have asked God's pardon. The keenest of my pains was the thought that our good Mother was not pleased with me, that I had not her approbation—*that* was the source of my greatest misery. Her maternal letter, so full of affection, has come to heal this wound and strengthen my heart, which is better able to meet any other adversity. Oh! may God return to this dear Mother the good she has done to her daughter of the Woods!

Forgive me, my Lord, for going into such details about my miseries, and permit me to thank you for the charity you had in sending money to us. It was like a gift from heaven, and is a new proof of the tender watchfulness of that divine Providence, of which we are in truth doubly the children. We had but one dollar remaining of what Mr. Byerley had lent us, and we did not know where to get a cent for the wants of the house. Still, how could I mistrust Divine Providence? Now I get flour on credit in the firm hope of soon being able to pay; so, my good Father, we have bread, shoes, etc., thanks to your liberality. May we not in truth call you our father?

Miss Bernard was admitted into our house against my will formally and strongly expressed. I had said that I would not receive her, and I wrote to the Bishop of Vincennes that having said No, I would never say Yes. Displeasure was the result. Our Sisters were consulted. It was settled with them that she might be admitted to the probation of the novitiate. Sister St. Francis more particularly took her in charge. I thought I ought to yield for the sake of peace, persuaded that this person, when better known, would never be received. In fact every one could see that she was not made for the religious life, especially in America; however, I believe God has punished me for having yielded, from the trouble we had to get rid of her. She left only a week ago. Even in sending her away we could not avoid displeasing our good Bishop, who was vexed because we had sent away another at Christmas.

Those who remain appear to be animated by the best spirit. I believe you would be pleased with us, if you saw us. We are asked to form establishments in several towns of Indiana. Everything leads us to hope that our House is called upon to do a great deal of good in this country; but that miserable money is wanting, without which one cannot live even here.

All our Sisters offer you their respectful homage and thanks. Give us all your paternal blessing and deign to pray for us. Pray especially, I entreat you, for the pressing needs of the one who is with the most filial attachment, my Lord, of Your Lordship,

The most humble and most submissive daughter,

SISTER ST. THEODORE.

TO VERY REVEREND A. MARTIN, VINCENNES

March 10, 1843

Respected Sir, Dear Vicar General,

I should like to have been the first to present good wishes and to offer you the greetings of all your daughters of the forest. I expected to do so by an opportunity which, however, escaped me. I beg you to believe that our wishes are none the less sincere and comprehensive than those you have had the goodness to offer for all of us in general, and for myself, in particular, who stand in so great need of help from on high.

I feel confident that you have the charity to pray for me often; and what gives me this confidence is less the tender interest that you are pleased to take in our house than a certain sympathy of soul, which inspires me to pray often for you and to feel deeply all your tribulations. The expression of your good will towards us has consoled my heart and sustained my courage. Sometimes I feel almost sinking under the weight, not only of present miseries, but still more, perhaps, under the apprehension of future misfortunes with which we are threatened. Pray, O pray, for our poor Congregation, so young and yet already so tried. Do not say that you can do nothing for it. Indeed you can hope much from God and from man.

Father Buteux brought me the books and the letter you had intrusted to his care. I have distributed the former according to your instructions. All were received with great joy and lively gratitude, no one being more grateful than I in receiving what the Bishop destined for Saint Mary's.

We began today to read the books publicly. They will undoubtedly edify us by putting before our minds the labors and virtues of the first apostles of Kentucky, which we see every day reproduced by the evangelical workers in Indiana who, also, amid tears scatter the good seed, the seed of the Holy Word, upon the unresponsive soil of our land. We shall be only too happy to have part, be it only in a small measure, in their labors and sacrifices, as we also hope to have a share in their reward. (Kindness of Father Buteux.)

Reverend Stanislaus Buteux, S.E., the first chaplain at Saint Mary-of-the-Woods, was introduced by Mother Theodore herself in her first *Journal*. Little can be added to the encomium she there bestowed upon him:—"A Parisian of brilliant education, appearing incomparable in learning and piety, who has renounced everything to come to gain souls to Christ."

He was one of the Eudists whom Bishop Bruté brought to the diocese in 1836 to found a college in Vincennes. As the college grew slowly Father Buteux could be spared for parochial work; accordingly, he was given the care of the Catholics in the Illinois district of the diocese, which at that time, besides North Arm of the Grand Prairie, Paris, Coffee-town, and Lawrenceville, included Thrawls' Station in Indiana. The latter on the west side of the Wabash was more easily accessible from Illinois than from Terre Haute, especially at highwater stages. In this small settlement (if three or four families living in log huts, a saw mill, and a black-smith shop can be called a settlement), Father Buteux built a frame church in 1838, on land purchased from Joseph Thralls by Bishop Bruté. In February, 1840, this church burned down, having caught fire from the over-heated stove. Instead of rebuilding it, Father Buteux began to erect on the same spot, the following summer, a house for the Religious, then en route to the diocese. Not able to finish this house until the next spring, he united his efforts with those of Bishop de la Hailandière in securing the Thralls home for the Sisters. The parish remained without a church until 1844, services being held either in the small convent chapel or in the priest's residence.

Father Buteux also built St. Joseph's Church in Terre Haute. This was a brick structure, of large dimensions for those days, erected in 1839–1840; "quite good for this country," Mother Theodore remarked, as she visited it and heard Mass there, Father Buteux celebrating, October 22, 1840, when the Sisters were on their way to their new home—Saint Mary-of-the-Woods.

With the addition of a steeple and other modifications made by Father Chassé (1866–1872), this church served the parish until 1912. Plans were then made to enlarge the edifice, but in the end the pastor, the Reverend Camillus Eichenlaub, O.M.C. (1905–1912), erected an entirely new and beautiful church. This last was greatly injured by fire in January, 1934, but was at once handsomely restored by the pastor, the Reverend Paschal Murray, O.M.C. The present church encloses the foundations of the first church, built by Father Buteux.

After the arrival of the Sisters at Saint Mary-of-the-Woods Father Buteux ceased to have charge of St. Joseph's. He was pastor of Saint Mary's parish church and chaplain of the convent until August 1841. He labored devotedly to establish the Community, the Annals say, and "even worked like a common laborer on the building of the Academy." As soon as he had dedicated it (July 18) he withdrew, going to New Orleans for his health. Two years later he was back at Saint Mary-of-the-Woods to be nursed through a spell of sickness.

After his recovery he left the diocese and went back to France. Though the mild climate of his native land seemed necessary for more robust health, the lure of the New World eventually brought him back. Not to Indiana, however: he settled in the Diocese of Boston. There he labored zealously for many years. A letter of Father Chassé to Mother Anastasie says that Father Buteux asked Bishop de St. Palais, then Bishop of Vincennes, to let him come back to die at Saint Mary-of-the-Woods and that before the Bishop's permission, arrived he had gone to his eternal reward.

In reply to an enquiry about the career in the East of Saint Mary's first chaplain, a letter from the secretary of the Cardinal Archbishop of Boston, dated October 18, 1931, stated: "Reverend Stanislaus Buteux died on June 14, 1875, and was buried in the old mortuary chapel in St. Augustine's Cemetery, South Boston. Outside the sanctuary of this chapel, in separate brick vaults, suitably marked, lie the bodies of some twenty priests, who, in their day, were very influential in promoting the growth of Catholicity in the Archdiocese of Boston, and among them is the body of Father Buteux."

Father Chassé was also a Eudist and a companion of Father Buteux in the College of Vincennes. When the College closed in 1847, and the faculty scattered, Father Chassé chose to remain in the diocese. After twenty years of arduous labors in various positions, he came to Saint Mary-of-the-Woods as chaplain and died here September 1, 1879. A Terre Haute paper, quoted here in part, paid the following tribute to his memory:

"The Reverend Jean Baptiste Chassé, late Chaplain of the Sisters of Providence, is no more. He died yesterday morning at Saint Mary's at precisely forty minutes after two o'clock. His death, like his life, was the full embodiment of courage and hope mingled with faith and resignation.

"The deceased was born at Rennes, France, January 6, 1815. At a very tender age he entered upon his academic course, at the seminary attached to the university of his native city, where he completed the full curriculum of classical, mathematical, and philosophical studies, in preparation for the holy orders he longed to espouse. He came to the United States in 1839, then only in deacon's orders, and was here raised to the priesthood, in Vincennes, by Right Reverend Celestine de la Hailandière. He was soon afterwards appointed assistant priest at the Vincennes Cathedral, which station he filled most acceptably for a considerable period. He was for some years professor of Greek and Latin languages at the University of Vincennes. While there he was active and efficient in the establishment and development of the St. Vincent Orphan Boys' Asylum, which was founded at Highland, three miles east of Vincennes. He was perhaps the first Chaplain of that institution.

"About 1855 he was sent as pastor to St. Simon's parish, at Washington, Indiana, where he discharged his good, benevolent, faithful ministerial offices for twelve years. When Reverend P. B. O'Connor was called to fill the office of Chancellor and Vicar General at Vincennes, 1866, Father Chassé was installed in his place as pastor of St. Joseph's parish in this city. He remained here until June, 1872, when after the death of Father Corbe he was sent to Saint Mary-of-the-Woods as Chaplain of the Sisters of Providence. There he meekly and patiently labored in the service of his divine Master to the hour of his peaceful death. After a lingering indisposition, his coveted rest came at last, in that beautiful place of flowers and love, dedicated as his whole life had been to the aims and uses of moral and Christian culture. A fit death for the place, and a place suitable for such a death."

March 20, 1843

My very dear Sisters:

Your letters have gladdened my heart and called forth more than one *Te Deum*, not for your victories, for you are not yet triumphant over your enemies, but for the sentiments you express. If, as you say, you would lay down your lives for the souls that must be won over to God, I am sure He will grant our prayer without requiring so great a sacrifice.

You know, my dear daughters, that your position requires great circumspection. Carefully guard every word; watch over yourselves that nothing imprudent may escape you and thus give the ill-disposed a reason for their complaints. You may have to wait longer than you would like, you may have to bear privations; but, bear and forbear. Have confidence in the Providence that so far has never failed us. The way is not yet clear. Grope along slowly. Do not press matters; be patient, be trustful.

I fully enter into all your difficulties; this is the same as telling you that I suffer with you. Need I tell you that I pray for you? Every thought of my dear Sisters in Jasper is a prayer. You are lonesome, and so are we; but of this separation we do not complain. We cannot do our work if we all stay in the nest. As soon as the birds can fly they must be on the wing, looking after the interests of our Saviour Jesus. We shall make no account of our personal feelings except to sacrifice them. Say often, My God, I thank Thee that I have this to suffer. Offer it to Him. He will be pleased with your child-like simplicity. And rest assured, my dear daughters, if you lean with all your weight upon Providence you will find yourselves well supported. I approve of the practices you have imposed upon yourselves in honor of St. Joseph. Pray,

be humble, be charitable, and God's blessing will be
with you.

We are sending you letters that came from France, knowing
that it will give you pleasure to share in our joys. Take good
care of them and bring them home with you when you come to
the retreat.

May our Saviour Jesus Christ fill your hearts with His love;
may the Blessed Virgin Mary, our sweet Mother, have you in
her holy keeping; may the angels guard and direct you. Love
us all at home as we love you, in the Hearts of Jesus and Mary,
and pray much for your

SISTER ST. THEODORE.

Impoverished by the fire of October, 1842, and in need
of means for the expansion of the institute, desiring moreover to consult about the difficult situation of Saint Mary-of-
the-Woods, which could not well be done by letter, the
Sisters agreed that Mother Theodore should return to
France for the spiritual and temporal interests of their little
Congregation.

The Bishop of Vincennes approved the project, replying
to the proposal with the following letter addressed to
Mother Theodore:

"Respected Sister:
"I have weighed before God your reasons for
undertaking a journey to France. I approve of this
measure and hope that God may give you success and
bring you back to your daughters rich in the alms that
will have been bestowed on you. Go, therefore, my
dear Sister, to that France which is so charitable, so
zealous for poor missionaries, and whose resources
seem to increase in proportion as it gives. Make the
faithful understand well your position and your
wants. Tell them that, notwithstanding what I
have done to establish you, you are far from being
securely founded; that my resources are exhausted and

that you have heavy debts. Speak of your log house, your accidents, your farm house and your loss by fire; of the distress of the country, of the children whom you are obliged to teach *gratis*; all this is the truth and you cannot fail to excite lively interest in your favor.

"I authorize you to make use of this letter as you please. I beg of those among my venerable colleagues who will read it to be favorable to you and to aid you with their alms and prayers. I bless you with all my heart and remain, with deep respect and affection,

"Your very humble servant,

CELESTIN, BP. OF VINCENNES

"VINCENNES, IND., U.S.A., April 30, 1843."

To this letter the Bishop added the following notes:

"Auspice Mariae

"The object of this voyage must be to interest the faithful in your establishment.

"1st—They can aid you by their prayers; ask many, especially from those who pray well, who seem to have power with God.

"2nd—They may procure novices for you. A few good ones would be very desirable: (a) those who have talents, particularly for music, which is needed so much here; (b) those that have fortunes, by which means the house would be maintained. Of course, it is well understood, whatever might be their talents or their fortune, *that* would not suffice; there must be a true religious vocation. The love of suffering, not in speculation, but in practice, and true humility, are necessary; for it must be borne in mind that we are founding a religious house, and that there ought to be in its members the sanctity of founders of communities. Great care should be exercised and enquiries made about the persons whom you might think of admitting.

"3d—They can give you money. They will do so

if you explain your needs sufficiently, stating that your establishment is not self-sustaining, that you have contracted heavy debts, that you have been obliged to refuse postulants who were unable to pay their expenses, as you did not have the wherewith to support them—how could you support and educate them without funds at your command?

"Moreover, you must purchase more land in order to raise enough for your sustenance. The Bishop is no longer able to continue his assistance; had he anything to invest it should be in a seminary, the first stone of which is not yet laid, nor has he even the ground on which to build. Must you now abandon a work which Almighty God blesses in so special a manner? I think there is not an institution in the United States which has developed so rapidly as Saint Mary-of-the-Woods. Without education Catholicity cannot be spread to any extent; even the Faith cannot be preserved without it. The great majority of Catholics cannot pay for their education; and if they could, they would not find teachers to make known to them the truth. What we need for them is free schools. But for these we must have money. Solicit, therefore, freely and earnestly. Such an object must appeal to the charity of the devout, who need but to be convinced."

Bishop de la Hailandière then wrote in behalf of the undertaking to Bishop Bouvier.

"Vincennes, April 30, 1843

"My Lord:

"Behold our dear Sister Theodore again at your feet. It is with my full consent that she has left for a time the work in which God has engaged her here, in order to try to elicit in France the charity of the faithful in behalf of her institution. Of myself I should not have advised her to make the journey, although it is evident that the numerous sacrifices I have made for the Sisters cannot be continued any longer. To my great regret it becomes impossible to provide for the establishment as should be done. But seeing in this good Sister so much devotedness, and such a strong desire, despite her poor health, to go and entreat help among her friends, I could not but applaud her zeal and allow her to go under the guidance of Divine Providence. I beg of you, my Lord, to receive her favorably and assist her to interest the charitable people of your rich diocese in behalf of her Congregation, already so numerous but so poor.

"France sends here her priests and her religious women; she shares with us the merit of her prayers; she also gives alms. As for myself, I have for my immense diocese no other resources than those that come through the Society for the Propagation of the Faith. Unfortunately, the resources diminish as our needs increase. If a more abundant allowance be not granted us this year we shall not be able to do anything more. Sister Theodore will endeavor to explain. I beg that she be given credence. She will also express my gratitude to you, present you my homage. She can never say fully how much I venerate and admire you. I have the honor to be,

"My Lord,

"of Your Lordship

"the most humble servant,

CEL., BP. OF VENCENNES"

Mother Theodore had intended going to Jasper before leaving for France; therefore, after her farewell visit to the Bishop, she set out from Vincennes but had proceeded only nine miles when high fever obliged her to return without seeing the Sisters. It was her intention, also, to bring back with her her Assistant, Sister St. Vincent Ferrer, to preside at the Motherhouse during her absence. Why she reversed her decision in regard to Sister St. Vincent is told in the following lines:

TO FATHER KUNDEK, JASPER

Saint Mary's, April 20, 1843

Monsieur le Missionnaire:

Having reflected seriously on what you told me, I have decided to leave you Sister St. Vincent until the retreat, unless

some unforeseen event obliges the Sisters to recall her before
that time. Continue, then, your efforts and try to render her fit
for God's work. I look for this favor from your zeal and good
will.

It was very painful for me not to have seen my dear Sisters.
I console myself, however, by the thought that it was the will of
our good Master; at least, He permitted it. I beg Him to bless
them and make them Religious according to His Heart.

Do not forget, I entreat you, your promise of praying for me
at the Holy Sacrifice. I too shall pray for you—you who are the
father of my Sisters and, consequently, mine.

In these sentiments, I am, with the most profound veneration, *Monsieur le Missionnaire*,

Your very humble servant,

SISTER ST. THEODORE.

In great haste.

PART III

SECOND JOURNAL OF TRAVEL

MOTHER THEODORE set out for Europe on April 26, 1843. She had as traveling companion Sister Mary Cecilia, an American novice, a person of superior qualifications, capable not only of appreciating the advantages of travel but of valuing the opportunity of intimate association with one like Mother Theodore. Her mind and heart were equally benefited by the contact.

Sister Mary Cecilia was Eleanor Bailly, a daughter of the noted Joseph Bailly who, at the beginning of the nineteenth century, established an agency of the American Fur Trading Company near Calumet (now Chesterton) in northern Indiana. Her grandfather, Michael Bailly, or Baillie, was a Norman nobleman who had come over from France and become associated with John Jacob Astor of New York. Traffic in pelts took him to Quebec where his children were born. He traversed Canada westward as far as the Great Lakes and finally settled at Mackinac, Michigan. His son Joseph married Marie le Fèvre de la Vigne, an Ottawa princess, a devout Christian who had purchased her freedom from her tribe according to the Indian law, and at Mackinac their children were born.

Joseph Bailly succeeded his father in the business, and to his commercial activities with the Indians joined the labors of an apostle, evangelizing and, in a measure, civilizing them. He eventually moved from his northern home on the Straits to the country bordering Lake Michigan on the southeast. After trying several locations, he fixed his abode in Porter County, Indiana, and called the settlement Baillytown. There his daughter, Eleanor, then in her twenty-sixth year, met Father

de St. Palais (later Bishop) during one of his missionary trips
through the Calumet region, and conferred with him about her
vocation.[1]

Eleanor had been educated in the convent schools of
Detroit and Canada. In social life she was called "the belle of
Detroit." Forsaking the world to embrace the religious life, she
cast her lot with the one-year-old Community of Saint. Mary-
of-the-Woods, arriving on the twenty-first of November, 1841;
thus she had been in the novitiate about a year and a half
when the trip abroad took place.

On her return from France she began teaching at the
Academy. In the year 1848, when a general election was held,
she was chosen First Assistant and was appointed directress
of the Academy, a position she held until the death of the
Mistress of Novices, Sister St. Francis, which occurred
January 31, 1856. Sister Mary Cecilia was then recalled to the
Motherhouse to take charge of the novitiate. In August of the
same year she was elected Superior General, Mother Theodore
having died on the fourteenth of May.

Mother Cecilia's administration lasted twelve years and was
signalized by many developments; notably, the building
of the fine new Academy and a temporary frame chapel adja-
cent to the convent. Her after years were passed in various missions—at the Bailly homestead, near Chesterton (then
Calumet); at Lafayette, Fort Wayne, and, finally, at St. Ann's
orphanage for girls at Terre Haute where, on August 4, 1898,
she closed her eventful life, being then eighty-four years of age.

The sagacious Foundress had previsioned a career of
great usefulness for her novice and directed her powers
accordingly. Sister Mary Cecilia responded with affectionate
loyalty to Mother Theodore in the ensuing years, and supported her valiantly through the difficulties that crossed
their path. If later times brought some disappointments,
they could not have been foreseen that early spring day

---

[1] "Joseph Bailly" in *History of Porter County, Indiana*; Vol. 1, p. 33.

John O. Bowers, *The Old Bailly Homestead*.

"Joseph Bailly" in *South Bend and Many Miles Around*; Chicago South
Shore and South Bend Railroad Broadcast, No. 33—South Bend *Tribune*
Station WSBT, March 26, 1929.

Necrology, Community archives, Saint Mary-of-the-Woods.

when Mother Theodore and her companion set out upon their memorable voyage.

The diary entry of May fifteenth (1843) reads: "All Mother's good letters have come by Coliche" (an employee who brought the mail from Terre Haute).

Why those letters are missing cannot be explained except on the supposition that they were burned in sacrifice, as it is known that the Sisters sometimes destroyed their precious letters when they sought favors through prayer.

Another inexplicable thing is, there is no account of this journey east other than a brief statement to the effect that the travelers went by way of Pittsburgh, that their habit was everywhere respected, and that certain provisions had been sent from New York to Saint Mary-of-the-Woods by Mother Theodore through her friends, Mrs. Parmentier and Mr. Byerley.

The only surviving letter of this period is to a novice who had come over with the Sisters in 1840. In the rush before sailing, Mother Theodore took time to write her a little letter. It bears no outside address, hence it must have been an enclosure with the letters mentioned above.

TO SISTER MARY XAVIER

Brooklyn, N. Y., May 10, 1843

My dear Sister:

Only in trembling do I write these few lines. I fear you will weep again. O my dear daughter, do not weep, for those tears cannot be pleasing to God. He is jealous of the heart, especially of the heart of a Religious. Perhaps it is to detach you that He has permitted me to leave Saint Mary's. Let us adore the designs of this good Master and be resigned to His Holy Will. Accustom yourself to break your will. It will kill your soul if you do not kill it beforehand. Never act under the impulse of self-will. Ask your permissions—more rather than less; be very exact as to regular observance; let your conduct be such that you may be held up as an example for your Sisters. Never speak when you are excited, but wait for the impulse of nature to pass away and that of grace to succeed it. Give your Sisters whatever they need in all that regards your employment; in a word, be kind to all.

I will not tell you to pray for me—you do that—but I do say, *Be good*, in order to obtain for me the graces I need. If you are not all *good*, I shall die on the way. My lot is in your hands, for it is written that God does the will of those who love Him. Adieu, dear Sister. Always your devoted

SISTER ST. THEODORE.

The voyage was made on the *Silvia*, an American ship. It lasted thirty days, was prosperous and uneventful.

Arrived in France Mother Theodore was cheered up by the warm reception she received at Ruillé-sur-Loir. She presented her letters from Bishop de la Hailandière to Bishop Bouvier and received his blessing on her work. Not only did he give permission, but he volunteered to interest the other French bishops in her behalf. He went to Ruillé to consult with her and the Superiors of the Motherhouse. She had a complete understanding with him regarding the affairs of the Community in Indiana, and was strengthened by his wise counsels and encouragement. All were most sympathetic and generous towards her. Sister Mary Cecilia improved her opportunity by taking lessons on the guitar and in voice culture, as Bishop de la Hailandière had directed.

While in the north of France on her quest, Mother Theodore visited the family of Sister St. Francis Xavier (Irma le Fer de la Motte) residing at St. Servan. It was a happiness for them to learn from her own lips all about Irma and the home she had found in the wilderness of far-away Indiana; and a happiness, too, for Mother Theodore to become acquainted with the family so remarkable for its deeply Christian spirit and devotedness, so honored in having a son in the priesthood and a daughter a foreign missionary.

The first letter of Mother Theodore to the family—the beginning of an intimate correspondence—is addressed to Irma's mother:

Ruillé-sur-Loir (Sarthe) Sept. 16, 1843

Madame and very dear Friend,

I should have written long ago to tell you again how happy I was to become acquainted with you, to see you, to converse with you. My stay was short, it is true, but the memory of it will be everlasting. I should wish to say this to each member of your estimable family, especially to the worthy Monsier le Fer and to our dear little future Sisters, Eugenie and Cecile; but this is a sacrifice which we shall all unite in offering to the Almighty. He will accept it and put it to good account. He loves us so much. I have recommended your Abbé to the community of Ruillé, and to that of Saint Mary-of-the-Woods.

I have received news of my children in the "Woods." All write to me except the one from whom I expected a long letter. Sister St. Francis did not put in a single word for me, but was careful to enclose messages for everyone else. Tell me, could we not chastise her for her mortification? I can find no other reason for her silence than this. Our dear child is well, they tell me; she had had sick headache but rarely since my departure. As to what you wish to send your daughter, I leave you entirely free in your choice. The time of my departure is not yet fixed. I hope it will be before the winter is too far advanced.

You may send the box at once, if you feel more easy about it, but I must tell you that in this season it is more than probable that it will not reach St. Mary's as soon as we shall. What you sent in May, and what I bought in New York for our house and sent in care of our Bishop had not arrived on the first of August. Perhaps they are not there even yet. If you send a trunk by us be so kind as to forward it to the dock. I shall let you know as soon as I learn at what port we shall embark.

We shall be in Paris with the Ladies of the Visitation whose address I enclose in this letter. Have the kindness to send me there any letters you think will be useful to me, with addresses, recommendations, and so forth.

If I did not mention Mlle. Lavienville, it was because I flattered myself that I would have the pleasure of seeing her in Paris. Please tell her that I love her always and that I recommend myself and my little family to her good prayers. The same petition I make to all who, like herself, take interest in the good of souls.

It is impossible to answer all the kind things you say to me except by a sentiment of profound gratitude. I can express it only to God, Who understands the language of the heart. I thank Him over and over for the unexpected favor He granted me in the midst of your family. Let us all beg of Him the grace to draw from it the fruit which He intended in giving it. My dear friend, far from diminishing my esteem and affection by what you have confided to me, you have, on the contrary, increased both. Mutual confidence is the sweet secret of gaining hearts. No, I was not disedified at the manner in which you received our little humiliation—I could even shed tears over it myself. Humiliation is the food of strong souls. It is not surprising, then, that we who are weak should suffer from it.

I thank Mlle. Eugenie for her letter and for the suggestion she makes to address myself to the *Ministre de la Marine*. Bishop Bouvier will make the request for us.

I beg you to accept for yourself and all your family the assurance of the most tender affection and lively gratitude with which I am, dear Madame, in a most special manner,

Your most sincere friend in Our Lord,

SISTER ST. THEODORE.

I have some news to announce which, I know, you will be pleased to learn—our good Mother Mary has been re-elected! Adieu! My conscience reproaches me for writing so much.

SR. ST. T.

It soon became evident to Mother Theodore that the time was inopportune for collecting funds, and that the difficult and disagreeable task she had undertaken would likely prove a failure. Under this impression she wrote from Paris, September 22, 1843:

TO THE RIGHT REVEREND J. B. BOUVIER, BISHOP

OF LE MANS

My Lord and Father:

I have just learned for a certainty that the Society of the Propagation of the Faith will do nothing more for us than it has already done through His Lordship, the Bishop of Vincennes, for the Councils have made it a law not to give to Congregations of women; hence, no alternative is left us but to solicit private contributions. It is very difficult to do so at Paris, not being known here; besides, Paris, like our provincial towns, is deserted at present. I had letters of recommendation to several persons all of whom are absent. We should have to resign ourselves to remain in France during the winter if we hoped for any success. But, then, what would become of our Sisters at Saint Mary-of-the Woods? Which of these two evils is to be preferred? I leave it to Your Lordship to decide. Were it left to me I believe I would start with the little money I have, on account of the difficulties which have arisen since my departure between our good Bishop and the Sisters.

I say this, my Lord, simply as my opinion on the subject, but I assure you I am not at all anxious to follow it, being on the contrary perfectly submissive to what it may please Your Lordship to direct. If, my Lord, you adopt the project of having us leave before winter, it would be high time to write to the Ministry to know whether we shall have our passage free, and at which seaport of France we shall have to embark in order to go to New Orleans. This is very important. As we are four to return we should have to give the sum of 750 francs for each one on a passenger vessel. This would be impossible for us to do. I shall await your answer in Paris. We are with the Ladies of the Visitation, *rue d'Enfer*, 72. You will please tell me whether we ought to remain or to prepare for our departure. I have debts at Paris and I do not know how to pay them. However, I am not too much discouraged. I see in all this the Will of God and I submit to it.

I beg you to give me your blessing and deign to accept the homage of the most profound veneration with which I am, my Lord, of Your Lordship

The very submissive daughter and obedient servant,

SISTER ST. THEODORE.

The Bishop replied immediately (September 25, 1843), saying, "I fear that a prolonged absence on your part may bring to your establishments in America more prejudice than the advantages you would procure by gathering up a little more money. You seem to understand it as I do. When I received your letter the day before yesterday, I had already written to the *Ministre de la Marine*, urging him strongly to grant free passage for you and your three companions. We shall see what his answer will be."

And three days later the Bishop wrote, "Having time only for two lines before the mail leaves, I shall confine myself to saying that last evening the reply came from the *Ministre de la Marine*. He answered at once and the tone of his letter gives me to understand that he would have been favorable to your request had a French government vessel been going to the United States."

If Bishop Bouvier did not succeed in obtaining free passage for the Sisters, he was fortunate in winning coöperation among the prelates of France for the work of his "dear Daughters of Indiana." Moreover, his letters to the Society of the Propagation of the Faith, also to officials of the government, if not immediately effective, opened the way to future assistance. Mother Theodore was encouraged, therefore, by finally securing a little more aid than she had anticipated after her first failures, and she would have prolonged her stay had not some peculiar difficulties arisen at Saint Mary-of-the-Woods during her absence. While she was still in Paris, collecting, before her return to the Motherhouse for her final adieux, she received the following letter from Mother Mary of Ruillé:

"October 16, 1843

"My dear Sister Theodore:

"I am sending you a letter from Mr. Hardy which seems pressing. I am keeping until your arrival here one for Sister Mary Cecilia which is, I believe, from your Bishop, and another from your Sisters of Vincennes, but as I am not sure that they would find you at Paris I shall not mail them. The most interesting thing they say is that Sisters Mary and Agnes made their vows at the retreat, which took place in the month of August, and that after this retreat the election of the Superior took place—that you received five votes out of six and that, consequently, you are still the Superior of Saint Mary-of-the-Woods.

"Sister Celestia of Vincennes has been admitted into your Congregation, a thing that had to be submitted to, notwithstanding the reluctance of Sister St. Francis. The separation of the two Congregations has also caused throbbings to poor Sister St. Francis. I have written to Sister Basilide that upon this point no opposition should be raised, as it has to be so, it not being reasonably possible otherwise. To conclude, I persist in believing and in thinking that your presence is of absolute necessity at Saint Mary's and that not all the gold of France could repay you for the injury that your absence may cause to the spiritual good of your infant Congregation.

"Provide yourself well at the feet of the Immaculate Virgin, Our Lady of Victory, in order to go and sustain a combat with no other arms than humility, meekness, and firmness. The one will cause you to examine the proposals that may be made to you with diffidence in your own judgment; the other will lead you to proceed in all in a becoming manner; and firmness will prevent your ever taking part in what evidently appears contrary to the good of your institute, and enable you to suffer it with courage when, by Christian and religious means, you could not prevent it. Ask these graces of our good Mother before you leave the spot where she loves to pour down her favors. . . . Make haste, my dear Sister Theodore, fly back to Vincennes to mend the broken platters. Watch over your little flock, prevent the enemy from sowing cockle among the good seed and the wolf from entering the sheepfold. If your return to France has been useful, your presence at home is still more necessary.

"Your affectionate

"SISTER MARY"

As there were only three professed Sisters, young and inexperienced, and a few postulants at St. Mary's, and as Mother Theodore had expected to be back by the end of September, it had been agreed that the retreat would be deferred until after her return. The two professed Sisters and three novices on mission were to make their retreat privately. But Bishop de la Hailandière did not approve of postponing the retreat, as an earlier letter from Indiana had told Mother Theodore. It was a matter of regret to all that she had not informed the Bishop of her plan before she left. She acknowledged her mistake and offered her apologies.

The retreat took place and the Bishop himself gave it. The Sisters on the missions had been hastily notified, but only Sister Mary Liguori and her novice companion from St. Francisville were able to be present. What happened after the retreat is thus described by Sister St. Francis in a letter dated August 16, 1843:

THE RIGHT REVEREND J. B. BOUVIER
Bishop of Le Mans

MOTHER MARY LECOR
Superior General of the
Sisters of Providence
of Ruillé-sur-Loir in 1840

MOTHERHOUSE OF THE SISTERS OF PROVIDENCE
RUILLÉ-SUR-LOIR

From a drawing made in 1866 by Sister Mary Joseph le Fer de la Motte

"My dear and esteemed Mother [she says], I give
you a hundred thousand guesses as to what we did
yesterday, feast of the Assumption, from two to three
o'clock. The preceding Sunday we finished our retreat.
Sister Agnes and Sister Mary had the happiness to
pronounce their vows; so we were six professed Sisters. Monseigneur called us into your room and then told
us that it was for the purpose of holding an election of a Superior, as your three years had expired.
I say nothing of the general consternation. All were
pale, trembling, praying. Twenty minutes later, of
the six votes cast, five were for "Sister Theodore" and
on the sixth was written "Ma Mère," which did not
prevent your election from being unanimous. So the
good God wishes you to be again upon the cross.
Will it be at Saint Mary-of-the-Woods? God knows—
that is sufficient for me. How fortunate we are, my
Mother, my poor Mother, that only God knows this
new and dark future. All during my retreat I tried
so hard to *thank* Him for our separation from Ruillé
that, at the end, I thought my soul would be separated from my body."

The outlook of Mother Theodore's work in France was
brighter now than at any time during her quest, as several
influential friends had become interested and were forming
plans that promised better results. In fact, some of these plans
were realized the following year. However, the advice of the
Bishop of Le Mans and of the Superior General of Ruillé determined Mother Theodore to prepare at once for her departure.
She embarked at Havre, November 28, 1843, on the *Nashville*,
an American vessel, which on account of the winter season
took the southern route by way of the Gulf of Mexico.

The narrative of her last days in France, given with her
usual detail of "episode and incident," here follows.

THE SECOND JOURNAL

We had no trouble [she says] in arranging the affairs of
our Congregation. The Bishop of Le Mans always showed

himself a father. With our temporal concerns it was different. We wished to appeal to the benevolence of our friends
and to the charity of the faithful, but we arrived at a very
unpropitious time. Works of charity which had been multiplying under every form had drained the purses; besides,
those people who belonged to the higher classes were at
their country seats. The towns through which we passed
were deserted. A calamity was added to our distress—continued rains had inundated the lower parts of France.
Almost all the hay was lost and the crops were threatened.
In some towns, particularly noted for their generosity, there
was another obstacle—we found Vitre and Fougères in desolation. The people earned their living in these towns by
making linen in their homes. Some months back, they had
been ordered to discontinue that kind of work, as goods
coming from the manufactories were alone sanctioned in
commerce. In fine, it almost seemed as if we would have
to remain in France, far from our dear mission, for want of
money to pay our way back.

Sister Mary Cecilia and I had resolved to return to
America by taking passage on the lower deck. In this case
we would have to change our costume to secular dress. But
God saw our good will and was satisfied with that, for He
came to our aid in a very extraordinary manner. Having
gone to see the castle of Brissac [the home of the Countess
of Marescot], only a league from where we were staying, I
was calling Sister's attention to the fine architecture, those
superb towers which make this castle a precious monument
of the gigantic structures of the Middle Ages. Sister was
still lost in admiration of these beauties when some one
came to tell us that the Marchioness of Brissac would give
us an audience. We had not asked this favor on arriving
because, having walked through the mud a considerable distance, we were not fit to go into a drawing room. However,

we entered and were received by the pious Marquis and Marchioness with demonstrations of the most tender benevolence. The next day they came to return our visit at the home of M. Perrault de la Bertaudière [at Soulaines] whose guests we were, and a storm obliged them to remain all night and a part of the next day. They presented us their offerings and gave us letters of recommendation for those persons in the capital who were most renowned for their charity and position in society.

Not having been able to go to Paris until after the retreat at Ruillé, where the Bishop of Le Mans had given us an interview to conclude our affairs, it so happened that when we arrived in Paris we found none of those persons to whom we had letters of introduction. The residences were closed; only the caretakers were there. One letter alone remained; it was addressed to Mlle. Labrouche at the Chancellor's office. We supposed it would be of no service, so we decided not to present ourselves there. More than once we passed the Place Vendôme without even turning our eyes toward the Chancery.

A clergyman of our acquaintance took us to the Monastery of the Visitation. The Sisters received us with that charity which characterizes them, and which renders them true daughters of St. Francis de Sales and his worthy cooperatrix. Their house, situated at the extremity of *rue d'Enfer*, was far from the center of the city where we were obliged to go for our little affairs and to look up those to whom we had letters of recommendation. Seeing at length that all was useless, we resolved to leave the capital and return to Ruillé, there to pack up and set out with the little money we had collected, which was scarcely enough to pay our passage.

Before leaving we wished to have the happiness of assisting at Mass in the holy sanctuary of Our Lady of Victory, and, at the same time, to do all in our power to obtain that our Congregation of Saint Mary-of-the-Woods (which had just been separated from that of Ruillé and made a distinct Congregation) might be associated to the Archconfraternity of the Immaculate Heart of Mary, which had lately been erected in this church. The priest who conducted us to the "Visitation" had the kindness to accompany us on this occasion.

On entering the sanctuary where God causes the power of the Immaculate Mary to be manifested daily by the most striking prodigies, the soul is seized with an indefinable sentiment. One seems to feel something divine. Great concourses before the shrine of the Mother of Jesus indicated the place she occupies in this ancient spot.

When we entered we saw a priest hearing confessions. It was the curé, that good Father Desgenettes, founder and director of the Archconfraternity. He had the charity to hear us also, and to promise that he would associate us, as a congregation, to the Archconfraternity. It was on this precious day that we became in a particular manner Children of Mary, that the Blessed Virgin deigned to take the poor children of the Woods of Indiana under her maternal protection. It was not long before we experienced the effects of this protection.

On this same day Sister Mary Cecilia begged me to make one more attempt with the one remaining letter. I had the greatest repugnance to present myself at the Chancery. Ministers of Louis Philippe resided there—the men now in power. What were two unknown persons to expect from them, and especially two Religious women? However, as I had several times refused Sister's request, I granted it this time, but it was only out of pure complaisance that I did so.

We presented ourselves and asked for Mlle. Labrouche. We were told that she was with her young pupils. We afterwards learned, that she was the governess of the children of Monsieur Martin du Nord [Keeper of the Seals, Minister of Justice and of Religious Worship]. She received us very kindly and seemed to have the most tender sympathy for our work. She promised to speak to the Keeper of the Seals; in fact, the next morning before eight o'clock, a courier came with a letter which informed us that His Excellency would give us an audience at nine o'clock. We found the Minister very well disposed toward us. He promised to do all in his power, and indeed he kept his word; for from that day until our departure from France, he was like a father to us. The first thing he suggested was that we address ourselves to the Queen. "You must write," he said, "to Her Majesty, the Queen. I will deliver your letter myself. Ask for an audience and nothing more." We did so, and the Keeper of the Seals not only took the letter himself to St. Cloud, but, not being able to deliver it to the Queen, he gave it to the King and begged His Majesty to be our advocate with his royal consort.

As soon as M. Martin returned from the Court he informed us of what he had done and told us to hope. He wished us to let him know when we would have received an answer from the Queen. Furthermore, any time we had any business we were to have free access to the Chancery. One day an official refusing to let us in was severely reprimanded and received orders to admit us any time we presented ourselves. We used to go first to the Mlles Martin du Nord, who then went with us to their father's office; he was always ready for us.

The Queen's answer did not arrive for a week. M. Martin was uneasy. On Saturday he sent for us and told us we ought to write again to the Queen. I was obliged to improvise a letter on the Minister's desk. That was quite unnecessary, however, for on our return to the "Visitation" in the evening, the Superior handed me a letter from the Queen. She and all the community were delighted, for charity made them rejoice in our good fortune as if it had been their own.

The Queen said she would leave St. Cloud and repair to the Tuilleries the next day at one o'clock to meet us there. We informed M. Martin and he awaited the issue with paternal interest. At the hour stated we went to the Tuilleries. Her Majesty had been there some minutes. We were ushered into the Queen's apartment. She entered a moment later, gave us seats herself, and had us sit beside her, giving us the most gracious reception. She inquired about our situation like a tender mother, and listened to the details with the greatest interest. She had the kindness to show particular benevolence toward Sister Mary Cecilia and spoke English with her.

Finally, after having manifested the most tender sympathy for our work, she asked us what we wished of her. We replied that as a signal favor, we begged of her to pay our passage. She immediately answered: "Your passage shall be paid. How many are you?" "Four," we answered; which was indeed true, since we had two postulants. "Well," she said, "the voyage shall be paid for four." Then she added, but this is not enough; you will need something when you are in your Woods. I shall solicit here for you, and the King and my children will contribute. I shall ask them for you. But, on your side, you must do something also—you must ask the bishops to contribute; the Bishop of Le Mans will no doubt do so."

After that she continued to speak with touching kindness of all that might contribute to the welfare of our work. In a moment of holy exaltation she said, "Ah, yes, Sisters, let us save souls!" There was in her manner, her eyes, and above all in her voice so intimate a conviction of the price of a soul that my heart was touched by it, and is so even yet in recalling that incident to my mind. During the course of this conversation, which had become quite easy, almost familiar, I might say, I said "Mother" to her. Perceiving what I had said in a distraction, I begged Her Majesty to excuse me. "That is right," she said; "call me 'Mother'; it is a name that is very dear to me."

His Majesty the King now appeared and we were presented. They then condescended to take us to see the royal chapel. While going through, His Majesty said, "There is the Queen's confessional." Sister Mary Cecilia, who was at the side of the King, said, "And yours, Sire?" He laughed and passed on. After nearly an hour's interview we took leave of Her Majesty, kissed her hand and returned thanks to the best of our ability.

From the Queen's apartments we went to those of Madame Adelaide, the King's sister. We were admitted as soon as we had made known that we were guests at the Visitation Monastery. Her Royal Highness received us well, informed herself in detail about all that concerned our undertaking and seemed to take true interest in it. She asked us how much our passage would cost, and began to calculate the expenses. We could see the difference between these two royal women in a simple interview, and the comparison that we drew was not in favor of Madame Adelaide. But I am convinced that if we had not seen the Queen first, her Royal Highness would have enchanted us; for she was, in fact, very kind. Every one has not a soul like Amelia.

Assured now of the protection of the Queen and her sister-in-law, we left the Tuilleries, our hearts full of gratitude and affection for the Queen. We were not certain, however, that our passage would be paid; for Madame Adelaide, after having made the calculation, said that the Queen did not know to what she was engaging herself, and that,

seeing the numerous good works in which she took part,
she was obliged to restrain the ardor of Her Majesty's good
heart.

These observations were indeed true. We might well
fear that the Queen, who had not asked anything about the
cost of the voyage, might not be able to fulfil her promise.
But these thoughts did not trouble us. She had spoken sweet
words which went straight to the heart, words consoling and
strengthening, which poor solicitors seldom receive. How
many times after having gone up and down stairs, climbing
to the third and fourth stories, I wept in the streets before
beginning another ascent to receive only a half franc with
more contempt! This time it had not been thus. My heart
full of gratitude, longed to go to the sanctuary of Mary
Immaculate to thank her for having granted this day of
consolation to us. Happy to be free, we went straightway
to the church of Our Lady of Victory, to pour out our hearts
in tears of joy in the presence of our heavenly Protector and
Mother.

The next day we went to see M. Martin. He was awaiting us
and received us with his usual kindness. He was touched by
our account of the Queen's benevolence, and said with profound emotion, the tears glistening in his eyes, "The Queen is
a saint." His Excellency told us that we must address petitions
to the Ministers of State. We wrote one to M. Guizot, Minister
of Foreign Affairs, and one to the Minister of the Interior.
M. Martin gave them to the Queen with another letter from us
in which we begged Her Majesty to present them herself,
which she willingly consented to do. M. Guizot promised the
Queen that he would give us assistance. If he has not done it
so far it is not the Queen's fault. She has constantly shown
herself a mother to us.

We learned one day from M. Martin that Madame
Adelaide had said to the Queen, "If you are willing, sister,

we will give five hundred francs to Sister Theodore." The
Queen answered with dignity: "No, sister, I promised Sister
Theodore to pay her passage; it will be paid." Finally,
when we were at Havre we received the last mark of the
Queen's constant kindness—her portrait, which we keep as a
treasure.

Thanks to the favor of the Queen, we soon had that of
several other persons. We already enjoyed that of Bishop
Forbin-Janson, who was at Paris. He was like a father to us.
His residence was open to us at any hour. Several times. His
Lordship admitted us to his table, contrary to his custom in
regard to persons of our sex. He said to his Coadjutor, laugh-
ingly, "My dear, the Sisters of Saint Mary-of-the-Woods are not
women; they are angels; that is the reason you see them here."
He would not allow us to go on foot on the streets of Paris. I
objected that it was too expensive to have a carriage every
time that we went out. He answered, "My daughter, that is my
affair. I shall pay for it." And he did. After our departure he
continued his interest in us. He preached a charity sermon
that brought two thousand francs for our establishment.

A number of persons of every station have shown such
interest, such a desire for the prosperity of our work, and
so many prayers have been and are still being offered, I
doubt not but God will bless this dear little Congregation,
notwithstanding the trials which it pleases Him to send it;
even though there were no others to pray for it than the good
holy Carmelites of Le Mans, with whom we are united closely
in the Heart of Jesus. The Archbishop of Paris granted permission to preach in favor of our work only at the recommendation
of the Keeper of the Seals. It was the same with the Bishops of
Orleans, St. Brieuc, Rennes, and Versailles. The Archbishop of
Tours evinced the deepest sympathy and all gave unequivocal
proofs of their generosity.

Thus Far the Second Journal

The Queen's interest followed the Sisters to America, for the year after their return Her Majesty sent them, fifteen hundred dollars. This sum included her own gift and also donations she had solicited. Referring to these contributions, Mlle. Henriette, the daughter of the Baroness de la Valette, of Tours, had written to Mother Theodore (November 4, 1843), "If the Queen continues to favor you, she will give one of her ladies to make the collection, a thing she frequently does." The money from the Queen came to Saint Mary-of-the-Woods by a draft from M. Guizot, Minister of Foreign Affairs in France, through the French Minister at Washington, D. C.

After reading the second *Journal*, one naturally asks: Why was Mother Theodore directed to apply to the Queen rather than to the King?

The answer is: Louis Philippe was proverbially close, while Amelia was renowned for her generosity. Out of the five hundred thousand francs annually allowed her from her own family, she spent four hundred thousand in charity.

Amelia was an Italian princess born in Naples, the daughter of Ferdinand of the Two Sicilies. Her mother was the sister of Marie Antoinette. In 1809, when twenty-seven years of age, she married Louis Philippe, Duke of Orleans, at Palermo. There was no thought whatever of rising above the ducal rank. But the revolution of 1830 put on the throne of France Louis Philippe who, on account of his sympathies with the middle class, was called the Citizen King. Thus Amelia became "Queen of the French." Latimer's *France in the Nineteenth Century* says: "No breath of scandal ever disturbed the matrimonial happiness of Louis Philippe and Marie Amélie. They had a noble family of five sons and three daughters; all distinguished by their ability and virtues. . . . Amelia never interfered in politics. . . . No description could do justice to the purity and charity of this admirable woman." When the Keeper of the Seals said to Mother Theodore, "The Queen is a saint," he was only forestalling the verdict of the historian.

Among the trials that weighed heavily on Mother Theodore at the period of her visit to France was the decision that the Community in Indiana had to be separated from the Motherhouse of Ruillé-sur-Loir. She suffered deeply and she knew how deeply the Sisters at Saint Mary-of-the-Woods would suffer in the separation.

Sister Basilide in a letter of August 1, 1843, having expressed her anxiety on this subject, had added: "If the constitutions and habit have to be changed, I should think myself in another Community, and I really would be. So I shall withdraw myself, for I would give my life rather than leave the Community that has reared me and is dearer to me than my own family." The other Sisters, without going so far, had also told of their anxieties. They knew some modifications of the Rule would be necessary in a different country and they were ready to accept changes if the essentials were retained. Yet they had fears and misgivings about the security of their poor little foundation when deprived of the guidance of their Superiors in France, and of the authority and protection of the devoted Bishop of Le Mans.

To allay fears and adjust matters satisfactorily, if possible, was the task awaiting Mother Theodore. One marvels at the balance of mind she maintained amid the vicissitudes of her life. She could hide her grave thoughts under a cheerful exterior and a lively interest in outer things, and her facile pen lent itself to the fertility of her mind. After a dangerous passage, the *Nashville* was detained by fog on approaching New Orleans. Here she availed herself of the opportunity of writing to her good friend and trusted adviser:

TO THE RIGHT REVEREND J. BOUVIER, BISHOP OF LE MANS

At the Mouth of the Mississippi, January 24, 1844

My Lord and venerated Father:

Half an hour ago we cast anchor upon the Mississippi which we cannot ascend on account of a dense fog that hides its banks. The terrible sea is passed. That painful voyage which lasted eight weeks is over, that voyage during which we had forty days of tempests, one in particular being most frightful. Never had the sailors seen the like, they said, and I easily believe it. During six days it only diminished a little from time to time to begin again with renewed fury.

It carried off our long boat, a part of the capstan, broke the main yard, the masts, etc. It tossed the vessel on the waves, which were as high as mountains. We were foundered. It was all over for us, if the Lord had not come to our aid. The wind which was blowing with very great violence from the southwest, quick as lightning (this is the expression of the captain) shifted to the northwest, and, blowing with equal force, raised enormous masses of water and lifted the vessel, which was being filled with water with fearful rapidity.

We look upon this reversal as a real miracle, and we believe we owe it to Mary Immaculate and to her august mother, St. Ann. At least, it is a very perceptible mark of the protection of heaven. No doubt we are also indebted to the very fervent prayers which you have had the charity to address to Heaven for us. Be so good now as to ask of the Almighty that the life. He has so mercifully spared may be employed to serve Him with much love and fervor.

We took a far-off route in order to avoid the sand banks of the Bahamas and passed San Domingo, Cuba, Tortuga, Jamaica, etc. As these islands lie between the tropic and the equator the heat was suffocating. We suffered from it—a singular suffering for the month of January.

The island of San Domingo is covered with green trees, orange, lemon, etc. Its coasts are very high, not so high, however, as those of Cuba. One point in particular rises to such a prodigious height that its summit can seldom be seen. We saw it, but much above the clouds that surround it and hide it from those who are at its base. It is called Torquino Peak.

In these warm seas there are numerous fishes of various species, especially flying fish; they are as large as our mackerel.

This letter remained unfinished. Five days later Mother Theodore had something quite different to relate to Bishop Bouvier. She was ill at the Ursuline Convent, but would now conclude her letter with the following few lines:

New Orleans, La., January 29 [1844]

Feast of St. Francis of Sales

It is from my sick bed that I am writing to you, my Father. I was seized with fever on arriving. There was a letter awaiting me here from our Sisters at Saint Mary-of-the-Woods. Since the last news that I received at Ruillé, His Lordship has formed two new establishments, withdrawn the Sisters from one which we had, given the habit to two postulants, admitted two novices to their vows, and received three Sisters from another Community—all without the advice or consent of the Sisters. They tried to make representations but he answered that he had foreseen their objections and would be obeyed.

Ask for me the spirit of understanding and of counsel. I shall need both gifts if the Lord sends me to Vincennes. If He should call me to Himself, you are sufficiently informed of the facts. Your Lordship will judge in your wisdom what would have to be done. May I beg of you, my Lord, to have our Mother of Ruillé informed of our arrival? I have begun a letter to her but I cannot finish it today, as I am permitted only a few minutes to write to you. As soon as I am better I shall write to Père Lottin and to Mlle. de Tucée. Sister Mary Cecilia offers you her respects and thanks.

Deign to accept the homage of the filial affection and of the most profound respect with which I am, my Lord, of Your Lordship

The most humble servant,

SISTER ST. THEODORE.

The establishment mentioned in the foregoing letter as having been closed by Bishop de la Hailandière was that of St. Francisville, Illinois. Just at that time, November, 1843, the Diocese of Chicago was formed, which took the thirty-five counties of Illinois that had formerly belonged to the Diocese of Vincennes; hence the Sisters were recalled from St. Francisville and sent to open a school at St. Peters, now Montgomery, Indiana.

The other establishment formed was the taking over from another Community one already existing. The Sisters of Charity of Nazareth, Kentucky, had a school at Vincennes as early as 1824. They were succeeded in 1838 by Sisters of Charity from Emmitsburg, Maryland. These in turn were now withdrawing, October 1843, and the Sisters of Providence were called to replace them.

Concerning this change the *Annals*, which were written by Sister St. Francis Xavier, relate: "Our chaplain received a letter for himself alone in which, however, His Lordship requested our opinion on three things: 1st—If we would receive Sister Celestia and Sister Ann Austin (Sisters of Charity) in case they should present themselves. 2nd—If we would leave to him the choice of the persons to be put there. He added, 'Answer me Yes or No, and do not make the absence of the Mother or anything similar an objection.'

"Sister St. Francis answered that since the Sisters of Charity were doing good in Vincennes, she did not see the necessity of taking that mission from them, since the diocese was vast enough for them and for us. As to accepting their Sisters, if they were good subjects she would be sorry to take them away, as she would not like the Sisters of Charity to take away our Sisters; and, as to letting the Bishop name the Sisters for the establishments, she would do so only when commanded."

Nevertheless, the Bishop asked that the two postulants, whom he specified, be vested and sent to Vincennes, and he called Sister St. Vincent from Jasper to take charge. He wrote to Sister Basilide, October 15, 1843, "It is understood you consent to leave Sister Marie Joseph Superior at Jasper. Their school is not large; two Sisters will suffice there unless their health should fail." The two Sisters were still only novices.

Hoping to clear away some of the misunderstandings, the Bishop of Le Mans, on November 8, 1843, had addressed the following letter to the Bishop of Vincennes:

"*Monseigneur*:—Having learned that the Society of the Propagation of the Faith had granted funds directly to M. Moreau, I wrote to the treasurer in Paris, M. Choiselat, and recommended Sister Theodore and her house to him; well understood, my Lord, without any prejudice to you. I expressed myself formally, and, by the way, I have been in circumstances several times to make the observation that it seemed to me your manner of administrating was judged of too severely by the Society without giving you a hearing. At Paris, at Rennes, and elsewhere they take the liberty to speak thus. Sister Theodore has been perfectly loyal to you. M. Choiselat answered that the Society of the Propagation of the Faith had for rule to give nothing directly to establishments of women, but that you had in your request included the Sisters of Providence for quite a large sum; that the council at Paris had taken into consideration the motives of this request and had, in consequence, given you an allowance for which he would give Sister Theodore a note for the amount destined for her. What she has obtained through your recommendations and mine together, was given directly and only for her establishment. No other use could be made of it. Hence, I feel assured that with the aid thus obtained and with what the Propagation already granted you for them, these devoted Sisters will extricate themselves little by little.

"Permit me, my Lord, to speak to you with fraternal liberty in the charity of J. C. The excellent Superior General, who has just been re-elected unanimously, is full of uneasiness in regard to the future of her daughters in America. While Sister Theodore was traveling about with admirable devotedness on her begging mission, several letters arrived addressed to her. The Superior thus learned that you had believed you might decide as to the admission of subjects, of their vocation, of their profession, etc., without considering the Constitutions and Rules. She entreated me to make an observation to you, viz., that a Congregation could not, under pain of death, be led in this manner. The Bishop must have the superintendence and the high direction; but he must leave to the body its free action and abstain from whatever could appear arbitrary. He might not consent to the admission of a subject whom he believed to be dangerous, nor accept a contract which he would judge to be prejudicial to the Congregation, or to one of the houses of the Congregation; but, not only must he not force, he must not even urge the admission of any one whomsoever, nor regulate their temporal affairs himself in any way whatsoever. The Sisters have the management, as I said before, under his superintendence, because he is their guardian and protector, but he does not manage for them. It is in following largely this way, consecrated by the experience of centuries, that I have the consolation of seeing my two fine Congregations of Evron and of Ruillé develop with admirable prosperity, and the other edifying Communities with which my diocese is enriched.

"At Rome a long examination was made of the Constitution and Rules of the Sisters of Ruillé. They did not think that they should finally approve them yet, but the Pope highly praised them by a special decree. This is already a great deal. I believe I shall give you pleasure by sending you a copy of this decree.

"If, as I have been told, you are shortly going to make a voyage to France, I hope you will do me the honor of paying me a visit. Then we can speak at length of the Sisters and of many other things.

"I cannot understand how you have, my Lord, deposed Sister Theodore and caused an election during an absence endured in her quality of Superior, and with your full consent given in writing. Happily this fact is not known, for, I can assure you, it would have produced a very bad effect around here.

J. B. Bp. Le Mans"

Accompanying Mother Theodore, besides Sister Mary Cecilia, were two postulants, Sister Monique Tiennou and

Sister Laurence Cheminant; also John Delahay and his sister, coming to work at Saint Mary's. As Mother Theodore's illness was more than a few days' indisposition, Sister Mary Cecilia, Sister Monique, the young man and his sister were sent on to Indiana. Mother Theodore remained seven weeks in New Orleans, nursed back to health by the devoted Ursulines. On the nineteenth of March, though still very weak, she set out for home, with the postulant, Sister Laurence, whom, she had kept with her. The journey was made by steamboat up the Mississippi and the Ohio, thence by stage to Vincennes, and again by boat up the Wabash to Terre Haute. Finally, after an absence of eleven months, she was back again with her Community at Saint Mary-of-the-Woods, April 1, 1844, as recorded in her diary.

Resuming her correspondence, she addresses one of her old friends now bearing a new title—Superior of the Seminary.

TO THE VERY REVEREND A. MARTIN, VINCENNES

Saint Mary's, April 7, 1844

Respected Superior:

I have been so fortunate as to find the little package that was destined for you. I shall send it by the first opportunity. You have a letter to be returned by the Bishop. Our purchases abroad have arrived. Be so kind as to note down briefly whatever would be pleasing or useful to you in the way of objects of piety, stationery, patterns and paper for drawing and painting, etc. We shall be happy to divide with you.

Please give me a little share in your prayers. After a life of such activity and dissipation, I need special grace in order to bring myself back to recollection of spirit and become a true Religious. Surely it is time.

Sister St. Francis offers you her respects. She is indeed a good daughter of Providence. Really, I am humiliated in seeing her run in the way of perfection while I just drag along. Adieu. I am afraid you will not be able to read this, as I am writing in the dark.

With sentiments of deep veneration I remain

Your very humble servant,

SISTER ST. THEODORE.

Mention has been made of the portrait of Queen Amelia that reached Mother Theodore at the moment when she was embarking at Havre. To thank for this gift comes the next letter.

TO QUEEN AMELIA

Saint Mary-of-the-Woods, Indiana

April 28, 1844

To Her Majesty the Queen of the French

Madame and most dear Mother:

Before leaving my beloved country I wished to tell you the pleasure it gave me to receive the portrait of Your Majesty. I was writing to you when the Commissary General came to say that the ship was waiting for me. I was thus obliged to hasten to embark, as the *Nashville* was already under sail. In a few minutes we had left France.

The voyage was long and perilous. On the twenty-second of December, beginning at two o'clock in the morning, there was a frightful tempest. At one time the ship was turned on end by the angry waves. In this moment of danger, after the example of one of our Kings, we invoked the God of the Queen. We asked Him sadly why He let us find favor with her, if we were to perish now. He heard our supplications and reversed the ship to natural position in a manner quite miraculous.

Having arrived at New Orleans I was attacked by a grave

AMELIA, QUEEN OF THE FRENCH FROM 1830 to 1848
From an oil painting presented by the Queen to Mother Theodore in 1843

illness, which kept me seven weeks longer away from my dear home in the woods. It is only a few days since I saw it again and embraced the cherished daughters whom I had left here. At this moment of pure happiness I needed their assistance to express my thanks to God. With tearful eyes, and hearts full of the deepest gratitude, we were but one heart and one soul. We went to the chapel to beseech our Lord to pour abundant blessings upon Your Majesty, upon the King, and upon Her Highness, Madame Adelaide; indeed, upon all the members of your august family.

This did not satisfy our hearts; we have therefore ordered a special prayer to be said daily for this intention. More-over, to perpetuate the remembrance of your great goodness to us, we shall inscribe on the first page of the register of this nascent Congregation what you have done for us. Your portrait, which is our dearest treasure, shall be put in the most conspicuous place, so that we may have continually before our eyes the picture of her who is truly our mother. The sight of it will recall your tender piety, your ardent zeal for the salvation of souls; it will be to us what the glance of the prince's eye is to the soldier in battle, and it will encourage us in our trials and privations.

Notwithstanding my desire to speak of you to the inhabi-tants of the New World, I was not the first to proclaim your admirable virtues. Their lustre has shone beyond the sea to confound impiety and to console the dear Americans, of whom your royal spouse had such tender recollections.

The holy Bishop Flaget, more than any one else, never tires speaking of His Majesty the King. The Right Reverend C. de la Hailandière, our Bishop, was also deeply touched at the interest you have taken in our little Congregation. He admits your august family to a share in his prayers and apos-tolic labors, thus to give the tribute of thanks which he feels are due to you. In fine, I can say, Madame, you reign here over all hearts. Strangers envy our happiness in having you for our Sovereign. The old French of Louisiana and Vincennes take pride in being your subjects. But I will not let it be said that even in France there is a heart more sincerely and gratefully yours than that of her who is, with the most profound veneration,

> Madame,
>> Of Your Majesty
>>> The most humble and obedient servant,
>>>> SISTER ST. THEODORE.

Having despatched her letter to the Queen, Mother Theodore set out to visit the missions. Immediately on her return she explains to her friend in New York the cause of her delayed correspondence.

TO MRS. PARMENTIER, BROOKLYN, N. Y.

May 22, 1844

Madame and venerable Friend,

It has been impossible for me to reply sooner to your very good letter of the sixteenth of April, which I received just as I was setting out to visit our dear Sisters who are in the establishments. I arrived home last evening worn out with fatigue and overcome with work. I come now to refresh myself with you for a few minutes. But again I must talk about money. When will the day come that we shall be able to be occupied only with God? Our consolation is that it is for Him we engage in other things. To Him, too, dear mother, my heart longs to express my gratitude to you and to good Mr. Byerley. If the Lord deigns to hear the prayers that we offer for you and for him, He will load you with His most precious gifts and will give you all that your heart desires.

I await almost with impatience the fulfillment of the promise you made me to give detailed news of yourself and of your dear family. Assuredly I shall always find time to read your letters and I shall do so with great satisfaction. It will be a recreation for me and I shall expect it from your goodness, to which I already owe so much.

You will also learn with pleasure that the good God blesses the House that your charity has caused you to adopt and which looks upon you as its mother. We are now thirty in the Community all told. Nine postulants are to receive the habit in August; these, added to the fifteen that have already had that happiness, will make twenty-four [novices]. See how we have multiplied in three years! Sisters are asked for in several places and we already have five houses in all. God be blest!

Let us come down to business. I have given to Mr. Crawford a note on Mr. Edward, but only for $1,800. There remains due to you $62.00. I beg you, dear friend, to take this amount from what you have collected for us; if there is any left over, please send us some white calico, or muslin, fine enough for necker-chiefs. It is impossible to and any out here that is wide enough according to the Rule. I enclose a piece of thread to show the exact width required.

Our Sisters think perhaps you might be able to have some medals made for us, if you think it is expedient to do so. A model is enclosed. Do not put in too much silver. On one side there should be engraved in English *Providence First Class* on three medals; *Providence Second Class* on the other three. On the reverse side of the six *Excellence*.

For all these things, should you not have money enough, as I suspect, I shall send the balance in the near future. If, per-chance, a few dollars are left over, send some unbleached sheeting. Kindly ship all by the Lakes to the address of M. Webb, Esq., at Lafayette. He will forward it to us.

Pardon me the liberty I am taking to trouble you thus, and be well assured that it is impossible to add to the affection of her who will always remain in Our Lord, my very dear friend,

Yours very sincerely,

SISTER ST. THEODORE.

On one occasion, when Mother Theodore was visiting the Sisters in Vincennes, she wrote the following concerning a misunderstanding that had occurred:

TO THE VERY REVEREND A. MARTIN

Very dear Vicar General:

Permit me to say how grieved I am at what has happened. I gave you pain—I realized it this morning—but I can assure you it was not done intentionally.

I must admit that I was somewhat "put out" when reading in Sister's letter that you opposed the Sisters' returning to Saint Mary's before the time you had specified. What preceded and what followed in that letter confirmed my idea that it was merely formal opposition. You have made it clear that I was mistaken. I am very sorry about it. Interiorly, I rejoice; but I can truly say that, apart from the momentary contradiction that I felt, it never entered my mind to mention it. If I did so yesterday to the Bishop it was without bitterness, without premeditation, and without making the statements that you report. If upon reflection I had attached the least importance to the incident, I would have written to you yourself. I positively did not know that Father Corbe remembered it, much less that he spoke of it to His Lordship.

I do not say this by way of excusing myself. I see very clearly that I did wrong and I ask your pardon. You will be good enough, dear Father Martin, to forgive me, will you not? Do not let me return to my solitude with the painful thought that you are displeased with me. I have sorrows enough without that.

Please add to this favor, which I ask so earnestly, that of remembering sometimes before the Lord one who never ceases to be, with sentiments of profound veneration,

Monsieur le Grand Vicaire,

Your very humble and devoted servant,

SISTER ST. THEODORE.

Providence of Vincennes, July 18, 1844

P. S. I would be very glad to see you a moment before I leave. It might be for the last time.

With another much esteemed friend there were other matters to be settled. The school at Jasper differed from all the other schools conducted by the Sisters in that it was a public school, supported by the county and under the supervision of the county school authorities. For the stability of the establishment and its peaceful administration, Mother Theodore believed that certain conditions should be a matter of contract. Hence the letter that now follows:

TO THE REVEREND JOSEPH KUNDEK, JASPER

Saint Mary-of-the-Woods, July 28, 1844

Respected Sir:

It is with deep regret that we feel ourselves compelled not to admit the conditions which you propose for your establishment, because they are contrary to our Rules and to the usages we have adopted for our houses in America. For three years we have been acting only tentatively; it is time now come to something positive for the foundation of our missions.

The great desire we have of seconding your zeal, the special affection which we bear toward the good people whom you direct, the attachment, quite maternal, which we feel for this mission, our eldest daughter, cause us to depart as much as possible from the common rule in favor of your work. You will see this by the explanation of our conditions.

In the first place, we ask you to give each year the sum of one hundred dollars in cash, payable by installments of twenty-five dollars at the beginning of each quarter. Secondly, that you provide the Sisters with flour, meat, sugar, and coffee, they themselves to provide for their other wants. Thirdly, that they may have, as they already have had, the use of the house, the furniture, the garden, etc.

On these conditions they will receive *gratis* the children of the county. The county will pay you. If among the parishioners in easy circumstances there are any who can make a small compensation for the higher education of their children, this shall be received by the Sisters, who shall not have to give an account of it except to us.

We engage ourselves, on our side, to keep in your school two Sisters able to teach—the one German, the other English—for as long a time as the above conditions are fulfilled, and to do all we can to accomplish good under your direction.

We would be extremely grieved if you would not be able to comply with our wishes; for, as I have said, we love the mission of Jasper very much; yet, we believe we ought not to give Sisters if we cannot fulfil our other duties. The future of the establishment, then, is in your hands. See before God what you can do. The money you will receive from the county will greatly reduce your expenses.

Convinced that you will do all that you can, I am, awaiting your answer, with the most sincere respect,

Your very humble servant,

SISTER ST. THEODORE
Superior.

TO THE SAME

[Some days later; without date.]

Monsieur le Missionnaire:

I thank you for your charity in giving me the holy counsels which your letter contains. Now obtain for me by your prayers that I may put them in practice. How much I stand in need of help from above.

It is a great comfort for us to find so satisfactory all the arrangements you have made. Our gratitude cannot be well told, but our prayers for you shall never fail. We indeed owe a great debt to the one who is almost our first bene-factor in Indiana. May God reward you in the way of His munificence. Continue, I entreat you, to assist us by your coun-sels and prayers, that. God's work may not suffer be-cause of our imperfections.

Your humble servant,

SISTER ST. THEODORE

The records show that for several years some young stu-dents from the Seminary spent their vacation months at Saint Mary's, helping on the farm. In a letter dated October 3, 1844, Mother Theodore replies to enquiries about them.

TO THE VERY REVEREND A. MARTIN, VINCENNES

Respected Superior,

I am happy to be able to tell you very candidly that I have not observed anything blameworthy in the conduct of the dear seminarians. I wish it had been in our power to do more for them than we did, but this year we could not do it. I hope that later on we shall have the consolation of being more useful. In the meantime, I rely on your indulgence, particularly in sending Sister M. Therese's straw mats. The dear daughter did her best on them.

I must close now, for I am obliged to go to Terre Haute, where I am called to court to explain my conduct and defend myself against accusations relative to counterfeit money that was said to have been received from me. One has to come to America to be treated thus! Sometimes I am so disheartened with this country that I feel as if I were carrying on my shoulders the weight of its highest mountains, and in my heart all the thorns of its wilderness. Pray for me occasionally that I may not lose courage; nay, more, that I may be brave enough to hold up others who falter sometimes.

Sister St. Francis thanks you a thousand times for your letter. She is happy to find for once a compassionate heart. Poor child! How much she has suffered and still suffers.

Receive the renewed assurance of the deepest veneration with which I remain,

Your very humble servant,
SISTER ST. THEODORE.

TO THE SAME

Saint Mary's, December 13, 1844

Respected Vicar General:

I thank you sincerely for your gracious kindness in telling us about the departure of the Bishop. [He was making his first visit to Rome.] I regret that he has gone without my letter, but it is the Will of God, so it seems. If you would be so good as to return it to me I should be greatly pleased. Also, give us the address of His Lordship in France. I expect to write to him there some of these days. We unite our prayers with yours for the dear traveler, and we shall continue to pray for him daily as long as the shepherd shall be separated from his flock. We pray also for you, that God may assist you in carrying the burden [the administratorship] laid upon you; finally, we pray the God of peace and love to come and establish His reign in our poor diocese. Heaven grant that our unworthiness, and mine in particular, may not be an obstacle to this favor.

A letter from France received yesterday says all your family are well. Madame le Fer went to see the ladies to get tidings of all for you. The Sisters thank you for your goodness in sending their letters by Mr. Moore. They have been returned. When you shall have a similar occasion we shall be happy to profit by it. All the commissions prepared for Monseigneur are waiting here.

Do not forget our needs when in prayer, I entreat you. How strongly I feel that it is necessary to be holy! But more strongly do I realize that I am far from being so. Obtain this grace for me, and deign to accept the homage of the most profound veneration with which I am, dear Vicar General,

Your very humble servant,
SISTER ST. THEODORE.

There are no other letters on hand belonging to this period. There is a *Journal*, however, describing the return voyage from France, addressed by Mother Theodore to two good friends in Paris, Louis Veuillot, editor of the *Univers*, and Leon Aubineau, an associate in the work. The *Univers* was the organ of a strong Catholic party headed by Montalembert, whose object was to promote religion and to protect the rights of the Church and of the Catholics of France.

Louis Veuillot, a gifted young journalist, though born of a Catholic family, had grown up with but little knowledge of God or of the teachings of the Church. In the brief sketch of his early life, written by himself in 1841 as an introduction to his book, *Rome et Lorette*, he says, speaking of the training given him by his parents, "And not a word of God" —"*Et pas un mot de Dieu. Je le dis à la honte de mon temps, mon à la leur; ils ne connaissaient pas Dieu.*"[2]

In 1838, in company with a friend, a devout Catholic, he had made a visit to Rome and while there embraced the Faith. Returning to Paris, he resolved to devote his talents and energies to the spread of religion, the increase of devotion, and the defense of the Church. The *Univers*, just then in need of new and vigorous management, afforded him the opportunity he desired. Offered the editorship, he eagerly accepted it. This Catholic daily newspaper, that during its few years of existence had scarcely been noticed, now began to command attention and consideration because of the brilliant style, the wit, and the fearlessnes of its editor.

Veuillot had not been long in charge of the *Univers* when Mother Theodore made her visit to France in quest of funds. While at Tours she received hospitality at the home of the Baroness de la Valette, an aunt of Sister St. Francis (le Fer de la Motte). The Baroness, an admirer of the *Univers*, invited M. Aubineau to meet Mother Theodore and to hear about Saint Mary-of-the-Woods, feeling sure he would be interested. Aubineau divided his time between that city and Paris—between his labors for the St. Vincent de Paul Society in Tours and his work for the *Univers* in Paris.

Referring to the interview between Aubineau and Mother Theodore, the Baroness wrote to the latter on November 8, 1843, "This good and pious young man seized upon the details you gave him with the greatest delight and retained them wonderfully well, as you have seen in the *Univers*, which has given your story almost a European publicity. Though this journal has not as many subscribers as have the secular papers, yet it reaches nearly everywhere, and we must not doubt that this publicity will bear good fruit. . . .

---

[2] *Rome et Lorette* (5e édition; Tours, 1853), p. 14.

"And I must inform you, my very dear Sister, that the intimate friend of M. Aubineau, M. Veuillot, the director, editor, and support of the *Univers*, charmed by the sketch [about St. Mary-of-the-Woods] contributed by his friend, has just had printed 500 copies of the two articles that appeared in the *Univers*—the articles that opened the hearts and purses of the good people of Le Mans. The pamphlets will be sold at fifty centimes each for the benefit of your work. You will appreciate this noble act the more, when I tell you that M. Veuillot is poor only because of his having sacrificed a fine position and all the advantages which the government would have conferred upon him in consideration of his talents, that he might have the happiness of devoting himself to the service of Religion."

In return for so much disinterested generosity toward her work, Mother Theodore had only the promise of prayer to give. And on several occasions she spoke and wrote assurances that the Sisters of Providence in Indiana would remember in their prayers these two good friends in France. Hence, even five years later, July, 1848, Aubineau could write with confidence from Tours, "I trust that a part of the strength of both M. Veuillot and myself will come to us from the chapel of St. Mary-of-the-Woods."

Of Aubineau himself Mme. de la Valette makes comment in a letter to her niece, Sister St. Francis [November 30, 1844]: "Here is M. Aubineau [she writes], who wishes me to tell you that the young men of the Conference of St. Vincent de Paul pray for your work, as he also recommends his work to your prayers. We may truly say *his*, for he is the soul of this association, which takes charge of instructing the ignorant and of relieving every kind of misfortune."

That he continued in his devotion to all kinds of works of mercy is apparent from a letter written by Veuillot in June, 1853, to "my good Sister Francis Xavier, and my much honored and much loved Mother Theodore." "I shall go and read your letters to M. Aubineau [he said]. He will not fail to write to you, but I must tell you one thing he will not tell you. He has received the Cross of Honor for the courage he displayed during the cholera epidemic. He shut himself up in the penitentiary and remained there three or four days, nursing, consoling, and burying the unfortunate prisoners, and did not leave them until he himself was stricken. Almighty God preserved him for us. Bonaparte has conferred marks of esteem upon him, but he is more grateful to God than to Bonaparte."[3]

Aubineau in his introduction to the French life of Sister St. Francis Xavier (Irma le Fer de la Motte), written in 1879 by her sister Clementine, says, "The first pious book I published was a little sketch of Saint Mary-of-the-Woods written under the charm of Mother Theodore's recital and, so to speak, in her own words."[4] Opposite the title page of Aubineau's book this notice was printed: "Offerings intended for Saint Mary-of-the-Woods will always be received at Paris at the office of the *Univers*. They may be addressed to M. Louis Veuillot, who will send them to the Superior of the Religious of the Visitation of St. Mary, appointed to transmit them to their destination."[5]

From the sale of this book and from the contributions sent to the *Univers* a modest sum was realized and forwarded to Mother Theodore after her return to Indiana. Much of the same story told in *Sainte Marie-des-Bois*, with additional material, is included in a later book written by Aubineau in 1875, an octavo volume of over 500 pages, entitled "*Les Serviteurs de Dieu au XIXième Siècle*."

Because of Veuillot's connection with Mother Theodore and his great and lasting service to her, it will not be deemed a digression here to make brief mention of this champion of the Truth during the middle years of the nineteenth century in France. In praise of Veuillot much has been written —of his life and work, his letters and other writings. Fifty-eight volumes, many of them in defense of the Church and her rights, testify to his powerful trenchant style. Even the French "free-thinkers themselves," whose principles Veuillot had attacked vigorously, acknowledged him "not only as an incomparable journalist but as one of the greatest writers of France."[6]

---

[3] Letter in the Community archives.

[4] Mme. Clementine de la Corbinière, *Une Femme Apôtre ou Vie et Lettres d'Irma le Fer de la Motte* (2e édition; Paris, 1880).

[5] *Sainte Marie-des-Bois—Publié au Profit de la Communauté* (Paris, 1846).

[6] Eugene Tavernier, "Louis Veuillot," *Catholic Encyclopedia*, Vol. XV, p. 394.

Around the first of the year 1860, Veuillot published in the *Univers* a beautiful address to Pope Pius IX, proclaiming in the name of the Catholics of France their defense of his independence in the Papal States, then being threatened by Napoleon III of France and his allies in Italy. "The high-souled chief editor, as well as the members of his staff," says the Reverend Bernard O'Reilly in his life of Pius IX, "had but one care and one thought, and that was to do their duty toward the Holy Father and the Church, fearless of every personal consequence."[7]

When, disregarding official warnings, the editors, late on the night of January 28, 1860, were preparing to publish in the morning issue of their paper, the Holy Father's encyclical, *Nullis certis verbis*, Veuillot said, holding in his hand the Pope's letter that had just reached them, "This is our death warrant; our paper will not be living tomorrow night."

Later the "chivalrous journalist" added—quoting again from O'Reilly—"We felt rather a sentiment of deep joy to have found so glorious an opportunity of perishing; and we set about translating the encyclical, in order to have it inserted in the morning edition, before any prohibition could be sent us, and to prevent the paper from being seized in the printing room." The next morning the encyclical was all over Paris and out on its way to the other cities of France and beyond. The same day, January 29, the *Univers* was suppressed by government decree.

O'Reilly adds: "The great journalist and the paper which his genius had raised so high had had many warm opponents among Catholics; but this suppression made friends of former foes." Seven years later the publication of the *Univers* was resumed and Veuillot was again at its head, as ardent, devoted, valiant as before.

In the letter written to Mother Theodore and Sister St. Francis, already quoted, Veuillot relates some of the circumstances connected with a previous attack upon himself and the *Univers*. That time the opposition came from the episcopal authority in Paris. There can be no doubt about the good intention and the sincerity on both sides—ecclesiastical authority on the one hand, and the editor of the *Univers* on the other.

[7] *Life of Pope Pius IX* (19th edition; New York: P. J. Kennedy, 1892), p. 365.

I had hardly recovered from this terrible stroke [the death of Mme. Veuillot]," he wrote, "when I met with the contradictions that have echoed even in your forests. By the adorable permission of that Providence which has always visibly assisted our work, I was in Rome at the time they attacked me in Paris. I can tell you, my dear Sisters, they attacked me without charity, without justice, and even without reason. The Pope judged thus of it. I saw him four times. I had with him two long conversations *tête-à-tête*. I assisted at his Mass in his private chapel, the only secular present, and had the happiness of receiving Holy Communion from his hands. Finally he took our defense, and our powerful adversaries, recognizing that they had been deceived, have given a beautiful example of obedience to the Vicar of Jesus Christ. This has done them a great good and has given more honor to them than to us.

"No words can express, my dear Sisters, the benignity of the Holy Father. He has a smile which goes to the depths of the soul. I felt as much at my ease near him as near the tenderest of fathers. I was kneeling close beside him, almost touching his armchair, more than once, whilst listening to him, forgetting everything else save his goodness. I dared to take his hand and cover it with kisses.

"He listened to all I wished to say. He blessed my children, my parents; my partners, as I named them one after the other; my friends. Among the latter you were not forgotten, for, interiorly, I named all those in the entire world who assist us in their prayers. For some moments he rested his hand upon my head. I think I feel it still. I returned consoled, encouraged, ready for the combat. You were right in thinking, my dear Sisters, that even had it been otherwise, we would not have given the scandal of resistance; we would have submitted with joy—finding more joy, perhaps, in submitting than in triumphing.

"We were all resolved—(I began by saying to the Holy Father in the name of all my associates)—we were all resolved that we would continue our work only if he thought it useful, and in the measure that he would permit. I added that even if Rome should not think it proper to mix in an affair in which the authority of the Bishop was exercised against some laymen, we would not ask for justice, but would unhesitatingly suppress the journal—purely and simply, without protestation or explanation. We shall always have the same sentiments. Nothing will make us relinquish them. You can rely upon this.

"In case anything of the kind should ever arise again, wait not for the news; reply boldly that your friends are Catholics, that is to say, children of obedience. Yes, my dear Sisters, if we seek a word that suffices to give the definition of the Catholic, such as he ought to be, it is this one: *He is obedient*. This is the word that best portrays and praises him."

Such were the men—Veuillot and Aubineau—who became the advocates of the humble, unknown foundress and of her little Community in the Indiana forest. To these men Mother Theodore sent the long narrative that constitutes the following section.

PART IV

THIRD JOURNEY OF TRAVEL

ENTLEMEN:

The good will you have shown us makes us feel that you will welcome some news from over the sea. Your piety will appreciate our feelings of thankfulness to God for having called us hither to be instruments in His hands for the fulfilment of the gracious works of His Providence, of which one of you is the happy conquest, and of our holy Religion, of which both of you are zealous propagators. May this divine Religion, to which you have consecrated the light of your intellect and the warmth of your hearts, sweeten for you the fatigues endured in the battle of the Lord and crown you with laurels that will never fade.

On the twenty-eighth of November, after having communicated as on the preceding days with the intention that Jesus might be our Viaticum from France to America, perhaps even from the ocean to Heaven, we were busy in finishing some letters. The Queen, in addition to her other favors, had deigned to send us her portrait to Havre. We could not think of leaving without returning our thanks to her, also to *M. le Ministre des Cultes*, who had constantly shown us such paternal interest. Quite absorbed in paying these debts of gratitude, I was not thinking of the *Nashville*, whose time of departure had been left undetermined.

At two in the afternoon the captain sent word that we must come at once as they had been waiting for us since six in the morning. We had only a minute to recommend ourselves to God, and to throw our papers pell-mell with our other belongings. When we arrived at the quay great was our consternation to see the vessel start, and we not able to go aboard because the police were demanding our passports and we had none. Happily the *Commissaire de Marine* was informed of our difficulty and sent the order to let us pass. The ship was already some distance out, but we overtook it in a rowboat and, shortly after, the steam tug towed us out to sea.

It is a painful moment when the steamer alone takes the direction of the port, carrying back the friends and the children of the poor voyagers who, long after all has disappeared, continue looking towards the coast of France. At that moment we felt that we were going to prove, even better than by letters, our gratitude to our dear friends in France, as we were going to make them participate with us in the merit of our long and perilous voyage. Accepting for this intention the fatigues and dangers of the passage, we said with all our hearts: For us be the sufferings of the sea and the storms of the ocean; for them, our dear friends of France, the sweet pleasures of home and country, the beautiful feasts of our holy religion and the happiness of multiplying for many years the works of mercy towards others. How often since then have I made the same prayers.

A contrary wind kept us five days in the channel. Scarcely were we on the main before the rolling of the ship increased, and again we were paying our tribute to the ocean. There is nothing, perhaps, more diverting than the first gust of wind which changes the decks of a ship into a hospital ward: children crying, women moaning, men holding their head in one hand and a basin in the other; *l'eau de cologne*, smelling salts spread over all the handkerchiefs—but to laugh at all the different sounds of this improvised concert, one would have to be a non-participant; for truly it is one of the most pitiful rôles that one can play.

On the fourteenth of December at sunset after a glorious day I was watching the twilight gradually waning until it finally gave place to the darkness. The stars shone forth in the blue sky above and were reflected in the depths below, while a fresh breeze was speeding our vessel over the waves. Nothing so lifts the soul to God as a beautiful night on the ocean. I was lost in thoughts of the past. It was a Thursday evening. I fancied myself to be again in the beautiful chapel of our dear Visitandines in Paris, where I had received the last Benediction of the Blessed Sacrament. I recalled the fervent piety of the good Carmelites of Le Mans and thought perhaps at that very moment they were praying for us. I united myself to their prayers. The passengers scarcely spoke at all. Suddenly fearful cries resounded throughout the ship.

My first impulse was to rush towards the unfortunate one, but it was so dark on that side of the ship that I did not dare venture. I congratulated myself when I learned that the screams proceeded from a sailor who was being punished for having imbibed too freely. Some minutes afterwards we witnessed another scene more alarming. On going down we found that the captain had fallen. He lay stretched out, motionless, and so flushed as to make us fear he had congestion of the brain. I proposed to bleed him. You cannot imagine how distressed I was to see him in such a condition. We were beginning a long voyage at the worst season of the year, and he was the only one capable of managing our vessel. But God had pity on us; scarcely was the vein opened when the captain recovered. The exertion he had made of throwing the drunken sailor into the hold, joined to his choleric temperament, put him in this state.

The weather during the next few days until the

twenty-fifth was magnificent and so hopeful were we of a good voyage that I expected to have but two words to say about it; namely, that it was prosperous and monotonous. Little did I dream of those terrible scenes which I must now describe.

In the night between Saturday and Sunday the wind changed. On Monday, toward five o'clock in the evening, it commenced to blow furiously, and the waves rose to a prodigious height. The captain recognized the danger in a moment and put the ship to drive before the wind. So violent was the storm that it took the sailors more than two hours to reef the main sail alone. The waves broke over our heads with a frightful roar. We thought each moment would be our last. During this time we were shut up in our little cabins, six feet in length by four in breadth, a space scarcely larger than a grave. Sister Cecilia and I occupied one cabin, the postulants another. I need not tell you that we did not sleep (death seemed too near), we prayed. Those ocean heaps, those thunderings of mighty waters that kept rolling over our heads, had in them something so awful that, not hoping alone to appease the anger of God, I went for our young postulants. We then began prayers in common, offering to God the sacrifice of our lives with all the earnestness in our power. The waves seemed impatient to accept it, and to put an end to that terrible scene. It was now nearly two o'clock in the morning. We were bathed in perspiration from the mere fatigue occasioned by the violent motion of the vessel and the exertions we were obliged to make in order to keep from falling. The billows struck the ship with redoubled fury, and during one shock, more fearful than the others, the water burst in at the aftermost part of the vessel, ten feet from us and, rushing through a broken porthole, threatened to inundate our cabin.

Poor Sister Cecilia exclaimed, "Oh, the time for us to die

has come! Mother, take me near you!" But no, the hour had not yet come. The captain followed by one of his sailors rushed to close up the opening, and he almost succeeded in making fast the portholes; they could not, however, entirely prevent the water from reaching us. The sea now caused another disturbance on deck by breaking asunder some of the ropes and pulleys. Three huge chains that held the boats in which the animals and fowl were confined were broken. Some of the fowl were swept away by the waves, and the remainder were left on the brink of the yawning abyss. The passengers amidships were soaked completely through. Some were screaming, others weeping, and all believed their last moment had come.

But, "they that go down to the sea in ships, doing business in the great waters; these have seen the works of the Lord, and His wonders in the deep" [Psalm 106:23–24], and it is their duty to give glory to Him, and to tell His wonderful works to the children of men. We have a keen sense of this sweet obligation, and it is a pleasure to relate to you, who are so well able to appreciate them, the gracious acts of God.

At eight o'clock the wind ceased; at nine the captain informed us that the danger was over for the present. He did well to say "for the present," for in a winter voyage on the ocean, as in that from earth to heaven, we are never really out of danger until we are in port.

The clouds were of a yellowish tinge, the atmosphere was dense, and although the wind no longer raged, yet the sea continued to heave and to utter, as it were, ominous groans. Tuesday was spent in profiting by this treacherous calm to repair the damages of the night. The fireplaces and so forth which had been displaced by the storm were restored. As for us, we spent the day in thanking God. Towards evening a gale sprang up, and our poor chickens, having lost their coop the

night before, were carried off into the sea; also a pretty little
rabbit with which we had made such intimate acquaintance
that it crept into our pockets.

The night was rough. The morning of the next day,
Wednesday, again brought the wind and storm, together with
the repetition of the same scene of horror as before, only in a
more frightful degree. The *Nashville* was again "brought to,"
and even the ropes were coiled to prevent their being caught
by the wind. The second storm began about eight o'clock. An
hour later our only boat was swept away, and with it all hope
of salvation in case of shipwreck.

One cannot conceive how frightful it is to see nothing
between oneself and eternity but a few planks nailed together, against which the winds and waves have let loose
all their fury. The Holy Ghost has revealed to us these
feelings of anguish [Psalm 106:25–26]. Yes, how true it is
that the soul melts and pines away at the sight of the dangers, when one is lifted up to the heavens by the waves and
then hurried down again to the depths. Not a billow but
dragged away with it something from off the deck. The brooms,
the pails, the benches were quickly engulfed; they seemed to
say to us as they fell into the sea, *Hodie mihi,
cras tibi*.

It was not yet four o'clock in the afternoon and darkness
had already spread over the horizon. If a storm is dreadful by
day, it is still more awful by night. The lamps cannot be lighted, nor can anything be distinguished, save the white foam of
the waves which seem greedy to devour us.

We assembled together for prayer. We looked no more
for repose in this world and though we were covered with
perspiration from the tossing of the ship, which trembled like
a person in a nervous attack, we did not notice our fatigue. We
had begun again the Way of the Cross, and had offered anew to

our dying Saviour the sacrifice of our lives. In spite of
the terrors of our weak nature, we could say to Him with
confidence *My God, into Thy hands I commend my spirit*. We
addressed ourselves also to our Blessed Mother, for it was
Mary who had chosen our ship, and we had made a vow to her
Immaculate Heart. In examining if at the period of undertaking this voyage I had had any human views in the selection of
our route, my conscience reassured me, for I had entrusted all
to the Blessed Virgin.

I do not know how long the devotion of the Way of the Cross
lasted; but the storm raged terribly the whole time; nevertheless, when we followed Jesus to Calvary and thought upon His
sorrows, our own became less. It was for us, for our love, that
He died upon the Cross; it was for Him that we were going to
perish on board the *Nashville*. But we were not worthy to con-
summate that sacrifice.

What strength the soul draws from prayer! In the midst of
a storm, how sweet is the calm it finds in the Heart of Jesus.
But what comfort is there for those who do not pray? Often
this thought that struck me when reading *Rome et Lorette*
comes back to my mind. How much consolation I found in
reading that excellent work. Heaven will repay you, I hope, for
the good it has done to me.

When we had finished the Way of the Cross we felt
strengthened, and it seemed our Lord said to us, as heretofore
to His disciples, Now rest awhile. I induced my Sisters therefore to try to sleep. I remained watching by their side. While
looking upon those poor dear children, I asked our Lord
whether a frightful death was the hundredfold. He had promised in this world to those who leave all to follow Him. I prayed
Him to pardon my weakness and to give me some little token
of hope. Opening a book of devotion, I lighted upon this passage of the 106th Psalm [28–29], "They cried to the Lord in

their affliction and He brought them out of their distresses; He turned the storm into a breeze; and its waves were still."

Shortly after, the captain came to tell us that the danger was now over, but that he feared another storm, and that then the rolling would become more intolerable than ever. It was now four o'clock in the morning. I thanked God heartily when I learned that we were out of danger, for I must admit that it would cost me to die without seeing once more my dear mission of Saint Mary-of-the-Woods.

After we had returned thanks in common to our heavenly Father we crept out of our cabins. It was impossible to stand upright; we reeled like drunken men. On deck we learned that a child eight years old had died during the night. Some said he had been frightened to death by a gush of water into the hold; others that he had died of starvation as the poor people below had not, since the first storm, been able to prepare any food, all their cooking utensils having been washed away. The captain told us that he would bury the child himself, because the poor little thing was a German Protestant, but that if it had been a Catholic, he would have me do it.

A bell was rung. All the passengers came on deck. Never shall I forget the scene we then witnessed. It was ten o'clock in the morning. The sky was overspread with thick dark clouds. It looked like a vast temple at night, as the fitful, lurid sun cast a yellowish tinge resembling the pale light of the tapers near a catafalque. The foaming waves opened like immense tombs that seemed avid to swallow their first victim.

When all was ready a porthole was opened, and a plank painted black, six feet long and three broad, was suspended over the deep. The body of the child, wrapped in a winding sheet, was placed upon it, with a large stone attached to the feet. For a minute or two the captain read—I do not know what prayer. Profound silence reigned. The father scarcely shed a tear. The mother seemed quite unmoved. At a word spoken by the captain, the plank was raised in the air, and the next instant the light corpse glided into the waters. I made the Sign of the Cross over it, but alas, I do not know whether the child was even baptized. The passengers withdrew, apparently untouched by the scene, and some even smiled. How impiety deadens the heart!

That day was an anxious one. It was dark at four o'clock. Unfavorable signs appeared in the horizon. At five the waves dashed with such fury that Madam Thomas, who occupied the adjoining cabin, came with her sister and daughter and begged to join in our prayers. We received them joyfully. From that day forward these good Creoles have continued to come and say the Rosary with us and to assist at our other exercises of piety. Jammed, bruised, and knocked against one another, we prayed, expecting that God would soon call us to himself.

We had no means of estimating the danger of the ship otherwise than from a small window which, when the sea was calm, was fourteen or fifteen feet above the surface but was now plunged beneath the waters that deluged us. I had stuffed a woolen blanket into the opening, but it was thrust back by the violence of the waves. Little globules of phosphoric light shot out from under my fingers. As the storm increased in violence we began once more our Way of the Cross, thinking that this time surely we would not live to finish it.

Happy those who are able to pray!

Towards two o'clock the next morning we completed our holy exercise in which, for the third time, we offered the sacrifice of our lives. Nevertheless I felt great confidence in my heart, for we had just vowed a Mass in honor of St. Anne

NATIONAL SHRINE OF SAINT ANNE
Brittany, France

d'Auray and an inscription on the walls of that chapel, testifying that the *Nashville* had been saved by Saint Anne.[1] As the storm grew in violence, the Sisters wished to make other vows. I would not permit it, telling them that we must stay calmly by the Cross of Jesus and await in peace the end of our long agony. Poor Sister Cecilia had great difficulty in resigning herself to death by drowning, which seemed to her the most terrible kind of death. Oh, how much she suffered! I proposed that all go to rest for awhile, and so fatigued were they that they readily consented.

For some minutes there was absolute silence, then suddenly it was broken by an extraordinary crash as if the vessel had completely broken asunder. The ship had, in fact, been thrown upon the beam end, and was now under water. The keel was above the surface and the tops of the masts below.

The water was rushing in through every opening. It found its way into the hold, the cabin, and indeed everywhere. Soon our little bunk was almost submerged. Several passengers of the lower deck burst from their prison, and went half dressed to the captain to compel him to let them have a sort of boat in which the cow was kept. Others, fiercer than the American savages, drew their knives to cut their throats, that they might thus escape the horrors of a more tedious death. Imagine if you can the cries, the con-

---

[1] The shrine of St. Anne d'Auray, the patron of sailors, overlooks the sea on the west coast of Brittany. It has been renowned for centuries for the many and great favors obtained there through the intercession of the Saint. While devotion to St. Anne began among the Bretons with their conversion to Christianity, it received a new impulse in 1624 when St. Anne appeared to the peasant Nicolaic and directed him where to find her statue, hidden away long ages before in a time of danger. She further directed that a chapel be built there in her honor. To commemorate these events, there takes place annually on the feast of St. Anne, July 26, a solemn celebration called St. Anne's Pardon because of the indulgence attached. Thousands make this great pilgrimage, and other thousands frequent the shrine throughout the year, as St. Anne is invoked not only in sea-faring needs but in all necessities. *Catholic Encyclopedia*, Vol. 1, p. 39; Vol. XI, p. 577.

fusion, the fright, the terror of the women and children, who, in the middle of the night felt themselves sinking in an icy sea that pressed about them on all sides.

We had all been thrown to the floor by the same shock, but kept clinging to one another, that we might die together. "O Jesus! O Mary! O Saint Anne, have pity on us!" Ah! They heard our cry.

The wind, which blew furiously from the southwest, veered around with the quickness of lightning (that was the captain's word) and blowing with the same violence from the northwest, reversed the wave which was engulfing us and saved the ship. A few minutes more and it would have been too late. The tempest however continued to rage, but, having just escaped so imminent a danger, we no longer were afraid. "The gifts of God are without repentance" we said; so, though still exposed to the fury of the sea and wind, we spent the following days in thanksgiving.

The incident I am about to relate will show clearly that God was watching over our ship. On New Year's Day at six o'clock in the morning, the captain ordered the sails to be reefed. The tars began with the largest, but the wind caught it inside. The whole crew, consisting of twelve men, got upon the yard, but all to no purpose. Two hours later that same yard, disburdened of its human load which naturally would have been expected to break it, had it been in any way damaged, fell of itself into two pieces, one on each side of the main mast. If the yard had broken when the crew were upon it, they must all have perished. The damaged condition of the vessel hindered the captain from taking the Bahama route where we would have been exposed to the current from the Gulf of Mexico. We sailed with a fair wind towards the Antilles, in the direction of San Domingo, which lengthened our way about 585 kilometers.

On the first of January, which was the thirty-fourth day of

our voyage, we had still 2,200 miles to traverse. Our provisions were getting frightfully low, but God Who watched over us sent a small vessel in our direction the following day. It was thought that they might have provisions to spare; so on being signaled by the captain it came up to us and we bought some maize, biscuit, and salt-fish.

The next day we crossed the Line with the usual ceremonies. The heat was stifling, and the awnings that were spread above us were very ineffective screens from the burning rays of the sun. Such a temperature in the month of January told us too plainly how far we were from our dear France.

At length on the fourteenth we saw land. It was the island of San Domingo with its high forest-clad shores. We were a day and a half in passing it. We saw no inhabitants, but a thick smoke that rose out of the woods made us suppose that the negroes must be burning their trees for the purpose of cultivating the land. After the massacre of the whites in 1793, the negroes remained masters of the beautiful island.

On the nineteenth we sailed past the Isle of Tortuga, so called from the number of turtles that frequent it. Shortly after, we saw the large and beautiful island of Cuba. The summit of the peak of Tarquino rose above the clouds floating several hundred feet below. In this island, conquered by Velasquez[2] without the loss of a single man to Spain, there is a Catholic Church to which the remains of Christopher Columbus have been transferred.

For us Religious, a thought more consoling than all the glory of conquests moved our hearts. Our Lord Jesus Christ

[2] "In 1511, Captain Diego Velasquez, who had accompanied Columbus on his second voyage [1494], was sent to Cuba to subjugate and colonize the island." "Cuba," *Catholic Encyclopedia*, Vol. IV, p. 559.

dwelt in that land. Oh! how happy for us could we have gone and cast ourselves at His Feet to return thanks for His having preserved our lives which are consecrated to Him, We could thank Him only from afar. In calling to mind the labors and fatigues of the conquerors of the New World, we were humiliated by our want of courage. They conquered a hemisphere; but one soul alone is worth more than the whole world. Pray to God for us that we may become less unworthy of our beautiful vocation. To Him alone be the glory of our labors, and to you, dear friends, the recompense on account of the assistance you will give us.

The wind continued favorable. A calm had succeeded the storm. We were improved in health and the outward appearance of the vessel changed for the better. I say "the outward appearance"; for had our crew been capable of improvement, they certainly ought to have been touched after the signal favors they had witnessed at the hand of Divine Providence; yet, though they all agreed that so imminent a danger had not been escaped in the memory of man, not one of them was grateful for the mercy vouchsafed.

The cabin passengers, although of a more elevated rank in society, rivaled in irreligion those of the lower deck: an atheist, a skeptic, a Protestant afflicted with consumption, and his wife; two young men of the world, utterly without faith, such as are unhappily found in our modern French colleges; a lady of the class called freethinkers, the mother of a young person who was far from edifying. But on the lower deck was the worst kind of rabble you can imagine. Quarreling, drunkenness, fighting, blaspheming—every kind of vice was to be met with there. It was in truth a very antechamber of hell. I do not know why it was that they treated us with respect; yet, if any of them were ill, the others would stand by in two rows for me to pass through whenever I went to attend them. They chose me to baptize a newly born infant. I felt a deep sense of gratitude for this favor. Thou, poor little child, born upon the bosom of the heaving billows and exposed to far different storms from those of the *Nashville*, may it be granted me to see thee again, in that beautiful heaven the gate of which I have opened to thee!

Every evening at the same hour when the weather was calm, I used to go on deck and bless God for all the wonders of His creation. I loved to consider the care of God's Providence which extends even to the little fishes. In the Gulf of Mexico there are vast numbers of flying fish, which would be the prey of the larger ones, were it not that God, as if to supply for their exceeding weakness, has given them wings wherewith to escape the voracity of their enemies. This, too, is our state, was my reflection; God has given us the wings of prayer to enable us to escape the snares of the devil. But, although these little fishes find safety in the air, they are unable to support themselves in it long, owing to the structure of their wings; thus their nature in this respect is not unlike ours, since they are obliged to live a good deal among their enemies.

It was always with regret that I left the deck, for to me the whole world presents no more admirable scene than the setting sun at the tropics. It pours forth streams of pure and soft light, coloring the sky and the waves with a thousand tints, ravishing in beauty. One evening I noticed a long wave of light coming to us from this luminary. It seemed to trace by its splendor a path all sprinkled with diamonds and other precious stones. Suddenly Sister Cecilia, pale as death, came running towards me exclaiming, "Mother! Do you not hear those terrible cries? They will kill each other." I turned round and beheld the mate, a man of Herculean strength, struggling with the captain, who was endeavoring to handcuff him. In the midst of blasphemies and imprecations, the offender was finally overpowered, and they pushed him thus fettered towards a little trap door and threw him into the hold like a heavy log. This trap door was just by the stairway to our room, which we could not enter without passing it.

Imagine a Goliath of six feet, about thirty years of age, half intoxicated, and pouring forth blasphemies and curses. He threatened to set fire to the ship, etc., etc. It made one's very heart stand still. A verbal process was drawn up and he was condemned to prison for five years, for having struck the captain. The next day what was our surprise on seeing this same man giving his orders as usual. Nevertheless, as he feared "some token of remembrance" from the captain, as soon as we reached New Orleans he landed quietly without asking for his pay.

On the morning of the twenty-sixth at nine o'clock we got out of the Gulf of Mexico in a thick fog; but we were espied by a steamer that had come in search of us to guide us into the Mississippi. The sea seemed already more disturbed, owing to the intermingling of the water from the river, and the mud kept thickening in proportion as we neared the land. At this spot are seen large fish, particularly dolphins, ever playful and active and several kinds of water fowl, especially the pelican. I dearly love this bird.

On approaching the mouth of the Mississippi, one sees a great deal of dead wood that has been borne down the course of the stream, a distance of perhaps more than three thousand miles. The sea exerts all its strength to force back the foreign substance that thus enters upons its bosom, and from this contest of the mighty river with the ocean is produced a kind of floating island, formed of mud, dead leaves, trees, etc. Each year makes an addition to the preceding formation. Lower Louisiana may be said to be built on the sea, for it is on this drift of the Mississippi held back by the ocean that the pilots' houses are built. But why do those people live there under a burning sun, in an unhealthy place? To earn a little money. And we, Religious, can we complain of living in a wilderness to gain souls to Christ?

At length we cast anchor and the perils of the sea were over. I cannot express the feelings which at that time moved our grateful hearts. The fog had disappeared and we were lost in admiration of one of the fairest scenes of the world. The vast sea which we were on the point of quitting; the sea of another kind which we were about to enter; that forest of ships from all parts of the world, either preparing to cope with distant storms, or coming, like ourselves, to repose after their voyage—it was a magnificent spectacle.

Here I saw again the *Cincinnati*, the boat that had first carried us to a foreign land. The sight of it gave me those feelings of pleasure that one experiences again on seeing an old friend with whom one had undergone adventure and sufferings.

We soon left this innocent recreation, however, to go to the poor consumptive. His end was approaching. We had done our best for him during the whole voyage; but now his cough had so greatly increased as to make his danger perceptible to every one except himself and his unfortunate companion, whom he was about to leave alone in the world. Fearing that the sudden death of her husband might be fatal to this lady, who was in a critical condition, I ventured to tell her, with all the delicacy I could, that she must make haste if she had any matters that required settling, as soon it would be too late. I then returned to the poor patient to speak to him of God. Oh, how troubled he was! How earnestly he promised that when his health was better he would be good! Truly he had not a bad heart; but he was a son and a son-in-law of Protestant ministers, and he could not make up his mind to embrace the Catholic faith, though he admitted that it was the only true religion. Poor man! He died the next night while I was at his bedside, all the others, even his wife, having left him. How devoid of consolation is the death of a Protestant. In speaking to him of his Saviour the words died away on my lips. Nor could I bid him hope in Blessed Mary's intercession—he had blasphemed her name a few days before.

Having closed his eyes I went to his widow. What could I say to console her? I gave her my own little room, and we watched with her during the two days that we continued on board. On reaching New Orleans we put her in the hands of a friend. She had never before spoken to a Catholic. She had now become better disposed toward our Holy religion. Let us hope that the few seeds sown may not remain unproductive of fruit.

After we had waited twenty-four hours, a steamer in company with another ship came to tow us to port. At a few miles from the mouth of the river one sees a great number of dead trees and countless reeds. The aspect of those vast, desolate areas imparts to the soul something of their sadness. There is no habitation, no living creature to be seen, nothing in fact but some crows; which make me think that this wet land must resemble the surface of the globe when Noah left the Ark. Farther on vegetation flourished with a rich and wild luxuriance; orange and lemon trees, loaded with the finest fruit, were interspersed with the rose and the laurel, and altogether it was a delightful country. Herds of roe deer sported and gamboled on the plains. On the banks of the streams were the most lovely swans. They were dazzling white, much larger than those of Europe, and they always went together in pairs. To catch them, trappers set the woods on fire and take them as they escape from the smoke.

After some years the ground, formed by the debris brought by the streams, becomes solid enough to build on. The houses which are erected on it by the rich planters look like miniature chateaux encircled by splendid gardens. Rice grows perfectly well on this crust of earth. Each planter has his slaves. The cabins of these poor negroes resemble the cells of the cenobites. They are made of planks, are about twelve feet square, and have a little garden in the rear. Every negro family is thus lodged. Some planters own as many as fifteen or twenty families of these slaves, which constitute the chief wealth of the lords of Louisiana. Nearly all the inhabitants are Catholics; it was easy to detect this from the little cross which guards their humble cemetery. The Sign of Salvation touched us tenderly. Tears moistened our eyes as we prayed for those of our brethren, the French of Louisiana, who repose there in the shadow of the cross.

As we approached New Orleans the houses became more numerous and the land was better cultivated. The quantity of rice stacked in the fields showed that the last crop was good. Finally we arrived at New Orleans. We wrote to the Bishop, Monsignor Blanc, who had the kindness to send his Vicar General to get us. The Customs officer was favorable to us and did not require that our baggage be sent to the Customhouse. The examiners scarcely looked at our effects. At last, on the twenty-seventh of January, we left the poor *Nashville*, on which we had suffered so much. A few minutes later we were at the good Ursuline Sisters, who lavished upon us the most hospitable and affectionate attentions.

I need not say with what haste we proceeded to the chapel to adore our Lord. At His feet we poured forth our thanksgivings for the preservation of our lives, and for the fatherly love with which He had watched over our dear Sisters of the Woods during our absence. (We had just received a letter from them; all were well and in good spirits.) We also invoked the blessings of Heaven on our dear and generous friends beyond the sea, who were so truly present to my thoughts and affections that I seemed actually in the midst of them. For true hearts there is no separating ocean; or, rather, God is their ocean, in Whom they meet and are united. They love, they lose themselves in Him.

This happy day of joy and gratitude was a Saturday, the day consecrated to the Blessed Virgin Mary, as was also the day of our first arrival in New York. But in this land of exile, happiness has no morrow! The very next morning, while assisting at the Holy Sacrifice, a burning fever obliged me to leave the church and go to bed. There I lay for seven weeks, the object of the most affectionate and tender nursing and attention on the part of the good Ursulines. Oh, how compassionate, how universal and beautiful is charity!

They regarded me not in the light of a troublesome stranger but of a suffering sister. I seemed to be still at that dear Ruillé, where, at the beginning of my religious life, my bad state of health so frequently brought my superiors to the infirmary to visit me. Years had passed by since our Mother watched by my bedside; but I saw that at all times, and in all places, there is a source of compassionate charity in the hearts of true Religious. The Ursulines have a magnificent house in New Orleans. It has two hundred columns and five hundred doors and windows. Nevertheless, great as is the outward splendor of this Community, when I think of the virtues of those who dwell therein I cannot but reflect that all the beauty of the King's daughter is from within. We found a father and friend in their chaplain, Father Perché. He uses his distinguished talents in defense of the Church and in behalf of the Bishop of the diocese, now so unjustly persecuted.

Notwithstanding the constant and affectionate care of

those pious, devoted Ursulines, my heart could find no rest away from my dear Sisters of Saint Mary-of-the-Woods. I had been obliged to separate from my traveling companion, Sister Cecilia, in order to send her on with one of the postulants. The other remained with me. I was burning with the desire to join them all again.

To try my strength I took a drive in a carriage. This enabled me to see the city, which in my opinion, is not very remarkable. Each quarter is appropriated by a different European nation, the French being the oldest. The streets are badly paved. Schismatic church guardians profaned the Cathedral, which is nearly abandoned, and the walls are falling into ruins. A little farther off is a pretty church dedicated to St. Augustine, The ground was given by the good Ursulines. We drove through what is called the American part of the town, in order to visit the hospital, kept by the Sisters of Charity of the Order of St. Joseph. This section is new and well built, and the hospital is fine; but it is still quite inferior to those we have in France. It commands a view of the whole town, which is surrounded by the Mississippi. The river rises many feet above the ground level; this renders the city very malarial. The continued miasma, joined with the extreme heat, causes that terrible malady known as yellow fever.

The most painful sight I saw in New Orleans was the selling of slaves. Every day in the streets at appointed places, negroes and negresses in holiday attire are exposed for this shameful traffic, like the meanest animals at our fairs. This spectacle oppressed my heart. Lo! I said to myself, these Americans, so proud of their liberty, thus make game of the liberty of others. Poor negroes! I would have wished to buy them all that I might say to them, "Go! Bless Providence. You are free!" But such feelings must be concealed from the Louisianians, as this is a point on which they are sensitive.

St. Joseph's day, which had been fixed for our departure, at length arrived. Having assisted at the Holy Sacrifice of the Mass and listened to a beautiful discourse on the virtues of the great Master of the interior life, we left New Orleans. On board the steamer, which was at least two hundred feet long and capable of carrying two thousand passengers, I looked out upon the moving panorama that was being exhibited around this finest river in the world. There were ships from all nations, of all sizes, and of every shape, and suitable to all purposes. I counted thirty steamboats in motion at once. The air was darkened by the clouds of their smoke. The noise of their wheels and engines surpassed belief, and I fancied I was looking upon the great Tyre of ancient days, with its merchants from every clime and its commerce with all the isles of the sea. Then I asked myself: What was New Orleans a few years ago? Nothing but the sea; afterwards, a few savage tribes, and today, it is a world of itself. But—tomorrow?

Shortly after, the steamboat had started, and everything was disappearing from us; the last object we saw was the dome of the Hotel St. Charles. The country through which the river winds is very flat. The Mississippi is exceedingly sinuous in its course. It seems to turn back upon itself, as if it dreaded to lose its waters and its name in the depths of the sea. On the banks may be seen hanging from the trees a vine from fifteen to eighteen feet long, of an ashy green, whose filaments are no thicker than a thread. This species of moss, which is very soft, is dried by the inhabitants and is the only material they use for their mattresses.

We had scarcely passed two days on the steamboat when the spring weather enjoyed at New Orleans was gone. The sweet smelling fruit and flowers were succeeded by majestic trees still bare of foliage. The farther north we went, the lower became the temperature and bleaker the landscape.

MEMORIAL
in fulfillment of
promise made by
MOTHER THEODORE
during storm at sea

ST. ANN'S SHELL CHAPEL
Saint Mary-of-the-Woods
1844
From original drawing made in 1852 by
Sister Maurice Schnell
Reproduced by Sister Margaret Marie McCormick

ST. ANN'S SHELL CHAPEL REBUILT IN 1876

This severe change was sweet to me, for it meant I was nearing home. Finally on the fifth day, with inexpressible joy I saw once more my Indiana. I would have loved to kiss its soil.

This land was no longer for me the land of exile; it was the portion of my inheritance, and in it I hope to dwell all the days of my life. I saluted the Guardian Angels of Indiana and prayed them to take the souls of these poor people under their protection, especially those whom we are called upon to benefit. Towards midnight we reached Evansville, one of the largest cities in Indiana. The father of one of our novices,[3] came to meet us and took us to his home. The next day, which was the Feast of the Annunciation, we had the happiness of receiving the sacraments of Penance and Holy Eucharist. O Mary, my good Mother, be thou forever blest for thy tender protection! Again on one of thy feasts do I receive new favors from God. Assist me, I beseech thee, to fulfil the promises I made to thee during the storm at sea.[4] Oh, how happy shall I be to make Thee known and loved.

Had I not already known that I was in Indiana, in the Diocese of Vincennes, I might have guessed it from the extreme poverty that surrounded us. On coming out of the brick church, whose only ornament was bare walls, we were taken by a

[3] Sister Mary Magdalen Linck.

[4] During the terrific storm at sea described above, Mother Theodore renewed the vow she had made in 1840 to propagate devotion to the Blessed Virgin and make it one of the Community's special works. She further promised, besides the memorial at "Notre Dame des Victoires," an ex-voto of some kind at Saint Mary-of-the-Woods. This materialized in what is known as St. Ann's Shell Chapel; so called because the interior walls are covered with shells, the altar and other decorations being uniquely and artistically formed of shells.

The original chapel, built in 1844, was of logs. Eventually falling into decay, it was replaced in 1876 by a stone structure on the same spot, of the same dimensions, and lined with the same shells.

The celebration of St. Ann's Day (July 26) brings hundreds of visitors at sunset on the eve, to witness the procession of over a thousand Religious and many visiting clergymen, with which the solemnities begin. Mass is sometimes said at the Shrine on the feast, and visits of devotion are made throughout the day.

Catholic lady to the priest's house. He was absent, but we pushed open a door and entered a room, if room it could be called, about eight or nine feet square. An unpainted wooden chest served as a table. The good lady showed me the inside of it. There I beheld the bed of the servant of God [Reverend Anthony Deydier]. We may indeed consider his bed as his tomb and his life a continual death. Before the church was built he offered the Adorable Sacrifice on the same board. A few books (English and French), a wooden chair, and a little stove constituted all the furnishings. On the stove was a cast-iron pan in which he baked his corn bread, his only article of food, and of which he partakes only once a day.

Such is the penitential life that he has led for several years—this Apostle of Evansville—and yet, he is happy! He has made several conversions among the Protestants. The mother of one of our dear novices, the Catholic lady who took us to his house, was one of his converts. He desires greatly that the interior of his poor church might be ornamented a little. We shall try to help him as, thanks to our dear brothers in France, we are now almost rich in devotional articles.

The next day I took the stage for Vincennes. I was touched by the sight of those magnificent forests traversed so often by Bishop Bruté in visiting his flock. And my heart throbbed when I saw by the light of the setting sun, the beautiful spire of the Cathedral of Vincennes, surmounted by the cross.

In a few minutes I was surrounded by my dear missionary Sisters; there are four at Vincennes. In worthy emulation of the priest of Evansville, they had neither a tumbler nor a table napkin for me, and the sum of the delicacies they could set before me was a little corned beef. But what of that! We did not even notice it. On the following morning I had the happiness of receiving Holy Communion from the hands of my own Bishop and Superior. Shortly after, I was at his feet receiving his blessing.

My joy would have been complete had I only been with my dear Solitaries in the Woods. So greatly did I long to see them again that the next morning I took a steamboat for Terre Haute, and at eight o'clock that evening reached Saint Mary-of-the-Woods [April 1, 1844].

What more can I say? After almost a year of separation, of anxieties, and of sufferings, I saw them all again. Imagine our feelings when, with emotion too deep for words, we went to kneel before Him to Whom we owed all our happiness. Before Jesus Who so lovingly watched over us we could pour forth our hearts. Our first prayer was made for you, our dear and generous friends. Yes, in that poor, holy chapel, we renewed our promises to associate you with all our hopes for the future. And from that happy day not one has passed in which our prayers have not been offered up to God, that He may shed on you the sweetest lights and the most abundant blessings of His grace.

I expected to send you these pages several weeks ago, but I had to leave Saint Mary's to visit our three establishments. I am glad of the delay because I can give you some religious items that I gathered in my trip.

I arrived at Vincennes during the retreat for the clergy. Sunday, the fifth of May, was the day of general Communion. The missionaries, to the number of twenty-five, vested in their priestly robes, received Communion from the hands of the Bishop, and so heavenly was their appearance that they scarcely seemed any longer to belong to this world of misery.

After Mass took place the truly grand and solemn ceremony of the opening of the synod. It began with the chanting of the *Veni Creator*, the litany of the Saints, and a passage from the Gospel. The Decrees of the Council of Trent were read and

a long profession of faith; then each priest, resting his hand
upon the Gospel, swore at the feet of the Bishop that he
believed firmly all that had just been read as well as the
whole doctrine of the Catholic, Apostolic, Roman Church. The
preacher of the retreat, Father Deydier, delivered an appropriate sermon.

Meanwhile I reflected with admiration on the wonders
effected by the Divine Mercy in this diocese. Ten years ago
there was not a priest in it, and now they are holding a synod!
There is a Bishop, a cathedral, and there are more than thirty
churches. How quickly has the grain of the mustard seed
grown into a tree!

After Vespers there was a private session. On Monday
the same ceremonies took place in the cathedral as on the
preceding day. On Tuesday a solemn Mass was celebrated
for the missionaries of the diocese who had died, working in
the vineyard of the Lord. The saintly priest of Evansville
ascended the pulpit to deliver the funeral oration of these
Christian heroes. He had been for several years the companion, the friend, and the confidant of Bishop Bruté. Would
that I could here produce the eloquent simplicity with which
he spoke of the virtues of the holy Bishop! Oh, but it was
touching!

He began by speaking of his interior and mortified life
when only a simple priest, of his labors, of his zeal. He related
some of the thousand acts of charity which made him a hero of
the missionary life. "One cannot stir a foot," he said, "in the
neighborhood of the Mountain [Emmitsburg] where he dwelt,
without finding traces of his goodness and foresight. In one
place it is a bridge, in another a grotto which offers to the
traveler a welcome shelter from the heat and to the devout a
consoling remembrance."

Like his friend who was delivering this panegyric, Bishop Bruté slept upon the floor, exposed to all the rigors of the seasons. He never retired to rest until after midnight, rose again at three and employed in the recitation of his Breviary and in meditation the time that elapsed until Mass, which he used to say at six o'clock at St. Joseph's, the house of the Sisters of Emmitsburg, distant from his own log house about two miles.

He was obliged to cross a creek, a kind of torrent, very common in America. Wet sometimes through and through, his clothes in winter would freeze upon his body and almost hinder him from walking. Nevertheless, in this condition he would hear confessions, say Mass, and give Holy Communion to the good Religious then so poor.

After a few words of consolation and of love, which came so readily from his heart, he would leave them, and go to devote his brilliant talents to the service of a college near Emmitsburg, that has since become the nursery of the clergy of the United States. Almost all the Bishops of the present time were the pupils of Bishop Bruté at this place.

In his leisure moments this devoted priest would go to visit the families of his extensive mission. Returning to his hut, he devoted the first portion of the night to writing, either in favor of Catholicism or combating error. Many times also has an afflicted soul been the object of the night watches of this holy priest. He wrote thousands of letters in the hours snatched from the night's rest. Even his recreations were spent in doing good. Quotations happily chosen, pleasing talents, a prodigious and extensive memory, made his company as interesting as it was beautiful. He could not remain idle. His own activity he imparted to his friends and made them do wonders.

Who can tell the marvelous works of Simon Bruté as Bishop? What a diocese! Good God! A vast country without churches, without priests, still occupied by the Indians from whom it takes its name. In 1834 Bishop Bruté received from the saintly Flaget a priest about three years ordained. Father Lalumière constituted all his clergy.

The following year Bishop Bruté returned to France in company with Bishop Flaget whom he regarded as a father. Displaying there the zeal of his heart and the great needs of his poor diocese, he inspired generous sentiments. Several priests and young levites [nineteen] volunteered to share his labors and to follow him into the foreign land. While on sea a violent storm threatened to swallow them up. He gave them a general absolution to reassure them, but at the same time he said, "My dear children, fear nothing; it is a ruse of the devil. We shall not perish." And so it happened. Contrary to all human expectation, they arrived safe at New York and thence set out for their mission. It would be impossible to say all that the good Bishop, enriched by this happy reinforcement, did for the diocese which God had given him.

The preacher went on to recall him to their memories by saying: "In this church, in this very sanctuary where you are seated, you have seen him serve your Mass with a humility surpassed only by his piety. Look at this church so often swept by his own hands. In this spot he would get on a chair to ring the bell; in that, he chopped the wood wherewith to warm you. Yes, it is to you, my dear brethren, it is to you he gave the example of all the virtues of the deepest brotherly affection. So strong is the memory of all this in your hearts, that to try to recall it would only weaken the impression."

He said the truth. Oh, how deeply touched were all the clergy in this recollection of their venerated father! I saw them burying their heads in their hands to hide their tears from the bystanders. There they were, those dear children of the good Bishop Bruté! There was he, that venerable prelate who had been called to replace him in the sacred functions of the apostolate, who was in fact his eldest son, the well-beloved of his heart! There also was our good Father Corbe, to whom the Bishop with the tenderness of a mother's heart, had so many times carried in his pockets bread and little lumps of sugar! There they were who had shared in his watchings, his privations, his labors; but in that moment everything else was forgotten, save the charity of their good father.

"Is it not true," said the preacher, "that when he was with us, we did not feel our fatigue? Is it not true that nothing was hard to us, that we scarcely knew we were poor, though really lacking the very necessaries of life? Look at those who died before him! What fervor he inspired in them—the good Father Deseille, who died among the savages, and who, when alone and forsaken, had the courage to drag himself into his little log chapel and to administer to himself the Blessed Sacrament, and then amid his savages expired in the arms of Jesus.[5] And the seraphic Benjamin Petit,[6] devoured with so burning a zeal for the Indians, did he feel the labors that so early snatched him away from our love, and at the same time placed him among the martyrs of charity? And the dear Father Hamion, the last whom we have lost, would he have been so quickly spent had he not inherited the zealous spirit of his worthy Bishop? He counted his life as naught, if he might but gain souls to Jesus Christ; and he showed even in the ravings of his delirium,

[5] Cf. Alerding, *History of the Catholic Church in the Diocese of Vincennes*, p. 137.

[6] Cf. Sister Mary Salesia Goedecker, O.S.B., *Simon Bruté de Remut*, p. 364.

that in that missionary heart of his there was nothing but God, God alone. These are the models in life and in death that we are to copy, we who are continuing their labors. *Beati mortui qui in Domino moriuntur.* Without anticipating the decisions of Holy Church, we love to look upon them as inhabitants of Heaven, those friends of ours who have left us. It is sweet to think that the happiness with which they are inebriated does not make them forget us, exiles, their brethren of Indiana."

How beautiful that funeral oration was! How it touched me, and how heartily I thanked God for the little share he has given me in this dear mission, where so many saints have labored and shall still labor. That share I would not give, I do not say for a crown—for what are all the treasures of earth to the heart of a Religious?—I would not give it, I say, for all the spiritual consolations to be found in the service of God.

The Synod ended with the chanting of the *Te Deum* and the reading of the last Decrees of the Council of Baltimore for all the United States, as well as those regulations which were for the diocese of Vincennes in particular. When all was over, these good missionaries, renewed now in the spirit of God, began to get ready to return to their dear though hard missionary life. Several came to beg me to let them have Sisters to aid them in their labors. Two in particular, stationed in the largest towns, were very insistent. Father Delaune, a priest from St. Brieuc, eagerly desired to have some at Madison, where he is in charge of a daily increasing congregation. "The Protestants," he said, "try to steal away from me my poor Catholic children by giving them books, clothing, and even money; but my people pay dearly for these presents. The proselytizers begin by ruining the mind, and then they corrupt the heart. Will you not take pity on so many souls whom the evil one is snatching away from us? Will you not come and wrestle with this wicked foe?"

You know, Gentlemen, that I would have wished for nothing better. We would be able to give Sisters, but funds would be necessary to start with, and neither he nor we had any. One was as rich as the other. He appealed to His Lordship, who said that he desired with all his heart to have an establishment at Madison, but that it was impossible for him to assist us. We were obliged to separate, postponing our good work to some future day. And before that time, how many souls will be lost!

You will see presently, however, that the expenses of an establishment of ours ought not to be ruinous. The next day I set out on a visit to our Sisters at St. Peter's,[7] an establishment formed during my absence in France. They occupy what was the first Motherhouse of the Brothers of Father Moreau[8] in America. It is in the midst of the forest, a log house open to all the winds. The furniture consists of a table with an old bench on each side, two sorts of cupboards, or presses, if such they could be called; two school desks, some wooden bedsteads equally sumptuous, one chair made of the bark of trees, and another of wood; this, exactly, is all the furniture. There were besides a few cooking utensils.

But their food! *Bon Dieu!* Some cornmeal and salted pork! Later they were able to add some milk and butter, the Bishop having, at a sacrifice to himself, sent them 100 francs to buy a cow. I gave them some of the articles I had received from our friends in France, but I must say that if I had been here, I would not have allowed them to pass the winter in such a house. I cannot conceive how the good Brothers of St. Joseph

[7] Montgomery, Indiana.
[8] Brothers of the Holy Cross.

could have lived there for the space of a year. Without doubt their love of suffering sustained them, and I think they must have left behind them their spirit of poverty, for when I proposed to the Sisters that they quit their old log hut and return with me to Saint Mary-of-the-Woods, those dear daughters pressed me so urgently and extolled so highly their happy situation and the good they could do, and had already done, that I decided to leave them there until the retreat.

Three of the principal persons of the district came as a deputation to entreat me to leave them their Sisters. However, if after the month of August they are not rich enough to repair the log house and buy a lock, some bedding, furniture, etc., I shall order the removal, notwithstanding. Imagine how heartily we laughed in the evening when, before retiring to what we called our dormitory, we were obliged to drag the furniture up against the door, which had neither latch nor lock.

I visited the classes. The children are very well disposed and generally docile. They have all arrived at the age of reason; a great many of them are over twenty. Oh, what good might be done if we but had that wretched money, often so badly expended! After encouraging the parents and the children we gave the latter a holiday, and then in order to give some recreation to the dear Sisters of St. Peter's I took them with me to Jasper.

The beauty of the forests of Indiana in the rich and lovely month of May surpasses all description. The rivers, swollen by the rains, flow through long lanes of verdure, caressing the islands they seem to carry with them in their course and which look like floating nosegays. The trees raise their straight trunks to the height of more than a hundred and twenty feet and are crowned with tops of admirable beauty. The magnolia, the dog-wood, the catalpa, covered with white flowers, the perfumed snow of the springtime, intermingle with the delicate green of the other trees. Wild lianas climb up to the top of the loftiest trees and then fall down in festoons of every shape, only to begin again upon the ground a new life, thence to climb up again to other heights. How truly is this part of the globe named the *New World*.

Animals of every kind are the quiet possessors of the woods; and here also are the hummingbird and a multitude of other birds. And all stay willingly near the habitations of man. The stag and the roe were not at all frightened at our approach. There is one creature, however, whose confidences we would willingly dispense with, and that is the serpent. There are specimens of all colors and sizes. The Sisters at Jasper told us that they had killed two very large ones in their school rooms. The snakes glide in under the logs, and only the Lord can protect us.

The congregation at Jasper is a very fervent one. During six months when the pastor was away from his parish, these good Germans came every Sunday seven or ten miles to sing hymns in the church. Thursday last, which was Ascension Day, I saw a whole parish that had walked ten miles in procession. They were in double file, the cross being carried by a young man who walked at the head. Arrived at the church, after assisting at Mass they listened to two sermons, one in English, the other in German. The service ended only about two o'clock.

I must admit I was very tired; and I say to my shame that my fervor was put to the blush when I saw all these fervent Christians begin again their pious procession. All the people, a parish of *musicians*, formed ranks again and, in chanting hymns and sacred songs, returned to their own villages praising God.

That evening we amused ourselves watching the fireflies that flew around by the thousands and would have clouded the air if they had not lighted it with their glow. All day the heat had been stifling. Toward evening we had one of those American storms which present a spectacle so terrifying. The lowering clouds mingle with the shade of the woods. Suddenly a cloud bursts. The lightning darts forth a rapid ball of flame. A high wind heaps in vast confusion clouds upon clouds. From time to time the atmosphere partly clears, and then through gaps in the clouds appear, as it were, new heavens and tracts of fire.

Such storms are admirably described by Chateaubriand, and, the phantom shrieks only excepted, we have witnessed the same scenes. The roaring of the winds, the howling of the wild beasts, the rolling of the thunder, the cracking of buildings, the torrents of water—all these sounds, multiplied by the echoes, seem as though they would proclaim to man that nature is in her last agony. Oh, how terrible will be the day of God's justice, when even under the reign of His mercy, nay, in the sweet month of May consecrated to the mild and gentle Mary, we are the daily witnesses of these majestic terrors!

Whilst writing this I was interrupted by one of the Sisters who rushed into the room exclaiming, "Mother, a snake! Oh, come!" I went out and saw at the door a snake six feet long, which one of the boys was trying to kill. There was enmity between this serpent and the woman, for I felt a sudden horror creep into my heart at the sight of it. But terrifying as are the snakes I must add that we have another plague still more disagreeable. I know not if we have a Pharaoh in the country but we are overwhelmed, harassed, and almost devoured by the mosquitoes. While writing to you this long and often interrupted journal, I have been beating them off, right and left. My hands are covered with wounds, and my eyes are dimmed by the thick smoke which we are obliged to use as our only defense against these "powers of the air." I hope all these causes together will claim some indulgence for this poor narrative, which has no other recommendation than its being the expression of a heart that is sincerely devoted to you, and feels that you will find a little pleasure in reading these details.

I should indeed have begun my letter by thanking you for the precious offering you had the kindness to send to the Sisters of the Visitation for us; but there arises within me such a sense of gratitude when I reflect on your benevolence and charity and that of your generous friends, that I postponed the expression of my grateful sentiments for the last page of my journal, so that the paper might limit what otherwise is without limit.

We would love to tell you again that every day we include you all in our labors and prayers. Being poor we can only plant; you must water; and to God alone be the glory of the increase. Would you suffer so many delicate plants to wither? Oh, no! You have understood the *Sitio* of Jesus dying and you will not refuse them the drop of water.

We consign these pages to your prudence and kindness. If you think their publication can contribute to the glory of God and to the welfare of our dear mission, we beg you to consider them as your own. Change, retrench, destroy, embellish, as you please. If you find any grains of gold among the base metal, when you will have presented the matter according to your art, we pray you in your unfailing kindness to send a copy to the Superior of the Visitation (your know our other friends in Paris); to Abbé Sevin, chaplain of St. Yves (Rennes); to M. le Fer de la Motte (St. Servan); to Abbé Hardy, chaplain at Fougères, Abbé Percheron (Chateaudun); to M. Prudhomme, bookseller (St. Brieuc); to Mme Letouzè-Guérin (Portrieux near St. Brieuc Binic), and to the Bishop of Le Mans.

Father Perché at New Orleans gets your paper and appreciates it. Being the editor of a Catholic weekly, he engaged me to ask if you would be willing to accept his paper in exchange for yours. He would send it to you regularly.

Be pleased to accept the homage of my deepest gratitude and of the most sincere esteem with which I am,

Gentlemen,

Your very humble servant,

SISTER ST. THEODORE.

Superior

Saint Mary-of-the-Woods
May 28, 1844

PART V

A RECORD OF DIFFICULTIES

W HEN Mother Theodore arrived at Vincennes in the spring of 1844 after her long illness in New Orleans, Bishop de la Hailandière received her most graciously. He seemed well pleased with what she had accomplished in France and urged her to begin at once the enlarging of the academy building. Thus encouraged she reached St. Mary's with a lighter heart, and the united Community were happy in the bright prospect that now opened before them.

Peace and encouragement, however, did not last long. Clouds were gathering. Thus on the twenty-eighth of October, 1844, Mother Theodore inscribed in her diary: "Today we receive the prohibition to visit our establishments." This prohibition applied chiefly to the two houses the Bishop had opened during Mother Theodore's absence in France— Vincennes, and St. Peter's (Montgomery)—which houses he wished to be entirely exempt from her jurisdiction. The Sisters were to be named by him and were to be responsible only to him. This, virtually, meant a division of the Community. The Sisters said they could not consent to go to these establishments under such conditions. Mother Theodore represented the case to the Bishop. He temporized, and finally withdrew his protection from the Congregation and appointed Father Corbe to be its Ecclesiastical Superior.

Although the Rule did not provide for an Ecclesiastical Superior the Sisters willingly acquiesced. Father Corbe hoped to conciliate the Bishop and restore relations to normal. As to visiting the other missions, Mother Theodore would have to obtain a written permission from the Bishop, or, in his absence, from Father Corbe.

Difficulties were not confined to Saint Mary-of-the-Woods. The conflict in the diocese is a matter of history. Alerding says:

"He [Bishop de la Hailandière] saw dissatisfaction around him, caused by his active energy, which, ever bent on pushing things in the way he thought proper, brooked no contradiction. It grew all around him; the institutions he had established with so much labor were suffering. . . .

"During his absence [in Rome] the discontent had taken greater proportions. But he never relented in his activity, and his fertile mind continued, as before, on the alert for what could be done, and he would attend to this himself. Therein, however, was the chief source of all his troubles. He attended to everything personally, and, although he had a Vicar General near him, a superior of his seminary, a superior over the community at St. Mary's, a rector for his Cathedral, he hardly would allow them to do anything. All over the diocese, as far as his hand could stretch out, it was about the same. There was, in consequence, a general feeling of uneasiness, nobody knowing what he was to do or not to do; . . . also real and, now, loud dissatisfaction. He saw it, he felt it. He reproached himself for it. Yet his ardent and lofty spirit could not well check itself."[1]

The letters of the succeeding years reveal how painfully the Community at Saint Mary-of-the-Woods had become involved; and they show also how Providence surrounded it with friends who sacrificed their own peace and comfort to sustain the harassed Sisters.

At the beginning it was hoped that the good will of the Bishop might be secured by concessions. The Sisters were willing to do all that could be done consistently with their Rules, and Father Corbe, noted for his forbearance, agreed with their views. Writing to Mother Theodore from Vincennes (April 26, no year given—evidently 1844), he said: "It is difficult, but the peace, the good, the very existence of the Community depend on such sacrifices. Let us make them generously, since they are so essential. Have courage. Pray, pray much, and God in strengthening you will enlighten you and will inspire you as to the manner in which He wishes you to succeed in this work, which is His own."

In November, 1844, Bishop de la Hailandière left suddenly for Europe. Father Corbe, who had recently been appointed Ecclesiastical Superior, then went to Vincennes to confer with Father Martin, the Vicar General, concerning

---

[1] H. Alerding, *The Diocese of Vincennes*, pp. 177, 178. The Reverend H. Alerding later became the fourth Bishop of Fort Wayne (1900–1924).

the affairs of the Community. By him Mother Theodore sent the following letter:

TO THE VERY REVEREND A. MARTIN

January 10, 1845

Monsieur L'Abbé:

Although I wrote to you yesterday, I cannot let our Father leave without a word for you, were it only to ask pardon and indulgence for my indescribable scribbling of yesterday, done in the midst of the noise made by five or six of the Sisters saying good-by to Father Buteux—conversation in which I also was engaged. So, please, leniency this time.

Father Corbe will tell you that we have just learned some news that will rejoice everybody except yourself, if it is true. If it is not, I do not want to be responsible for paining you unnecessarily. It will be time enough later.

I was pleased to see Father Corbe setting out to visit you. The reunion, I think, will be pleasant for both. I pray you encourage this estimable Superior to bear the burden of his new office quietly. He, too, had to come to St. Mary's to find the cup of tribulation and drink it. If ever this poor little Community becomes settled, it will be established on the cross; and that is what gives me confidence and makes me hope, sometimes even against hope. In the midst of all our storms, however, we have the consolation of seeing the religious spirit become solid amongst the Sisters, and that is not a little thing. If we are good Religious, God will protect us; and if He be with us, who shall be against us?

Permit me to recommend to you our Sisters at Vincennes. They have great need of your fatherly counsels and, I believe, are well disposed to follow them.

Allow me to repeat the assurance of my veneration, remaining, *Monsieur L'Abbé,*

Your very humble and obedient servant,

SISTER ST. THEODORE.

Father Corbe having returned from Vincennes wrote to
Father Martin (Feb. 1, 1845): "I would love to tell you
how much good it did my heart to see you, but I cannot
express it. I was tired, depressed, isolated at St. Mary's, feeling
there was no longer any one in the world who would
interest himself in me; and at Vincennes I met with a reception so cordial and frank it filled my heart with true joy, and
I returned to Saint Mary's animated with new courage.
Of courage I surely had great need at my arrival. I found
Mother Theodore attacked by what at first seemed only a passing indisposition, but which has increased so much the last
three or four days that I now have fear for her life."

Recovered from this attack Mother Theodore left in
April for Vincennes and Evansville. Upon her return home
she wrote again to the Vicar General, giving him news local
and foreign.

Saint Mary's, May 21, 1845

Venerable Sir:

Here I am again at Saint Mary's after all our hardships of
travel. Sister St. Vincent must have told you how distressed
we were by having to remain eight days on the steamboat, so
near the time of the First Communion of our dear little girls.
And, too, I could not have been more disappointed than at
having to pass Vincennes without seeing you, or even learning
whether your health was in the least improved since the time
of our departure.

I wished to tell you also that Father Deydier is very willing to give our retreat. It will begin the fifth of August; he fixed
this date in order that he could be back at Evansville for the
Feast of the Assumption. Had we the hope of having you we
would have deferred it for some days; but, since that favor cannot be ours this year, we have acquiesced in the choice of time
made by Father Deydier.

On my arrival home I found a good and paternal letter
from the Bishop of Le Mans. He said he had had two

conversations with the Bishop of Vincennes and had also written to him at Rennes, all without any satisfactory results. I was accused of many things which His Lordship mentions with reserve; which proves, I infer, that the issue was not as happy as might have been expected. He closes by giving us the permission to return to our Community in France, which he says will receive us with open arms, or *to go* and *try to establish* ourselves elswhere; although he himself regards as absurd the idea of leaving Vincennes. As this wise prelate considers us, in a way, obliged to stay here, you said well to wait before troubling myself too much.

Bishop Bouvier added that in saying this he acted in concert with our Superiors in France. Moreover, he said that in case we leave we should take with us the money we received at our departure from France the first time, and also the second, from the persons he named. It was given to us, not to Vincennes. Dear good Bishop Bouvier! He does not know it is all gone, gone into the gulf that swallows immense fortunes without ever being filled. The interest that you bear us assures me that you will be pleased to know all these details. Our good Father Corbe tells me that you have not written to him since his return. That grieves him—I whisper it to you.

Accept the expression of the deepest veneration and gratitude with which I remain, *Monsieur l'Abbé,*

Your very humble servant,

SISTER ST. THEODORE.

While in Europe Bishop de la Hailandière visited the Community at Ruillé and also the Bishop of Le Mans. At Rome he offered his resignation to the Holy Father, but Gregory XVI did not accept it. The Pope, seeing him in the prime of life and so pious and zealous, encouraged him to return to his diocese, confident that the difficulties would soon pass away. He enriched the Bishop with several valuable presents, notably the precious relics of St. Urban, Pope, and St. Theodore, Soldier and Martyr. Eventually these relics came to the convent at Saint Mary-of-the-Woods, and may yet be seen under the side altars in the sanctuary of the conventual church.

The Bishop returned in October, 1845, after an absence of eleven months. His dissatisfaction with the Community increased, notwithstanding Father Corbe's tact and his efforts at conciliation. Mother Theodore proposed to resign as Superior. The Sisters would not hear of it. The members of the Council had previously written to the Bishop of Le Mans for advice regarding these anticipated difficulties. Bishop Bouvier, writing from Laval, October 4, 1845, replied formally:

TO THE VERY DEAR SISTER COUNCILORS OF THE
ESTABLISHMENT OF PROVIDENCE AT SAINT MARY-OF-THE-
WOODS, DIOCESE OF VINCENNES, UNITED STATES OF AMERICA

"The sentiments that you express to me in your letter of August 10, my very dear Sisters, touch me to the very core of my heart. I am always deeply interested in you and if I could I would help you. It would be a true happiness for me to do so.

"But, my good Sisters, you are no longer under my jurisdiction. I can assist you by my counsels only, and the counsels that I could give must, in no way, injure the authority of the prelate charged with the government of the diocese in which you are.

"Two things appear to me certain: first, those among you who have made Vows according to the Rules and Constitutions of Ruillé are not obliged, in virtue of your religious consecration, to submit to substantial changes which might be made without your consent; second, those who belonged to the Congregation and were given for the American Foundation have not lost their title as Daughters of Providence of Ruillé; by it they even have the right to return to the Motherhouse (so long as they will not have merited to be excluded as unworthy) if circumstances oblige them to return.

"I do not retract the permission I have given to Mother Theodore to settle with her companions in another diocese, in case she must leave that of Vincennes; but she would do it at her own risk and peril, the House of Ruillé not wishing to be a party to any such arrangement. How much I desire, my very dear Sisters, that all might be for the best at Vincennes, and that you might continue in that diocese the good that you have so happily begun.

"Notwithstanding the tender interest which I bear you and the desire I have to be useful to you, I am obliged to end with my recommendations. Be holy at any price, and I am confident that we shall meet in a better life, never to be separated.

"I often recommend you to God as daughters most dear to me. Remember me before Him and accept the expresson of my most paternal sentiments.

"J. B. BP. LE MANS"

Fortified by the decisions of Bishop Bouvier and unable to come to agreement with Bishop de la Hailandière, Mother Theodore addressed herself to another Bishop who had previously assured her of a welcome to his diocese.[2]

TO THE RIGHT REVEREND PETER PAUL LEFEVRE

BISHOP OF DETROIT

Saint Mary's, December 18, 1845

My Lord:

Before taking the liberty of writing to you about the important affairs with which we are engaged, we wished to consult our Superiors in France, the Bishop of Le Mans and our Reverend Mother, and beg their permission to settle elsewhere than in Indiana. We have obtained the permission. We desired also to see the Bishop of Vincennes and to correspond with him. We have done both; and, although our affairs are not entirely terminated, the nature of our relations

---

[2] Letter of the Reverend William Chartier to Mother Theodore, June 20, 1845; in the Community archives, Saint Mary-of-the-Woods.

leaves scarcely any doubt but that we shall leave Terre Haute shortly. Persuaded of this, we have cast our eyes upon your diocese, drawn by the reputation of your prudence and zeal, also by the thought that we could fulfil more perfectly the end of our holy vocation which, being entirely that of charity and other works of zeal, would find with you more opportunity for its exercise than in a diocese of the East.

We come, then, to ask whether Your Lordship is still disposed to bestow upon us shelter and protection, and on what conditions. The first we propose is that you would deign to approve our Rules and Constitutions. An experience of five years has convinced us that, with some slight exceptions, they can be observed here as in France. However, if after examining them you should, in your wisdom, judge that some points would be observed with difficulty in your diocese, we would beg of you to let us know what they are, that we may see if it be possible for us to admit the changes without altering the spirit of our Congregation. I think I may safely advance that our Sisters are disposed to do all that will depend on them in order to do good, provided that our Constitutions be not altered in any essential points. As the other conditions are mostly about material things, we simply ask what you will be able to do for us.

As to our temporal affairs I shall tell you candidly how we stand, so that you may better know what you would have to do. If we remained here, we should be well enough off as to the temporalities. We have no debts, but having spent our money in founding our House, our pecuniary resources would be very small for a new establishment. The Council of the Propagation of the Faith, however, being acquainted with our work and appreciating it, would, undoubtedly, not refuse to continue its assistance, especially if requested by you to do so.

In honoring us with a reply you will be kind enough to

tell us whether to send a copy of our Rules and Constitutions by mail, or whether you know of any other means of conveying it to you.

We are authorized to write you this letter by our Very Reverend Superior [Father Corbe], who will address some lines to you himself.

Deign to accept the homage of the most profound veneration with which I am, my Lord, of Your Lordship

The most humble and obedient servant,

SISTER ST. THEODORE.

Sup'r Gen'l

The reply of the Bishop of Detroit to the foregoing letter was addressed to Father Corbe, who hastened to communicate to Father Martin the information received for the Sisters. Father Corbe wrote, February 1, 1846:

"...I have just received a letter from the Bishop of the North which is very urgent and quite satisfactory to me and to the Community. He promises a piece of ground and the approbation of the Constitutions in advance. The locality offers very great advantages on account of the number of Catholics and the easy communication through the lakes and rivers. Here there is nothing of that. And the Bishop instead of protecting the Sisters has already turned priests against them. Now, what is to be done? I ask you as a friend. Oh, tell me frankly what you think. You know that by a single word I can decide the fate of the Community at this moment. I can prevail on them to remain if, as I think, His Lordship is obliged to grant them what they are asking for; or I can decide for them to leave even though he would yield everything. As for myself, personally, we could never get along together after what he has said to me. As to the Sisters, I could expect them to come to definite terms with him, but not for long. I take my resolutions always slowly and even then with difficulty. After that, the matter is ended. It is not possible for me to retrace my steps. I desire with all my heart that you speak to me on all this with entire frankness.

"Good Mother Theodore is very sick, very weak, and truly in danger. However, I am hopeful that the good God will spare her under these circumstances. She is much worse since receiving a *beautiful* letter of eight or ten pages from His Lordship, full of calumnies, almost scandalous; and he wishes all the Sisters to read it, too, although he reproaches her with things she had spoken to him about only *in direction*, confidentially."

Writing on another occasion to Father Martin, Father Corbe said:

"Good Mother Theodore has at last decided to go to see His Lordship. I pray you to help her by your counsel, your influence. Encourage her. The good God will inspire you with the means of being useful to her. I tell you again, and I write it, she is the only one capable of directing the Community. I shall tender my resignation if she is sent away or forced to go by the Bishop."

And later:

"Good Mother Theodore is back again at St. Mary's, this time quite disheartened. It could not be otherwise. She will probably quit entirely and then—what will become of St. Mary's?—a flock of poor innocents who are no more capable of forming a community than I am of biting the moon."

Again he wrote:

"I shall certainly go to Vincennes as soon as I learn that the Bishop is there. This will not be for me a visit of pleasure or recreation; for, truly, it costs me to leave a diocese for which I have sacrificed my best years. It seems, however, the only course to pursue."[3]

Mother's Theodore's illness referred to by Father Corbe lasted six weeks. Scarcely recovered, she takes up the suspended correspondence and lays the matter before the Sisters of the Council, some of whom were on the missions.

LETTER CIRCULAR

Saint Mary-of-the-Woods, March 8, 1846

Very dear Sisters,

It is a joy to me to be able myself to tell you that, thanks to

[3] Original letters in Community archives.

your fervent prayers, Our Lord still permits me to live and to suffer with you. We will thank Him together, and to prove our gratitude we will repeat to Him from the depth of our hearts that we will belong to Him more perfectly than ever. And this we will more particularly prove to Him by the tender charity that unites us; for it is by this that we shall preserve the spirit of God amongst us, and that we can rely on His assistance—assistance of which we have now greater need than ever before; as, my dear daughters, the moment has come when we must leave the distressing state in which we have been for so long a time.

During the first days of my illness we received a letter from the Bishop whom you know about [the Bishop of Detroit]. He offered, together with his fatherly protection, to approve our Rules and Constitutions for his diocese, and he entreated our Father [Corbe] to come with us to continue to be our Superior. But this is all he can do for us at the present time.

I also received on the 27th of January a letter of ten pages from the Bishop of Vincennes. It is full of accusations and reproaches which are personal, three-fourths of which are palpably untrue. I am obliged to communicate this to you, for in a little corner your names are written; as is also that of Father Corbe, who read only two pages of it and then threw it aside with the greatest indignation.

Notwithstanding, we think here that before taking the final step it would be more according to the spirit of God to renew again our petitions to His Lordship, the Bishop of Vincennes, without mention of the past. In view of this we are sending you the letter that we are addressing to him, in order that you may sign it, if, as we do not doubt, you share our opinion in the matter.

Let us take courage, my very dear Sisters; the cross, it is true, awaits us at every turn, but it is the way to heaven. If we remain here we shall have many painful contradictions;

but the greatest would be the possibility of losing our very worthy and venerated Superior, who is our only true friend. If we leave we shall have peace; yet a host of privations awaits us. Let us beg our Lord to choose for us that which will unite us more closely to Him; and beseech Him for the light, the grace, the strength we need to do in all things His adorable Will. In Him I am, with the tenderest affection as always,

Your devoted

SISTER ST. THEODORE.
Sup'r Gen'l

You know, my dear Sisters, you are not obliged to sign the letter I am sending, if it is contrary to your views. You also know that in signing it you engage yourselves to remain in the diocese of Vincennes, if the Bishop grants us what we ask, and of leaving soon if he does not grant it. Reflect well and act according to your lights and intentions. Write to me as soon as you will have taken your determination. You understand that this letter is for *you alone*.

Always yours in our Lord,
SR. ST. T.

The letter addressed to Bishop de la Hailandière to be signed by the members of the Council, should they so choose, here follows:

TO THE RIGHT REVEREND CEL. DE LA HAILANDIERE
BISHOP OF VINCENNES

Saint Mary-of-the-Woods, March 8, 1846

My Lord:

It has not been possible to reply sooner to your letter of January 25; even today we can speak of only one item of that letter. We are confronting circumstances too grave to be deterred by personal considerations.

You say that we are mistaken in thinking that your refusal to reply to our letter of the month of August is equivalent to a refusal of those things we asked of you. If such is the case, we take the liberty to renew, once more, those same requests.

The first is, as you know, that you give in writing, with your signature and under your episcopal seal, permission to dwell in your diocese according to the Rules and Constitutions which we brought from France, in order that we may have the assurance of being allowed to follow them as perfectly as is possible for a body not yet organized. The second is that you give us the deed of the property of Saint Mary's so that we may begin to build. Your Lordship knows that we have never asked aught but these things in order to establish ourselves in Indiana as a Congregation subject to you. Many times you have said, and even written, that you intended to grant us these things, but that we had put obstacles. These obstacles are now all removed—all the Sisters of Providence can now hold property legally;[4] therefore, we dare hope that you will not delay to give us this last proof of your good will, which, in putting an end to a state so painful for all, will open to our view a brighter future and afford us the occasion to prove to you by our gratitude and submission how it has pained us to be, in a way, compelled to afflict your heart.

However, faithful to the spirit of candor which we have always followed, we must say that, after all that has occurred since our first request, your silence, or any reply which would not be the Acts we ask for, could not but be regarded by us, this time, as a formal refusal; in which case we would consider ourselves obliged to take a definitive resolution, and that with very little delay.

[4] The French Sisters had become naturalized as citizens of the United States and the institution had been incorporated by the State of Indiana.

The fate of our Congregation is yet in your hands. We shall pray with even greater fervor than in the past that God may inspire you to act in the manner that will procure Him more glory and unite us more closely to Him. In these sentiments we remain, with the most profound respect, my Lord,

Of Your Lordship

The very humble and obedient servants,

SISTER ST. VINCENT   SISTER MARY JOSEPH
SISTER ST. FRANCIS XAVIER   SISTER MARY CECILIA
SISTER ST. LIGUORI   SISTER ST. THEODORE

Bishop de la Hailandière's reply was a demand for an "Act of Reparation" from the Sisters as a prerequisite to his granting their petition. He maintained that they had calumniated him to their Superiors in France and he insisted on a retraction. The Sisters, having only stated facts, considered that they had nothing to retract; but they would do what they could, so they sent him the following declaration:

Saint Mary-of-the-Woods, April 6, 1846

My Lord:

Deign to be persuaded that it costs us less to acknowledge our faults than to treat of the painful matters which have occupied us for so long a time. We are going to prove it to you by replying the best we can to the letter you addressed to us last week.

Art. I—Our Congregation, not having been incorporated until the month of January last, it is clear that it could not hold property as a body before that time; until then, the American Sisters only had the right to possess individually, those from France not yet being naturalized. We do not think that we have either said or written the contrary. If we are mistaken, we declare that it was the result of error and we disavow it.

Art. II—We thought we explained ourselves sufficiently

in our preceding letter, but if we did not, we now declare formally that we have asked the approbation of our Rules and Constitutions only that we may be settled in Indiana in a final manner. Until we shall have obtained said approbation from another Bishop, we shall regard ourselves as still subject to the Bishop of Le Mans, and we shall be, in reality, a branch of the House in France. But, as it is recognized that such a state of affairs cannot continue long, and as you yourself oppose it, we have consented to the separation. We have insisted with Your Lordship to obtain this approval (even, it may be, to importunity), only because we consider it, as it really is, the foundation of our Congregation in America. We declare that as soon as you have given us this approval we shall acknowledge ourselves to be your daughters, and shall recognize in you, without exception, all the rights of the Bishop of Le Mans over our Congregation in France. These are, and always have been, our dispositions. It is surprising that they have not been understood; for, if we may ever have overstepped the rules of politeness and, perhaps, even those of respect for episcopal authority (which would grieve us very much), we can say that we have never infringed those of uprightness and candor; so we are astonished at finding ourselves accused of deceit.

Art. III—If the state of our Congregation, yet in its infancy, does not permit us to fulfill all our Rules in their perfection, very willingly we admit that at the beginning the observance was more difficult for you and for us. It is with our whole soul, it is even a consolation for our heart, not only to ask your pardon and offer our apologies for anything that in our conduct, in our intercourse, or in our letters may have escaped us contrary to the respect that we owe to Your Lordship, for whom we wish to preserve the most profound veneration, but we would all wish to be at your feet to ask pardon most humbly; and we would not rise until you had said: Go, I pardon and bless you. These are the sentiments of all the Sisters of Providence, and especially of those who are, my Lord,

Of Your Lordship

The most humble and obedient servants,

SISTER ST. THEODORE   SISTER ST. VINCENT
SISTER ST. FRANCES XAVIER   SISTER MARY CECILIA

The signatures of the other two Councilors who signed the letter of March 8th are missing here, because those Sisters were at distant missions now, and delay was not advisable; moreover, their sentiments were known to be the same as of those who signed.

The Sisters were just now facing the imperative need of enlarging the Academy. "The time had come," the *Annals* state, "when we must either build or send away our pupils. The bricks destined for the construction were deteriorating day by day." That first building, it will be recalled, as described by Mother Theodore, was only "fifty feet wide by twenty-six feet deep." And there were now forty boarding pupils. But the Sisters were unwilling to build on property that was not their own and the deed of the property had not yet been conveyed to them.

The Community's claim to the property rested on the following points:

(a) The Bishop had promised the Superiors in France that he would give the Sisters their home in Indiana, and in his letter of November 22, 1840, one month after their arrival at Saint Mary's, he wrote to Mother Theodore, "You are soon going to become rich proprietors. I have bought the Thralls property and paid two hundred dollars less by waiting for it." The Sisters themselves had contributed to this purchase, as is seen in the "Minutes of the Council," the first session of which was held "for the purpose of deciding whether to give two hundred dollars of our money, requested by the Reverend Stanislaus Buteux, to complete the purchase of the farm—project unanimously adopted." (Council Proceedings, November 10, 1840.)

(b)   The Society of the Propagation of the Faith, in its annual allotment of funds to the Diocese of Vincennes, had included a specified sum for the Sisters. Mother Theodore mentions this contribution in her letter to Bishop Bouvier, September 22, 1843, and Bishop Bouvier, himself, speaks of it at length in his letter of November 8, 1843, addressed to Bishop de la Hailandière.

(c)   The sum of twenty-five thousand francs had been given, through Joseph Picquet of Sainte Marie, Illinois, to the Bishop of Vincennes to establish Sisters in his diocese. "The Picquet family," according to the *Annals*, "had long been wondering that His Lordship had not given us the deed of our property, for it was a gentleman of Alsace, an uncle of theirs, M. Mertian, who had left by will the first amount necessary for a religious establishment in Indiana. The rest of the money had been given by the Society of the Propagation of the Faith, and all expected that the Sisters of Providence would be put in possession as soon as they arrived at Saint Mary-of-the-Woods."

(d)   The Bishop of Vincennes had told Mother Theodore when she was setting out for France in 1843, that if she would bring back four thousand dollars he would give her the deed of the property at St. Mary's; she brought back a little more than that amount and still the deed was not given.

Another question remained unsettled: the Bishop had not yet approved the Rules. This five-year delay could be interpreted, the Sisters thought, as tacit disapproval. When a settlement of these two matters was urged, the Bishop saw in the Sisters only ingratitude and rebellion.

During these years of stress a trial of another nature had come to the Community. Father Martin, the Vicar General and their staunch friend, was about to leave the diocese. He had tried the baths of his native land without experiencing permanent results; now he was determined to go to Louisiana, as his health was better in a mild climate; moreover, he could no longer endure the conflict at Vincennes. The announcement of his intention to leave the diocese plunged into amazed sorrow his old and greatly attached friend, Father Corbe, who thus tells him of his consternation and grief, in a few lines dated February, 1846:

"Your letter has pained me more than you could ever imagine. I did not sleep at all last night. What is going to become of our poor diocese? You have been a good friend to me and I hope if kind Providence wills that we be separated, our friendship will not suffer. I wrote to the Bishop of Rennes about the end of November and am expecting his reply from day to day. As soon as I shall have received it I shall let you know. I wrote also to the Bishop of Le Mans. Oh, but I regret not having done so sooner, and of not having persuaded the Sisters of St. Mary's to accept the first offers that were made to them. All would be settled now. Good Mother Theodore is not well and it is grief that nails her to her couch, that crucifies her. That letter could be the cause of her death; for since its reception she has had fever again. I beg of you write."

Again he says on March 9:

"The Sisters sent their *ultimatum* today; that is to say, they will remain or they will go if—all depends on His Lordship. What will be the issue? I am fearful of the consequences; but, after all, there must be an end. Let us still hope, however, and pray."[5]

When sufficiently recovered, Mother Theodore also wrote to the Vicar General concerning his departure from the diocese.

TO THE VERY REVEREND A. MARTIN

THE BISHOP'S HOUSE, NEW ORLEANS

April 1, 1846

Dear Father Martin:

So you have really left Vincennes? You are no longer in Indiana? There is no longer any hope? While I am writing this you are being carried rapidly away by steam on the muddy waters of the Mississippi, far from the land you had adopted. Oh, how your leaving grieves me! I understand your sorrow; I even feel it. We shall pray much for you during your journey. I am confident these prayers will not be unavailing for, besides coming from the heart, they are made by poor orphans abandoned in the woods; and you

[5] Originals in Community archives.

know God is always disposed to hear the prayers of the poor and afflicted. Your departure has terribly upset Father Corbe. He cannot last long in this state. We have not yet had any news from Vincennes, none whatever, but we know our letter is in the hands of His Lordship.

If you have had the goodness to buy the altar wine for us, and it has not yet been sent, kindly put it in care of Mr. John Crawford [of Terre Haute], who will deliver this letter to you. He is a gentleman who has always shown us much good will. We wrote to the uncle of our Jane to deposit the sum he owes us with Father Perché. May I ask you to inquire whether the latter has received it, and if he has, give it also to Mr. Crawford.

Pardon me the liberty I take in giving you so much to do on the eve of a voyage. That is what one gets by being so good.

I shall write you again as soon as we shall have received a reply from His Lordship. If it comes after your departure, I shall send my letter to Madame de France for you. I wish you a happy voyage and beg you to accept the homage of the deepest respect with which I remain

Your very humble servant,

SISTER ST. THEODORE.

After a short stay in New Orleans with Archbishop Blanc, Father Martin proceeded to Baltimore to lay before the Sixth Provincial Council held in May, 1846, at the request of the priests of Indiana, the situation in the Diocese of Vincennes. The Most Reverend Samuel Eccleston, Archbishop of Baltimore, advised him to take the matter directly to Rome, which he did. While he was in France, on his way back to America, Mother Theodore again wrote him.

TO THE VERY REVEREND A. MARTIN

Saint Mary-of-the-Woods, July 3, 1846

Monsieur l'Abbé:

Only a few days ago I returned from visiting the establishments, hence I was deprived of the pleasure of replying sooner to the letter you had the kindness to write to me before your departure. That letter pierced my heart. In reading it I said to myself, this venerated protector of our Congregation, this devoted friend, is no longer on American soil; an ocean separates us. Who will now protect us? I turned to my God and felt my confidence reanimated. If He takes away our last support, is it not because He wishes to be the sole support of His Daughters of the Woods? There never was such pressing need of His help as now.

I leave to Father Corbe to tell you some peculiar things that are said to be going on in America since you left. I content myself with speaking of our own affairs which, as you know, were not too promising when you visited us the last time. Conditions had not changed when our good Father decided, after much hesitation, to go to the retreat. I wished very much that he would go in order to confer with Father Timon, whom you had so well recommended.[6] We thought Father Corbe still at Vincennes when one fine morning he walked in on us to get his trunk and other belongings. He was no longer our Superior. He intended to set out immediately for St. Louis to consult the Bishop of that city, to whom you had also spoken in our favor.

You can imagine we opposed that project with all our might. What were we going to do—poor sheep without a shepherd—but stray away and get lost! After many plans, adopted and rejected, it was decided that Father Corbe

---

[6] Very Reverend John Timon, C.M., Vicar Apostolic of the Mississippi Valley; later, first Bishop of Buffalo (1847–1867).

should go back to Vincennes, and that after the retreat we would take our final resolution. He will tell you, no doubt, what passed between himself and His Lordship. He returned as Superior and was charged to present to us a formula to sign, a formula he himself had drafted. This Act contained an abridgement of what we had already done, some vague excuses, and a positive promise that we would remain in the Diocese of Vincennes if what we asked was granted. Those of the Sister Councilors that were at Saint Mary's agreed to sign it. Father Corbe made known this resolution to Bishop de la Hailandière, who was then at the Council. His Lordship replied at once that he would now give the official approbation to our Rules, and also that he would give us the property of Saint Mary's.

After we had transmitted to the Bishop this Act, bearing the signatures of all the Sisters of the Council, we concluded to let the contract for the enlarging of the school building. These additions will cost us about $5,000. Marcile and Roquet are the contractors.

You will say now: At last you are settled in Indiana; peace is going to be restored. Wait a moment before chanting the *Te Deum*. Never were we so near our extermination. The Bishop, not having been able to make me leave the diocese without returning to Saint Mary's (Father Corbe had to go to Vincennes to get me), now takes another course: he wishes to have elections. But it is not only as Superior that he does not want me here any longer. Most probably I shall go.

If in leaving this dear mission I could bear away with me the consoling thought that my Sisters were happy and in the enjoyment of peace, I would say, like you, what does it matter what becomes of us, provided God's work be accomplished? God's work—ah, it will ever be accomplished. What can men do against it? Here I cease. I shall say nothing further except, pray for your Daughters in Indiana. Get prayers said for them by pious and fervent souls, whose numbers are so great in our dear Brittany. You will not have to go far to find them. As soon as there shall be anything new I shall write to you.

I long to know how you stood the voyage, what time you landed, whether you have seen the Bishop of Le Mans and our good Mother and the Sisters at Ruillé. You will tell me everything, will you not? I can see you happy in the bosom of friendship, enjoying in peace a happiness you have not had for a long time. The thought of Vincennes must come only occasionally to darken your countenance. You have hope for our future, you say. What future? Soon we shall have lost everything.

The kind and virtuous Father Delaune no longer has powers for Indiana. He has been accepted with the most tender benevolence by the Bishop of Louisville. He is going to help Father Sorin in a new foundation in Kentucky. The Bishop of Vincennes said, also, that he is going to dismiss the Brothers [of the Holy Cross]. New priests are being ordained to replace the older ones. Three are going to receive ordination in a few days. They are your pupils, I think. Who will educate those that are to come? Nothing is changed at the Seminary since you left it. Father Dupontavice remains the Superior in the interior administration. Everybody has hopes of seeing you return to Vincennes and desires it most earnestly. I myself think you will return, but not so very soon. Now what *will* you do?

If I go back to France after the retreat I shall be there about the beginning of September. I hope to have the happiness of seeing you there. What things I shall be able to tell you— things that could never be written! ... With the most sincere gratitude and profound respect, I remain, *Monsieur l'Abbé*,

Your very humble servant,

SISTER ST. THEODORE.

In the lull that followed the signing of the document required by the Bishop, Mother Theodore issued to the Community the letter calling them to the retreat.

LETTER CIRCULAR

July 4, 1846

May the peace of God which surpasses all understanding be with you all, said the Apostle to the Christians of his time. It is very sweet, my dear Sisters, after a year of anxieties, to address the same words of peace to you. Yes, very dear Sisters, our affairs are at last terminated. Our Bishop has granted what we asked—what we asked with so much importunity— the approbation of our holy Rules and the property of Saint Mary's. He has pardoned us everything that, in our days of difficulty, he thought wanting in respect. His Lordship also leaves us our Father Corbe.

We in turn have promised in the name of the Congregation that we will remain in the diocese of Indiana; this, then, is the portion of the vineyard of the Lord which we are called upon to cultivate. In order that you may work therein with fresh ardor, we invite you to come to renew your souls in the retreat. Our venerable prelate has fixed the date for the 8th of August. Come, then, very dear Sisters, to consider the one thing necessary, the only thing that is truly our own. Sad experience teaches us that exterior occupations, even the holiest, dry up the soul and, in separating it from God, make it forget, like Martha, the one thing necessary which Mary had chosen.

We desire that you prepare yourselves to receive the graces

of the retreat by great exactitude in the observance of the chapter of our Rules that relates to traveling. We direct you to read it.

We wish you to be here the first days of August in order to recreate yourselves a little before the retreat.

SISTER ST. THEODORE

Sup'r. Gen'l

Father Martin, after receiving Mother Theodore's letter of July 3, wrote from Rennes to Bishop Bouvier, September 20, 1846, saying in part:

"Since my last visit to Le Mans where I had the honor of seeing Your Lordship, I have received a letter from Sister. Theodore, dated July 3. The sum of the news is, that, tired of the warfare, the Sisters of the Council have consented to sign an *Act* of complaisance, a sort of retraction or reparation, demanded by the Bishop. The signing of this document was exacted by. His Lordship prior to any concession on his part, and he had given to their Superior, Rev. J. Corbe, his word as Bishop that as soon as it should be signed he would approve the Constitutions and Rules and give the property to the Sisters at the date of the letter. The *Act* was in the hands of His Lordship in May and as yet nothing had been done. I do not blame these poor Sisters, they have yielded to a moral torture.

"Sister Theodore says also that His Lordship has openly declared his will that not only shall she not be the Superior, but that she shall have to leave the Establishment. She expected to leave after the retreat in the middle of August and return to France. If this comes to pass I do not give the Community one year of existence. But I do not believe it will happen. He wants them to build; they cannot do it without Sister Theodore, She would build, contract debts, and then be forced to leave! Finally she tells me that His Lordship has formally declared, that he is going to send all of Father Moreau's priests [of Holy Cross] out of the diocese.

"I shall be in Louisiana, God willing, the first of December. There I am going to exhaust what remains to me of health and strength. If things come to the point that Sister Theodore will have to leave Indiana, I shall do all in my power to open a door to her zeal in the South. It was a thing arranged with Bishop Blanc last April."

Upon receiving this intelligence from the Vicar General of Vincennes, Bishop Bouvier wrote to Archbishop Eccleston of Baltimore, who replied thus to the Bishop of Le Mans:[7]

"Baltimore, September 29, 1846

"My Lord:

"I have received the letter with which you have honored me regarding the Sisters of Providence in the Diocese of Vincennes, and about the passage through Baltimore of the worthy Superior of the Eudists in the United States, Rev. Father Chassé, who is going back to France.

"When the Bishop of Vincennes came here in the month of May for the Provincial Council, motives of propriety and delicacy, which you will understand, did not allow me to speak to him of this matter. It is, then, from other sources that I have drawn the little information that I have to communicate to you.

"It seems that these good Sisters have met with many obstacles and have had to struggle against grave difficulties, for which it would not be at all possible for me at present to state the remedy. Besides, the Bishop of Vincennes appears to be singularly tired of his position, and, they say, he is using his utmost endeavors to free himself from the administration of his diocese. Will he succeed in doing so? This is what we shall probably know before long.

"In the meantime, I think that the best that can be done for the present is to leave things as they are. Later on, in case the Sisters of Providence should wish to settle themselves elsewhere, I do not doubt but that they will find in some diocese every facility and all the encouragement they could desire.

"I am, with respect,

"Of Your Lordship

"The most humble and obedient servant,

"SAMUEL, ABP. BALT."

[7] Originals in the archives of the Diocese of Le Mans.

Letters had gone to Ruillé from time to time keeping the authorities in France informed of the state of things at Saint Mary's, and now Mother Theodore gives other important details.

TO THE RIGHT REVEREND J. BOUVIER, BISHOP OF LE MANS

Saint Mary-of-the-Woods, July 21, 1846

My Lord and venerated Father:

I would have been pleased to write sooner and to console your paternal heart which has suffered so much for your Daughters of the Forest; but I would, at the same time, have desired to tell you that all was settled and that the Congregation that you have protected with so much benevolence was at last firmly established in Indiana. If it does not yet please Our Lord to grant me this consolation, at least He permits us to hope that we shall soon have it. We may even tell you that much has been done. No doubt our good Mother Mary has informed you of the news that I imparted to her in my letter of last month, in sending from Vincennes a copy of the letter Mgr. de la Hailandiére sent to our Superior [Father Corbe]. His Lordship promised to approve our Rules and to give us the property of Saint Mary's. He granted everything we had asked for. We were happy to learn this, so much the more as we had little expected it.

As the Bishop had told Father Corbe before setting out for the Council that he would never approve our Rules, we were all convinced that this change was due to what you had written to Baltimore. It is a deep joy for us to think that, after God, it is to you we owe our happiness. This happiness assuredly will not be without clouds, but I feel certain that nothing will happen except what God will permit. He has protected us with so much love until the present day that I should consider it a crime to doubt His mercy now. It

FIRST ACADEMY OF SAINT
MARY-OF-THE-WOODS
1841
From a water color by Sister
St. Francis le Fer de la Motte

THE ACADEMY, ENLARGED IN 1846
Drawing by Sister Edith Pfau, from original made in 1854 by
Sister Mary Joseph le Fer de la Motte

PROVIDENCE CONVENT
1848
From a water color by
Sister St. Francis

matters little, who governs, it seems to me, provided the Rule be followed. I should be only too happy if my task were accomplished and I might be allowed to retire, to think of myself and prepare for death, which I believe is not far off. However, I do not will or desire anything but the fulfillment of the Divine Will.

His Lordship having promised to come to Saint Mary's, we were expecting him from week to week; finally he did come on the fourteenth of this month and brought us the deed for a portion of the land—about eighty acres. He reserves the rest for himself. The deed contains things which the Sisters dislike very much; for example, we are not permitted to do the least thing on his land without the approbation of His Lordship or his heirs, etc., etc. As the law in this country admits of no conditions, it is very probable the deed will not be valid. I took it to a lawyer who is going to examine it and let us know whether it is legal or not. I am afraid it is not properly made.

I am so tired of treating of these matters with His Lordship. As to our Rules—we are going to translate them into English, with the few changes agreed upon long ago; then, when they will have received the approbation of the Ordinary we shall have them printed.

It was not possible to defer any longer the enlarging of the Academy. The builders have been working on it for ten days. His Lordship advanced the money—$600 received from the Propagation of the Faith for us last year. The whole will cost from $5,000 to $6,000. Should His Lordship not require anything else from us, I believe we could raise that amount in the course of the coming year, if God continues to bless our Institution. We have now forty-six pupils. Although all do not pay, we were able to put aside something last year. This Academy is our only source of income to keep up the priest's house, the novitiate, some of the establishments, five orphans, and the Academy itself. I assure you, my Lord, we have to look out rather closely in order not to contract debts. We have at this moment no debts except one in Paris for dry goods. This we contracted reckoning on money which we had at Le Mans in the hands of a banker who has failed and has thus done us an injury. Had we known of his bankruptcy sooner we would not have ordered the goods.

We have at present only five postulants, but there are three girls at the Academy who desire to enter the novitiate. And there are several young girls who are receiving instructions for Baptism; one of these will be baptized this week and make her First Communion. A great deal of good is being done in our schools; we are much consoled in visiting them this year. After the retreat we shall take a new mission, Fort Wayne, in the northern part of the state. They intend to give us a brick house with a small meadow. That is all they can do.

You will continue to pray for us, my Lord, and deign to give us your blessing. We shall write immediately after the retreat to inform you of what we shall have done.

Permit me to offer you the homage of the deep veneration with which I am, my Lord, of Your Lordship

The most humble servant and submissive daughter,

SISTER ST. THEODORE.

When Bishop de la Hailandière was in Rome in the winter of 1844–45 he asked for a coadjutor. Not obtaining his request, he tendered his resignation, which, as has been said, was not accepted. The next time he offered it (at the Provincial Council of Baltimore in 1846) it was taken under advisement.

In the meantime Father Martin had been to Rome; Father Sorin of Notre Dame had transferred his Brothers to the Diocese of Louisville; Father Delaune, pastor at Madison, had gone to take the presidency of Father Sorin's college in Kentucky; Father Corbe was contemplating returning to France; and now, Father Chassé, a Eudist, was in the Eternal City in the interests of the St. Gabriel College at Vincennes. As Father Chassé entered into audience with the Holy Father, Pius IX said in greeting him: "You are the little priest from Indiana? I have good news for you. I have named a new bishop for Vincennes. The papers are signed there on my table."[8] Father Chassé immediately sent the news to his Superior, Father Bellier, S. E., who dispatched it to Terre Haute, and Father Lalumière lost no time in bringing it to Saint Mary-of-the-Woods. But in those days of slow communication, many weeks were to pass before the word from Rome could reach Saint Mary's. Even after the news was finally received there—early in June, 1847—the Sisters refrained from mentioning the subject until the appointment of the Bishop's successor, the Reverend John Stephen Bazin of Mobile, Alabama, had been publicly announced.

After Father Martin had returned to America, Mother Theodore wrote him again:

TO THE REVEREND A. MARTIN, BATON ROUGE, LA.

Saint Mary's, Jan. 22, 1847

My good Father:

It is very true that you are again on American soil, but it is also, unfortunately, very true that that soil is not Indiana. You are lost to us, lost to the unfortunate Diocese of Vincennes. For myself and for many others it is a real grief of soul. After you, good and generous friend, whom have we to lose? Our venerated Father Corbe? Well, yes; twenty-six days ago he went to Vincennes by order of His Lordship, and we have not heard a word from him since. Not one word has come to relieve the anxiety, frightful anxiety, caused by his protracted absence. To lose him or to keep him is a question of life or death for our poor Congregation,

---

[8] Alerding, *The Diocese of Vincennes*, p. 450.

unless God works a miracle to conserve it. He can do it, and—He loves us; this is our comfort and our only consolation.

Death is soon going to take from us our dear Sister Mary Liguori. She will be an immense loss to us. Adieu. My heart is so oppressed I no longer have the strength to pour out my soul. Pray for us all, for Father Corbe, who loves you faithfully, and for

Your very grateful servant,

SISTER ST. THEODORE.

During the year new difficulties had arisen from month to month. The deed of the property, having been pronounced illegal, had to be returned. The formal apology or "Act" given by the Sisters was no longer considered satisfactory and a full retraction was required. Though Mother Theodore had been named Superior General as well as Foundress, and although it had been decided that the Community was not yet sufficiently organized to hold regular elections, election was a matter the Bishop insisted upon. In this connection Father Corbe wrote (May 19, 1847) to Mother Theodore who had gone to Vincennes to visit the mission and to confer about the deed of the property:

"I beg you do not enter into any discussion with His Lordship, and if he speaks to you about an election you can extricate yourself by simply telling him that if the Community wishes it you will not oppose it. If he tries to force you to give in your resignation, or makes any other proposals for you to sign, excuse yourself by leaving everything to the decision of the Community. God, I trust, will help you. Notwithstanding my confidence in God, my soul is sad; it is truly tired of this sort of warfare, so long a time, no respite, no peace, and such a feeble hope for the future! Truly at present we can chant the *De profundis*. However, I trust the good God will let us go to the depths of misery only to manifest His goodness so much the more and to let us see that only in Him and by Him can we accomplish His Work. I have just written a letter to the Bishop. I tremble for the consequences; but I was forced to it by his letters.

"Well, now, my dear Mother Theodore, pray well to the Blessed Virgin and she will bring you back to us. Sister Olympiade is burning a good many candles these days. All are praying as much as they can. Let us hope for better times."

Mother Theodore had often proposed to resign, for the sake of peace, and to return to France. Mother Mary of Ruillé had assured the Sisters that they would be received back with open arms; yet, when the event seemed imminent, she pursued a line of argument hedged in with maternal encouragement and fortifying advice. Writing to Mother Theodore, January 29, 1847, she said:

"The opinion of our venerable prelate, Bishop Bouvier, and our opinion, also, is that you remain in peace and continue to direct that good work as in the past, without being troubled to know whether your venerable prelate is pleased or not. As to sending some Sisters to you, as you request, especially one to take your place, this is what our Bishop and we ourselves think regarding it: In case the resignation of the Bishop of Vincennes should not be accepted, it is perfectly useless to try anyone else, no matter who she may be; it is certain that no one could stand it there and do good; on the contrary, if the resignation should be accepted nothing will prevent you from keeping your post and continuing what God has begun with you. And I hope Heaven will give you time to form your successor.

"Consider, my dear Sister Theodore, that your case is a very uncommon one. You received the graces of the beginning; you speak the language of the country; you know the customs and the spirit. You were the one called to found that good work. It is from you it expects its life, increase and stability. I mean, of course, that you are the instrument of Providence, nothing more; for, do we not say every day in our office, *Nisi Dominus aedificaverit domum, etc.?*

"As to what you say to Bishop Bouvier concerning your fear of being no longer in the place intended by God for you (considering you are there against the will of your Bishop), our venerable prelate charged me to tell you not to be disturbed about the matter and even to remain there as long as possible. This is his opinion; and he wishes you to stay there whether or no, but without any anxiety of conscience. And we also give you the same advice."

What occurred in Vincennes during Mother Theodore's visit is thus described in an account sent to the Archbishop of Baltimore, May 31, 1847, by Sister St. Francis Xavier:

"The time for visiting the missions having come [she says], and this visitation being a point of Rule, Mother Theodore set out from Saint Mary-of-the-Woods April 19, 1847. She left the mission of Vincennes for the last. On the day before her departure from Vincennes, having already engaged her place in the stagecoach for the following morning, she went to see the Bishop. I shall relate only the end of her conversation with His Lordship, He accused her of wishing to remain Superior, despite everything. Mother then offered to propose an election to the assembled Community, and if they accepted it, she would consider herself freed from the duties of her charge; but until such time she would not leave her daughters."[9]

Her interview at the Bishop's house ended abruptly. The Bishop dismissed the Sister companion but told Mother Theodore she must remain until she would agree to all his requirements. She repeated that she never could agree to everything. Whereupon he left her in the reception room, turned the key in the door and went to his dinner. The Sisters, not knowing where she was, went later in the day to the Bishop to find out. He unlocked the door; Mother Theodore fell on her knees, begging his blessing. He blessed her and silently motioned her out. That evening, May 20, 1847, he went over to the Sister's house and there pronounced his sentence against the Foundress. Quoting again from Sister St. Francis' report to Archbishop Eccleston:

"The Bishop declared to our Mother that not only was she no longer the Superior but that she was not now even a Sister of Providence, for he released her from her vows; that she had to leave the diocese immediately and go elsewhere to hide her disgrace; that he forbade her to write to the Sisters at Saint Mary's —they had no need of her letters."

After hearing her sentence, which she received without reply and on her knees, Mother Theodore began at once to make arrangements for her departure the next morning, although she was already ill with pleurisy. Her anguish of

---

[9] Original in the archives of the Archdiocese of Baltimore.

mind increased the fever and the doctor had to be called during the night. He forbade her to leave Vincennes. For three weeks she remained under his care, sometimes at the point of death.

The statement of the situation of affairs sent to the Archbishop brought this reply to Sister St. Francis Xavier:

Baltimore, June 18, 1847

"Dear Sister,

"I have read your letter with the most painful interest, as I had heard from other sources that your position is perplexing in the extreme. Be assured that I am not insensible to your trials, but situated as I am I cannot, consistently with delicacy and propriety, take an active part in your affairs. Should I even attempt it I would but aggravate your troubles, as I have in such matters no jurisdiction out of my diocese. I feel, however, no hesitancy in encouraging you to be guided by the venerable Bishop of Le Mans, whom I venerate as one of the most holy and learned prelates in Europe. Of course I address myself on this point only to the Sisters who came from his diocese or were under his charge.

"May the God of all peace and consolation be with you and enable you to bear your cross with humility, obedience, and resignation.

"SAMUEL, ABP. BALT."

When Sister Mary Xavier, who had witnessed Mother Theodore's expulsion at Vincennes, returned to Saint Mary's the following day and related what had taken place, Father Corbe deliberated with the Sisters on the measures to be taken. The *Annals* give in detail what is here summarized: Mother Theodore had been expelled from the diocese; they would all go with her. Father Corbe wrote to the Bishop of Detroit and Sister St. Francis informed the postulants that as the Community expected to leave Indiana, they were free to return to their homes or to accompany the Sisters elsewhere. Without exception they chose to remain with the Community. The workmen also determined to follow Mother

Theodore wherever she would go. The Sisters made known their determination to the Bishop, and Father Corbe at the same time sent in his resignation. The Bishop answered Father Corbe but returned the Sisters' letter unopened. He had four times deprived Father Corbe of his office without having been asked, but this time he countered: "What do you want to leave the diocese for? Those who make the trouble ought to be the ones to stay and settle it."

The annalist added: "Sister Olympiade and Sister Mary Cecilia went to Vincennes to console and care for Mother. Sister Olympiade carried with her in a large bag all the most important papers and the little money we had, in order that Mother might have it when she would start for another diocese."

Sister Mary Cecilia returned to Saint Mary's after a few days. There, preparations were continuing: the trunks were being packed, the gardener was planning to carry off with him his young apple trees, and Sister Basilide was arranging to sell the cows and buy four good horses to draw the heavy wagons that would be needed for the migration.

In her report to the Archbishop of Baltimore, Sister St. Francis had already written, "We have decided not to remain at Saint Mary's with Mother Theodore as Superior, contrary to the will of the Bishop of Vincennes. On the other hand, the Bishop has declared that those of us who would follow her 'would depart under *une bonne excommunication*, to be released from which they would have to go to their dear Bishop of Le Mans.' "

The announcement that the diocese had a new Bishop came while Mother Theodore was still at Vincennes. Accordingly as soon as she was well enough to travel she went back to Saint Mary's. When her convalescence permitted she informed the Archbishop of her return.

TO THE MOST REVEREND SAMUEL ECCLESTON

ARCHBISHOP OF BALTIMORE

Saint Mary-of-the-Woods, July 6, 1847

My Lord:

The interest that your benevolent charity causes you to take in our Congregation makes me think you will receive with goodness some details concerning the late events that have taken place here since Sister St. Francis took the liberty of writing to your Grace.

You learned from her that the Bishop of Vincennes, dissatisfied with my administration, had deposed me as superior and forbidden me to remain in his diocese, or to have any communication whatever, even by letter, with the Community. I received this order the 20th of May at seven o'clock in the evening and began at once to prepare to obey by taking the first stage. But that very night I was attacked with pleurisy accompanied by a fever so violent that I was soon on the brink of the grave.

Ignorant of everything that was going on around me, I was occupied only in preparing myself for death, which I believed was not far away. But I was mistaken. I must still live and be engaged with our affairs. Without doubt I was not ripe for Heaven. I recovered slowly, too deeply concerned about the Community which I was forced to abandon under circumstances so critical.

During these days of anguish Bishop de la Hailandière received a letter from his brother, who had gone to Rome, telling him that the Holy Father had accepted his resignation and had appointed his successor. As soon as the Bishop received this news he wrote to the Community that he would have nothing more to do with us, that he left us entirely in the hands of our Superior. He added that whatever Father Corbe could not do alone he would have to arrange with his successor, who would not long delay coming to Vincennes.

Having read this letter, I considered that I should yield to the wishes of the Community and to the order of the Superior, who recalled me to Saint Mary's. I returned as soon as I was able to travel, and I now await in peace whatever it may please Our Lord to ordain for the future of our institution.

Deign to give us the assistance of your prayers and to bestow your paternal blessing upon her who is, my Lord,

Of your Lordship,

The very humble and obedient servant,

SISTER ST. THEODORE.

There were many among the clergy who were pleading the Sisters' cause. Besides Father Corbe and Father Martin may be instanced Father Lalumière of Terre Haute, who wrote to Father Martin, "The poor Sisters have had grievous things to suffer. I was almost exterminated myself, but I survived." Father de St. Palais, then pastor at Madison, wrote to Mother Theodore, "While you were imprisoned at Vincennes, I was carrying on a vigorous correspondence with His Lordship, which nearly ended in my extermination." Father Benoit, of Fort Wayne, writing congratulations, said in part: "Mother, more dear than ever because more suffering, at last I have received the news of your deliverance. Oh what good that letter of Sister St. Francis has done to my heart! *Vive Jésus!* Would that I could say, as you do, Mother, 'Hail crosses, great and small, spiritual and temporal, exterior and interior, hail! I kiss your feet, unworthy as I am even of your shadow.' I shall soon go to see you. I hope to find you not only recuperated but able to continue your labors for a long time."[10] Father Deydier of Evansville, who had given two retreats to the Sisters, did his utmost to assure the Bishop of the good dispositions of the Community; but to no avail. He was able, however, to speak in their favor when he met the Bishop-elect at Evansville, as the *Annals* say, and accompanied him to Vincennes for his consecration.

Concluding the record of these events in the *Annals*, Sister St. Francis says that there are certain circumstances that should be "well understood": "Bishop de la Hailandière liked to come to Saint Mary-of-the-Woods," she writes, "for this spot was his place of predilection, the object of his dearest affections. He would never have suffered so much, he would never have caused us to suffer so much had he loved us less. . . . As he understood his rights as Bishop and

[10] Original letters in the Community archives.

Superior in a manner contrary to the spirit of our Rules, he regarded our opposition to his views as contempt of episcopal authority, an act of the blackest ingratitude.

"It is necessary that this be well understood; for there are in the history of our Congregation facts which might be imputed to His Lordship as acts of tyranny, and which will be explained with less difficulty when one reflects that he considered as criminal disobedience what we look upon as sacred obligations."

("Monseigneur aurait bien voulu venir à Ste Marie-des-Bois car cette place était l'endroit de son choix, l'objet de ses plus chères affections. Il n'aurait jamais suffert, il ne nous aurait jamais fait tant souffrir, s'il nous avait moins aimées. . . . Comme il entendait ses droits d'évêque et de Supérieur d'une manière contraire à l'esprit de nos Règies, il considérait notre opposition à ses vues comme un mépris de l'autorité ecclésiastique, et comme un acte de la plus noire ingratitude.

"Il est nécessaire que ceci soit bien compris; car, il y aurait des faits dans l'histoire de notre Congrégation qui pourraient être imputés à Monseigneur comme actes de tyrannie et qui s'expliqueront un peu moins difficilement quand on réfléchira qu'il regardait comme des désobèissances criminelles ce que nous considérons nos obligations sacrées.")

Sister St. Francis had informed the Bishop of Le Mans of the events that marked the crisis in their difficulties, but before her letter reached him he had heard of Bishop Bazin's nomination to the See of Vincennes. Mother Mary, replying to the letter received from Saint Mary's by Bishop Bouvier, wrote from Ruillé-sur-Loir, July 8, 1847:

"Dear and ever-beloved Sister St. Francis Xavier:

"We have shared the profound sorrow which the premature death of our dear Sister Mary Liguori has caused you. Her loss is the more to be deplored since you relied on her to be your mariner's compass after your present guide would be wrecked by the waves and tempests of all kinds of tribulations. This double misfortune has just happened to you, as is stated in the letter you wrote to Monseigneur, which he has communicated to us, and in which you announce to him, not only the deposition of Sister Theodore and her unmerited expulsion from the society which she had founded with the help of God, but even her being sent away from the Diocese of Vincennes.

"All this is very hard to digest and difficult to conceive; but God has permitted it to try your faith and your confidence in Divine Providence. This painful trial is the last, however, by which He wishes you to show your love and obedience. He tries you as He did Abraham. He will also console you as He did that holy patriarch in restoring to him his son by the ministry of an angel. He will restore to you your Mother also (if she is not already given back to you) by means of a saint named by the Holy Father to replace your present Bishop. Thus you see that at the moment you believed all lost, God in His divine decrees was occupied in your deliverance.

"Remain then in humility and when your new prelate shall think fit to ask of you an account of your line of conduct with his predecessor, explain yourselves with great simplicity and sincerity, without showing either resentment or bitterness of heart against the one who put upon you such heavy crosses, though by Divine permission, as men are but the instruments and the secondary causes in all that happens to us, good or bad. Consequently, give to your new Bishop unequivocal proof that you are the disciples of a crucified God and that, following His example, you know how to forgive from your heart your enemies, your persecutors, and even your executioners, if necessary.

"Our venerable Bishop has written to us from Paris, where he now is, that he has heard from a good source that the resignation of Bishop de la Hailandière has been accepted by our Holy Father; that a most worthy new Bishop has been nominated for the bishopric of Vincennes, and that the person commissioned to deliver the papal bulls had embarked at Havre on the fifteenth of June last. His Lordship in this letter asks me to write to you immediately and engage you to persevere in your patience; which means to say that he desires you to remain at your post, notwithstanding the anathema hurled at you by Bishop de la Hailandière which, after all, cannot last long. By doing so you will add to your crown, bearing on your head, and not in your soul, the weight of an unjust excommunication. So, let Sister Theodore remain in Indiana; and if by some necessity she is obliged to quit your house for some days, let her not go far from her little flock. She will govern it later with peace and in security; for I think that the new Bishop will do her justice."

Reassuring words came also from the Bishop of Le Mans to Mother Theodore herself. He was at the Motherhouse of Ruillé when he wrote, September 9, 1847:

"We have spoken of you often at Le Mans, at Ruillé, and elsewhere. Our best wishes attend you in your efforts to do good, and in the various trials through which God is pleased that you should pass. Do not forget that the elect are formed under the press of tribulation, and that you are never more sure of being pleasing to Our Lord, your Divine Spouse, than when you have reason to believe that He unites you with Him in His humiliations and sufferings. Your Superiors and we cannot but approve your line of conduct in the hard circumstances in which you have found yourself. We are greatly pleased also at the unity of sentiment your dear Sisters have shown, which must be truly consoling for you."

Bishop Bazin was consecrated Bishop of Vincennes in the episcopal city, October 24, 1847. Mother Theodore being seriously ill could not attend the ceremonies. The Sisters, fearful, wondered what would be the attitude of the new Bishop toward the Community. His first letter to Mother Theodore written only four days after his consecration answers the question:

'Vincennes, October 28, 1847.

"Good and respected Mother,

"I write two words in haste, for I am still over-burdened with occupations. I am much pained to learn that you are seriously indisposed. I hope that when this letter reaches you, you will be already nearly restored; this is at least the desire of my heart.

"I was deeply moved in reading your letter. My tears flowed. Bury the past in oblivion, or think of it only to bless the Providence of God who sent you crosses because He loved you; for God never fails to try His true children.

"Father Corbe and your *méchante* Sister Xavier have

informed me of your difficulties. The future is yours. I shall judge you only by the future and according to your Constitutions. Please tell your daughters of the Woods that I will also be a father to them. I have the sweet hope that the enemy of all good will never succeed in troubling the happy harmony that should exist between religious Communities and their chief pastor. It seems to me that if on both sides we seek the greater glory of God, we must necessarily agree.

"As soon as I can get off for a day I shall go to see you, and I hope that this will be soon.

"While awaiting this pleasure, I beg of you to present to your dear Community my sentiments of devotedness and affection, and you in particular accept the expression of my respect and consideration.

JOHN STEPHEN
Bp. of Vin."

On November 19, 1847, Bishop Bouvier wrote again to Mother Theodore, saying in part:

"Your letter of September 20, to the Reverend Mother Superior General has been communicated to me. Regarding you and your companions as Daughters most dear to me, I have written to your new Bishop as a father full of solicitude for his children. I hope that in this worthy colleague you will find another father who will love you in our Lord with all his heart, and to whom you will be respectfully devoted. You will find him a man of God, and you will be docile instruments in his hands, to aid him efficaciously in the accomplishment of the great obligations of his charge. On the other hand, I have the firm conviction that he will know how, like other bishops who have your Sisters in their dioceses, to respect your rights and maintain your Rules."

As soon as Bishop Bazin received the letter from Bishop Bouvier he informed Mother Theodore:

"Vincennes, November 30, 1847

"My very dear Mother,

"Your father having learned that you are very much better and wishing for your entire restoration, hastens to send you a letter from the Bishop of Le Mans, which he received this morning.

"Yes, dear Mother, the wishes and hopes of the saintly Bishop Bouvier will be realized. I hope you will ever find in me a father, a friend in Jesus Christ, to whom you will be able to confide, without fear, all your anxieties. You will feel my authority only as a support to assist you to observe your Rule in all its perfection. A bishop ought to be for a superior who has the spirit of her state a lever to raise up the heaviest burdens, a light to enlighten her in her doubts, and a confidant to whom she may confide her pains and from whom she may draw the consolations she needs.

"Your good Sisters give me the hope that you will come to complete your recovery at Vincennes. If that be possible, it will be a real satisfaction to me; we should then have the time to converse at leisure. I do not see that I can go to Terre Haute yet—at least not for some weeks.

"I think Bishop de la Hailandière will leave to-morrow by stage. His effects went yesterday by steam-boat.

"I recommend myself to your fervent prayers and to those of the Community. Believe me always, in the hearts of Jesus and Mary,

"Yours very devotedly,

JOHN STEPHEN,
"Bp. of Vin."

A week later Mother Theodore went to Vincennes and met Bishop Bazin for the first time. There were many explanations to be made, questions to be settled, and plans to be formed. The interviews were mutually satisfying and comforting. Mother Theodore returned to Saint Mary's with, the promise of an early visit from the Bishop to their home in the Woods.

Bishop Bazin was not able to visit Saint Mary's until the last week of January. He remained six days. The *Annals* say: "He was like a father amongst us. He gave us several instructions, heard our confessions, visited our pupils, and showed the greatest interest in the health of our Mother who had fallen sick again. With her he changed several points of the Rule, which could not easily be observed in America. He was pained to see our buildings so far apart and so distant from the church."

Though Bishop de la Hailandière had finally approved the Rule, he had not settled about the deed of the property. This matter was now going to receive the new Bishop's early attention.

Thus after nearly seven years of incessant struggle, the coming of Bishop Bazin brought peace and happiness and a feeling of security hitherto unknown at Saint Mary-of-the-Woods. The account of the Bishop's visit thus concludes: "At his return to Vincennes he wrote to all our Sisters on the missions, to Mobile, and to the Propagation at Rome. All his letters were full of expressions of the joy that his visit to Saint Mary's had afforded him. He promised to return in August to preach our retreat and to see reunited all the dear daughters upon whom his sweetest hopes now rested. But God in His impenetrable decrees had ordained that this good Bishop should have this consolation only in Heaven."

———

Among those who enjoyed the tranquillity that reigned at Saint Mary-of-the-Woods after the advent of Bishop Bazin was Father Corbe, the worthy chaplain and Ecclesiastical Superior of the Sisters. As his name is closely linked with the history of the Community for a period of thirty years, a brief sketch of his life seems to be in place here.

It was Father Corbe who welcomed the Sisters to Vincennes at the end of their long journey from France in 1840. He there sustained their courage while they were awaiting in tedium and suspense the return of their Bishop, whom they had met at Madison and who had there informed them that they were to be located not in the episcopal city, as they had supposed, but in a country place. It was Father Corbe who upheld them again in their struggles in the heart of the wilderness sixty miles away when, in 1842, he came to be their chaplain, and who, two years later, was appointed their Ecclesiastical Superior—an office he held until his death, which occurred June 3, 1872. Father Corbe is the only one who has ever held this office, as the Rule of the

Congregation does not provide for an Ecclesiastical Superior. His appointment was brought about, as has been seen, by circumstances.

Father Corbe was at once father and friend, and more— he saved the Community to Indiana. During the crisis he wrote to his very dear friend, Father Martin, it will be recalled: "You know that by a single word I can decide the fate of the Community at this moment. I can prevail on them to remain . . . or I can decide for them to leave."[11]

Had the Sisters gone, they would have had their good Father Corbe with them, for Bishop Lefevre had made it clear that their welcome to Detroit included their chaplain. And Father Corbe himself had written to Father Martin, February 23, 1845, "If the Sisters go I shall follow them; that will be to the North." But God in His merciful designs had decreed the Sisters of Providence for Indiana, and the Diocese of Vincennes was not to lose one of its most zealous early missionaries, a learned and holy priest, a distinguished theologian, and a wise director of souls.

Father Corbe was born November 4, 1806, in the Diocese of Rennes, Brittany. In Baptism he received the name John, the Baptist being his patron. He was educated in the College of Rennes, where he developed a vocation to the priesthood. His ecclesiastical studies were made in the diocesan seminary, where he was ordained on Ember Saturday, of Pentecost week, 1832. He said his first Mass the following day, Trinity Sunday. His first assignment was to a professorship in the College of Rennes. At the same time he was private tutor to some children of the nobility.

Bishop Bruté, the first Bishop of Vincennes, having gone back to Rennes, his native city, in 1836, to procure missionaries for his needy diocese (in which at the time of his installation in 1834 he had found only one priest), brought back with him to Indiana nineteen colaborers. Father Corbe was one of that number. He pledged himself for only ten years,[12] but he never returned to his native land, having felt that he could do more for the interests of the Church and the welfare of souls as a foreign missionary. God spared him to this work thirty-six years.

[11] Letter of Father Corbe to Father Martin, February 1, 1846; in the Community archives.

[12] "Soon will be completed the ten years that I promised Bishop Bruté to remain in America." Letter of Father Corbe to Father Martin. No date given; probably early in 1846. Original in the Community archives.

Further details of his career are here subjoined, taken from a memoir written at the time of his death by one of the Sisters who did not sign her name:

"Father Corbe's first mission was St. Francisville, a little French settlement in Illinois, then in the diocese of Vincennes. For subsistence there he depended almost entirely upon his gun. When he shot any game, he would bring it home and hang it over the fireplace to cook while he went to say Mass. Bishop Bruté would often go to see him and take him some little refreshment and, perhaps, leave him a small donation. When Father Corbe would put his hand into his pocket, and find there a dollar, he would say smilingly, 'I am richer than I thought I was.' In relating to us the poverty in which he lived during the first years of his missionary life, especially at St. Francisville, he would add, 'But, oh, I was so happy in those days!'

"When concluding his sermon he never failed to say, 'Well, let us try to love God with all our heart.'

"Time rolled on, and Almighty God seeing the love our dear Father had for Him wished to perfect it by sending him sufferings. He Was attacked with rheumatism with which he was afflicted to the end of his life. During his last year his pains became excruciating; still, he edified all by his patience and charity. Whitsunday [1872] he said the Community Mass as usual, but the Bishop gave Holy Communion. Poor Father Corbe felt greatly humbled to have the Bishop wait on him. During the week he seemed a little better; however, on Trinity Sunday he said his last Mass, a low Mass. (He had said his first Mass on Trinity Sunday forty years before.) Oh, how he suffered during this, his last Mass. It took him an hour to say it. The grief which we felt cannot be expressed as we thought of losing him who was to us a spiritual father, who had watched over this Community for thirty years and instilled the lessons of virtue into the hearts of those who were here. . . .

"The feast of Corpus Christi came. He was preparing to say Mass. Seeing how weak he was, we urged him to go to bed and take some remedy. He replied, 'If I cannot say Mass on Corpus Christi, it is time for me to die, I have nothing more to do on this earth. I will ask our Lord to take me.' He soon became much worse and on Saturday evening received the last Sacraments. We asked for his

FATHER MARTIN
Consecrated First Bishop
of Natchitoches 1854

FATHER CORBE
Chaplain at Saint Mary-of-the-Woods,
1842–1872
Ecclesiastical Superior of
The Sister of Providence
1844 until his death in 1872

blessing. At first he refused, saying, 'I am not so sick as you think I am. I shall be better tomorrow, then I shall give it to you.' But, as we pressed him, he finally consented, and thereafter, even when unconscious, he had his hand continually extended in benediction over us. . . . His happy death occurred on Monday morning, the third of June."

Mother Anastasie, then Superior General, in her circular, which embraced many of the details here given, said besides: "While grieving over his loss, we cannot but gratefully thank our dear Lord for granting him all the spiritual assistance which the Church can give at the time of death. . . . We have no doubt it was a special grace vouchsafed to him as a recompense for the untiring zeal and tender charity which urged him to bring this solace to the sick, even when he could scarcely walk from excess of pain; as well as a reward for his ardent love of our Lord in the Blessed Sacrament. . . . Without the slightest struggle his holy spirit took its flight leaving its impress on his countenance which was radiantly serene and placid, his eyes and mouth naturally closed as if in a sweet peaceful slumber.

"On Tuesday evening the precious remains were borne in solemn procession to the chapel, where they reposed till noon on Wednesday, when they were conveyed to their last resting place.

"Our dear Father shrank from honor during life, but in death he received all that could be bestowed. His funeral obsequies were grand and imposing. There were twenty-three clergymen present, besides our beloved and bereaved Bishop, who officiated though almost overcome with emotion.

"After the Mass of Requiem the Vicar General, Father Bede O'Connor, a Benedictine, delivered a most touching and beautiful discourse on the virtues of our saintly Father. Sublime panegyric that it was, every one could feel that it was but the simple truth, yet falling short, far short, of the whole truth; for his true worth is known to God alone. The discourse was closed by inviting all present to join in saying for the soul of the departed five times the Our Father and Hail Mary in honor of the Five Wounds of our Lord.

"Then began the funeral procession, the coffin being borne by the members of the Sodality of the Passion from Terre Haute, who had volunteered their services. The body of our beloved and venerated Father rests in our little cemetery, according to his own expressed desire. He was all for us in life, so he wished to remain with us in death. As we have his body in our midst, let us strive to preserve amongst us his spirit by endeavoring always to be faithful to the holy lessons he taught us both by word and example."

Father Corbe was a man not only of profound thought and deep spiritual-mindedness, but of many-sided interests. When at leisure he was always with his books, a constant reader, a close student, especially of history and theology. Like his great friend Father Martin, nature had a strong appeal to him, and like him also, he delighted in excursions for geological specimens, which he added to the collection donated to the Academy by Father Martin. He was also fond of painting. With James Roquet, a parishioner of the village, an architect and builder and likewise an artist, many pleasant hours were spent with brush and pencil. Several sacred subjects done in oil, while not displaying professional skill, were at least fair specimens of creditable amateur work and artistic sentiment. Photography also attracted him. Writing to Mother Theodore, then visiting in Madison, he said (May 9, 1847); "I shall be glad if you would bring me from Louisville a small quantity of hyposulphite of soda. For your recompense I shall daguerreotype you on your return."

There was comparatively little leisure, however, for these pleasant diversions. From 1842 until 1865, besides having the care of the Community, Father Corbe was pastor of St. Mary's parish, which comprised all Vigo County west of the Wabash River. He had been made Vicar General by Bishop de St. Palais in 1849 and, during the Bishop's absence in Europe in 1851–52, he was Administrator of the diocese. He also accompanied the Bishop as theologian to the Seventh Provincial Council of Baltimore.

Writing from that city to Mother Theodore (May 8, 1849), he is still mindful of his charge: "The Sisters of Saint Mary's—I love to picture them to myself," he says, "praying to the Blessed Virgin, our good Mother, and their special protectress, with so much fervor and simple faith. Here we too pray to Holy Mary, and it is very gratifying for me to be a member of the Council where, by order of the Pope, the question concerning the dogma of the Immaculate Conception was decided. Yesterday the deliberations on this subject occupied the whole day; and now all the bishops of the entire world are going to be engaged with the same question. Undoubtedly it will be declared an article of faith. It is a happiness for me to contribute to the honor of the Blessed Virgin, at least by my official approbation. It gives me an occasion of returning thanks for all she has done for us at Saint Mary-of-the-Woods."

PART VI

LATER LETTERS
(1846-1856)

AMID the vicissitudes of the sorrow-burdened years, recorded in the foregoing pages, the institution at Saint Mary-of-the- Woods had been making fair progress. The boarding school was growing from year to year, the novitiate had an encouraging increase, and the missions were prospering.

Besides her duties as Superior General, Mother Theodore had the spiritual training of the early subjects, and when these went forth upon their missionary career she kept in touch with them by her pen. Her correspondence included, moreover, response to the many and varied claims of business, friendship, and courtesy. No one seems to have been overlooked, no message to have been forgotten, no detail too small to receive her attention. Her diary, as has been said, records nearly five thousand letters written by her; less than two hundred of these, however, have been recovered. The originals of nearly all the letters published in this volume are in the archives at Saint Mary-of-the-Woods. The exceptions are indicated as they occur.

As the formal endings used by Mother Theodore in addressing persons outside the Community are similar to those already given in earlier parts of this book, most of these endings will in future be omitted. Not to break the sequence of events described in Part V, some of Mother Theodore's letters of that period were passed over in the regular order of time. These will now find place with those that followed them.

TO THE REVEREND J. KUNDEK, JASPER

Saint Mary's, January 13, 1846

Monsieur le Missionnaire:

With heartfelt gratitude I have received the wishes you had the kindness to offer in the letter of December 22d with which you honored me. Mine for you were expressed in a letter to Sister St. Vincent, which she must have at present. You will learn from it that we frequently beg of Our Lord for you all the graces you need in order to keep your dear flock in the edifying fervor in which I beheld it.

I take this opportunity to thank you for the paternal kindness you show to our dear daughters of Jasper; we are, truly, deeply grateful. God will render you a hundredfold for what you do for the poor children of the forest of Indiana. Beg of Him to bless them and to make them Spouses according to His Heart by the practice of all the religious virtues. Ask the same especially for me, so destitute and yet in such great need of them. I have the greatest confidence in your prayers.

Please tell our Sisters that at last I have received their letters. I longed to have news of them. Poor Sisters! How very near they came to being cruelly punished for their negligence. [They had had a fire.] I hope that will make them more careful. I shall profit by the first occasion to send them things that they need, but I fear I shall not have the opportunity during the winter; so, perhaps they better buy what is indispensable. A thousand pardons for troubling you with these little details. That is what one gains by being good. . . .

TO THE SAME

Saint Mary's, August 17, 1846

Monsieur le Missionnaire:

It was not possible for me to answer you any sooner, our retreat ending only yesterday. Like yourself we have the happiness of possessing the precious relics of a holy martyr of Jesus Christ. It is an inestimable favor.

I thank you very much for the charity you have had in giving me the holy counsels contained in your letter. Now obtain for me grace to put them into practice. How much I am in need of help from above! Here I am, Superior again for my constant humiliation, and to cause some one, whom you know, to practice patience. In fine, I shall say again that *fiat* which sometimes costs so much. It costs much at the present moment to our good Sister Mary Margaret. His Lordship wished that she should be sent to St. Peter's; we did not think we ought to oppose him in that. Besides, you form so well your "Philotheas" in the ways of God that we are much pleased to give you our dear little Sister Seraphine, convinced that she will make progress under your direction.

The conditions that the Community proposes are the same as last year: first that you will give the property, or at least the use of the house occupied by the Sisters and its dependencies; secondly, that you will give the sum of one hundred dollars each year to the Sisters, and that you will leave them the profit of the schools whether German or American. Such has always been the rule. I thought I had already told you this and had written it to you. But it appears you did not understand me, or perhaps I did not explain myself well. I hope that this time there is no ambiguity in my words. The Sisters are not to give an account of the profit from their school to any one but to their Superiors.

On our side we engage ourselves to supply you with two Sisters capable of teaching German and English to the children of your congregation, and to receive gratuitously those belonging to indigent families, when you shall certify that they are unable to pay. The girls are received in our school at any age, but the boys cannot be received after they are thirteen years old.

If you give the house to the Community, it will take charge of the repairs and additions judged necessary; in the contrary case, such expenses will fall to your account.

I must close now to let Sister Marie Joseph say a few words to you. . . .

On the same sheet with Mother Theodore's letter, Sister Marie Joseph, the Superior of the mission, tells Father Kundek when he may expect his contingent for the coming year. She asks him to announce in church the next Sunday the opening of school on September first, and to say that boys over thirteen years of age will not be received. She adds though, that the boys of that age who had not made their First Communion would be permitted to attend religious instruction during the hour that it is given in the school, but must leave when it is over.

Referring to Sister Mary Margaret she adds: "As I had feared, I am obliged to return without my former companion. God does not wish me to lead so easy and sweet a life. That would be to gain heaven without the works of penance, and you know such is not what we can expect."

Again, but without date, though it must have been about this time, judging from Father Kundek's letters, Mother Theodore writes to him:

I cannot think that St. Joseph will let your work fail. We are making a novena for you. Please tell our dear Sisters that they know how interested everybody here at St. Mary's is in our first establishment. Prayer must make it prosper. I know nothing will be wanting as far as the good will of the Sisters you have is concerned. While they suffer from the coldness of those who ought to be devoted to them and to contribute to the welfare of the mission, so long as they have daily Mass and the Sacraments regularly, and experience your fatherly solicitude in many other ways, which they recognize with gratitude, I do not fear they will become discouraged or desire to discontinue their efforts. . . .

In an emergency trip to visit Sister Mary Liguori, seriously ill at Madison, Mother Theodore writes a hurried message enroute. Though begun at Edinburg, Indiana, the letter seems to have been finished in some other town—Columbus perhaps.

Edinburg, Oct. 28, 1846

My very dear Daughters:

Voyages, which are an image of life, are generally accompanied by a crowd of unavoidable contradictions; we are experiencing some just now. You know our great desire to hasten to our dear sick Sister. Well, we arrived here at Edinburg two hours after the departure of the steamboat. Last evening in the fear of delaying them we waited an hour and a half, expecting, listening, hoping, up to half-past five, the hour at which we finally learned that the stage had gone without thinking of the nuns.

As it was the fault of the agent we required that they furnish us a special carriage; but despite the swiftness of our horses, running thirty miles on a *Rail-road* [corduroy?] of Indiana, which sometimes caused us to ask ourselves if we were still entire in our individual being, we arrived only at 1:30 and the cars had gone before noon. Hence we are obliged to remain here until the return of the boat. I profit by the delay to write a few words and to ask you to send a prospectus to our bakery woman at Terre Haute. She is only waiting for that to send you her little girl. I bought butter at Mr. Smith's, next door to the bakery. Have Sister Olympiade send for it tomorrow by a boy on horseback.

I suppose John has told you to pen up the hogs; they would not now find food enough in the fields and would get thin. If you have not sufficient flour, empty the sacks and send the remainder of the wheat to the mill, sooner rather than later, for you know how long they kept us waiting. I suppose the oxen will be able to travel in a few days.

All who have not put on their heavy underwear must do so at once. The mornings and evenings are very cold. It was well I was inspired to bring my old cloak. I pray Sister Olympiade to be so kind as to see that our good Father Corbe has *all* his winter clothes in good condition, especially if he goes to Vincennes. It is very cold in the stages. Do not fail to offer my profound respects to this venerated Father, and tell him he must not have the fever while I am not there to give him his sweet doses. I also beg my dear Sisters of the Academy to see that the children are warmly clad.

The nearer I get to Madison the more my anxiety increases. Shall I find my poor dear Sister Mary Liguori alive? Loss of sleep and the rough roads of this route have disturbed my stomach a little, together with the hot bread and butter; but I am not sick. Those good little boiled squirrels at St. Mary's will quickly put me all right when I get there. I shall do everything possible not to return by this route; it is truly killing. Sister Augustine is somewhat consoled as to leaving you, but I have not succeeded in curing her entirely. I was too uneasy to be very amiable.

Pray much, especially during your retreat. I do not flatter myself that I shall have a spark of devotion left to celebrate the beautiful feast of our brothers in heaven; according to appearances, my piety will all have vanished.

At Indianapolis I saw Mrs. Drake. She received us very kindly. Ruth also; both send their kind remembrances to the Sisters at the Academy and to Sister Ann.

I am writing with an iron stick they call a pen, and am obliged to plunge it to the bottom of the bottle to get the ink, at the peril of my fingers—a great pity, is it not? You understand at least, my dearly loved Sisters, that I do not have to get down deep in my heart before finding the tender love that fills it for you all. . . .

The Mrs. Drake mentioned in this letter was the wife of General Drake, State Treasurer, who owned a hotel at Indianapolis. Their daughters, Ruth, Almeria, and Anna were pupils at Saint Mary-of-the-Woods from 1845 to 1857; Ruth for five years, Almeria seven, and Anna five, two at a time during some years. Almeria embraced the Catholic faith while at the Academy, her Baptism taking place June 23, 1850.

Sister Ann was a great favorite with the little girls. Their visits to her at the bakehouse were rewarded with cookies and milk, or fruit in season. Besides her generous treats, however, her religious influence gained their hearts. Radiant kindness, sweet humility, and happiness in hard labor left a lasting impression on all who knew her. She went to her reward on February 7, 1897, having passed fifty-five years in the religious life.

Though Mother Theodore returned home in November hopeful of Sister Mary Liguori's recovery, she was soon disillusioned. Sister's health continued to decline. She had contracted a cold in 1844 at St. Peter's, through exposure, and unable to procure needed remedies had become predisposed to lung trouble. Removed to Madison the same year, she grew stronger, but in the fall of 1846 her condition became critical.

On January 13, 1847, Mother Theodore wrote in her diary: "We receive the news that Sister Mary Liguori in a dying state left Madison on the 29th of December. We do not know what has become of her. The only consolation we have is to know that this poor Sister is accompanied by Rev. M. de St. Palais. Sister Mary Celeste also is with her."

On account of the rigor of the winter and the slow travel in stage coaches on almost impassable roads, the journey took over two weeks. Arriving finally at Terre Haute on January 14, 1847, the party found the Wabash River and the bottoms to the west covered with ice.

As soon as Mother Theodore learned of their arrival in the city she set out to get them. The roads were frightful. At the bottoms she had to leave the wagon and cross the frozen river, now nearly a mile wide, on foot. Of what followed she added in the diary: "Three times we endeavored to have our invalid taken over this sea of ice in a carriage, but we had to give it up and carry her in a chair. Four strong men rendered us this service with the greatest of difficulty, for it was almost impossible for them to keep on their feet. Finally, after much fatigue and all kinds of dangers, we were happy to see this dear invalid installed in our infirmary at Saint Mary's with our good Sister Seraphine who has been there two months."

Concerning Sister M. Celeste (Sophia Kennedy) here mentioned, a few words may be of interest. She had been a Sister of Charity of Emmitsburg stationed at Vincennes when those Sisters had a school in that city (1838-1843). She was a native of Ireland and belonged to the family of the Gill Publishing House of Dublin. She was well educated and could teach music. Learning that there was no music teacher among the Sisters at St. Mary's, and knowing, moreover, that the Sisters of Emmitsburg were to withdraw as soon as the Sisters of Providence should be able to take over the school at Vincennes, she offered herself, at the suggestion of Bishop de la Hailandière, to the new Community. The period covered by her vows having expired, she was free to make the change, though she always remained attached to her first Community. She arrived at Saint Mary-of-the-Woods on Christmas Day, 1841, brought by the Reverend Napoleon Perché of Portland, Kentucky, an ecclesiastic whom Mother Theodore had known in France.

A diary item of January 10, 1842, reads, "Sister Mary Celeste begins to teach music at the boarding school." (A "Music Master," no name given, had been employed the preceding year.) In 1844 she was one of the Sisters sent with Sister Mary Liguori to open the school at Madison. There she remained seven years. Transferred then to Fort Wayne she taught there ten years. The three succeeding years she was at Terre Haute, after which she was retained at Saint Mary-of-the-Woods to be engaged in literary work. She died at the Motherhouse December 12, 1878, her life of zealous labors and happiness in her new Community crowned with the esteem of all who had known her.

Of Father Perché, who had accompanied Sister Mary Celeste to St. Mary's, the diary item of January 6, 1842, says: "He remained here ten days during which time he gave us an instruction lasting an hour and a quarter every day upon our duties in the religious life. In leaving he made a present to us of an altar garniture, books, medals, etc. He left for New Orleans on the day of the Epiphany." In June of the same year a diary entry is: "The 15th we received a trunk from New Orleans full of things for our chapel. It is sent by Father Perché, a benefactor and friend of our House."

From time to time in after years, books and altar furnishings, a barrel of Mass wine, and "pictures of the Sacred Heart and of the Immaculate Heart of Mary, framed" were among his gifts to Mother Theodore. On one occasion he wrote: "I transport myself in spirit to your pretty little chapel of Saint Mary-of-the-Woods, uniting myself in heart with you and your daughters who pray with so much fervor, beseeching Our Lord that He would let fall on my poor soul some drops of those graces which He showers in torrents upon those souls so pure and so well prepared to receive them."

While stationed in Kentucky, Father Perché had been zealous in securing subjects for Saint Mary's; and in the far South, if he could not aid in the same way, his interest continued even after he became Archbishop of New Orleans.

Less than two weeks had passed after Sister Mary Liguori was brought home to the infirmary when, at the early age of twenty-nine years, she was called by the Master to the reward of her brief but fervent labors. Mother Theodore must now send out to the Community the first death circular from Saint Mary-of-the-Woods.

LETTER CIRCULAR

January 25, 1847

Our very dear Sisters:

In feelings of grief, the most keen and profound, we come to announce to you the loss we have sustained in the death of our dearly beloved Sister Mary Liguori Tiercin. It pleased God to take her away from our tenderness this morning at eight o'clock, after a cruel illness which she bore for three months and a half with a patience so heroic that she was the admiration of all who saw her upon her bed of suffering.

You will share our sorrow, very dear Sisters, for you tenderly loved this virtuous companion. The first tidings of her illness brought consternation to your hearts. You implored the Almighty with all the fervor of your souls to preserve her; several among you have even generously offered your lives to save hers (as you have told me in confidence). Notwithstanding, the Lord has been deaf to our supplications; He has not accepted our offerings.

Let us be careful now not to murmur against Him. In our having to give Him the first fruits of our Congregation, who, more than she, merits the honor of being chosen?

You are aware with what greatness of soul she advanced with a firm step in the constant practice of all the Christian and religious virtues, not of those that are only the product of a wrought-up fancy, but of those solid virtues that consist in fulfilling the obligations of one's state with all the perfection possible. You have seen her, very dear Sisters, practice with the most exemplary fidelity all the Rules of our Institute, which she loved so much. You have been witnesses of her charity, her zeal, her perfect obedience, her devotedness, her tender piety, and her courage. You have loved the noble candor and happy disposition which rendered her so dear to us all. You know that in everything she has been the model of a missionary Sister and of a true Daughter of Providence. She has been for me in particular, and very constantly, a subject of consolation, and has never given me a single instant of displeasure. Hence, her death has made in my soul a wound that will not be healed until we shall be reunited in heaven, where she now awaits us, I have the firm confidence.

If her life was edifying, her death was not less so. Would that I could reproduce in detail the circumstances that accompanied her last moments, give a sketch of the deep religious sentiments that she manifested up to her last breath. Let us content ourselves with saying that not only did she receive the Last Sacraments of the Church with faith and love, but all that accompanied her last sacrifice leaves no doubt but that her death was precious in the sight of God, and that she is now united to her dear and divine Spouse.

Let us not lose the stern but salutary lesson which we have received, my very dear Sisters. We all would wish to die as our beloved Sister Mary Liguori did. Let us live as she did and the same favor will be ours. A good life is the best preparation for a good death.

In our combats, our labors, and our tribulations, let us raise our eyes to heaven, our true country. Let us see there the crown that awaits us. That of our dear Sister Mary Liguori, we like to think, already graces her brow. Let us be courageous. The combat will not be long. Our turn will soon arrive. Death comes to cut down his first victims amongst us. His arm is still raised to immolate another. Dear Sister Seraphine is but waiting for the sign to follow the one who, only yesterday, was the companion of her sufferings, and with whom tomorrow she will be united in the bosom of God. How well prepared our dear Sister Seraphine is. She is so innocent and pure, it is impossible to look upon her without feeling a heavenly consolation. She ardently desires to die, especially since we have permitted her to take her vows. Soon her prayers will be heard.

Which of us shall be the first to follow her? I do not know. Perhaps it will be you, my daughter, who think it the least and who reckon upon your strength and your youth. Consider, I entreat you, that death sports with human calculations. The youngest and the most robust of the six who came to found this House has been taken. Let us always have in hand our lamps burning, that we may not be surprised. We urge you to make a very exact review of the dispositions of your souls on the day of the monthly retreat. Let us suffer nothing in ourselves that could trouble us ever so little in our last hour; thus, our death will prove to be but the begining of our eternal felicity.

Whatever reason we may have for hoping that our dear Sister is already in possession of her everlasting happiness, we must not cease to offer to God our prayers and supplications for the repose of her soul, for we know that nothing defiled can enter into the Kingdom of Heaven. Here we have fulfilled all the obligations that our holy Rules impose upon us, with much ceremony and a sort of veneration. We continue to pray for her, and you, dear Sisters, will unite with us in fulfilling faithfully Art. 224, Chapter 23 of our Rules.

Beg our Lord our Saviour since He has been pleased to call to Himself our dear Sister Mary Liguori that He would be pleased, also, to inspire some fervent and devoted souls to come to fill the immense void she has left in our Congregation. You, especially, above all, dear Sisters, be other Sister Mary Liguoris to us; that will be the way of consoling the broken heart of

Your affectionate,

SISTER ST. THEODORE,

Sup'r Gen'l.

The second sad announcement followed soon:

LETTER CIRCULAR

February 17, 1847

Our very dear Sisters:

As we had well thought, our good little Sister Seraphine did not long delay to follow Sister Liguori. On the first of February she received the Last Sacraments and after that she gradually declined. On the tenth she again received the Holy Viaticum; finally, Tuesday evening about eight o'clock she became much worse. We alone suffered in her agony; as for her, one thought, one desire occupied her soul entirely—to live until midnight that she might have the happiness of receiving her Saviour in Holy Communion.

With what solicitude she questioned us to know whether she was very sick! Poor child! When we remarked that since a single drop of water could not go down, she would not be able to swallow the Sacred Host, she replied with that charming simplicity and tender confidence which characterized her: "Mother, Our Lord will help me, I am sure I shall." She had us prepare her room and all that was necessary, and after midnight our good Father Corbe had the kindness to bring her Holy Communion. She swallowed the Sacred Host without difficulty. Her last act upon earth was to receive her God. A few moments later she went to finish her thanksgiving among the angels whose innocence she had imitated. For us, sinners, Lent is about to begin; for her it opens an eternity of joy; we do not doubt it.

Let us endeavor, my dear Sisters, to imitate the simplicity and openness of our dear Sister Seraphine. And if it is not granted to us to have her innocence and candor, let us try to efface by penance what is wanting in us in these respects. During the holy season of Lent we should apply ourselves particularly to acquire the spirit of interior mortification, which little by little destroys the old man in us and renders us more humble, more obedient, and more united to God.

Offer for the repose of the soul of Sister Seraphine the prayers prescribed by our holy Rules, and pray also for her who is, with true affection, all yours in Our Lord,

Sister St. Theodore,

Sup'r Gen'l.

Sister Seraphine Carroll, "Laughing Eliza," entered the novitiate July 28, 1842, at the age of sixteen years. She had been sent from Logansport by Father de St. Palais, who jestingly told her that she would never be permitted to laugh again if she became a Sister. Her amazement was amusing when, at the first general recreation, she heard gay laughter all around her.

Her first mission was in 1844 at Vincennes. There she remained two years. In August, 1846, she was assigned to Jasper, but succumbing soon to an affection of the lungs, she was recalled in November to Saint Mary-of-the-Woods. She had the happiness to take her vows on her deathbed, being then twenty-one years old, the age the Rule at that time required for profession.

In journeyings often, Mother Theodore now writes another letter en route.

TO THE SISTERS OF SAINT MARY'S

[No date.]

My dear Sisters,

Here I am at Terre Haute where I did not hear Mass, but I went to the church to make my meditation and to say my office. There I united with you in spirit during the Holy Sacrifice.

I went to Mr. Crawford's. As you know, two ladies of his family leave with me this morning between eight and nine o'clock for New Albany on the steamboat *James Ross*. I shall get Sister St. Vincent at Vincennes and, God helping, shall go to Madison on the same boat as it is freighted for Cincinnati. It is a very beautiful boat and seems to be very good.

I send you some meat by the butcher. He will go over tomorrow if he can, and he will give you this scribbling, which I doubt much that you will be able to read. The ink marks no better than dishwater. Perhaps it will become black in getting old.

I am very *fachée* at Finette [the mare]; she covered me with her miserable hairs. Fancy the effect on my beautiful habit. I believe I would willingly have given her to Mr. Crawford's mother, but the little rogue, guessing my thoughts, gave me so many caresses and showed herself so gentle that I was disarmed.

Good-bye, my too-dear Sisters; far from you my heart is sad. Let us meet in the Heart of Jesus, where I am entirely yours. . . .

TO THE REVEREND J. KUNDEK

Saint Mary's, The Holy Day of Easter, 1847

Reverend Sir and venerable Friend:

The duties of Holy Week have prevented me from writing to thank you for your kindness in taking Sister Augustine to Vincennes. May she there secure the health which she needs in order to fulfill the duties of the employment which Divine Providence has assigned her.

I am happy to learn that our two Sisters are doing what they can for the good of their schools. I beg of Our Lord to bless them. Truly the crosses of our venerated prelate are not all of gold. Let us pray for him, for the diocese, for that poor Ferdinand! What will become of it? What is my dear little girl doing in the midst of all these troubles? I am afraid she will lose her vocation, which I believe comes from God. After all I am ashamed of my want of faith and confidence. Is not the Divine Spouse of Virgins able to preserve this child? It would be blasphemy to think otherwise.

I rejoiced to learn that good Father Kutassi was better. I hope he will be well very soon. I hope, also that Our Lord has kept you from all harm during the holy season that has just passed away; you had so much to do for His glory. I beg of you, dear and venerated Pastor, to extend your zeal to me for I have such great need of the help of God. It seems to me that if I were really good all the Sisters would be so, too. I ought to be their model, and there are so many who march far ahead of me in the way of perfection.

I wish very much that you may be at Jasper when I go there. I expect to be there the third Sunday after Easter. Is

there any sure means of getting to Jasper from Evansville? Be
so kind as to answer me, and to address your letter to
Madison, where I am to be in ten or twelve days. . . .

Traveling southward by boat after visiting the Fort Wayne
mission, Mother Theodore writes:

TO SISTER ST. FRANCIS XAVIER, SAINT MARY'S

On the Canal, May 6, 1847
My very dear Sister:

Is it really true that you are well, even for you? I have terrible suspicions about your veracity in this respect. See what it
is to have deceived once, twice, twice-and-a-half and more. We
cannot help being diffident of such people.

I know, Sister St. Francis, yes, I know well that you love me,
that you love me more than you love the others—that is understood; let us say nothing more about it.

I am very anxious to be at Madison where I expect to find
news of you. I shall be glad especially to know whether your
health, Sister Mary Cecilia's and, in general, everybody's is
good. I wish much also to know something of our very dear
Father Corbe—whether he continually carries his cross, and
whether the promises of His Lordship made no impression on
his soul nor shook his resolution; but, especially whether the
Bishop continues to be unfavorably disposed. Give me details
on all these points. Give me also the advice you judge useful for my sojourn in that dreaded city—Vincennes! Before
addressing your letters there, get Sister Mary Cecilia to seal
them for you in a way that they cannot be opened. We never
know into whose hands they may fall.

The establishment of Fort Wayne is not doing very well. The
Superior is too exacting with her Sisters, and she shows some

distrust. As she does not open her heart freely to them, theirs remain cold. She would obtain much more by requiring less. But who is perfect in this world of misery and imperfection? Sister Mary Magdalen has a great infirmity and is very feeble; she had one of her attacks last Sunday during high Mass, She got up and went towards the altar. That has happened several times. Everybody knows that she has epilepsy. It is truly sad. If you obtain the cure of this dear child, well, then, I shall have confidence in your relics; but, my dear Sister St. Francis, if you do not obtain it I shall not have any.

Have you any important letters since my departure? In any case keep them. I shall not be long at Vincennes if I am permitted to leave when I wish. How much I regret the time we spend on these boats or away from our houses. I do not think Fort Wayne can be visited every year until the ways of travel become easier; anyhow, I shall not go back next year.

There is here on the boat a Sister of——in disguise. Her efforts not to be known, however, are not very successful. But she is a good daughter. I feel more fervent in praying with her. We are yet one hundred miles from Cincinnati. I shall mail my letters there. Always as ever in Jesus and Mary. . . .

Whatever may have been Mother Theodore's apprehensions regarding "that dreaded city—Vincennes," she could scarcely have foreseen that the climax of her trials would be reached so soon. Only two weeks were to pass. But that story has been told at length in the preceding Part V. Mother Theodore was back again with her Community at Saint Mary's, the new Bishop was awaited, and the annual retreat for the Sisters was approaching.

During this time, the summer of 1847, there was a rumor in Indiana concerning a new Vicar General as well as a new Bishop. In regard to it Father Corbe wrote to Father Martin: "Some one told me, and even Bishop de la Hailandière himself said it, that Bishop Bazin would bring you back with him to be his Vicar General. Oh, would that it were so! Oh, if the good God would but deign to add this new favor to the other which He has granted to our prayers, then I would believe that He has not abandoned this mission of Indiana!" Mother Theodore now speaks on the same subject.

TO THE REVEREND A. MARTIN, NEW ORLEANS, LA.

Saint Mary-of-the-Woods, August 17, 1847

My good Father,

In learning of our late trials and the manner in which Our Lord has extricated us, you must have said: There is a Providence and the Sisters at Saint Mary's are truly Its daughters. I thank you with all my heart for the interest you have so kindly taken in all our troubles. Oh, if you but knew the happiness you have procured for the poor afflicted ones! I hope that this joy is awaiting you and that one day we shall have part in it.

A new era is beginning for the Diocese of Vincennes. Will it be one of happiness? If you would only return we might hope for peace, unknown so long in our cold Indiana. We are asking this favor of Our Lord. Perhaps He has already granted it, since we are asking it through Blessed Mary. Are we not her well-beloved children? Oh, yes, Father, we shall have you again. Is not the Church of Vincennes your cherished spouse, for which you left everything. Oh, with what joy it would welcome you back!

I do not know when the new Bishop will arrive, nor what he will do for our Congregation. Without doubt he will have heard enough to have given him strong prejudices against us. Well, no matter! I have confidence in the future. The One who took up our defense will protect us again. His arm is not shortened.

I did not think it necessary to write to His Lordship. We shall see him at Vincennes. Oh, but Father Corbe is good!

So devoted! His firmness has saved our Congregation. Is it not almost a miracle? Under what colors has not he himself been represented! After all, our only support, our only strength is God. I hear you say: My daughter, He suffices.

I have not found any opportunity to send the twenty dollars we owe to the Vicar General of New Orleans. If you were rich I would beg you to pay him for me, and I would settle up when we meet. To be frank, I cannot pay it now. We are bankrupt. Our retreat will begin next Sunday. We have no retreat master. Father Corbe will have to give it. Father Lalumière will help him to hear the confessions. The Sisters have arrived from the missions. They are all around me making a great noise. All offer you their respects and recommend themselves to your prayers. Our Father assures you of his friendship. He says he is going to write to you soon, but I say do not count on it too surely. He is always inclined to his pet sin [procrastination].

Adieu, dear Father Martin. Pray for your daughter and give her your blessing. . . .

In the letter next presented appears the name of another friend of the Community, the Reverend J. P. Bellier, a Eudist. Father Bellier was president of the College of St. Gabriel at Vincennes, and as the College could not support itself he was unable to meet his obligations. He was struggling with debts incurred by his predecessor in purchasing the property and also by himself through improvements made on it. In this difficulty he besought Bishop de la Hailandière to assume the debt, but the matter was not arranged and he had to seek aid beyond the diocese.

In a letter to Mother Theodore written from Louisville, Kentucky, September 26, 1847, Father Bellier spoke of the haste in which he was obliged to leave Vincennes, and added, "I shall not leave America before having paid, through one means or another, every cent that I owe." But only three months would pass, however, before Bishop de la Hailandière's successor, Bishop Bazin, would write to Mother Theodore: "Yesterday I took upon myself a very heavy cross by assuming all the debts of the Eudists. I had to do so or see our holy religion brought into disgrace by the bankruptcy of St. Gabriel's College, which was to be disposed of by the sheriff on the 8th of January."

Mother Theodore's letter mentioning Father Bellier was addressed to one of her companions from France, until now always at St. Mary's, but at present stationed temporarily at Vincennes:

TO SISTER MARY XAVIER

Saint Mary's, September 25, 1847

My poor dear Sister:

I suspect you have enough of mission life and that you would like just as well to be at Saint Mary's, at the risk of meeting with some of the difficulties you left behind. I have often told you, my poor child, that a change of place or of employment is only a change of miseries. These exist everywhere, for our true country is not here below. We are in exile; let us never forget it. I am happy that you can have your Communions. When we have our good God with us we are strong.

I do not doubt you were sorry to find that our dear Father Corbe left Vincennes without going to see you. He could not do so without running the risk of remaining over some days longer. He did not have any too much pleasure there, I can assure you. He feared His Lordship would prevent him from returning, which would have been a great misfortune for us. This good Father sends you his kindest regards. He loves you sincerely in Our Lord. All our Sisters send a thousand loving messages.

I knew that you would be very much surprised to see Sister St. Francis, but I knew, also, how glad you would be. *For God and the welfare of our Sisters, you know, we must be ready to make any kind of sacrifice.* I am sure you will take all possible care of the health of our dear Sister St. Francis; on this account I send her. If you were not at Vincennes I could never have made up my mind to let her go.

I pity poor Father Bellier. How he must suffer! If I were in his place I would not remain in America. Perhaps in a few days, I, too, shall be banished; but he does not leave behind him as many orphans as I shall have to leave. Ask Father Chassé to offer my respects and sympathy to the poor exile when he writes to him. Present also my profound respects to good Father Chassé and say I thank him sincerely for the interest he takes in our Community. I should be much pleased both to see and hear him.

Remember me kindly to Dr. Baty and his wife. Eliza arrived in very good health and spirits. She seems happy and sends love to all. Offer my respects also to Mr. Hayes and family. Alice is well and will become accustomed to school life after awhile, but it is hard for her to be away from home. She is worried about her good mother. She sends much love to you all.

Do not be discouraged about the school. God will help you. Tell me the exact amount Father Chassé lent you. Sister Marie Joseph is in a bad state of health, but it is believed she is not in danger. . . .

TO THE RIGHT REVEREND J. BOUVIER, BISHOP OF LE MANS

Saint Mary-of-the-Woods, Indiana

December 4, 1847

My very dear Father:

It seems that God wishes to render His gifts still dearer to us by causing them to pass through your hands before reaching us. I have just had a new proof of this. Your good letter of October 30th came to Bishop Bazin on the last day of November. He hastened to send it to us with the greatest protestations of devotedness for our Congregation and for myself in particular. I am sending you his letter that you may judge of the effect of your recommendations.[1]

Good and venerated Father, how shall we ever express to you our gratitude? Without you where should we be now? And so the most pressing desire of the hearts of your Daughters of the Woods is to pray for you with all the fervor of which they are capable, not only on the first of the year, but every day of their lives. Oh, could you but know, my Lord, all the petitions we address to Heaven for your happiness, it would be a little satisfaction; but, after all, God knows it well.

The tribulations which have afflicted our Community have produced very precious fruits. Besides the admirable union that exists between persons of different nationalities, of dispositions so opposite, some well informed, others without education, there is also among the Sisters a great spirit of faith, of piety, and a confidence in God which goes as far, I believe, as it can go. Could you see with what confidence and perseverance they ask of God all that they wish to obtain, you would be touched. I can assure you they know how to pray. And, indeed, they have never asked for anything which they have not obtained. I, myself, often put their zeal to the test. As I was preparing to go to Vincennes with several of the Sisters to assist at the consecration of our new Bishop, I was attacked, as last spring, with inflammation of the lungs. At the end of three days they despaired of my life. But here I am again on foot, though very weak and unable to render any service to the Community. As it is the beginning of winter I fear I shall remain a long time in this state; but—whatever God wills!

[1] Original letter of Bishop Bazin to Mother Theodore, November 3, 1847, in the archives of the Diocese of Le Mans.

My illness has deprived me of seeing Bishop Bazin, but, from what I am told by persons who have seen him, I am led to hope that better days will soon dawn for Indiana, and in particular for our Congregation. It is said he has much of the kindness of Bishop Bruté, though not his talents. No one regrets that he has not such preëminent gilts. He is pious, humble, and of an amiable simplicity. He seems also to have a very tender heart. Everyone believes that he will do much good.

All our establishments are progressing. The number of pupils is everywhere increasing, except here at the Academy where we have only thirty-one boarders this year. Sister St. Francis Xavier has been ill since her return from Vincennes. She is better now, though still very weak. Both of us put together do not make a half. She offers you her profound respects, as do all your other daughters. Deign to bless them and to remember them before God. Be so kind, above all, as to pray for me, so very needy.

If you should have occasion of seeing our Mothers of Ruillé, may I beg of you, my Lord, to remember me to them? I shall write as soon as I shall have seen Bishop Bazin.

It appears that Bishop de la Hailandière has gone. His sacrifice has cost him much. He is very unhappy. I entreat you to pray for him. I hope he will be better out of Vincennes. It is said he will be canon of St. Denis. If that is so, I shall bless God for it with all my heart.

You will see by my letter that I write with difficulty, and will excuse my scribbling and the rest. All our Sisters beg of me to present to you their homage and to ask for your paternal blessing. . . .[2]

After the consecration of Bishop Bazin on October 24, 1847, Bishop de la Hailandière stayed at the episcopal resi-

[2] Original in the archives of the Diocese of Le Mans.

dence for nearly two months. "He was determined to remain at Vincennes," wrote Father Corbe to Father Martin, January 4, 1848, "and was building a fine house for himself called 'Highland' on the road to Petersburg, two miles from Vincennes." And the *Annals* say: "He told his friends that Bishop Bazin would have the spiritual authority only, but that he would reserve the temporal for himself." Such proposals not being acceptable to Bishop Bazin, Bishop de la Hailandière finally left Vincennes, December 13, 1847, and spent the winter in Philadelphia.

On his way to France from Vincennes he made brief sojourns in Louisville, Madison, Pittsburgh, and New York. "Arrived in Philadelphia," says Alerding, "he had already heard of the death of his successor, and consoled some of his former clergy by announcing to them the probable appointment of one of their own number whom he would not name (Dr. St. Palais). In New York, he made with Bishop Hughes, arrangements which he thought final, for the publication he had at heart—that of the life of his ever loved, ever honored predecessor, Simon G. Bruté—and entered the vessel which was to convey him back to France, a Bishop without a See."[3]

The Bishop went to his ancestral home, Triandin, a short distance from Combourg, Brittany. There he dwelt in retirement for nearly thirty-five years, assisting other bishops when called upon from time to time, in preaching, confirming, and ordaining. He died May 1, 1882, at the age of eighty-four and was buried in the parish church of Combourg. In the fall of the same year, during the episcopate of Bishop Chatard of Vincennes, the remains were brought back to Indiana by the nephew of the deceased Bishop, the Reverend Ernest Audran, pastor of Jeffersonville, Indiana, and on November 22, 1882, were placed beside those of the three other Bishops of Vincennes—Bruté, Bazin, and de St. Palais—in the little chapel under the sanctuary of the Old Cathedral.

It will be recalled that Bishop Bazin visited Saint Mary-of-the-Woods at the end of January, 1848, and was much concerned about the health of Mother Theodore. Shortly before his arrival she had been stricken with what she herself calls "inflammation of the lungs." It was not until April that her

[3] *The Diocese of Vincennes*, p. 179.

health warranted her to travel. On the fourteenth, accompanied by Sister Mary Cecilia, she set out to begin the annual visitation of her houses. Arriving at Vincennes she found Bishop Bazin seriously ill and hastened to inform the Sisters at Saint Mary's.

TO SISTER ST. FRANCIS XAVIER

Vincennes, April 16, 1848

My beloved Sister:

I write you only a few lines today to tell you news that will afflict your heart, as it does mine. Our good Bishop is very sick. He has been sick since the beginning of Lent, but worse the last two weeks. This, however, did not prevent him from preaching in his turn and in that of Father Audran, who is not strong. Though the good Bishop was already quite indisposed, on Saturday he spent six consecutive hours in the confessional. While there he was taken with a violent fever which obliged him to go to bed. Doctor Baty saw him this morning and found him very sick. I can tell you nothing from my own observation, because he does not wish us to go to see him, but everybody finds him in a serious condition. Pray much for him. It would be an immense loss if he should die, and especially would it be sad if he went suddently, as the good Bishop Quarter did, who died before it was known that he was sick.

Angelique, too, has pneumonia. Jeannette is alone to attend to all these, to do the cooking, and to take care of the sacristy.[4] Imagine what she has to do. There are a great many sick here. On of our boarders was in danger but she is better today. Sister Marie Joseph and Sister Augustine are better also, and I think now they are out of danger. I am not very well myself, having had to leave church during high Mass. Perhaps I shall be better soon.

[4] Angelique and Jeannette, French servants at the Cathedral rectory.

Our journey was fairly good, except that we could not sleep, thinking ourselves nearly arrived at Vincennes. I believe that it is owing to the sleepless night that I feel so miserable.

Sister Mary Cecilia says a thousand nice things to you. All the Sisters send much love to all, first of all to our venerated Father Corbe. I shall write to him when I dare do so. Tell him not to persevere in the way in which he was when he said he did not pray for me any more, for truly I have great need of prayers. I am quite a grumbler. No matter; even in these bad days I love you all very much. . . .

Their worst apprehensions were quickly realized. On Palm Sunday Bishop Bazin was judged to have pneumonia. One week later the Sisters learned of the fatal issue and received the detailed account written by Mother Theodore.

TO THE SISTERS AT SAINT MARY'S

Vincennes, The Holy Day of Easter, 1848

How painful it is, my dear daughters, to fulfill the duty that devolves upon me today! You will hardly believe the sad news that I must announce to you. Alas! it is none the less true. He is dead, our worthy prelate, our dear and venerated Father, our Bishop, John Stephen Bazin! Only a few hours ago we assisted at his death, which was so edifying, so Christian, and received his last sigh. He gave us for you his last blessing. It will be for us a precious heritage.

Had you been here, my dear Sisters, during that cruel illness which in eight days took our dear father away from us, and which he bore with so much patience—had you been here, especially last evening when he received the Last Sacrament, you would have been touched at the burning words that came from his loving and charitable heart. I wish never to forget them!

Do not think, my dear daughters, that because you were far away he forgot you. No, every day he spoke to me of you. He was occupied about you even during his great sufferings. Some moments after receiving Extreme Unction he called me to his bedside to say, among other things: "Assure all your dear Sisters that I tenderly love your Congregation. If I were to live longer I would not spare any sacrifice for its prosperity, spiritual or temporal. Assure them such was my intention." A half hour before his death he again proved how truly paternal were his sentiments toward us.

We must not dissemble it, my dear daughters, our loss is immense and can have for us the most serious consequences; however, let us take care not to become discouraged. Let us submit with love to the will of God. He is never more a father than when He afflicts His children. He has always protected us; if we love Him He will never abandon us. Especially let us never forget that if we wish to die like the Saints we must live like them. Let us force ourselves to imitate their virtues, in particular humility and charity, of which virtues Bishop Bazin gave us such rare examples; for by the continual practice of these two virtues we shall be recognized as the daughters of this holy prelate, who was so humble and so filled with love for his brethren.

Although we may have the firm confidence that the one we mourn is already possessing eternal joy, nevertheless, we must offer our prayers to God in whose sight even the angels are not pure, so that if He finds some stains in the soul of this His elect, it will soon be admitted to union with its God Whom it loved so well. To this end you will fulfil faithfully the 98th article of the Rule, Chap. XIII.

Easter Monday—

I do not know what I wrote yesterday, my poor daughters. Did I give you any details about his last moments? I do not think so. I was writing to you or to our good Father Corbe on Holy Saturday when they came for me to go and open a vein for him. At five o'clock I found the Bishop more oppressed. He had me count his pulse; it was about 120. He told me he wished to see the doctor. I sent at once for him. Then he asked for Father de St. Palais and Father Audran. They were with him until six o'clock regulating the temporal affairs, after which he made his confession. At seven o'clock he received the Holy Viaticum. He spoke to us in English. Oh, if you had heard with what ardor he spoke, he who was charity itself. We were bathed in tears. We were in his room with the priests, accompanying the Blessed Sacrament with lights, when he received Extreme Unction. Father de St. Palais asked his blessing for all. Then he spoke again in English, the death rattle mingling with the sound of the words of this dear dying one who spoke so tenderly, with such difficulty, owing to the pressure on his chest. He finished by giving pontifical benediction; that was the last act of this kind. They then withdrew.

I remained with a few others. Sister Joachim and I stayed until eleven o'clock. The doctor wanted me to leave sooner but I did not wish to go. It was now impossible for me to hold out any longer. The doctor also went to rest. I threw myself on my bed but I could not sleep. Too uneasy to stay there longer, Sister and I got up at three o'clock and went back to his room. I feared he was dead. But no, he was even a little better. Father de St. Palais was alone with him. He asked who entered. He was told it was I. A little later, after I had given him a drink, he said I must go to rest; and a short time after, seeing me on my knees, he said that we did not need to tire ourselves praying continually for him, as some elevations of the heart sufficed.

Later he told me that he claimed our prayers, not that he merited them, but that he depended on our generosity, etc.

Finally, about half-past five o'clock, he called me loudly by my name and said: "Do not call your Sisters for this scene, it is too painful; they will suffer too much. There is no further hope. I hope only in God."

Five minutes before expiring, with a hand cold in death, and trembling in the cold sweat that always accompanies the last effort of nature struggling against dissolution, he blessed us—Father de St. Palais, Father Chassé, Dr. Thomas, Sister Joachim, and myself. In a few moments his soul had returned to its Creator. I had left the room at six o'clock to give your letters and some directions to the man who was to take them, and to pay him. I returned at once just in time to receive the Bishop's last blessing.

I shall have a great many edifying particulars to relate when we are together again. The Bishop died at 6:20 a. m. They say he will not be buried until Thursday. His parlor has been made into a mortuary chamber. Our Sisters are very tired, and I also. This letter must be for yourselves alone, for there is so little order in my thoughts I doubt that you can understand me. Sister Olympiade would say that I have *fatigue fever*. . . .

TO THE RIGHT REVEREND J. BOUVIER, BISHOP OF LE MANS

Vincennes, April 24, 1848

My Lord:

I have to pay very dear today for the joy I had in writing you my last letter. This one will afflict your heart. Mine is broken.

It is almost in the light of the funeral tapers burning near the mortal remains of Bishop John Bazin, that I trace, in weeping, these few lines to you.

Yes, my Father, he is dead, this venerable prelate who in six months had healed so many wounds, and whose loss inflicts such a deep wound in the hearts of all those who have known him, but more particularly in those of his poor Daughters of the Woods whom he protected with such paternal kindness, and whom he leaves once more without a support and a protector. How God tries our poor diocese! What will become of it? Nevertheless, we shall not cease to hope, for He Who had protected us with so much love dies not. He will still protect us. Besides, we have the firm confidence that the one over whom we weep will intercede for us in heaven, where I hope he already is or, at least, will soon be. The sublime virtues he practiced with such perfection until the end do not allow a doubt of it. I should never have known him well, if Providence had not afforded me the occasion of being with him during his last moments.

Wishing to make the visitation of our establishments, it was agreed with this good Father that we should begin with Vincennes. On Friday in Passion week, we took a steamboat at Terre Haute, which brought us to Vincennes that night. The next morning we assisted at the Mass of the Bishop who gave us Holy Communion. As soon as he had finished his thanksgiving (which always lasted a half hour at least) he came to welcome us. He seemed so happy to see us. There were there three of us who had been extremely ill this winter. He felt happy and rejoiced that we were better. "You must take good care of yourselves," he said; "your little Congregation is too young to lose you; besides, you are not ripe for heaven, my children, you have too much work to do yet," etc., etc.

Later, having some particular business to treat of, I went alone to see him. I found him, as usual, extremely well disposed towards our House. I told him you were happy to learn that he approved our conduct, and that our Mother had just written me that every one at Ruillé was delighted that we now had so kind a Father, I said, too, that this good Mother recommended me to be very submissive, and that I was prepared to follow her advice with all my heart. He took occasion in this conversation to speak of a matter about which His Lordship and the Community did not quite agree, without there being anything serious on either side, His Lordship having simply manifested to the Community his desire of proposing the election of a Superior General, and the Community believing this action unnecessary. The question was put off until Easter, at which time the Bishop was to go to Saint Mary's and begin there the visitation of his diocese. My intention was to make known to him the reasons the Sisters believed they had for not holding an election; they were disposed, however, to obey the Bishop if he continued to desire it after their explanation. This had been spoken of at Saint Mary's and Father Corbe had written to him on the subject some days before, begging His Lordship not to say anything about it to the Sisters until he could see him, and assuring him that they would understand each other perfectly when they should meet. All this was planned at Saint Mary's without my knowledge. I only knew that they wished to present their reasons to His Lordship when he should make his proposals. I was pained at it. I spoke of it to our Mother in a letter written some days before my departure for Vincennes.

This good Father said to me: "I have a letter from the Reverend J. Corbe; he objects to an election." He gave me the letter. Our former Superior [Bishop de la Hailandière] had told him, he said, that I had a letter of Obedience, which ought to be consulted before acting. "How is this letter expressed?" His Lordship asked. I repeated the first sentence, which appointed me Superior of the establishment and Superior of all the houses which should be formed later on, etc. He turned toward me, saying: "You are, then, Superior General? You never told me that! I wished to give you the title, which I deemed necessary in order to give more weight to your authority. Besides, I was saying the other day to your Sisters of Vincennes, that they owed you this mark of confidence after all you had suffered; but since this action is useless, let us say no more about it." You see, dear Father, all the difficulties were removed at once.

Alas! this state of peace was not of long duration. In the afternoon at two o'clock on Saturday in Passion Week the Bishop went to the confessional. He left it only at eight o'clock. He had preached two or three times a week during Lent, although he had a bad cold. His zeal was truly apostolic. On leaving the confessional he was attacked by a high fever which obliged him to go to bed. On the morning of Palm Sunday they called the physician, who exhausted all the resources of his art to effect his cure. I was so fortunate as to be able to render some service, thereby having the opportunity of discovering in the dear patient some very precious qualities. Particularly did I admire two virtues very rare in our days, a profound humility and an immense charity. It was especially in his last moments that these virtues shone with the greatest lustre.

I shall never forget what he said before receiving the Last Sacraments. We were eight Sisters there at that moment. We accompanied the Blessed Sacrament bearing lights, The Superior of the Seminary was also there, as well as several other priests. With what fire he spoke, disclosing a heart burning with love for all without exception! Every one melted into tears. Nothing was heard but suppressed sobs mingling with the death rattle of the dying prelate. Then he called me to his bedside, gave me his blessing for the Community, and said: "Do tell your Sisters that I love your Congregation tenderly. God knows that were I to live longer I would shrink from no. kind of sacrifice for its spiritual and temporal prosperity. Assure them that such were my desires and intentions." This was Holy Saturday at seven in the evening. With one of the Sisters I remained till after eleven o'clock; he then sent me to rest and the doctor also insisted on my leaving. I returned at three o'clock in the morning. Several times he expressed the interest he bore towards us. Notwithstanding his state of agony, he was occupied more about others than about himself. He conversed with God continually by fervent colloquies. How pious he was! What a beautiful soul! Towards six o'clock he grew worse. We were now only five persons in his room—the Vicar General, another priest, the doctor, Sister Joachim, and myself. He asked us to pray for him. We sank to our knees around his bed. Having prayed some minutes, we received his last blessing, which he gave with a hand trembling and already cold in death. We had but a few minutes longer to possess him here below. At 6:20 on Easter morning, he breathed his last.

Scarcely was his death made known than the grief it caused became general. Protestants as well as Catholics are in great consternation. All weep as if they had lost a father.

We prepared a mortuary chamber where he is now exposed to the veneration of the faithful. There is an altar in this room, upon which the Holy Sacrifice was offered several times this morning. He will be interred only on Thursday, in order that his priests may have time to reach Vincennes. I sent a dispatch to Father Corbe. His Grace, the Archbishop of St. Louis,[5] and the Right Reverend Bishop of Cincinnati[6] sent word by telegraph that they will be here for this sad ceremony. It is six months today since they consecrated him.

Pardon me for sending you these long details, and so badly written; but I have been disturbed so often, and I have not the time to re-write my letter. I rely on your usual indulgence. I have heard from Saint Mary's; all are well. What a stroke for them when they learn of this death.

[5] The Most Reverend Peter Richard Kenrick, D. D.
[6] The Right Reverend John Baptist Purcell, D. D.

May I beg of you, my Lord, to send this letter to our Mothers of Ruillé? I offer my profound respects and entreat them not to fail to pray for our worthy Bishop. What is becoming of your Republic? I fear it will end badly. Adieu, my Father. Be pleased to give your blessing to your poor and much afflicted daughter in Our Lord. . . .[7]

LETTER CIRCULAR

Saint Mary-of-the-Woods, July 14, 1848

My very dear Daughters,

Notwithstanding the trials through which it has pleased Our Lord that we should pass, He has deigned to bless our Congregation. It has grown in the shadow of the Cross, which still covers it, and we hope that our Heavenly Father will never deprive us of this precious mark which distinguishes His children and His works.

It is time to begin to organize ourselves, as much as possible, according to our Rules and Constitutions. My duties have multiplied to such an extent that it is impossible for me to fulfill them. I feel deeply the need of sharing a burden which I can no longer carry alone.

Having seriously weighed the matter before God, I come, my very dear daughters, to beg you to choose from among you a Sister who has the spirit of her state and your confidence, to give me as my First Assistant. Another office, not less important, that of Mistress of Novices, must also be filled. The person having the charge should have the graces as well as the obligations of the office.

You understand, without doubt, how important these first nominations are. On them depend the success and all the future of a work which is the highest object of our hopes, and which has already cost so many sacrifices. Prepare your-

---

[7] Originals in the archives of the Diocese of Le Mans.

selves, then, for this great action by fervent prayers and Communions. I would do you an injustice to fear that in your choice you would be influenced by any other motives than the glory of God and the good of a work for which you have sacrificed so much.

Through a special privilege granted by our venerated Father Corbe, all the Sisters who made their vows at the retreat of 1845 are eligible, as well as all those whose profession was anterior to that date. Conformable to Chapter II, paragraph 20, of our Constitutions, the Professed Sisters will give, in sealed billets and not signed, their observations upon the two persons who seem to them suited to fulfil the offices of which I speak.

I am expecting a letter from Father de St. Palais, to learn from him what day next month our retreat will begin. Whatever the date may be, come as soon as you have everything in order, and console by your presence the one who loves you very tenderly in our Lord,

SISTER ST. THEODORE,

Sup'r Gen'l.

The election resulted in the choice of Sister Mary Cecilia as First Assistant and Sister St. Francis Xavier as Second Assistant and Mistress of Novices.

The next letter is the first of several written by Mother Theodore to one of her companions from France, who up to this time had always been at St. Mary's and, since 1842, had been directress of the Academy. She had performed also the duties of purchaser and general overseer of the buildings and grounds.

TO SISTER BASILIDE, MADISON

October 16, 1848

My dearly beloved Daughter:

I have just received your letter. How grieved I am about our poor Sister Alphonse. What a pity you did not send her during the fine weather. But the thing is done. Now beg of God that it may turn out for the best for our sick one. I shall wait until I have seen Father de St. Palais before speaking of a substitute. But where shall we find one? How poor we are, my daughter, how poor we are. Our dear Sister Mary Cecilia is no better. May God have pity on us!

Be very guarded, my daughter, in your words and actions, also in your affections. Be careful lest you show more affection for one pupil than for another; this would produce a bad effect among the children, since all wish to be loved by you. I say this by way of precaution, knowing the *gluey* nature of your poor heart, and the danger there is for you when coming in contact with persons who are amiable and educated.

I received a long letter from C——; not too bad for her. Bear with her, consult her from time to time; your charity will have its reward.

You cannot imagine how we suffer from your being absent. The whole family of swine have taken up their abode in the Academy grounds, the fences are down, the gates broken and left open; in fine, there is great disorder. "Where is Sister Basilide? We miss Sister Basilide badly," Father Corbe said the other day. It is not the first time he complained, and his complaints find an echo. Poor Sister Basilide! I, too, miss you very much. How happy we shall be in heaven where we shall never have to part. . . .

TO THE SAME

Saint Mary's, November 20, 1848

Good and dear Sister Basilide:

I thought I could tell you many things this morning, and write a long letter, but I am obliged to leave immediately for Potsville, and from there go to Terre Haute. I could not tell you all the trouble the house in Terre Haute is giving me. The work does not advance rapidly, notwithstanding that in a few days we shall have to open school there. Pray God that He may bless it. Sister St. Vincent is often low-spirited. I do not know what will become of her there. [She was to be the Superior.]

One of our little boarders is very ill of pneumonia—one of those I brought from Vincennes. She is an only daughter and has to die far, very far from her mother. You can imagine in what state this puts me, knowing how uneasy I always get in such circumstances. Oh, how much I have prayed, how much we all have prayed! You also will pray. This is the fifth day of her illness. She is not worse, which means, perhaps, that she is better.

I cannot answer your whole letter this morning. I am glad that you received the letter of poor Sophie. How easy it is to throw that child into a bad way. I wrote to her Saturday. I did not reproach her—that is not the way of doing anything with her—she must be taken by her affections. She tells me your partiality for Miss Duplessis did so much harm to the school that there is diffculty in keeping the pupils. I do not know to what extent this accusation is true, but I pray you, for the love of everything, to try to put an end to it. You know how easily offended children are.

Without believing you as culpable as is supposed, I am a little afraid you are not entirely free from some blame. You seem to take the part of that young lady very easily. Believe me, my dear Sister Basilide, you have to distrust your own heart very much—you know that well. It is very probable that the aversion others show for this girl is only the natural feeling that everybody has *for*, or rather *against*, those preferred to others. Show her less affection and soon they will show her more.

What weakness in our poor and miserable nature! How happy we shall be in heaven, my poor Sister Basilide! But before we get there we must suffer. Now, my dear daughter, make every effort to prevent that young girl seeing anything cold on your part towards those who disapprove you. And do not speak of what I tell you. I pray you, my dear child, do not do so for the love of God, for the sake of peace, and also in order to give a little pleasure to your poor Mother Theodore, who loves you so much, and who would like to see you perfect, but who is very far from being perfect herself. I am pleased to know that your little girls are improving. I have no doubt but that they will continue to do so under so good and capable a teacher.

I felt quite sure that Sister Marie Therese would please at Madison, because of her fine manners. She is truly very ladylike among those Germans. Give her my love. I shall write to her soon. Fond remembrance also to Sister Mary Celeste and Sister Joachim. I shall write to both of them when time permits.

Father Corbe and all the Sisters send you very much love. Every day they bring up to me such things as this: "Sister Basilide—if Sister Basilide were here this gate would be fixed," "that door would not be falling to the ground," "this pane of glass would be replaced," etc. I am obliged for the sake of truth to acknowledge they are right; otherwise I should be jealous, perhaps. . . .

Mother Theodore always gave personal care to the sick pupils whenever her own health permitted. Referring to the sick child mentioned in the preceding letter her diary states: "On the 15th one of our pupils, Miss Rogers, is taken sick with winter fever." The school register gives a Cecilia Rogers of New Harmony, Indiana. This is likely the same person, as New Harmony was, comparatively, "far, far away," and the child may have been brought to Vincennes

to meet someone there who would take her to Saint Mary's.
On the 20th, "she is better and appears out of danger." The
21st, "the little girl is worse." The 23rd, "she is much better."
The 25th, "Mrs. Rogers, mother of our sick little girl, arrives."
The 27th, "Mrs. Rogers and her sick little girl leave Saint
Mary's." Cecilia's name appears again in the school register
of 1854 for one year, and in the 'seventies she returns as
Mrs. Laird with a pupil for the school.

TO THE RIGHT REVEREND J. BOUVIER, BISHOP OF LE MANS

Saint Mary's, December 9, 1848

My Lord:

As the first thought of our afflicted hearts was to pour
out their sorrow into yours and to seek there a consolation
which we have never failed to find, so it is towards you that
they now turn in their joy and happiness, that you may
share in them. If your paternal heart renders you so sensitive to our sorrows, it cannot let you be indifferent to our
consolations.

We have just learned that we have a Bishop-elect, the
Reverend Maurice de St. Palais. God has given us the one
whom the whole diocese has earnestly asked for since the
death of Bishop Bazin. He belongs to an eminent Christian
family; three of his sisters are Daughters of Charity. I knew
one of them at Angers. Father de St. Palais made his studies at
St. Sulpice, where he was ordained. It was there that he
became acquainted with Bishop Bruté, who brought him to
his poor mission of Indiana. He has been working here for
twelve years with zeal and success, doing incalculable good
in the midst of the greatest privations. He built several
churches, and in leaving each one of them was everywhere
deeply regretted by the people, for the favor of possessing
such a pastor was fully appreciated. It was he who came

THE RIGHT REVEREND
JOHN STEPHEN BAZIN
Third Bishop of Vincennes
Consecrated, October 24, 1847

THE RIGHT REVEREND
MAURICE DE ST. PALAIS
Fourth Bishop of Vincennes
Consecrated, January 14, 1849

from Madison two years ago and brought over on the ice and snow of a rigorous winter our poor Sister Mary Liguori, who was in a dying condition.

During our years of trial he always showed himself a devoted friend and protector of our Congregation. As soon as Bishop Bazin was consecrated, Father de St. Palais was called to be Vicar General and Superior of the Seminary. He soon became the Bishop's counsellor and friend. Bishop Bazin did not do the least thing without consulting him. Just before dying he named him Administrator during the vacancy of the See, and gave him publicly marks of the greatest esteem and affection. The priests who were assembled for the funeral of Bishop Bazin made a petition to have Father de St. Palais for Bishop, This request was approved by His Grace the Archbishop of St. Louis, who was present, and it has been confirmed by our Holy Father the Pope, notwithstanding the many intrigues to prevent the appointment.

These details would be tedious for another, but for you they will be pleasing. You will be glad to know that your Daughters of the Woods have a protector, and to learn something about the one to whom they are confided.

We find Bishop de St. Palais' administration much resembling your own, which renders him still dearer to us. Far from destroying the Rule he will help us to fulfil it exactly, for he is full of piety and has very good judgment. He is so poor, and the diocese is in so destitute a condition, that he has just been obliged to close the Seminary. He could keep only a few students; they are now in the episcopal house. We have two here at our own expense. If the Council of the Propagation of the Faith does nothing more for our poor Indiana, I do not know what will become of the clergy.

And you, venerated Father, what is becoming of you? Or rather, what is becoming of your Republic? Is it a little less exacting? How I fear for France. Every day we offer to Almighty God fervent prayers for your happiness. Could we forget for one single day how much we owe to you?

We shall write again after the consecration, and then we shall speak a little of ourselves. It is very probable that the new Bishop will move our Motherhouse to Madison, where he intends to fix his See. The truth is, we are very badly located here. At the present moment we are entirely cut off from the world by the overflowing of the Wabash, which is higher than at any time since 1818. The river overflow is only half a league from our house, and so charged with drift that it is impossible to cross it.[8] I do not know when my letters can be sent. Be so good as to remember your Daughters of the Woods in your prayers and bless them. . . .[9]

At Vincennes for the consecration of Bishop de St. Palais, Mother Theodore writes about the plans:

TO SISTER BASILIDE, MADISON

Vincennes, January 8, 1849

My very dear Sister:

It is from Vincennes that I am writing to you. I came here last Friday with Father Corbe. We thought we should find several priests here, especially Father Dupontavice, but he is expected only tomorrow by the Louisville stage. He will bring news of you, I am awaiting it impatiently. I am uneasy about Sister Joachim. Your letter to our Bishop does not say anything about the illness of that dear Sister, so I conclude she is better; but I shall be entirely reassured only

[8] Under normal conditions the river is nearly five miles away.
[9] Original in the archives of the Diocese of Le Mans.

after receiving a long letter from you. Give me full details, good ones I hope, if such be the will of God. But I wish to know them just as they are.

I left you for a few moments to go to see our Bishop. He has received a telegram from the Bishop of Nashville[10] who says that he will surely come. Bishop Spalding[11] will also come, and the consecration will take place next Sunday. Until today it was feared that it would have to be postponed on account of the high water, for the Bishops of Cincinnati and St. Louis have sent word that they must not be expected; so, there will be only two bishops at the consecration. We are glad to have even that number.

You certainly did right not to come. The weather being so bad, and the roads so dangerous, you might have to stay a long time away from your mission; which would be to its prejudice. In this I recognize my Sister Basilide who knows how to make sacrifices when necessary. However, I feel very much being deprived of seeing you; but to make up for the disappointment, I shall go to Madison early this year, if God gives me a little health. I wish much to see you.

How is Sister Joachim? Give me all the details. I repeat it, I am very uneasy. Poor Sister Basilide! I share very much in all your anxieties. And how is good Sister Mary Celeste? I hope she has recovered. Give her my love.

Mr. Edward Doran is here. He wants to pay for Ann and Eliza. I find on your books that the latter is owing $117.50 for the whole year. You know that she was received for $100. I do not know how she spent $17.50 during the course of the year. You did not specify any details except up to the month of December, and those items amount to one dollar and a few cents. Do you remember what she got

[10] The Right Reverend Richard P. Miles, O.P., D.D.
[11] The Right Reverend Martin J. Spalding, D.D., Bishop of Louisville.

for the other fifteen dollars? I dare not ask for it without knowing for what it is due.

Of late I scarcely knew which way to turn for money, but Providence came to our help. Last week Mr. Benbridge sent $50; "Cousin Jane," $190; and what Mr. Doran is to give will "fill some holes." I think I told you that our Sisters at Terre Haute opened their school the day of the Circumcision, or rather, the day after. They have only a few pupils, all small girls; twenty-eight the first day and twenty-seven the second. I do not know whether they have continued to go on thus decreasing. But, then, almost nothing was ready. I hope things will be better in the spring.

I do not think Sister Mary Cecilia will come to the consecration, especially when she knows you are not coming. She is not very well. She has too much to do. As to Sister St. Vincent [the Superior of the newly opened school in Terre Haute], she has the greatest desire to come, but I am not sure that Father Lalumière will let her off. He is famously severe. We think Sister Augustine [the Superior in Jasper] will arrive one of these days, by land or by sea. Poor Sister Basilide! We were expecting you also. Your bed was ready. Anyhow, God will repay us for all we do for Him. . . .

TO THE SAME

Vincennes, January 13, 1849

My dear Sister Basilide:

I have just received your presents through your good pastor.[12] I thank you very much. And let me assure you, it gives me great pleasure—I mean your remembrance. The tokens of attachment that you give me constantly are among

---

[12] The Reverend Hippolite Dupontavice.

my joys. May I tell you, my dear child, I had feared that distance had cooled the heart of my Sister Basilide? It is a happiness to see that my fears are without foundation. Let us keep ever united in Our Lord. When we love one another in Him, we love Him better.

Be very sure, my dear daughter, that the Sisters at Saint Mary's love you much. You know how busy they are, especially Sister Mary Cecilia and Sister St. Urban, I am persuaded that the latter makes a real sacrifice by not writing to you. So does Sister Anastasie. She said to me the other day that she offered this sacrifice for—I do not know exactly for what, but it concerned you. You see from this that she loves you. However, my dear Sister Basilide, do not believe that any one loves you as your Mother Theodore does. No, I can answer for this. The name of Mother is not given in vain. Could I forget what you are to me? No, dear Sister Basilide, no. Be assured once for all—I am not always in my days of avowal—*No one will ever love you as your old Mother Theodore does*. Now this is enough on the subject.

I am happy to learn you are all united. Oh, may that blessed union last a long time! For that purpose it is necessary to bear the faults of others and try to correct our own in order not to make others suffer too much. I am always praying for you, but what are my poor prayers?

Your pupils, I think, will be more numerous in the spring. I am glad that you yourself take charge of the Catholic girls. Try to make them learn well—I mean those who come to you regularly; their progress more than anything else will induce others to come. What negligence among some Catholic parents! Let us try to make up for their forgetfulness of duty by our zeal and fervor.

I am glad that Sister Joachim is better. I should be sorry to lose that dear Sister; she is a good daughter. I would have been pleased if you had told me what your pastor has against our

Father and against me. I do not know that I did or said anything that could displease him in the least. Tomorrow he is going to officiate as a bishop or, rather, as an assistant. I do not believe that Bishop de St. Palais thinks now of taking him away from Madison; however, he has made him Vicar General, *of course*.

If the good God hears all the prayers of all of us, and if I be not sick this winter, I shall go to see you before spring. We have had steamboats nearly all the time this season at Terre Haute.

Do not press the Gwin ladies; they are already unfortunate enough. Edward Doran has paid, but Mrs. Batis is in a very bad humor because I *dared* to say to the lawyer that we had not been paid.

As I am writing to you before the ceremony I can tell you nothing. I shall send a letter by the pastor, if I can, and then give all details. Father Corbe, Sister Olympiade, and myself are the only ones here from Saint Mary's. I do not blame you for having done something for your pastor, but I cannot approve of your having taken refreshments at his house. I beseech you, dear Sister Basilide, do not do so again; you know that it is against our Rule. *We must not displease God to please men. . . .*

Sister St. Urban (Anna Maria McGowan), referred to in the foregoing letter, entered Saint Mary-of-the-Woods in 1846, and was for many years a prominent teacher at the Academy. She had formerly been at Emmitsburg, but wishing to be in an order in which perpetual vows are taken, she was recommended by Bishop Purcell of Cincinnati to consider the Sisters of Providence. In the aspirations of this Community and in the quiet of the surroundings at Saint Mary's, she found all that satisfied her yearnings. Her studies in philosophy had been made under Bishop Brute at Emmitsburg and from him she acquired scholarly tastes and high religious ideals. Small in stature but large in distinguished personality, Sister St. Urban exerted an influence at the Academy that was far-reaching and that contributed forcibly to the perpetuation of the culture and refinement instilled by the early teachers of the school. She died August 6, 1888.

Sister Anastasie (Jane Brown), mentioned also in Mother Theodore's letter, had been a pupil of the Academy within the first year of its foundation, having entered in September, 1841. This school year, however, was termed the Second Year, as the short session from July 4 to August 12 before the vacation was called the First Year. In January, 1844, she entered the novitiate. After her religious profession in August, 1847, she taught at Vincennes; then at Terre Haute from January, 1849, to July, 1855, being the Superior there from 1853. In 1855 she was sent to open the mission in Evansville. In 1856 she was elected First Assistant to Mother Mary Cecilia, who appointed her directress of the Academy. These positions she retained until 1868, when she was elected Superior General, an office she held six years, two terms. Her next sixteen years were passed in Lafayette and Madison, and again as directress of Saint Mary-of-the Woods Academy. In 1890 she was chosen Second Assistant to the newly-elected Superior General, Mother Mary Cleophas. After this term, now of six years, she was allowed to retire to enjoy the rest her years and her labor had merited.

In physical build Mother Anastasie was very tall and powerful. She was masterly in eloquent expression, yet gentle and benign. Her religious regularity was so perfect that one day, late in life, when she was not at morning prayers, investigation was made at once and she was found half-dressed, lying on the floor, having suffered a stroke of paralysis. She never walked again but spent several years in a wheel chair, though in good health otherwise. Another stroke then sent her to the infirmary where she lingered until her happy death, which occurred August 10, 1919, in her ninety-third year. Her faculties were well preserved to the end, and her sweetness of disposition increased day by day.

Confidence that springs from faith is the word that characterized the life of Mother Anastasie. She was optimistic, no matter what the outlook. Amid her trials (and she had great ones) she maintained a firm reliance on God; and in times of peace, on account of her childlike confidence, she enjoyed heartily the little pleasures and satisfactions that brightened her way, tokens, she called them, of the sweet Providence of God.

Her natural endowments had been well cultivated both in her childhood home and in the Community, and she had facility for acquiring what she did not possess. She was a real educator, spending most of the day in visiting the classes when in charge of a school. She excelled in art—in drawing and in water-color painting particularly. Even in her advanced years she painted burses and sick-call cases with exquisite touch. In 1910 it was Mother Anastasie's privilege to be a witness in the process for the beatification of the servant of God, the saintly Foundress, Mother Theodore Guérin, with whom she had lived fifteen years.

Sister Joachim (Jeanne Marie Bodin), a native of Brittany, born in 1815, arrived at Saint Mary-of-the-Woods August 6, 1844. In 1848 she was at Madison, as the preceding letter shows, and was pronounced to be a "good daughter." The next year she went to Vincennes to open a pharmacy at the girls' orphanage. In 1851, when the orphan boys were taken in charge by the Sisters of Providence, Sister Joachim was named Superior of the asylum. There she remained, exercising the most maternal care over the homeless little ones for twenty-four years. Suspecting then, and with good reason that another year would bring her a Silver Jubilee celebration, she requested her Superiors to give her a different assignment. Her wish was granted. She remained at the Motherhouse, a humble and industrious worker in the lingerie and an edification to the end of her life, which terminated peacefully May 2, 1901. Silent but pleasant always, she was looked upon as one who knew the secrets of habitual union with God.

TO THE RIGHT REVEREND J. BOUVIER, BISHOP OF LE MANS

Saint Mary's, February 8, 1849

My Lord:

I promised myself the pleasure of writing to you after the consecration of Bishop de St. Palais, at which I had the consolation of assisting. It took place on the 14th of January, Feast of the Holy Name of Jesus. There were only two

bishops present.[13] The Bishop of Nashville was the conse-
crator. The Archbishop of St. Louis[14] could not come on account
of the bad roads, and because the cholera, which was making
great havoc in New Orleans, threatened each day
to invade St. Louis through the steamboats which run between these two cities, and which are every day loaded with
people fleeing from the plague. The same reasons detained
the Bishop of Cincinnati.[15] The other two prelates came to
Vincennes in poor wagons, over frightful roads and with the
greatest difficulty; but they had even greater hardship on
their return journey.

On the day of the consecration a torrent of sleet fell. This is
of frequent occurrence in America. It forms a layer similar to
melted lead, or lava from a volcano, and covers whatever object
it falls upon, taking their forms. Woe to the man or beast
exposed to its violence.

Eight days later we started from Vincennes in open wagons
and with eight horses roughshod. They made particles of this
polished surface fly up and go rolling on the ice, shining in
the sun with a thousand colors. One might have fancied the
horses were trampling under foot millions of precious stones,
and that we were traveling in an enchanted country. The
enchantment, however, was only for the eyes. Never did I suffer so much in traveling. We broke down four wagons, and
finally our horses took fright four miles from Terre Haute and
exposed us to the greatest danger. We were preserved only by
a special protection from Heaven.

I do not know why I tell you all this adventure. I beg
of you to pardon me. That is what you get for having written that we can never give you too many details. If you but
knew, my good Father, how happy I am, as are also my com-

[13] The Right Reverend Richard P. Miles, O.P., D.D., Bishop of Nashville, and
the Right Reverend Martin J. Spalding, D.D., Bishop of Louisville.
[14] The Most Reverend Peter R. Kenrick, D.D.
[15] The Right Reverend John B. Purcell, D.D. (Made Archbishop, July, 1850.)

panions, in thinking of the paternal love which you have the kindness constantly to show to your Daughters of the Forest! God alone can render you what this generous devotedness deserves. All that we can do is to pray for you, and we do not omit a *single day* to fulfill this duty so dear to our hearts.

Our good Bishop is so poor that we are obliged to meet the expenses of his outfit—if we may use that term for the clothing of a bishop. Sister Olympiade was six weeks at Vincennes sewing for him. She makes cassocks, and so forth, perfectly. She really renders invaluable services with her needle to the missions as well as here at home. She makes the clothes of all our workmen, also of the orphans whom we have at the Seminary; thus she saves us considerable expense. She takes care of our sick also and goes to see the people of the neighborhood; all of which produces an excellent effect. As it is to you we owe this good Sister, I thought you would learn with pleasure that she is so very useful in this country.

The cholera is making terrible ravages at New Orleans. A cousin of Bishop de la Hailandière, Father Ducoudray, formerly of St. Francisville, Illinois, has just died there, having had but a few hours in which to prepare himself. As many as one hundred and twenty-five persons have died there in a day. When the weather becomes colder the disease diminishes, only to break out again with redoubled violence when it grows warmer. The towns which surround us are already attacked by this plague, St. Louis, Cincinnati, Louisville, etc. I do not think it is in Indiana yet, but all are in extreme fear of it. They, are convinced that in the spring it will come to those low places near the rivers, which have been under water almost all winter. The Bishop has announced in the paper that our Sisters would take care of the sick who might be attacked at Vincennes. Our intention is to devote ourselves in the same manner in all the towns of our state where we have establishments.

Some time ago I heard that the people of Terre Haute intend building a hospital in their city, and that they hope to have our Sisters take charge of it. If this news is true, it would be one of the most precious occasions of doing good that could be offered to us. It is impossible to say how much good we might do in fulfilling this portion of our Holy Rules; but it would be absolutely out of the question to undertake this work unless our dear Superiors at Ruillé would furnish us with the means. We should require two or three Sisters formed by Sister Athanasius, or by someone else who understands how to run a hospital. It seems to me it would be easier for our good Mother to find us persons thus qualified than persons to teach. I am confident that if you would ask this for us we should obtain it. All that contributed to the good of our establishment has come through your hands; from you we hold it. As soon as I know anything definite about the hospital I shall write to Ruillé and send the letter to you.

It is certain that the town of Terre Haute will become one of the largest in Indiana, on account of its location. They are already making railroads, canals, doing away with the obstructions in the Wabash which prevent the passage of steamboats, and so forth. They do here in one year what in the Old World would not be done in ten.

Our Congregation is everywhere appreciated. Sisters are called for in almost every town of the diocese. I have just written a letter of refusal to the pastor of a German Congregation near Cincinnati. Last week we declined to form an establishment in the capital of our state (Indianapolis), where the Protestants wish for us as much as the Catholics do.

Our house in Terre Haute is not yet finished, although the Sisters have been there a month. They have over fifty pupils and, it is said, will have more in the spring. If we had thirty Sisters more, ready to go out, we could employ them all. But there are scarcely any vocations in this country, except for the "great Confraternity." It is nearly a year since we received any postulants; besides that, we shall have to dismiss some of those we have who are not suitable.

Should you have an occasion of seeing our Mothers of Ruillé, or of writing to them, I beg you to offer them my profound respects. I am ashamed to send you this scribble. I have been obliged to write it piecemeal, and have not time to re-write it. Be so good as to excuse me, and deign to accept the homage of my most profound veneration. . . .[16]

In this letter Mother Theodore refers to the newly opened orphanage as the "Seminary." This building had been the old St. Gabriel's College of Vincennes taken over from the Eudists by Bishop Bazin. It was located on a small tract of land extending from Perry to Hart, and from Fourth to Sixth Streets. To this college building Bishop Bazin had transferred the seminarians from the old seminary on Second Street across from the Cathedral rectory. Thenceforward the old St. Gabriel's College was known as the "Seminary."

In the interest of history there may be added here a few lines from a letter of Father Corbe dated January 4, 1848, written to Father Martin, then in Louisiana. He says, speaking of Bishop Bazin, "He has bought the college and has made it his Major Seminary. . . . The seminary where you were has been raised a story and surmounted by a belfry; to this has been added a chapel, near the *factory*; and the frame house on the corner, rebuilt in brick, connects with the old house by a brick porch—all planned and accomplished by Bishop de la Hailandière. This seminary has been given to the Sisters of Providence" [for their convent].

Up to this time the Sisters had lived and taught school in an old house a story and a half high on Main Street between Fourth and Fifth, property still called the "Bishop's Block." Bishop Bazin moved the Sisters from Main Street (in those days Market Street) to the former seminary on Second Street east of the rectory, and wrote to Mother Theodore, December 30, 1847: "Great questions have been debated and decided

16 Original in the archives of the Diocese of Le Mans.

within the last few days. John Stephen Bazin is the owner of St. Gabriel's College which for the future will be at the same time Seminary and College, but for Catholic boys only. [Previously non-Catholics also had been admitted to the College.] The good Sisters of Providence will take the seminarians' old quarters where they will keep school and care for the orphans. The Sisters at Vincennes know nothing about this, as yet, but I feel confident none of them will cry at leaving Market Street and coming nearer to God."

By 1850 the cholera had left scores of homeless orphans in southern Indiana to be cared for by charity. On August fifth Mother Theodore wrote in her diary: "We learn that the cholera is making fearful ravages at Vincennes. Two Sisters are remaining to take care of those who are attacked."

Bishop de St. Palais, who had succeeded Bishop Bazin in 1849, finding he could not yet support a diocesan seminary, placed elsewhere his few candidates for the priesthood, closed the Seminary and College, and gave over the building to the use of the orphan boys. These children had been in temporary quarters in the care of seculars until the spring of 1851. The diary again says: "On the first day of April we took charge of the little orphan boys of Vincennes. There were forty-three of them. They occupy the old College, which has changed its name and is now called St. Vincent's."

The orphan boys were taken to Highland in 1863, and the "Seminary" then became the home of the orphan girls. After the transfer of the latter to Terre Haute, in 1876, it was occupied by the boarding pupils and the higher classes of the St. Rose Academy, removed from Second Street.

This "Seminary" building, erected in 1811, said to be the second oldest brick building in Vincennes—the first being the Harrison Mansion built in 1804—was itself historic. It replaced a small frame structure of 1807, used as the first common grammar school. It served as a meeting place for the Territorial Legislature in 1811, and then successively as a college for young men, a seminary for ecclesiastical students, a home for orphan boys, then for orphan girls, a hospital for sick soldiers during the Civil War, and, finally, an academy for young ladies. This famous old building was demolished in 1884, when Bishop Chatard sold the property to the city except the half square on Fifth Street extending from Seminary to Hart, on which the Sisters built a new St. Rose Academy.

Mother Theodore's fears and predictions concerning the epidemic were soon realized. The cholera did "come to those low places near the rivers," which had been under water almost all winter.

TO THE SISTERS AT MADISON

Saint Mary's, March 2, 1849

My very dear and beloved Daughters:

Just this moment I hear that the *cholera* has made its entrance into your dear Madison. I cannot tell you how anxious I am about you. I beseech you to be sure to write to me at least three times a week, even if only a few lines, to let me know how you are, whether the disease spreads, or whether it has disappeared,—in a word, *everything*. You understand that the least details are of interest in such moments of danger. I have confidence, however, that God will not permit any of you to be attacked by the epidemic. Be cheerful, kind to one another. Have nothing on your conscience that could trouble you. Do not fast. Let your food be wholesome and well prepared. Keep your house, the yard, and also your persons clean. Change your linen often, and have your children clean also, if they are still with you. Finally, my dear daughters, pray. Prepare yourselves, or rather, keep yourselves ready to answer the summons of your Divine Spouse if He calls you to Himself; but, let me repeat it, I hope He will not. At New Orleans the contagion attacked only those who were predisposed by an enfeebled constitution or by excesses.

We are going to have public prayers for you. You yourselves pray also as much as your occupations will permit. Say every day this prayer, revealed to a priest in Rome in a similar circumstance: "O Jesus, divine Redeemer, etc."—the prayer that they say every night at Ruillé after night prayers. Finally, if the plague makes great ravages in your city (which I do not anticipate, as its inhabitants are temperate and laborious), arm yourselves with courage, and devote yourselves generously to the care of your suffering brethren. Without distinction of persons, do good to all for the love of God, and if you have to die, well, my dear daughters, *die for Him who died for you.* I cannot feel, however, that our good and merciful God would demand of me the great and painful sacrifice by taking any one among you, because He knows that I cannot spare you now. Oh! no, my God, you will not take these dear children, even though they should devote themselves with heroic love to the victims of the cholera.

Adieu, my very dear children, or rather *à bientôt.* Whatever may please Our Lord! Pray and suffer—Heaven is the reward.

If the cholera is spreading much, you should dismiss your children, if you have not already done so. Write to me at once, be it only two lines. Everyone prays for you, loves you, and is uneasy about you. . . .

TO SISTER BASILIDE, MADISON

Saint Mary's, March 3, 1849

My dear Sister Basilide:

Since I learned that the cholera is at Madison I can talk of nothing but the plague. I had a thousand things to write to you, but all have escaped at the one word, *Cholera.* Read to the Sisters the few lines of my last letter; they were for all. Something reassures me and tells me that it is not going to be a great epidemic. I heartly desire that my presentiment may be confirmed by a letter from you.

I felt confident that you would be cheered up by a visit from Bishop de St. Palais. He is truly very kind. He is doing wonders. God only knows where he will find money to pay for his property at Evansville, at Madison, and his orphan asylum at Vincennes. As for ourselves, we get into debt terribly despite the strictest economy. The improvements at St. Mary's, and the house at Terre Haute have almost ruined us.

What would you wish to do, my poor daughter, with your big C————? You can never give good judgment to those persons to whom God has not given it; for, *He alone gives intelligence*, and He will not require what He has not bestowed. Those who have received less will have less to answer for. A man is just starting for Terre Haute. I must give him this letter to mail. . . .

The large wings added to the first Academy in 1846, and a small, two-story frame addition then needed, made a debt not yet entirely cancelled. Besides there was the cost now of the house in Terre Haute. This building was erected on a lot on which there stood a small school house that had to be incorporated in the new building. The lot was deeded to the Community on this condition. The new house was said to be one of the best brick buildings in the city. An early map of Terre Haute, now in the Public Library, has a picture of the school on the upper margin, as one of the prominent buildings of the city. It was called "St. Vincent's Academy," but some years later, it was given the name "St. Joseph Academy." This is the only one of the mission houses that was planned and built by Mother Theodore.

TO SISTER BASILIDE, MADISON

March 5,1849

Dear Sister:

I wrote to you Friday last when I learned that the cholera was at Madison. Your letter of the 26th has reassured us, but I feel inclined to scold you for not writing oftener. I have just heard that there were new cases on the 28th. I beg of you, my daughter, do not fail to write frequently while that ugly visitor is in your city.

I could embrace you heartily for what you tell me of your little Catholic children. I always feared that having so much to do in your school at St. Ann's you would be obliged to neglect these little pets. But no; you have given them attention, and they are improving. I owe this then to my Sister Basilide and shall thank her for it as soon as I get to Madison. If Mr. Cholera be still with you after Easter, I could not go; I should not be permitted to do so. Father Corbe will go with His Lordship, and I, also, if that villain, Cholera, is not in the way.

You gave the Bishop a grand reception at Madison—that was all very right. We Hoosiers of the Woods will receive him with all simplicity.

Yesterday your letters for our Sisters came to hand; they will write to you soon. Both are poorly, especially Sister St. Francis, who is in miserable health. Sister St. Vincent is pleased at Terre Haute; Sister Agnes and Sister Anastasie likewise. All the little troubles about the school are over. The children were never better than since the last examination. Try to sanctify yourself during Lent and pray for me. Goodbye. . . .

After Easter of this year Mother Theodore went to visit the mission at Fort Wayne. Returning by canal boat she was obliged to stop over in Lafayette. As the Sisters did not yet have a convent in this city, she was pleased to accept the hospitality offered her by a Mrs. Benbridge, the mother of two young ladies then attending the boarding school at Saint Mary's. Upon her return home she writes to this lady:

Saint Mary-of-the-Woods, May 30, 1849

My dear Madam:

It is with much pleasure I devote the few leisure moments now at my command to addressing you, as it has been my sincere wish to be able to testify my grateful acknowledgement for your amiable attentions to Sister Angelina and myself during our stay under your most hospitable roof. Notwithstanding the very leisurelike movement of the *Little Pink* we arrived at Terre Haute about half-past ten Saturday night, and finding our carriage waiting for us drove out to Saint Mary's very early on Sunday. To our great joy we found all our large family well, your dear daughters not excepted. They were delighted that we had spent our time at Lafayette with you. We trust your health has not suffered from the unusual coldness of the season and that you have heard from Mr. Benbridge and your interesting little boys.

Your dear little girls are looking very well and are applying themselves assiduously to their studies, particularly Mary, who does not indulge at all in "home-sickness" and gives much satisfaction in every respect. Sally is a good child, but she will not make the exertion necessary to over-come her own will at times, particularly as regards singing. This is a subject of deep regret for us, as we know you desire that she should apply herself to that. Mrs. Bradley's little daughter is well and appears very well contented.

As you had the kindness, my dear Madam, to offer to obtain from Mrs. G——the bill due us, I enclose it to you, making in her favor a deduction of one-third, provided she will pay at once, or as soon as possible. Her debt to us is $96.95 but we are willing to take $65 upon the above condition. Our bill of the full amount has been sent to Mrs. G——.

Have the kindness to present our compliments to your

family and receive for yourself the affectionate remembrance of my Sisters, with our best wishes that Heaven may bless you and your excellent family. . . .

An item in the diary, June twentieth, is interesting on account of the connection here. It says: "Mr. and Mrs. Benbridge and their children arrived at Saint Mary's fleeing from the cholera, which is at Lafayette." Cholera was all around, but it had not yet touched Saint Mary-of-the-Woods.

LETTER CIRCULAR

Saint Mary-of-the-Woods, June 28, 1849

My very dear Sisters:

It is with true consolation that we announce to you the opening of our retreat, fixed by our venerated prelate for August 8th. It will be given by a Jesuit.

Prepare yourselves, my dear daughters, for these days of grace and pardon by greater fidelity in the fulfillment of your duties and by greater recollection. Without this spirit of recollection, in vain shall we hope to receive the gifts of God.

Undoubtedly, my dear daughters, you feel sensibly the need of coming to refresh, your souls in solitude. A year will soon have passed since you returned to your labors. However good and holy your occupations may be, they leave distraction and fatigue. Come then, dear daughters, to enjoy yourselves a little in the Lord and prepare for what the future has in store for you. Who knows what will become of us in these times of calamity?

Let us ask with earnestness to be preserved at least before the retreat. Let us place this retreat under the protection of Mary conceived without sin. Place under the same guardianship the pupils that you leave for a while. Confide your journey and its dangers to this good and tender Mother. Who has ever perished that entrusted herself to Mary? Take her as your model on the way. Often repeat the *Memorare* in her honor for yourselves and for your traveling companions; thus will you avoid dissipation and prepare yourselves for the holy exercises.

In order to have time to rest a little before the retreat, you will begin vacation before the end of July, and when you will have put everything in order, leave at once for Saint Mary's.

Permit me to remind you that during the journey you should be silent and modest. Everybody here is anxiously awaiting you and will be happy to see you, but no one more happy than

Your devoted and affectionate

SISTER ST. THEODORE,

Sup'r Gen'l.

The first Jesuit to give a retreat at Saint Mary's was Father di Maria, who was at the time stationed at St. Joseph's Church, Terre Haute. From that year (1849) to the present day, except one year, the annual retreat has always been conducted by Jesuits.

In her diary Mother Theodore gives an interesting account of the closing of that retreat; she says: "August 15. We had a very beautiful ceremony today, Bishop de St. Palais officiating for the first time in our little chapel. This good Father gave Confirmation to five postulants before performing the double ceremony of the Profession and the taking of the habit. The retreat had been very edifying and it finished in the same manner. The Bishop, the Jesuit, and Father Corbe were well pleased with the silence, recollection, and fervor of the Community. The Bishop gave Confirmation with the mitre on; it was the first time we witnessed this ceremony. Three of the novices took their vows and seven postulants received the habit. In the evening of the same day His Lordship and Father di Maria left for Terre Haute in order to take the stage for Vincennes the next day. The Jesuit went to see about establishing a house of his order at Vincennes."

The news of the rapid spread and the frightful consequences of cholera in the United States had been appearing in
the newspapers of Europe. After sending out her circular calling the Sisters to the retreat, Mother Theodore writes to allay
the fear of her friends in France.

TO THE RIGHT REVEREND J. BOUVIER, BISHOP OF LE MANS

Saint Mary's, July 8, 1849

My Lord:

I understand sufficiently well your paternal heart to know
that you are quite uneasy about your daughters of the Woods,
if you have learned from the papers the ravages the cholera is
making in America. You will be happy to hear until now we
have been spared.

The epidemic is terrible all around us. The last news by
telegraph informs us that within twenty-four hours, on the
third of July, one hundred and sixty persons died at St.
Louis, one hundred and twenty-seven at Cincinnati, and in
the other cities of the West the same proportion. At Madison
our schools are closed and Sisters Basilide, Joachim, and
Felicitie are employed in taking care of the sick at their homes.
The people speak of making a hospital of the Sisters' house
temporarily; if they do this we shall send them help.
All our Sisters, or nearly all, offer themselves very generously
for this dangerous undertaking. A postulant whom we had to
dismiss last week also wanted to take part in this good work.
She would have preferred to die rather than return to the
world. It is painful to send away a young person with good
dispositions.

Very probably we shall have the occasion of satisfying
all those amongst us who wish to devote themselves to the
unfortunate victims. The plague has made its appearance at
Indianapolis, Vincennes, Lafayette, Washington, and several
other localities; at Terre Haute, and even in the village at

Saint Mary's. For several weeks there has been a sort of discomfort, colic, disordered stomach, dizziness. During the past few days all this has become more serious, *des cholérines*, or, as it is called here, cholera morbus, less dangerous than the malignant cholera, so called in English. The condition of the atmosphere tends to increase the fatal effects of the disease. The heat is suffocating; the air is charged with miasma and dampness often followed by storms. Inundations add still more to the insalubrity of the lowlands.

At New Orleans a sixth part of the city has been submerged for two months by the overflowing of the river. When the waters subside they leave exposed to view putrefied carcasses which corrupt the air, already so impure in this city of tombs, where death seems to have established its domicile. This, however, does not prevent the Americans from visiting the pestilential city, thus making its numerous steamboats the messengers, or rather the carriers, of destruction; for they go back and forth spreading death wherever they stop. It is to these steamboats that is due the presence of the cholera in our Indiana forests. But the Americans must have the "dollar." Their cupidity renders them daring and indifferent to everything else. It is nothing to them to expose their lives and those of others in order to gain money. How materialistic these people are! Not a single week passes that their indifference does not make our rivers the tombs of a great number of persons.

His Lordship and Father Corbe just lately escaped one of many accidents by a special intervention of Divine Providence. Being at New York on business after the Council, they were to have taken at six o'clock in the evening a large steamboat called *The Empire*. Detained by a trifling matter they missed the boat. While they were lamenting the mishap, *The Empire* collided with a merchant boat, which in its rapid course it could not avoid. This little vessel became almost entirely lodged in the flank of *The Empire* and dragged it with its hundreds of passengers down with itself to the bottom of the waters. A large number were drowned. Twenty bodies were found after the wreck; many have not been found.

These misfortunes of daily occurrence are not the only ones which afflict our unfortunate America. We hear of nothing but fires and murders. While at Fort Wayne last month we saw eleven of the finest houses in the city consumed by the flames in a very few hours. This fire was nothing compared with the terrible conflagration which happened about the same time in St. Louis. A steamboat in the dock took fire about ten o'clock at night; it is thought to have been set on fire through malevolence. The ropes and cables of the boat, cut or burnt, left it free to go down with the current, setting on fire in succession twenty-seven of those vast wharves. This terrible fire soon spread to the city, which was spared from general destruction only by sacrificing several of its beautiful buildings. The explosion cost the lives of several persons, but of this scarcely anything is said in the papers. Instead a long list is given of the loss of money and of property; the figure amounts up to thirty-five million francs. . . .[17]

Added to Mother Theodore's anxiety occasioned by the cholera, comes another of a different nature. The health of the Sisters always gave her concern and at this particular time that of Sister St. Francis Xavier, now Mistress of Novices, causes her special alarm. She thus describes a crisis:

TO THE SISTERS AT MADISON

Saint Mary's, Nov. 25, 1849

My dear Daughters:

What a day we spent yesterday! God only understands what passed in our hearts. After writing to you last evening

---

[17] Original in the archives of the Diocese of Le Mans.

I returned to our dear sick Sister St. Francis. Her weakness was such that she could not even open her eyes. Her words died on her lips; she could scarcely be heard. Her pulse was very weak, rapid, irregular. At eight o'clock she was still weaker. Father Corbe came to see her. For several hours the only signs of existence were a weak breathing and, from time to time, a spell of coughing. She had one while Father Corbe was there which tired her very much. She asked for a little of the dear water of La Salette. As soon as she had taken some she felt stronger. She sat up in bed and said. "I am cured. You must not doubt my cure. I owe it to the Blessed Virgin." She asked to have her bed arranged, and at ten o'clock she went to sleep. She had scarcely slept at all during her illness. At twelve o'clock I wished her to take some broth, but she begged so earnestly to be permitted to fast for Communion in the morning that I did not think I could refuse her. She received at six o'clock, and since then the improvement continues. She slept nearly all last night, and we believe she is now out of danger. Thank God with us and do not forget our Blessed Mother.

Is it not admirable to see how the Blessed Virgin loves us? It is to her that we owe everything, for she is the channel through which come all the graces that God showers upon us so profusely. Should the dear sick one get worse I shall write to you, but I am not much afraid this will happen. The gifts of God are without repentance; so if I do not write do not be uneasy. Goodbye. . . .

TO SISTER BASILIDE

January 11, 1850

My very dear Sister:

I begin my day by writing to you, hoping to find an occasion for Terre Haute. I hasten in order to be in time to tell you that I cannot, by any means, give you permission to have *meetings* of ladies of the world at your house—not under any pretext whatsoever. It is very possible that this society will not be able to subsist; but God will not ask of us an account of what we can do only by exposing the few religious virtues that we possess. I admire those fine ladies who have large and comfortable homes and are not willing to lend a little corner of their own houses once a week, but who wish to come and take our poor cottage the only day of the week that we are free and able to hold together our innocent recreations. Say to all of them, pastor and others, a *No* that will prevent them from returning to the charge. You can say that your Superiors are not willing; that will excuse you, especially to the pastor.

I believe it will be very difficult to get your house exempt from taxation. What shall I say? If you cannot do better, you must pay; but I find the amount exceedingly high. How is it that property which is worth only $3,000 is so excessively taxed, especially when it is against the formal law of Indiana? I read it myself. Those gentlemen of Madison are very conscientious!!

I do not think that the slight deafness of Sister Mary Therese can be cured. It might happen even that she would find herself worse after all those inefficacious remedies; however, if she desires to continue treatments let her do so.

Try to keep up the vocation of Jane. If you do not send her now, have her ready for the beginning of spring. It would be a great happiness for us if Celeste Duplessis would became a Religious at Saint Mary's, but I do not expect it. We have great need of a musician.

Sister Angelina continues to have severe hemorrhages. She is as pale as death, and leaves her bed only a few hours a day to give some lessons to the most advanced pupils. It truly seems against conscience to let her teach at all; she really is not able to give lessons. Sister St. Francis is not worth, much more, in her own way; she has not stepped out of doors yet. Our Bishop is still in the North. He has written a few lines to Father Corbe to say that he will be here the fifteenth of this month if the thaw continues. I do not know how he will get back, the roads are so dreadful, nor whether he still intends going to Madison. It seems to me your Madison is at its apogee. Our Terre Haute will rise higher. But what is all this? Cities and provinces disappear like individuals. God alone remains. Let us attach, ourselves to Him with all our hearts and He will take care of us. . . .

TO THE SAME

February 18, 1850

Truly, my dear Sister Basilide, man proposes and God disposes. Sister St. Theodore had planned to leave today to go to see her dear Sisters at Madison, with whom she intended to spend a part of Lent. God has disposed otherwise by sending her her old malady, which returns with renewed energy from time to time. Yes, my dear daughters, I am still sick with stomach ills, fever, and the rest. For nearly eight days, in fact even ever since my return from Vincennes, I have done almost nothing at all. I am not so sick as you have seen me sometimes, but I am very miserable. Pray for me and be resigned to the will of God. Ask the same favor for me also. I need it, for I can only send you much love when I wish I could embrace you. We must do penance in Lent.

It was not until two months after this letter that Mother Theodore, though only partially recovered, was able to visit Madison. While there she wrote to her greatly esteemed friend, Father Kundek, the pastor of Jasper, whose health had become so poor that he was contemplating a change of climate, perhaps permanent. With his prolonged absence in prospect, Mother Theodore wrote:

Madison, April 19, 1850

Dear Reverend Father:

I cannot tell you how much your project preoccupies me. I dread to see the arrival of the month of May, and I reproach myself for my uneasiness. What can befall us in the month set apart to honor our Blessed Mother but that which is good and right? I pray for you with all my heart. Pray also for me, that my presence here may contribute to the glory of God and the salvation of souls, bought at so great a price.

Two of the Sisters here are in poor health, Sister Catherine and Sister Philomene. The former offers you her respectful homage and commends herself earnestly to your prayers. She is always weak, but I do not think she is in danger. She still keeps her school, which is very heavy. The Sisters here, as everywhere, have more than they are able to do. Yesterday I told Father Dupontavice that they could no longer take care of his church. He agreed, realizing himself that they are overtaxed. Last evening he came to tell us that he had already found some one else to take the place of the Sisters in charge of the church. This will be a general regulation for all our establishments. I had previously spoken to you about it at Jasper. Perhaps you have already found some one else, and I thank you heartily; if not, I beg of you to get a woman who will wash and iron the church linen, etc. I intend writing to the Sisters about it, as you had told me you were entirely indifferent in the matter.

I sent you word that the Bishop had promised to be at Madison about Pentecost. From what I can foresee, he will not be at Vincennes until near Corpus Christi; at any rate, you will have more certain news by Father Contin, who arrived here in the city last evening.

Oh, may God grant you to decide on remaining in this little corner of the Lord's vineyard and continue to do the work of a good vine dresser! I wish it may be so for the sake of the Bishop, for the diocese, for my Sisters, for your congregation, and for myself, your very humble servant. . . .

Back at Saint Mary's again, Mother Theodore gives an account of her journey home.

TO SISTER BASILIDE

April 30, 1850

Dear Sister:

You are uneasy about me, about us all, and all your Sisters share in your anxiety? Well, my dear daughter, you have reason to be uneasy. Never in my whole life have I seen or even imagined such roads as we find from the capital to Terre Haute. I have no doubt of its being a miracle, owing to the way we were *fixed*, that we arrived *safe* at Terre Haute. I do not say *sound*, for we were so bruised, so sick, so tired, from our twenty-four hours in that crowded *Mud Wagin*.[18] Seated as I was on the corner of some big registers that were being sent to St. Louis, and which that day filled the so-called stage, I was half dead when we arrived. Jane was still worse than I, and poor Mary, so talkative in the cars, had lost all her animation. We were truly like *poules mouillées*. I had nosebleed all along the way. At last, on. Friday, we arrived with all our members. Rest gave us back the use of them and here we are, still living, I getting ready to be shaken up again, for I intend leaving for Lafayette, and so on, next Monday. You will pray for me. If you write to me, address your letter to Fort Wayne.

---

[18] Thus Mother Theodore attempted an English phrase.

We were obliged to spend one day more than we intended in Indianapolis on account of there being no place in the stage. We were cordially received by the Drake family, who speak well of our institution. I have succeeded in collecting some bills.

If you could have trees planted around the edge of your lot, I think it would be well. Ask Father Dupontavice whether he could have some planted for you. Choose pretty ones; those in front of Mr. Bright's frame house are nice. If what you plant are of slow growth, have locusts planted between them; then when the fine trees will have grown up, the locusts can be cut away. The latter are common, though pretty. Do not fail to have boxes made, very simple, to protect the young trees against the browsing of the cows and other animals. George will do that for you, but it must be done just at the time the trees are planted.

I expect a long letter from you some of these days. Much love to the Sisters. Those of Saint Mary's send you a large share. All are fairly well, and so is our good Father. Offer my respects and compliments to Father Dupontavice. The thought of him did me good all along the way; and ever since, I am always fancying I hear him singing his *Regina Coeli*. When he sings that, he is in heaven. What a devotional voice he has. . . .

TO THE RIGHT REVEREND J. BOUVIER, BISHOP OF LE MANS

Saint Mary-of-the-Woods, July 10, 1850

My Lord:

It seems a long time since I had the pleasure of writing to you. Although there is nothing remarkable to communicate to your Lordship, I feel none the less the desire of having a little chat with you, knowing you will be happy to learn that your daughters of the Woods continue to enjoy the peace so long awaited, so ardently desired—peace, the charms of which they would never have known, had you not aided them to endure the struggle which preceded it. Never, no never, my good Father (allow me to tell you this again), shall we forget the paternal tenderness which you have shown us, especially during our days of trial. God will render you a hundredfold for what you have done. You cannot imagine the happiness we all experience when we receive one of your letters. The last has gone the rounds of almost all our establishments, as Sister St. Francis does not want us here at Saint Mary's to be happy alone.

Bishop de St. Palais is ever kind. His conduct in our regard reminds us of the interest we have seen you take in the House of Ruillé. Like you, he is a devoted father to our Congregation. He could not start for France at the time he had appointed, as he has not yet finished the visitation of his diocese. At the present moment he is having the little girls' orphan asylum repaired; that for the boys will be ready in the month of September. His Lordship counts on giving us the charge of the latter also. I do not like to take the responsibility of bringing up boys. I fear we shall not succeed. It is a matter of great regret that Father Sorin cannot give Brothers for this work. Well, we shall do our best; besides, we shall have the boys only until they are twelve years old.

When the Bishop goes to France in the near future, he will give you more details about our mission than I can give you by correspondence. We have nothing special since my last letter, no new mission, and we shall not take any more this year, for our Sisters are overburdened with work and several of them are delicate. Sister St. Francis in particular is suffering much. I fear we cannot keep her long. She will be an immense loss to our little Congregation, as there is yet no one who can replace her in the novitiate. God has sent us several postulants who give hope for the future, but it requires time and care to form them. They are young; we prefer to have them young, for when they grow older in this world of America, it is very difficult to make good Religious out of them.

Sister Angelina, our principal music teacher, who also has been seriously ill for some time, is worse than usual this spring. She probably will not last much longer. She, too, will be a great loss, for in this country one must teach the children to make a noise on the piano or give up having school. But our hope is in the providence of God, which has protected us until the present, and which will provide, somehow, for our future needs, especially if you will have the charity to continue praying for the success of our work, which already owes so much to you.

Bishop de St. Palais wishes to have the Sisters in some of the more noted places in the diocese, but he does not press us. He allows us to settle our affairs with our Superior, Father Corbe.

There are always from six to seven hundred pupils in our schools. About two-thirds are Catholics. We might almost say that the other third are also Catholics, at least in heart, which is particularly true of the boarders at Saint Mary's. Three of these dear children received holy Baptism on the twenty-third of June. On the same day two made their First Communion, after a retreat of three days, during which time they edified the entire Community. I have seldom seen children more fervent and better disposed. Their first Communion day was for us a beautiful feast. After the ceremony I accompanied the dear children to the Academy. Their companions, from whom they had been separated during the retreat, received them with demonstrations of warmth and respectful affection. "Oh, I wish I were with you!" said these poor little girls who are not even baptized. Tears of tenderness were in the eyes of all.

Several of the pupils are taking instruction and have already received permission to be baptized, but there are others who cannot obtain permission. One who desires to be baptized before leaving, is seventeen or eighteen years old and belongs to a family remarkable as to high morality, but much opposed to Catholicism. The young girl is a model in every sense. Must we see her leave without being regenerated in the holy waters of Baptism? I cannot tell you what pain this thought causes to all her teachers. The Bishop and our Superior have not yet decided. I do not know what their decision will be. At this very moment I am in receipt of a letter from her father, who insists on her returning without Baptism. Poor child!

Several who have been educated in our houses, and are now married and in society, are advocates for our holy religion. We begin to see the good which our Congregation is doing in this country. Nevertheless, we must expect to suffer much here, surrounded by those who are interested in many ways of destroying, or at least weakening, our influence. We shall always have to struggle against their rivalry. This year they have made unheard-of efforts to ruin our schools.

The Episcopal minister of Vincennes has left his church to become a Catholic. The one who replaces him keeps a school; he has, besides his parishioners, a family of fourteen children. Poor man! I cannot get accustomed to the idea of one so burdened usurping the title of "Minister of the Lord." When returning from Fort Wayne, I found myself in the steam-boat with an individual whom they called "Bishop." In fact he was the Episcopal Bishop of Indiana. It is probable that he was not flattered to be in our company as he soon left the boat; however, he may have arrived then at his destination.

Besides the annoyances above mentioned, we have much to suffer from the climate. It is so changeable that in one day we sometimes experience extremes both of heat and cold. For three or four weeks the heat has been suffocating, varying from 80 to 95 degrees. When there is no breeze at all, one can scarcely breathe. The heat is due, I believe, to the drought. At Saint Mary's it has rained hard only once since the last days of April. Yesterday we had a heavy rain, which did great good to everything. It is surprising that the trees, and even the corn, etc., remain fresh-looking in such a drought. This is owing, unquestionably, to the heavy dew which falls every night.

We have gone out several times this summer to gather simples and linden blossoms, etc. In each excursion we discover something marvelous, beautiful, and useful in the magnificent forests of Indiana. At each step we can admire the grandeur, the power, the goodness of God. How bountifully He provides for all our wants—I would even say, for our pleasures! I love our woods and solitude very much; and yet, I surprise myself sometimes regretting my little Ruillé, going so far even as wishing to go back to prepare myself for death. In repose, far from temporals, should I not be nearer heaven?

Many thanks for having given us news of our beloved Mothers. We offer them the homage of our sincere and respectful affection, and to you, my Lord and Father, that of our lively and deep veneration. . . .[19]

TO THE REVEREND JOSEPH KUNDEK, JASPER

Saint Mary's, August 18, 1850

My good Father and Friend:

We felt the effects of your fervent prayers during our retreat. Notwithstanding the excessive heat and our poor accommodations, all our Sisters were able to make this dear

---

[19] Original in the archives of the Diocese of Le Mans.

retreat, to follow all the exercises until the end; this could not have happened without a special grace from God. I beg of you to thank Him for us and to ask that the fruits of this retreat may not be lost by dissipation and tepidity.

Sister M. Magdalen's health is poor, so poor in fact that we think of keeping her here, at least for some time, confident that you will not take it ill. Besides, she will always be at home, and should her presence at Jasper become necessary, we shall be able to send her back to you at any time. Meanwhile we give you Sister Agnes and two other Sisters; thus nothing will suffer from this new arrangement.

I was happy to learn that you also will have a retreat at Vincennes, as soon as the cholera shall have entirely disappeared; and I hope that this time the cholera will not prevent you from coming to pay us a little visit in our Woods, where everyone desires to see you.

The Jesuit Father who gave us the retreat has been sick ever since it closed; he is somewhat better today. The Bishop and Father Corbe are also indisposed. Father Lalumière complains a good deal while waiting for sickness to come. I think they will all be here at Saint Mary's this evening. You will be missed. I wish you could be with them.

Our Sisters will be at Vincennes on Sunday. If you could send for them during the early part of the week we should be greatly obliged to you. All offer you their profound respects and commend themselves to your prayers. . . .

TO THE SAME

Saint Mary's, December 4, 1850

Dear Reverend Father:

Long ago I should have answered the letter with which you honored me, dated the 8th of last month, had I not been sick—that is my excuse. I should be happy, Reverend Father, to second your zealous views, if it were possible; but there is not in all our Community now at Saint Mary's a single person who knows how to play the organ. You see I cannot give what God does not give to me. I am really sorry; however, I console myself thinking that you will easily find musicians among your Germans, who are born singers. I am very glad also that you have an organ. It will greatly add to the majesty of the holy ceremonies, already so devotional, in your beautiful church. Never shall I forget the happiness I experienced when assisting at one of your feasts, the first time in this country. Jasper reminds me of France, particularly of Brittany.

Here we are in Advent. Already we have entered upon the ecclesiastical new year. Permit me to offer my wishes for your perfect happiness, not upon earth—true happiness for a Christian, much less for a priest, is not found here—but for the grace to continue carrying your cross with courage and love, in order thereby to merit to enjoy God during all eternity. I doubt not but that you will ask the same for me, and for our poor little Congregation, which is so very needy. You are almost our first benefactor in this country; be also our protector, and obtain for us the grace to be very faithful to our holy vocation. . . .

TO THE RIGHT REVEREND J. BOUVIER, BISHOP OF LE MANS

December 18, 1850

My Lord:

I cannot allow these days to pass by without offering to Your Lordship the wishes which your Daughters of the Forest form for your happiness. Do not think, my Lord, that in order to call down upon you the blessings of heaven, it is necessary to be at a special season of the year. No, my good Father, as long as there will be a daughter of yours at Saint

Mary's, there will be a daily offering presented to God for the one to whom we owe not only the foundation of our dear mission but also its development and its preservation. What would become of this young Congregation in its days of trial without you, my Father? Could we ever forget it? You will excuse me for repeating it. Thanks to you, then, my Lord. The time of such events is passed for our Congregation of the Woods; or, if God has some in reserve for it later on, He gives it today as much peace as a work of this kind can have in the midst of a Protestant people.

We had our retreat as usual. It was given by a Jesuit and produced good effects. The Sisters follow the exercises with edifying assiduity. I am the only one of the house to break silence during that time. Silence is observed perfectly; hence, all the rest is well done. Five novices took their vows, making thirty-three professed Sisters. Four postulants received the habit. We have now twelve novices and twelve postulants. There were fifteen of the latter, but just lately we dismissed three. It is better to have fewer in number and good ones. We keep them about two years, sometimes more than two years, in the novitiate before giving them the habit, as many are so poorly instructed in their religion when they come, and are so far from being all that is implied in the religious life. When our schools will be more numerous and will have had some years of existence, we shall not have the same difficulties. There are a few of our own pupils among the postulants, and we can see the difference.

Our schools have suffered much this year from Protestant opposition. There are now only thirty-three pupils at the Academy. Moreover, several of the Catholics do not pay. We are as poor as Job. It is impossible to think of building. Bishop de St. Palais gave me four hundred dollars a month ago [advance salary for the teachers at Vincennes] to buy building material. I was obliged to use it for the purchasing of provisions, which are almost half as dear again as last year.

The pupils being less numerous in the establishments also, for the same reasons (hard times and bigotry), our income has diminished. We have a great many little orphans [at Vincennes], forty-seven girls; there are, besides, thirty-two boys, whom the Bishop wishes us to take in charge at once. We dare not refuse His Lordship, he is so good to us. However, I fear very much that we shall not succeed in bringing up little boys. I wish they were confided to Father Sorin; but he would want the Bishop to pay him a considerable sum for each of these children, and His Lordship cannot do it. We shall do what we can; perhaps later on there may be found some other means of caring for them.

I do not venture to speak again of our Bishop going to France. He has put it off so long that I think he will delay yet longer; nevertheless, he says he shall start in the spring. He thinks of leaving the diocese in charge of our Superior, Father Corbe; but the latter does not wish to accept the administration. I hope we shall induce him to take it, for it would be a great privilege for our Congregation to have him at the head of the diocese during the absence of our worthy prelate. Father Corbe is very kind to us. We, on our side, do all we can to show him gratitude. It is pleasant to live thus in union and to have peace.

Another establishment is offered to us; it is in Louisiana. There would be inconveniences in accepting it, but it would afford great advantages, especially in regard to pecuniary resources, which will be wanting for a long time in Indiana, as it is yet a new State. Notwithstanding, I do not believe that we can think of this foundation at the present time. The proposal of this establishment raised among us a slight contest or, rather, difference of opinion on two points of our Rules: one, a passage in Chapter XIV reading, "If there be an Ecclesiastical Superior named by the Bishop, it would be to him that the Superioress should address herself." Sister St. Francis thinks that we can take this establishment, send Sisters there when we please, with the permission of our Ecclesiastical Superior, without asking the permission of the Bishop. It appears to me that for this action, the Superior should have to be invested with a special authorization, conformable to the Article of Chapter IX, which says that the Bishop can always recall us to his diocese when he wishes. I conclude that we cannot send Sisters to Louisiana, nor elsewhere, without the permission of the Bishop of Vincennes. Be so kind, my Lord, as to tell us which one is right. The other submits in advance to your decision.[20]

What is now becoming of your Republic? I fear that the calm which you enjoy is only a forerunner of a storm. You are let alone at least. Faith and piety appear to be reanimated. Religion is respected, but how long will this last? I could not tell you how uneasy I am about you, Father, and about our Mothers and Sisters, and even about the whole of our poor France. She is ever our country, ever dear to a French heart, even though she be away off, almost at the antipodes!

We have learned indirectly that our Sisters of France have greatly increased in number this year and that they have several new establishments. We rejoice at the success of dear Ruillé. If you see anyone from there, I beg of you, my Lord, to remember me to them. Deign to pray for your Daughters of the Woods and bless them. . . .[21]

TO SISTER MARIE THERESE, MADISON

Saint Mary's, January 5, 1851

My dear Sister:

Your letters, your wishes, and your little presents have been received. I thank you heartily for all. The present for

[20] The decision was, of course, that the permission of the Bishop would be necessary. The Rule has been made explicit on this point.

[21] Original in the archives of the Diocese of Le Mans.

Nanon figured in my feast as though it had been for me. I shall forward it to its destination.

I hope to write soon to your sister Emily. If God calls her, He will furnish her the means to get here from France. I shall tell her frankly what I think; she will then do what she judges to be right. I have written to Francis advising him to come with the Bishop. I told him that you would be happy to see him and that John would be more than delighted. I am going to write to Nanon also, to thank her for taking such good care of the father and mother of two of my daughters.

You pray in a special manner for me these days? I likewise pray especially for you. This morning after Holy Communion I begged God with all the intensity of my soul to grant you the grace to overcome your propensity to anger. If you will it you can do it, for grace will not be wanting; and you will render yourself happy and *me also*. I do not hesitate to say that I would entreat you on my knees if by that act I were to be more persuasive. *Never speak when you are excited*. Keep back the words that would wound your loving Jesus. . . . Oh, how patient He was, and still is, even with you! Are you not His daughter, His disciple, His spouse? Will He recognize you by your gentle sweetness?

John has a big, new overcoat, and whiskers on his chin. He is always a good boy and loves you tenderly.[22]

Adieu, my daughter. Reflect well on the contents of this letter. If it makes no impression, if you do not try to do better, it is useless to write to me. I shall not look upon you as my daughter. In the hope that you will improve, I assure you of my constant affection. . . .

The next letter is addressed to Sister Maria (Caroline Vicaire). Born August 16, 1824, at St. Aubain du Cormier,

---

[22] John de la Haie (Delahay), Sister Marie Therese's brother, was employed as gardener at Saint Mary-of-the-Woods.

France, she entered the novitiate at Saint Mary-of-the Woods, November 25, 1845. She was a music teacher employed in various missions for many years. Finally, becoming disabled, she spent her declining days at the Mother-house. A little packet of twenty-five letters labeled, "Most precious letters from my beloved Mother Theodore," was her treasure. When the writings of Mother Theodore were being collected for translation Sister Maria selected those letters she cared to give, copied out portions of some she withheld, then, when those had been copied, destroyed all the originals; hence the noticeable omissions in the letters here produced. Despite a difficult character, Sister had fine qualities, especially an affectionate and forgiving heart and great generosity. She was strongly attached to Mother Theodore, thus was it possible for the one to administer stern rebuke and the other to receive it with profit.

TO SISTER MARIA, VINCENNES

Saint Mary's, January 6, 1851

Having just learned that you are better, my dear Sister, I thank God with all my heart. May you learn from this illness all the lessons He intended to teach you, and above all, may you profit by them. Be more prudent; never remain with wet feet, and do not expose yourself to an attack which is likely to return at the least imprudence. . . .

It pleases me much that you have read my letter and meditated upon it. Meditate on it still further while you are unable to do much for the house. Make serious reflections for the future. Your lightness causes me to fear much for you. When will you be firm and always yourself? But you are exactly like the weathercock on a steeple, ready to turn with every wind. In conclusion, I hope grace will triumph finally, and that you will become its conquest. See how the years are fleeing, and then — eternity! Are we ready to appear before God?

I thank you sincerely for your good wishes. You do well to pray for me. Ask for me especially the grace of a good death. Assure our dear Sisters Helena and Rose of my gratitude and good wishes in return for theirs. I intended writing a few lines to each of them, but I cannot do so now. A pack of letters is waiting for me to answer, and I am not well. They will be so kind as to excuse me this time. I shall soon see them on my way to Madison, if God gives me health enough to go. . . .

TO SISTER BASILIDE, MADISON

January 28, 1851

I have before me your letters of the 21st and 22nd of this month. My dear Basilide, I begin by telling you that I am very glad to hear that the arrival of Sister St. John has given you pleasure, and that she took the school immediately. I should like to think that she can take care of it by herself, but I am far from that conviction. Well, we shall see. You know, my dear daughter, that I always speak to you with candor and simplicity, convinced that this is a duty for me, and, too, I know that, after reflection, you prefer to be treated this way. Thus I am encouraged to proceed. It seems to me that a certain influence at Madison is harmful. This makes me feel more and more that some other change is necessary in your establishment rather than that of Sister Mary——. It is beginning to rain now, so it may be possible for me to go to see you soon; we shall then settle this matter together. . . .

Perhaps you are going to exclaim against my surmises? Well, Sister Basilide, listen. When I went to Rennes twenty-six years ago, there was a Sister there who was *detested*— this is the word. It was poor Sister Emanuel, a person with little training, abrupt as a Breton though she was a Norman.

Two months later, no one was to be compared with Sister Emanuel. The future of the establishment seemed to be in her hands. It is my conviction that if nothing had been said prejudicial to Sister Mary——, she would have the same standing with the pupils that she had last year, when I could not make them consent to leave her, although they were to be promoted to a higher class.

I am surprised that you do not know why the Misses D—— have left your school. I shall tell you when I see you. And I want to say to you now, my dear Sister Basilide, that I am happy to see that you can receive the advice I give without getting displeased with me. It is a great consolation for a Superior to be able to speak frankly to those of whom she has charge. You know this yourself. I have just received a letter from my "gros cherubin." She gives me news from Ruillé later than yours. Sister Eudoxie is not very well.[23] Our Mothers are in good health.

Not only can we not resuscitate the dead, but we can not even prevent the living from dying. Our poor Sister Marie Joseph is dying of consumption. I am greatly grieved about it. Pray for her.

Bishop de St. Palais no longer likes the first arrangements for the Sisters of Vincennes. He now proposes to give us $1,200 each year for four years. The condition he puts is that the Motherhouse be built before the end of these four years. God knows whether it will be. This good Bishop is truly a father to us. He imparts new life to our Woods whenever he comes to see us.

I believe I wrote you about the baker having embraced Presbyterianism last Sunday. What an example! I wish very much that you could get rid of your Armandine. We really have not the means to keep such children. We prefer to see a class fail entirely rather than to yield to the unreasonable-

---

[23] Mistress of Novices at Ruillé-sur-Loir.

ness or caprice of those who have no right to choose the Sisters, and who take a foot where they are given an inch. I shall tell you the rest when I see you. . . .

TO SISTER MARIA

Saint Mary's, January 30, 1851

You wish to get better? I also desire it, my dear Sister, if such be the will of God. But, as I have already told you, I would prefer to see you dead than unfaithful to the holy engagements you have contracted with God. No doubt but in His admirable designs in your regard. He has sent you this illness, or at least permitted it, for your sanctification. Profit by it, my daughter. Ah! be faithful to your holy promises . . . It sometimes seems to me that, having received so many graces, so many favors—being so unworthy—it seems to me, I say, that you will be severely punished if you are not faithful. You will be punished in an exemplary way. Take care. God is not mocked. He has His turn.

I do not think there is any danger for your life now, but be very prudent. Guard against getting wet, but if you do happen to be thus exposed you must change your clothes immediately.

All the Sisters send you much love. They are well. I think you will have the chance of seeing your Mother Theodore before long, just as soon as the river rises. Adieu, my dear daughter. Pray for me. . . .

TO THE REVEREND J. KUNDEK

Saint Mary's, February 22, 1851

Dear Reverend Father:

During the time Sister Bonaventure has been at Jasper she has had three, or rather four, different Superiors, and has never been satisfied with any one of them. She has always complained and constantly looked upon herself as a person unjustly persecuted. This disposition seems little adapted to the religious life. We gave her an extra year of trial, but she appears to be the same. It now seems to us that it would be well to try her in another place, under another Superior, in order to have nothing to reproach ourselves with when it shall be time to decide definitively on her admission or dismissal.

As we have great confidence in your judgment, we should appreciate it if you would tell us what you think of this novice; your advice would be of service to us. If another Sister is needed at present, I shall take one with me when I visit that mission, which will be during the holy season of Lent, if such be the will of God. I hope to have the honor and pleasure of finding you there, and of charging you with some commissions for Europe. It might be better for *me* to go back also, for I am good for nothing but to be put with the invalids. Please pray much for me. I do not forget you in the little that I do. I was very sorry about your accident. The Sisters wrote me that you scarcely felt it, so entirely are you disengaged from this earth. . . .

TO THE SAME

Vincennes, March 10, 1851

Dear Reverend Father:

I received your good letter here at Vincennes. It gave me pleasure, especially as to what you tell me concerning Sister Bonaventure. I should be very happy to see her form herself to the religious life. We shall try her at Vincennes with the orphan boys. I think this beautiful occupation will be very pleasing to her and will strengthen her vocation. As to the advice you give me for myself, I am very grateful; now obtain for me the grace to put it into practice and to become in the hands of God less useless for His glory.

In regard to the two little girls of whom you speak, if they are satisfied with the education they can obtain at Jasper, I have no longer any objection to their being received there. As to the charge for their board, that will depend on whether they are rich or poor. In the former case, I think they ought to pay sixty dollars, thirty dollars each, for a session of twenty-two weeks. If there be only one, she should pay thirty-five dollars. Besides, of course, they pay for their books, paper, pens, etc. If they are poor, the price can be reduced. I leave this matter to Sister Agnes. Arrange it together. I have written to Sister that the Community would keep an American teacher at Jasper only on condition that there would be at least twenty pupils in the school. If there are not that number, two Sisters will have to suffice, at least until the retreat.

I suppose you know that our dear Sister Marie Joseph is dying at Fort Wayne. They do not think she can live longer than this month. Please pray for her, asking especially for this dear daughter the grace of a happy death. And ask the same favor also for me, your humble servant. . . .

Only seven days were to pass before Mother Theodore must announce that the summons had come to her lamented daughter.

LETTER CIRCULAR

Madison, Indiana, March 17, 1851

It is with a heart oppressed with the most profound sorrow, my very dear Sisters, that I impart to you the news of the loss we have sustained in the death of our beloved

Sister Marie Joseph Pardeillan. On the fourteenth instant, at seven o'clock in the morning, she departed this life, a victim of consumption which had lasted six months. She bore her illness with a patience and longanimity truly admirable. You will share our deep affliction, my dear Sisters, for you loved Sister Marie Joseph and you were loved by her. What an affectionate heart was hers! What uprightness of mind she possessed! I have never found any one more candid, nor any one who had a greater aversion for the least shadow of duplicity. Her beautiful soul was visible on her open and benevolent countenance.

You, my dear children, have admired her obedience, her devotedness to her Congregation, her love for the Rules, and her tender piety. You have been consoled and edified especially by her universal charity, of which you have been the witnesses and many of you the objects. Those, for instance, who have lived with her, must remember how she labored to render life sweet and happy to her companions. But, my dear children, Sister Marie Joseph did not sanctify herself among us by any extraordinary or singular actions; she did it by the practice of the virtues of her state, for she was a good Sister of Providence. Very soon she will receive the reward of her devotedness and sacrifice and will be for us a new intercessor at the throne of God: such is my confidence.

My beloved children, our turn also will come before long. Thrice happy we shall be if, like those of our Congregation who have preceded us to the grave, we try every day to be what we desire to be at our entrance into eternity. If we love Our Lord with our whole heart, if we serve Him faithfully, we shall be happy even in this life. If there is any felicity to be found in this land of exile, it is undoubtedly for a good Religious. Death itself, far from being bitter to her, is the object of her most sanguine hope.

Although we have the firm confidence that our dear Sister

Marie Joseph has found favor with God, we are not dispensed from the obligation of praying for her. We know that, due to the infirmity of our corrupt nature, she contracted some debts towards the Divine Justice, but we do not know whether her reparations were sufficient to cancel them. Who is worthy to enter at once into the tabernacle of the Holy of Holies in leaving this world of sin and iniquity? Therefore you will offer for the repose of her soul the prayers prescribed in the 23rd chapter, paragraph 24 of our holy Rules, and remember her very often in your good works.

When I am visiting the establishments I have very little time to myself, especially when I am not very strong, as at present. I was not at Mass this morning. Tomorrow, though we celebrate the feast of our good patron St. Joseph, we are not to have Mass here, because our two priests will be absent.

I am awaiting an answer from our venerated Father Corbe to know whether I should go to Fort Wayne or not. I do not know when I shall have the pleasure of seeing you. *It will not be sooner than I wish.*

All the Sisters here are well and send you a thousand loving messages. Be always very fervent. Pray much and well. Do all your actions for God and He will be your recompense. All yours in Our Lord

SISTER ST. THEODORE,
Sup'r Gen'l.

From the account of Sister Marie Joseph in the Community necrology, the following details of her early life are an extract:

Mlle. Josephine Yvonne Pardeillan was born in Alsace of distinguished parents. Her father belonged to the bar of Savern. He provided for his children masters capable of forming their minds and their manners. Reverses of fortune made Josephine prize at an early age the advantages of a good education. Placed in a Badoise family, she was charged with the education of two young countesses. While there, as everywhere she went, she gained the love and respect of all. Some time later, she entered the Maison de Commerce of the Picquet family at Strasbourg, and her devotedness to its interests, and her sincere affection for the family rendered her the friend, the sister, and the confidante of all its members.

The pleasures and friendship and the enjoyments of life, however, did not satisfy her soul, and she eventually entered a religious community in Alsace. This community, in the summer of 1839, promised Bishop de la Hailandière to give him some of its members to found a house of the order at Vincennes, Indiana. They were to leave in a few weeks. Mlle. Pardeillan was one of the volunteers. She was then permitted to return home for a visit with her family, and was to meet the others at Havre. At the appointed time she was at Havre, but there she learned from the Bishop that her sisters were not coming, that for weighty reasons the community had withdrawn its promise, but that another order had been secured for the following year, and she might return to Alsace or go to Indiana at once and await the arrival of the Sisters of Providence. As all her preparations had been made for America, and her desire to go was great, she decided to seize the opportunity and join the party Father Martin was conducting to Vincennes, which arrived in July, 1839. The account continues: "A stranger, alone, and ignorant of the language of the country, living in the world after having renounced it, with no sure guide for her soul—thus she remained for the space of a year enduring sufferings that few can comprehend." It was a happy day for her when she extended greetings to Mother Theodore and her little band at Saint Mary-of-the-Woods. She then entered upon her novitiate here with admirable fervor, and ever afterwards gave example of generous devotedness. "Few persons," concludes the record, "have been gifted with more amiable qualities than Sister Marie Joseph. Her uprightness of mind, her open disposition and urbanity of manners, and her tender piety gained her the love and respect of all who knew her."

The death of relatives in the family of Sister St. Francis Xavier from time to time, called for words of condolence from her to her mother. With Sister's letter, on one occasion, Mother Theodore encloses one from herself.

TO MME. LE FER DE LA MOTTE, ST. SERVAN

Saint Mary-of-the-Woods, June 3, 1851

Madame and very dear Friend:

I reproach myself severely for having delayed the letter of your dear daughter for some days. I did not wish to let it go without telling you that I share in all your sorrows and pains from the bottom of my heart. God afflicts you. He has called away two who were the worthy objects of your affection. You have deeply felt these separations, but in the midst of your tears and sorrows, how consoled you have all been by the thought of the happiness which they enjoy in heaven. I am more inclined to invoke them than to pray for them. You have really a family of saints.

I often tell Sister St. Francis that I forgive her willingly for loving you so much. I gladly share her sentiments; for I feel in my heart an affection so tender and so full of respect for your whole family, that I sometimes fear lest I go too far, even Natalie[24] has already a great share in our love and prayers. I hope you will have embraced her when you receive this letter, and I trust she will be like your other daughters. God gives her to you for your consolation and, I

---

[24] Charles, eldest son of M. and Mme, le Fer de la Motte, was a navy officer. Once, when he was in the waters of the southern Pacific, he won the heart of an estimable Spanish lady, Mlle. Natalie Valdivieso, a native of Valparaiso, Chili. The young lady's mother being very ill at the time, Charles was obliged to return to his headquarters in France without her. Some months later, having learned of the death of Mme. Valdivieso, Charles claimed his affianced. But as his duties would not permit him to go to get her, "he was represented in Chili by a French gentleman, one of his friends, and contracted thus before God and man a union blessed and approved by the Church and sanctioned equally by the laws of Chili. During her long voyage from South America to France, Madame Natalie was exposed to great dangers from the sea, from fire, and from yellow fever." She was on a war ship. After several months of suffering on her part and anguish on the part of those awaiting her, she arrived at Lorient where her husband met her and introduced her into his family, which received her as one of themselves. The marriage by proxy was arranged on account of the risk attending the perilous voyage.

Cf. *Life and Letters of Sister St. Francis Xavier.* (Providence Press, Saint Mary-of-the-Woods, Indiana), p. 294.

believe, for the salvation of a soul which is very dear to us.

I suppose Sister St. Francis Xavier wrote you that we had both been ill in November, she at Saint Mary's and I at Vincennes. Never did I suffer more than in being far from this dear child during her illness. I had the presumption to think that no one could take care of her as well as I could. You must not be disedified. We truly love each other very tenderly, but I do not believe this affection is displeasing to God. If I were to lose Sister St. Francis now, where should I find a Mistress of Novices who would, by word and example, cause virtue to be loved and cherished as she does? These chosen and privileged souls are rare even in France, you know, dear Madame, and you will understand my predilection. Here no one is jealous of it. Every one else loves her also; who could help loving her? Oh! the good God does not forbid us to love—happily for Madame le Fer, is is not? To love in the right way is to accomplish the whole Law; it is to begin that happy life which will have its perfection only in heaven, where we shall live forever with a holy and perfect love.

I thank you very much for your kindness in sending me such excellent shoes. They made me feel that I am very far from being dead. I do not know who sent the delicacies. I suspect Mlle. Cecile has played that trick on me; she is the only one who could have guessed my stomach troubles and their remedies. I thank her very much for her attentions and beg of her to remember my spiritual needs before God.

If I were to try to thank you, dear Madame, for all your favors in particular, I should have to write a volume; for, what do we not owe to your generosity! We speak to God of our gratitude; to Him we confide the care of rewarding the good that you have done for His love to the poor Daughters of Saint Mary's. I dare hope that in His infinite bounty He will listen to the supplications we offer for you and all your family—prayers by which we ask His graces and blessings in time and the happiness of possessing Him in eternity. You will be, Madame, the interpreter to your dear children of my sentiments, and above all, do not forget Monsieur le Fer, for whom I entertain a profound veneration. . . .

LETTER CIRCULAR

Saint Mary-of-the-Woods, July 4, 1851

My beloved Sisters:

Once more I have the pleasure of calling you home for our retreat, which will begin August 8th. Come a few days before, my dear Sisters, in order to rest a little.

Be prepared to profit by those precious favors which for some of us are offered, perhaps, for the last time. Last year Sister Marie Joseph was with us; now she is no more. Sister Angelina is almost dying; who will be the next?

If the Apostles themselves were in need of retreat after having converted many persons, and having been obeyed even by devils, how much more are we in need of recollection, having neither the fervor nor the power of the Apostles. Be then, my dear Sisters, more united with God. Act with a purer intention. Be in your journey models of prudence and modesty; thus you will be the better disposed to receive the light of the Holy Ghost, which you especially need this year, having to make the election of an Assistant and of a Mistress of Novices. You know yourself how important that choice is, since on it depends the prosperity or the ruin of our dear Congregation. To ask for light you will say the *Veni Creator* and the *Ave Maris Stella*, as is the custom.

SISTER ST. THEODORE,
Sup'r Gen'l.

TO THE RIGHT REVEREND J. BOUVIER, BISHOP OF LE MANS

Saint Mary-of-the-Woods, July 10, 1851

My venerated Father:

At last our good Bishop has started off for France, where we hope he will arrive in a few days. I did not wish to write this to you any sooner for fear of causing some disarrangement in the plans for your intended journey. His Lordship has decided to go to see you wherever you may be, as soon as his business will permit him to do so.

I am convinced that you will be happy to learn from our good Bishop himself the details he will give you about your Daughters of the Woods. He will be able to tell you facts which will interest and console your paternal heart, and to show you that many souls still owe their salvation to the resolution you took of sending your Daughters to Indiana and to your kind protection during their days of trial. The trials are past, thank God. Bishop de St. Palais has made them disappear entirely. He has always shown himself the friend of our Congregation. Even as a simple priest, without fearing disgrace he was our defender. When Vicar General he was our advocate near good Bishop Bazin, who, ignorant of our affairs, scarcely knew what to believe regarding accusations brought against us. And finally, since he is our Bishop he has been a devoted father to us. He never causes us to feel his authority, except by the favors he bestows upon us. He never puts any obstacle to the administration. He gives counsels full of wisdom, yet leaves us at liberty if we find difficulties in the execution of them.

On our side, we regard it as a duty to second the beneficent views of this good prelate. Ten Sisters are employed in the asylum, whose inmates increase daily; yet there is no assurance for the future of the Sisters and of the children other than that Divine Providence takes care of the birds of the air and the grass of the field.

I hope, my Lord, that our Bishop will tell you that he is pleased with us; that will be some compensation for the past. When we compare the past with the present, we feel as if we were in heaven. The little miseries of life, even the prejudices and opposition of the Protestants, seem easy to bear in comparison. However, it has pleased the Almighty to try us this year in a very painful manner. We have lost our good Sister Marie Joseph, Superior of our house in Fort Wayne. She is a great loss for us as we have so few local superiors. The young people of this country are little qualified for government; their education renders them unfit. Women are not employed in any kind of business in America. It is said that in the East they are beginning to take up the French way, but as yet, we are strangers to this movement in our Woods.

Our American Sisters have not the tender piety of the French, but there is no hypocrisy nor dissimulation among them; they are, on the contrary, as a general thing, full of uprightness, of devotedness, and of simplicity, and some are models of innocence and of virtue.

St. Joseph has sent us a large number of postulants this year, several of whom seem very fine. It is a pity we cannot place them under local superiors, who could form them to mission work. Unfortunately, we have few of this kind. Oh, if Ruillé could but send us a few! Were you to say a word in our favor it would be very powerful. I know that you will intercede for us—you have always been so good towards us. Now is the time to come to our aid. Bishop de St. Palais would bring these dear Sisters; later on we might give back what they lent us. It is not necessary that they have great talents and a brilliant education; a solid and enlightened piety, a good head and sound judgment, joined to a good will—that is what we want.

As for the temporal, we could manage very well if our Motherhouse were built and paid for. We have very few debts now. They would all be paid off this year if we did not have to build. But it becomes absolutely necessary to build. We are literally piled upon one another, which is not only inconvenient, but very unhealthy during the extreme heat of the summer. And the heat is excessive this year. Every day we have storms, rain, etc. Our brickmakers are quite disconcerted. At this moment the Sisters are haymaking, because with so much rain the hay is spoiling. A storm the last night of April destroyed all the fruit in this part of the country. Even a large number of the trees were blown down.

Then there came a large swarm of locusts which made terrible ravages in our orchards. Our forests themselves look like vast orange groves, on account of the numberless little tender branches which have been cut down by these insects and now, having become yellow, are hanging down, from afar resembling oranges. The locusts are something like the May bug; we know not whence they come. They are armed with a kind of saw which is dangerous, not only to plants but to animals, and even to man. They make a sort of buzzing noise during the whole time of their existence, which lasts only five or six weeks. Then they die, after having deposited, one knows not where, the seed for another generation, which fortunately is not developed until seventeen years later; but they never fail to reappear after that time.

Sister Angelina, one of our dear daughters here, is dying. She is our principal music teacher and she paints admirably also. She did all my English correspondence. Her death will be a great loss. She is, and always has been, truly good and devoted. I beg of you to pray for this dear child.

We are going to write to Ruillé. We hope you will accompany Bishop de St. Palais in his visit there, if you possibly

[25] Original in the archives of the Diocese of Le Mans.

can. Our Reverend Father Corbe and all our Sisters offer you
the homage of their profound respect. . . .[25]

LETTER CIRCULAR

September 8, 1851

My beloved Sisters:

Scarcely six months have elapsed since we had the painful
duty of announcing to you the death of one of our dear Sisters.
Today, we have the same sad and difficult task.

Yesterday, September 7, at six o'clock in the evening, our
dear Sister Angelina Connery terminated her mortal career.
God had prepared her for her last hour by a painful sickness
lasting two years, and especially by her sufferings of the last
three months of her life.

Sister Angelina consecrated herself to God, while very
young, in the Convent of St. Joseph [at Emmitsburg] She
never loved the world. Far from its dangers she preserved,
throughout her whole life, her spotless innocence and childlike
simplicity.

During the eight years that she lived with us, she rendered important services to our Congregation. Her devotedness has been scarcely equalled by anyone; and her filial
affection for her Superiors is known to all. Her loss will be
severely felt, but no one will feel it more than I who lose in her
a devoted, useful, and loving daughter. If anything can console
us in this sorrowful circumstance, it is her edifying faith. She
died with sentiments of filial confidence in God, abandoning
herself to His holy will, and full of gratitude towards our
divine Saviour Who had always protected His fragile and
confiding child.

Some of her last words which touched us deeply were:
"Oh, how good Our Lord is!" We replied, "You will understand His goodness much better when you will have quitted
this body of sin." "O Mother," she said, "I understand it
even now." We cherish the hope that, fortified by the

Sacraments of the Church, which she received with a lively faith, she is numbered among those who follow the Lamb whithersoever He goeth.

Nevertheless, as we know that nothing defiled can enter the kingdom of heaven, and that it is very difficult to depart this life free from all penalties, you will join with us, my dear Sisters, in offering up for the repose of the soul of our dear Sister Angelina the prayers prescribed by our holy Rules. Pray also for

Your devoted

SISTER ST. THEODORE,

Sup'r Gen'l.

TO THE REVEREND A. MARTIN, NATCHITOCHES, LA.

Saint Mary's, September 11, 1851

Respected Sir and generous Friend:

This letter of our most dear Sister Philomene tells you that we have been on the point of losing her, but it does not tell you that her determination has cost me tears and anguish of soul. I realized then that it was not in vain that she called me Mother; however, our dear Lord has kept her this time. Pray, oh, pray much for her. We have felt, and we yet feel, that it is owing to your prayers that she is still with us. Please continue to pray very earnestly for her. She is so light and has so little piety.

We have lost our good little Sister Angelina. I regret her deeply. She is a great loss to us; but we feel sure that from heaven she will assist us. She was so pure, so frank, so confiding, and so devoted. I recommend her also to your prayers.

We heard that you have lost your Vicar General. This afflicts us especially on your account, as one seldom finds devoted friends nowadays. . . .

Saint Mary's, November 3, 1851

My beloved Daughter:

I do not wish to impose on you the girl of whom you spoke in your letter. If you do not care for her, do not take her. I shall not mind it in the least. Do as you judge convenient. Like you, I would rather keep the one who has pleased all the Sisters than try another.

No, my daughter, I was not surprised at the letter you know about. Some women's minds are so strange that nothing from them can surprise me. The one of whom I speak is afflicted with melancholy. That is a bad disease. One has to bear with such persons and suffer; but they themselves suffer more than anyone else.

I think Miss Rose Ann has left Terre Haute where, up to last Friday, she was still awaiting her brother. As I have not received any news since then, I do not know positively whether she has gone or not. I regret her very much, because she is a person who has much ability, one who might be very useful to us: but she is very hot-headed, and I would not like henceforth to receive subjects with faults which make others suffer too much and weaken union and charity. She is still very young and might correct herself, in which case she would be a very good acquisition. We shall see what will become of her. I gave her until the spring to consider. We must pray for her.

Sister Mary Cecilia has a very severe cold. Her lungs are so weak that I have fear when I hear her cough. She never complains. When she says she is sick it will be time to give her Extreme Unction. I do not see her for weeks, except in the chapel.

If you could attract more pupils for music I would be very glad; for, first, Sister Celestia can teach it very well, and, second, we are going to be in pressing need for our new house.

The carpenter asks thirty-five hundred dollars for the work alone, without even furnishing a nail. Imagine what will be needed for the whole—not a cent less than ten thousand dollars. Where shall we find this amount? But, after all, we are the daughters of Divine Providence. The sum will be paid in a short time, I mean in a few years. I wish I were as sure that we shall then be good Religious.

It is truly surprising that the Bishop does not give us a sign of life from France. I am really afflicted at his negligence in taking care of himself. It might finally be detrimental to him.

All the Sisters send you much love. They are all well. Adieu, my beloved Sister Basilide. Pray much for me. . . .

TO THE RIGHT REVEREND J. BOUVIER, BISHOP OF LE MANS

Saint Mary-of-the-Woods, January 1, 1852

My Lord and venerated Father:

To you I address the first lines that I write this year, which has just begun but which will have advanced far before this reaches you. Our wishes for your happiness would then be too late if we had not addressed them before to Him who alone can repay you. This morning we prayed with more than ordinary fervor begging that He would pay all we owe Your Lordship. It is asking a good deal, for we love to repeat it—after God we owe everything to you. Without you never would our mission of Indiana have existed.

For a long time we have been expecting a letter from Bishop de St. Palais telling us that he has been to see you, and given you news of your Daughters, who are also his. We feel convinced that his visit will be a consolation for your paternal heart. He will tell you of the good that God does in Indiana by the Sisters of Providence, and you will easily see that he is entirely devoted to us.

Since the departure of this good Bishop, we have received two postulants of superior merit, and we expect another who, to judge from her letters, will not be inferior to them either in talents or virtue. She is a privileged soul, one for whom God has done much. We begin to hope that even if we receive no help from Ruillé, we shall nevertheless be able to keep up and continue to form ourselves little by little. It is certain that our novices and postulants are, in general, very nice, and give us great consolation, and particularly, great hope for the future.

Did I tell you that, notwithstanding the losses we have sustained, we are fifty Sisters in the religious habit? Besides these we have fifteen postulants. This is not bad for our country. We have no new missions except the boys' asylum; but all our houses are completely supplied, and we could form a new establishment after the retreat, at Evansville or at Lafayette, Indiana. There is no prospect of going elsewhere. His Lordship is deaf in that ear. Our missions are all in a prosperous condition. There are forty-eight boarders here at the Academy; four are preparing to receive Baptism at Easter. This week another Protestant has asked to be associated with them, a privilege that will be granted her. Of the forty-eight boarders only twenty-two are Catholics. As many of the latter are poor, they bring little money to the house. But they repay us well by their good conduct. They are very fervent and set a good example to their companions.

As to our temporal affairs, we were doing well until we undertook to build a Motherhouse. This will soon throw us back into difficulties. No matter. We cannot go on longer without building; our old frame house is absolutely too small. Five hundred thousand bricks are made, and about two hundred dollars worth of lumber is on hand. This is little enough for an undertaking which must cost at least ten thousand dollars, more than fifty thousand francs. If God continues to send us pupils, the house will be paid for in four or five years, perhaps sooner. And if no accident happens, our House of America will be above want, and even in a condition to help the Motherhouse of France, should it be necessary. . . .

Our city of Terre Haute is becoming quite important. On the fifth of last month the steam cars began to run on the railroad here. The people are talking of making other roads in almost every direction. It will be a great saving of time for us in our travels when visiting the establishments.

Be pleased, my Father, to remember us to our Mothers and Sisters of Ruillé, and deign to bless your daughters of the Woods. . . .[26]

Mother Theodore's next lines are addressed, evidently, to a superior, but no name is given; the note bears only the date.

TO SOME SUPERIOR

January 1852

Sweetness   Self-possession   Charity   Support

Do not require from everybody the same virtue and qualities. When a fault is committed in your house, examine seriously before God whether you yourself are not the cause, I think if you examine yourself you will find that you are wanting in foresight, or in wisdom, perhaps in gentleness, or in charity, etc., etc.

When a duty is badly done, a utensil left out of place, and so forth, put the thing in its place yourself and tell the guilty person later about it. If you reprove, do it with sweetness, with a mere sign, and so on. Make it evident that it is always painful for you to afflict any of your Sisters by a reprimand. Take the

---

[26] Original in the archives of the Diocese of Le Mans.

Sister privately, show her her fault with affection, win her by pious suggestions and motives of faith. When the Sisters are sick take good care of them. . . .

TO THE REVEREND A. MARTIN, NEW ORLEANS, LA.

Saint Mary-of-the-Woods, January 22, 1852
Dear and venerable Friend:

It is always with great pleasure that we receive news from you, but we would be incomparably more pleased to see you in our Woods, our dear solitude, where you so greatly consoled us in our days of trial. It is not of that, however, that I come to speak to you today; it is of your protégée. You are such a good lawyer that your case is hardly gained when you address yourself to us.

This morning I assembled the Sisters to ask their opinion concerning the young lady you propose. We all much prefer that she had come before trying her vocation in another community. Notwithstanding our dislike in this particular, we are willing to receive her if she has not taken vows. So you may send her, and direct her to Mr. Linck at Evansville. She must have money for her journey and enough for her return, in case she is not pleased to remain here or that the Community cannot keep her. I hope that if Our Lord permits her to come such will not be the case, and that she will find amongst us the peace and happiness she seeks in vain in the world. The conditions mentioned here are considered essential by the Sisters.

I will say quite candidly that I fear the extreme difference which this young lady will find between the others—so grand, so worthy, so learned in the science of conducting souls—and the poor little daughters of Providence, who are so far from possessing any of these qualities; I fear, I say, that this difference will cause her to make comparisons which will render her obligations more painful by contrasting what she will have with what she has left. I suppose these reflections have not escaped you, for you know what we are; so, if you send her we shall feel that you assured yourself that her attitude of mind did not give you any fear on this subject. If she comes to us, we shall certainly love her tenderly, as we love all those whom the Lord confides to us. Affection is the only thing that we can give them.

Father Corbe is away. He had to set out for Vincennes on Monday where business required his presence immediately. It was so cold that I feared for his health. He will be happy to receive the letter you promised him. If it is as long on the way as yours to me was, it will be of ancient date. Only yesterday did I receive the one with which you honored me, dated November 29. Fearing that this may also be delayed on the way, I hasten to have it ready for the mail which is going to leave in a few minutes. Sister St. Francis will write to you soon. . . .

TO THE RIGHT REVEREND J. BOUVIER, BISHOP OF LE MANS

Saint Mary-of-the-Woods, February 18, 1852

My Lord and venerated Father:

I cannot resist the desire of expressing, if able, our sincere gratitude for the warm reception you gave to our good Bishop. When his Vicar General [Father Dupontavice] told me at Madison that the Bishop was so fortunate as to find you at Le Mans, the thought of the pleasure you would have in seeing him, and hearing him speak of your Daughters in Indiana, and of the good that God is pleased to do through them, caused me to experience one of those moments of happiness so rare in life, above all in the life of a poor missionary Sister. Your heart must have been somewhat compensated for all the pains and anxieties it had undergone for us.

The two pillars of our House of America, if I may thus say it, were reunited: you, my Father, its founder and support; he, its constant protector; for Bishop de St. Palais was our faithful friend before becoming our Father, and that, without being wanting in what he owed to His Lordship, Bishop de la Hailandière. We doubt not but that the interview of our good Bishop with your Lordship will confirm him in the favorable disposition which he has ever maintained toward us. We shall endeavor to render ourselves worthy of his protection and of yours.

You were not satisfied with receiving this good Bishop like a brother; you also bestowed upon him generous gifts for his poor mission, for his numerous family of orphans. I thank you, my Lord, I thank you for all you have done for our American Father. We are as grateful as if you had done it for us. He was also highly pleased with the way he was received at Ruillé. I write by the same post to Mother Mary to thank her.

There is nothing new in our Woods since my last letter, but the completion of the railroad from Terre Haute to Madison. Yesterday, for the first time, the cars started from this city to go in a few hours as far as the Ohio River.

I suppose you have my letter of January first. Deign to bless again your daughters of Saint Mary-of-the-Woods. . . .[27]

TO MOTHER MARY, SUPERIOR GENERAL, RUILLÉ-SUR-LOIR

February 18, 1852

We admire, as you do, my very dear Mother, the ways of Providence in the events which have taken place this winter

---

[27] Original in the archives of the Diocese of Le Mans.

in France. Truly, it is in vain that men revolt. The arm of God stops them at the moment they least expect it. It is impossible that He would allow the Mother and Nurse of so many good works to perish. Where, under the sun, is there any good work without the co-operation of France? Here in America her influence is deeply felt. Louis Napoleon seems a remarkable man. May God protect him! We pray for him with all our heart.

I forgot to tell you our Bishop wrote to us that he was much pleased with his visit to Le Mans and to Ruillé. I think you also must have been pleased to see him, to have details of our mission from the very one who could best give them, for he has seen all, has heard all. Even in the time of his predecessor, Bishop de la Hailandière, he always supported us. He was our staunch friend before he became our Father. I have written this to you before.

This very morning I have received letters from Sisters St. Vincent and Basilide. Both are well. The Protestants of Madison are annoying us a great deal. They are opening school after school in order to destroy ours. They want to subject our Sisters to their examination of the Catholic schools. Moreover, they wish to make us pay taxes, which is contrary to the laws of the State. We refuse positively. It embarrasses them a little to have women resist them and speak to them about the law. Woman in this country is only yet one-fourth of the family. I hope that, through the influence of religion and education, she will eventually become at least one half—the "better half."

I must tell you for your consolation that this year the good God has sent us some excellent subjects, who, we trust, will later do much for the glory of God. Please be so kind, my dear Mother, as to have a copy made for me, by anyone, of the changes in the new Ceremonial. We shall appreciate your sending it to us.

Adieu, my very dear and beloved Mother. I leave you now to write letters less agreeable than yours. I too, spend a great part of my days in writing. It takes me a long time to write in English, when the letter is not to one of our Sisters. I feel keenly the loss of my poor Sister Angelina.

This letter, like all I send to you, is for Mother St. Charles if she does me the honor of reading them. Much love to Sister Eudoxie, Sister St. Vincent—to all. And for you, my beloved Mother, all that a heart can say to a mother such as you are for your Theodore. . . .[28]

The death of M. le Fer de la Motte called for a message of sympathy from Mother Theodore to the family. Her letter was addressed to a married daughter.

TO MME. LE FER CHOISNET, ST. SERVAN

Saint Mary's, May 29, 1852

My very dear Cecile:

Let me write you a few lines to speak of your sorrow, of the dear object who causes your tears and ours to flow, of the holy man who was your father on earth and who is now your protector in heaven. Do not doubt it. It is he who obtains for all of you that courage and resignation which sustain you in these painful circumstances. We feel the effects of it here very keenly. I trembled in thinking of the consequences that the news would have on the frail, yet so precious, health of dear Sister St. Francis Xavier. We all knew beforehand that her virtue would sustain her soul; but it seemed impossible for her not to succumb after learning of the death of a father so cherished and so worthy of being loved. Since then I seem to hear Our Lord say to me: "Daughter of little faith, why didst thou doubt?"

---

[28] Original in the archives of the Motherhouse, Ruillé-sur-Loir.

The first days after receiving the dreaded tidings, this dear child could scarcely take any food; but for a week past she has come back to her normal health. I may even say that she is better than she was all last year. I should not have been so much afraid that God would take her from us. He knows how useful her life is to this rising Community. He knows that her every moment is consecrated to His glory and to the salvation of the neighbor.

Besides the care of a large novitiate, this dear Sister has been occupied in preparing four of the pupils for Baptism. Tomorrow is the longed-for-day, the great day for all. These little neophytes are very fervent. Their eyes sparkled with happiness this morning when they came and said to me, "O Mother, tomorrow!" They could say no more. Yes, indeed, tomorrow they will be washed in the regenerating waters and clad in the robe of innocence. They will be united to the Spouse of Virgins, to Jesus Christ, whose name they would never have pronounced in a manner worthy of Him if the Sisters of Providence had not exiled themselves to the forests of Indiana. Thank Him for us, dear friend, for having given us this beautiful, this sublime vocation. You must also thank Him for yourselves; for what do you not do for our mission in the Woods! You will be pleased to learn that this week we shall lay the cornerstone of our new Motherhouse. This building will be 110 feet long, 65 feet wide, and 40 feet high. *Veni Sancte Spiritus!*

The 30th. We have just come from the church. The ceremony was long and touching. Many tears of gladness were shed. Sister St. Francis was godmother for one of our young Christians; she is writing to you about it. She thinks her godchild will one day be a Religious of Saint Mary-of-the-Woods. The weather was magnificent. It seemed that heaven united with earth to add beauty to the feast. Never had I seen our solitude so charming. Why were you *not* here, dear little cherished sister? You also would have enjoyed it. I drew for you a gift of the Holy Ghost, that of Counsel. I said to Sister St. Francis, "See what gift I drew for Cecile; is it not suited to her dignity?" We laughed a little together.

You will forgive me for entertaining you with our joys, when you perhaps are in affliction on this day of joy in the Church. Your poor heart—has it not suffered much? Perhaps you weep in carrying the cross your Divine Master has sent. Oh! I would wish to suffer for you, or at least alleviate your affliction. Be assured I do share it. Day and night I am thinking about you all. I seem to see you, to hear you, and I am edified by the Christian conduct you manifest. Almighty God will be glorified by your crosses and trials, as they render you more worthy of Him. Have courage, my dear friends. Soon you will be united to those you have lost. "I will see you again," Our Lord said to His disciples, "and your heart shall rejoice, and no man shall take away your joy." No, dear Cecile, nothing can rob you of your joy when you will be reunited to those in heaven from whom you were obliged to be separated on earth.

June 2. I am so busy, my dear Cecile, that since Saturday when I began these lines, I have left off ten times or more. I did not want to send this, but Sister St. Francis will have me to make the act of humility, so I am letting it go. This time, my dear Madame Choisnet, you owe me a great many prayers. For more than two months I have scarcely prayed for anyone but you and yours, who are mine by affection. I drew the gift of Wisdom for Elvire. Please remember me to her.

Offer my love in a special manner to Mlle. Pépa and to all the others, but keep a good share for yourself; for certainly I love you very much. Sister St. Francis thanks God that you are not at Saint Mary's, because she says I love you too much. She would allow us to see each other but rarely. As we are far apart, she lets us do as we like.

Saint Mary's, June 9, 1852

I knew very well, my dear Sister Basilide, that you would be terrified at the simple account of the accident which came near depriving me of the little remainder of my life. Had I been well prepared, I think the good God would have taken me. It is well in His mercy that He granted me some days of *respite*. Beg of Him that I may profit by them. Oh, it is time, indeed, for me to be converted at last, for good.

Father Corbe has not come back from Vincennes yet. We expect him today or tomorrow. He has sent Father Contin to the asylum at St. Louis. The Sisters received him for nothing. Father Bessonies and two Brothers accompanied him. We begin a novena for him today. Oh, I hope God will give us back this good priest for the welfare of His Holy Church. We shall pray for him very much. Tell this to good Father Dupontavice, while thanking him for his sympathy for the poor daughters of the Woods. I would always tell you to offer him our profound respect and gratitude if I did not fear to be importunate, but those feelings are always in my heart.

No matter what the mayor may tell you concerning Father Purcell, never consent to take our books away from the Catholic children; this would be for the worst. Let those people keep their money and let us alone. I would rather throw the money into the river than expose the faith of our children. They do not want the Blessed Virgin, nor pictures of the Saints—those good people could even do without God! Such villains! They put me in bad humor.

Miss Mary Read has not yet gone to Madison. She expects to be there Sunday night by the packet from Cincinnati. If not on Sunday, then on Monday. It is possible that she will not stop. If she goes to you (do not go to meet her), tell her that

I wish her to come to Terre Haute by the first opportunity, that is to say, on the first train. You cannot easily have a stranger staying with you in the midst of your numerous occupations. I wrote to her in Cincinnati, but it might be that she would not receive my letter, which will wait for her at the post office. You will tell her to come at once, as I have already said.

You know, my dear Sister Basilide, how happy I should be if you had a little chapel; however, I cannot permit any extra expense before the retreat. You can easily understand that we are in pecuniary need at present. About forty workmen are now employed on the house, and they do not work for nothing, I can assure you. I bless God for having spared so long our poor old house; there would be no hope of restoring it now. I think we shall have the laying of the corner stone on Sunday, the day of the solemnity of Corpus Christi. It would be a beautiful day to begin a chapel and a convent.

Adieu, my very dear daughter, or rather au revoir. *July comes after June.*

TO THE SAME

Saint Mary's, June 14, 1852

My God, give her Your love, Your peace, Your wisdom, all the virtues of her holy state; give her the grace to correct in herself whatever may be displeasing to You—this is the prayer that I offered to Our dear Lord last Saturday after Holy Communion. You know for whom it was, my dear Sister Basilide, that I prayed with so much fervor. It was your feast day. I wished to write to you but found it impossible to do so, having been all day at the Academy finishing the monthly examination. Yesterday, you know, was the solemnity of the feast of Corpus Christi. The Blessed

Sacrament was exposed until after Vespers, which were followed immediately by the touching ceremony of the blessing and laying of the cornerstone of our house. Our Very Reverend Father Corbe performed the ceremony, and Father Lalumière delivered an appropriate discourse in presence of a large audience. It was learned and eloquent. Several persons from Terre Haute were present besides our boarders and the neighbors. We came in procession from the church, singing the Litany of the Blessed Virgin. Father Lalumière said, in concluding that we must live and die holily within these blessed walls. They are rising quickly; you will find them quite high.

You have seen Miss Read, I suppose. Tell me how she impresses you.

Adieu, my dear Sister Basilide. I have only time to add that I love you tenderly in Our Lord and Saviour. . . .

LETTER CIRCULAR

Saint Mary's, July 3, 1852

My beloved Sisters:

With heartfelt joy I write you again to bid you come to the retreat. Very soon a year will have elapsed since you left your dear home full of zeal and good will; but the weakness of our miserable nature and the multiplicity of our occupations have cooled those dispositions. It is time for us to repair our losses, to reanimate our fervor, and to refresh our souls. Our Lord knows our wants and He loves us. He has new favors to bestow upon us and it is through the channel of a retreat that He will communicate them. Let us be well prepared, my dearest Sisters, to receive them. Let us be more recollected, more faithful to our holy Rules. Let us pray often in order to obtain the light of the Holy Ghost to know well the state of our interior, so that we may render it an agreeable abode for Our Lord.

To facilitate as far as in our power your entire disengagement during the retreat, and also to strengthen among us the spirit of union and charity, and the spirit of poverty, I desire that you bring nothing with you but the things necessary for the journey and your flannels and stockings. Everything else you will find at your home.

The retreat will begin, as usual, on the 8th of August. Be ready to start so as to be here some days in advance in order to rest yourselves.

If it be deemed necessary for some of you to remain, we shall let you know before the first of August. Hoping to see you soon I remain, my beloved Sisters,

Your truly devoted,

SISTER ST. THEODORE,

Sup'r Gen'l.

TO SISTER BASILIDE, MADISON

July 5, 1852

My dear Sister:

Next week we shall send you the premium books, all that we can send. I shall try to have them at Madison by Tuesday's express. Your little rogues do not give a cent? I am very glad that your church has been enlarged and embellished. Congratulate your pastor for me and offer him my profound respects.

As to whom to leave in your house, I really do not know. Perhaps it would be well for all to remain until the time for the retreat and come together on the 5th or 6th, and two, at least, to return immediately after the retreat; or, better still, those who are to return immediately could come sooner;

could they not? In either case get a good woman, Mrs. Gunier [Jennier?], Maggie's mother, to take care of the house for twelve or fifteen days. After all, perhaps, it would be better to leave Sisters. Tell me what you think of these different plans. I cannot go to Madison; but I wish to see you, so you must come to see your old friend and your new house. One is going and the other is coming. Today they are putting the joists to the second story over the chapel. Adieu, or rather, au revoir. . . .

Several postulants, volunteers for the Indiana novitiate, were waiting at Ruillé until Bishop de St. Palais would return to America and bring them to Saint Mary-of-the-Woods. The following is addressed to them:

TO THE MISSES MARSHALL AND HERMANN

Saint Mary-of-the-Woods, Aug. 21, 1852

Young Ladies and dear Daughters in Our Lord:

We have learned with joy that you are at Ruillé, far from all who are dear to you in the world, already on the way to follow your beautiful, your sublime vocation. We earnestly beg of Our Lord to complete what He has begun in you. He will hear our prayers, for He loves you. He calls you not only to become His faithful spouses, but to be, in a certain respect, true apostles; not only to leave for His sake all who are dear to you in your family, but even to leave your country, in order that you may have nothing but yourself. He calls you to this land watered by the sweat and blood of so many holy missionaries who have come here before us to make known, loved, and served that God Who has chosen you.

You must understand, my dear young ladies, that in order to attain the perfection to which you are called, a solid foundation is required. One cannot belong to God in an imperfect manner and be happy here. The life of the world that surrounds us is a life of the senses, a mundane and sensual life. Its example is very dangerous. If we do not wish to be lost with it, but to save it without injury to ourselves, we must be very firm, very devoted to God. Think of this while it is yet time. If your hearts waver, if you are afraid of the cross, of poverty, of humiliations, do not leave France; you would not be suitable for our little Community. If, on the contrary, you are determined to belong entirely to God, to endeavor by His grace to become humble, pious, and above all, to renounce your own will by obedience, then come. Our Blessed Lord will assist you and protect you. He will be your guide in your long and hazardous voyage. He will bring you to our beloved Woods, where you will find Sisters who love you even now and who are praying for you. You will also find in your new country souls who do not love, who do not know God; but these whom you will instruct and direct in His service will be your crown in eternity.

And you, dear Miss Marshall, who have had the courage to bid adieu to a beloved mother, take your heart in your hands and offer it to God. He is so generous, He will reward you abundantly for what He enables you to do for Him. Oh, how much you will love Him in this blessed solitude if you continue to be entirely devoted to Him. Long ago we offered prayers for you, for your generous mother. When you write to her tell her that I shall try to be a mother to you, that I love you already as my beloved child, and that all the Sisters are anxiously waiting to have you among them. You will have for companion in your journey a young lady who is very good and very pious; she understands some English and will be able to converse with you.

I wrote a few lines in English for the one who is English.

This letter is also for another postulant (Elvire le Fer de la Motte) who is to come and whom I also love very tenderly. You will show it to her when she is with you.

A bientôt, very dear young ladies. In awaiting the pleasure of embracing you I am most devotedly in Our Lord all yours,

SISTER ST. THEODORE.

The young ladies to whom this letter was addressed were Nathalie and Justine Hermann and Mary Marshall. The Hermann sisters were Belgian lace-makers whom Bishop de St. Palais gained for Indiana. In securing them he foresaw, he thought, a new industry for his orphans that might prove lucrative. The young ladies, equipped with their bobbins and Brussels thread, embarked, but were notified by the custom officer that it was forbidden by law to make the lace for sale beyond the kingdom of Belgium. Very little Brussels lace, therefore, was made at Saint Mary's.

Justine Hermann, disappointed at not being permitted to ply her craft, returned home. Her little sister became Sister St. Antoine. The latter was considerably less than five feet tall, but she had great physical strength and a fearless character. After a number of years at the orphanage, where she rivaled the boys in tossing hay or shucking corn, she was employed at the Motherhouse in caring for the walks and shrubbery. In the winter she kept the chapel warm, carrying the coal and feeding the two immense stoves. When the age of steam heat superseded that of stoves and grates, Sister St. Antoine assisted in the care of the sick Sisters. Her ways were those of her care-free childhood, a childhood she never outlived; but she worked faithfully and rendered every service with alacrity. If she had a choice it was for the most repugnant duties. She went to receive her reward on December 13, 1913, aged eighty-seven years, sixty-one of which had been passed in the religious state.

Mary Marshall, Sister Mary Eudoxie, was born at Solihull, Warwickshire, England, July 26, 1829. After her first Communion, when she was twelve years of age, her mother took her and a younger sister to the continent to be educated. They had rooms in a French-speaking convent school in

Belgium, where they remained for eleven years, Mary in the latter years pursuing her studies in music and dramatic art under noted secular professors.

In 1852 Bishop de St. Palais visited the school and so forcibly portrayed the needs of the Church in Indiana that he captivated several of his hearers, among them Mary Marshall. Giving up her prospective career on the stage she chose instead that of missionary labor in the Diocese of Vincennes. She was then in her twenty-fourth year. She arrived with her companions at Saint Mary-of-the-Woods, October 18, 1852, having been brought from New York by Mother Theodore herself, who had been requested by the Bishop to be in that city when they should land so as to go with him to see certain buildings and furnishings, in view of the new Motherhouse then being built at Saint Mary's.

The Bishop gave Sister Mary Eudoxie her name, and, some years later, presented a fine large oil painting of St. Eudoxie, a penitent of the desert, for her music studio at the Academy. The picture remained there until the music department was transferred to the new Conservatory; then it found place in the Art Gallery where it is still to be seen.

Besides teaching music Sister Mary Eudoxie taught dramatics, her professional training being evident whether the presentation were a minstrel show or an elaborate Racine production in the Woodland primitive theatre.

After twenty-three years at the boarding school of Saint Mary-of-the Woods, she spent one year at Saint John's Academy, Indianapolis, four years at Madison, and one at Terre Haute as Superior of those houses. She was then recalled to Saint Mary's to begin preparations for a biography of the revered Foundress, Mother Theodore.

The collecting of materials entailed a correspondence covering many years. The translation from the French required many years more. Sister did not live to complete the task, but she had a large amount of material in readiness when ill health compelled her to relinquish the work to others. With what was then on hand, and contributions from other sources, a "Life" was published in 1904. Sister Mary Eudoxie was anxious that an additional volume should soon follow. The present long delayed work is the part-fulfillment of her wishes.

After her death, which occurred May 29, 1912, her sister, Miss Amelia Marshall, who was doing literary work in

England, wrote for the London *Chronicle* of July 10, a sketch of Sister Mary Eudoxie and of the family. Following is an excerpt:

"She came from an old and illustrious house, being the lineal descendant of Earl John Marshall who defended Dover Castle in the time of King John and who, in conjunction with Hubert de Burgh, 'served England for the English.' Sister Mary Eudoxie's father was the last to pay the tribute of five peppercorns for five lordships in Kent granted to John Marshall of Dover Castle. He obtained an Act of Parliament in 1839, and an amended Act in 1841, which enabled him to divide the property according to the wishes of his father among his brothers and sisters. On her mother's side she was descended from Sir Robert Blomart, Master of the household of Princess Elizabeth. In the reign of Elizabeth, Sir John Blomart, or Bloomer, built the Hatherop Manor House. It was superbly furnished in the old style. The collection of portraits was famous. Besides the pictures of the family of Bloomer and Webb (Sir Anthony Webb married a Bloomer) there was a series of whole length portraits of the Stuarts from James the First to James the Second, also of the three daughters of Sir John Webb and Mary Bloomer. These daughters married thus: Anna Maria to the Earl of Derwentwater; Mary to Earl Waldegrave, and Barbara to Viscount Montaente. Kudder in 1770 calls it a noble house. The Earl of Derwentwater was married to Ann Webb at Hatherop and from this manor house the Earl started on his ill-fated expedition, to join the Scotch army in 1715. Two of Sister Eudoxie's collateral ancestresses, Ann and Lucy, were nuns beyond the sea, supposed to be in a convent at Angers, where Lord Derwentwater's heart was sent. There is also a tradition that a monk of the family of Marshall, John Marshall, was hanged, drawn and quartered for the Faith."

Sister Mary Eudoxie would speak of the honor of having a martyr in the family, but to her illustrious ancestry she never made reference. The nobility she prized most was that of being a Spouse of Christ. Both Sister Mary Eudoxie and Sister St. Antoine lived to be witnesses in the cause of Mother Theodore.

Of the other young lady, Elvire le Fer de la Motte, who was soon to join the Indiana postulants waiting at Ruillé-sur-Loir, succeeding letters will have much to say. A sketch of her career, therefore, is reserved for a later date. Suffice to say here that she was the Sister of Sister St. Francis Xavier, ten years her junior, and at the time Mother Theodore made the acquaintance of the family at St. Servan, she was finishing her education in Paris, where her beautiful voice was under training and her harp studies were being perfected. In that year (1844) there was little thought that Elvire would find her way to Saint Mary-of-the-Woods. Although she was eighteen years old, Mother Theodore wrote when they met in Paris, "Elvire is only a child."

TO SISTER MARIA, MADISON

Saint Mary's, September 17, 1852

You are very foolish, my dear Sister, to be tormenting your imagination with the fear of losing your mind. To tell you plainly, this is my opinion, I do not think you are in any way similar to Father Contin. He had a good judgment, a fine intellect, a keen mind capable of delving to the bottom of things. He was very learned; not scrupulous nor anxious. See now how much this picture resembles you. Believe me, my daughter, we cannot lose what we never had. Be quiet, then, on this score and do not trouble yourself further about it.

We should not be any more surprised at temptations against faith than at those against any other virtue. The devil is the father of lies. It matters little to him in what way he troubles or disconcerts us; if only he can turn us away from God, that is all he wants. You must not listen to him. Now do believe me, dear Sister Maria. Occupy yourself less about yourself and more about God. Do what you do with uprightness, with the desire of pleasing God, without so much uneasiness about the future. Give yourself generously to Him with all that belongs to you. Oh, how many graces would be the fruit of this self-surrender!

I should be happy indeed to console and fortify your soul, but not being able to do so I can only pray for you, and this I do with all my heart. . . .

Saint Mary-of-the-Woods, November 2, 1852

Madame, my dear friend, the mother of my two beloved daughters, what can I say, what can I write? It would be very pleasing to me could I console you; but it is not given to man to heal the wounds of the heart—of a heart so good, so loving, so sensitive as yours. God alone can console you, strengthen you. He alone can give you the courage to overcome nature and to make to Him all the sacrifices He has required of you this year. What a year it has been for poor nature, and above all, what a year of grace! Only in heaven will you understand the treasure with which your soul has been enriched these months.

To pray for you is a necessity for me, but I am so occupied with what is called business that my prayers are very poor, very miserable. There are others who pray better than I do and who, frequently during the day, at the foot of the altar of our poor little chapel of the Woods, pray for a mother whom they cherish tenderly and whom they have left only for God, yes, for *God alone*.

You already know that I went to New York to meet our dear Elvire. How happy I was to embrace her, to offer for the first time with her my thanks to God! Some days later we were at Terre Haute where our dear and beloved Sister St. Francis awaited us. The presence of Elvire has given, as it were, a new life to Irma. She is well for her, but she has a cold. I appointed Elvire her superior to take care of her. You can imagine how devotedly she acquits herself of the duty. At New York Elvire herself made me very uneasy about her health; she coughed much, especially in the morning. Thank God, the cough has entirely left her and the dear child is well; yes, well in every respect. She has an angelic appearance, and what is more remarkable in my opinion is, that with all her qualities, she is charmingly simple. Every one already loves her and looks upon her as an old friend, or rather as an old Sister. I believe she is called upon to do very great good in this portion of the Lord's vineyard which is ours to cultivate; at least, such is my hope. If it were otherwise, if God did not call her to the religious life, I would restore her again to the arms of her mother. Let us beg of God that He would deign to continue to show us His will, and let us promise to follow it with all our heart.

It is probable that we shall start for Vincennes this week, as the Bishop wants to show his asylums to Elvire and her companions. I shall accompany them if my health permits, for I cannot send Sister St. Francis at present. The season is too far advanced and she is so susceptible to the least change of weather.

Be not uneasy about the expense of the journey. I have business to settle with the Bishop and we shall keep account of what he has advanced. We are not quite so poor as we used to be, so do not inconvenience yourself at all. Irma and Elvire are treasures that all the gold of California could not equal.

Elvire is here in my room now with her guitar near the fire. You seem to be with us. You will come some day, will you not? I have already selected a room for you in our new house. It is not ready for use just yet, but I hope that it will be next summer. I am very happy at what you tell me—that you prefer Elvire to be here with us than elsewhere. To justify this flattering preference I have only a heart to love your dear daughters, and I do love them, yes, very tenderly, and their mother too. . . .

TO SISTER BASILIDE, MADISON

Saint Mary-of-the-Woods, Dec. 9, 1852

My dear Sister:

I have just received your letter of the 5th instant. I can read it, but to be candid, I can hardly understand it. Is it true, then, that without asking anybody you have changed the books of the Catholic children upon your own authority? And the whole of last year you refused the mayor who asked this change as a favor! Is it true, also, that you told the inspector that he might visit your classes whenever he pleased? If it be so, my dear daughter, we must tell you that you will have the humiliation of seeing all your arrangements upset. If you did that, as your letter inclines me to fear, I know you no longer. I could say more, but I do not wish to condemn you before I know for certain. It seems impossible to me that you would have done this, knowing our positive will on the subject. . . . I declare to you that the Catholic books will be the only ones used in our school. I await only your answer before starting at once for Madison. The only fear I have is that you have consulted your pastor, and that he may have consented to the change. But I hope not. I am inclined to think that you did not treat him any better than you did me; you must have told him only when the thing was done. Dear me! What a head you have to take upon yourself to do such a rash thing. But—have you done it? I still doubt it. Write to me immediately and tell me plainly all that has been done.

I am so distressed about this affair that I cannot speak of anything else today. I shall be happy and shall have a weight taken off my mind if you can prove to me that I am mistaken, and that you have not compromised in any way the dignity of our Congregation in your dealings with those gentlemen. Much love to the Sisters.

TO SISTER MARIA, VINCENNES

December 20, 1852

My good Sister:

I must begin by telling you that I am much more pleased with your last letter than with the others. *Mon Dieu!* How happy I should be could I see you become some day what you ought to be. . . . As to what you say about your doing your own will from morning until night, I have more than once answered you on this point. You are not doing your own will when you are fulfilling the employment given you by your Superior; on the contrary, you are doing the will of God. If it were your own will, sometimes you would do the work and at other times you would not. So now be quiet about that. It would be better to be guarded in your words than always asking pardon. However, you must not fail to do this when you have given offense, even unintentionally.

You may write to me once a month, if you wish to do so. I shall reply whenever I deem it necessary, and if I am able to do it. Certainly, my poor daughter, you have many reasons for humbling yourself before God and man; but, after all, *it is never too late to begin to do well*. The mercies of the Lord are greater than our iniquities. He can pardon you more sins than you can commit, as your malice is finite and His mercy is infinite.[29] The peace that we may feel in this earth does not consist in not being tempted, but in keeping our heart firm and united with the will of God. As soon as we have fallen into a fault let us humble ourselves, ask pardon of God, and go on our way as before. In this manner not only temptations but not even sins will destroy our peace.

Adieu, my dear daughter. I wish you a good and holy year, a good and holy life, and what follows as a consequence, a happy eternity. . . .

The next letter is addressed to Sister Gabriella, who was one of the first postulants received at Saint Mary's after the arrival of the Sisters from France. She was, moreover, a year later, the first novice to leave the novitiate for mission life,

---

[29] Theologians differ concerning the degree of the malice of sin. For a complete discussion of this mooted point, cf. Tanquerey, *Synopsis Theologicae Dogmaticae*, II, pp. 718–719.

having been chosen as one of the three Sisters to open the first foundation from Saint Mary-of-the-Woods, that of Jasper, a German settlement. The Superior, Sister Vincent Ferrer, one of the foundresses from France, and Sister Marie Joseph, an Alsatian commanding French and German, could speak a little English but were not able to teach the language; Sister Gabriella therefore was sent for the English classes.

The Community necrology records that Sister Gabriella, Ann O'Neill Moore, was born in Ireland and came as a young woman to America. With an elder sister she kept a millinery shop in Pottsville, Pennsylvania, and in connection with it a circulating library, which brought her in contact with the finest people of the town. With these she was a great favorite on account of her amiable disposition and her remarkable conversational powers. Besides, she was very kind to the poor and helpful to the clergy in their works of zeal. Father Lalumière of Vincennes, returning from the East in the winter of 1840-1841, stopping at Pottsville, chanced to meet her. Learning that she was desirous of becoming a Religious, he suggested that she seek admission into the recently arrived Community at Saint Mary-of-the-Woods. She acted without delay and on February 2, 1841, entered the novitiate. Her future years were filled with unobtrusive good works. Mother Theodore always seemed to have had special regard for her. Sister Gabriella died November 30, 1875. At the date of this letter she had been transferred from Jasper to the northern part of the state.

TO SISTER GABRIELLA, FORT WAYNE

Saint Mary's, January 3, 1853

My dear Sister:

I have received with true pleasure your good and affectionate wishes. The heart understands the heart. As yours was speaking in your letter, mine understood its language. Be sure, my dear Sister Gabriella, that I wish and ask from God for you at least as much as you do for me. Oh, what a season for love, for fervor, for prayer! How often have you been, dear Sister, in the Stable of Bethlehem? Without doubt you have paid many visits there to adore our Divine Saviour. Have you considered, my dear Sister, with what rigor He treats His innocent Body, so tender and so young? What an example of mortification and self-denial! He gives us the graces which have cost him so much and which are so sweet to us! Oh, let us love Him! Let us, after His example, mortify our bodies of sin and corruption, in order that they may be glorified with Him one day in heaven. We have, both of us, a good opportunity for this, being not very well; and this is truly the time for mortification. Let us bear all we must suffer without complaint, without murmur, and also without taking unnecessary care of this dreadful carcass, which is today the object of our worship, and tomorrow will be the food of worms, maggots, etc.

I desire to see you very perfect in every way, and I do not like to know that you often have those miserable chills and fever. I hope by this time you are rid of them, but I fear they will come back again in your cold North.

I wish you could see the beautiful ornament we have received from our good Bishop, and also a pretty little Infant Jesus upon some straw. On pulling a string it opens both its arms and eyes and appears ready to speak. Sister Agatha seeing it for the first time exclaimed aloud. She thought it was a wonderful miracle. . . .

TO SISTER MARY XAVIER, VINCENNES

1853

I find you quite resuscitated, my dear Sister. If your actions correspond to your good resolutions, you will be like a seraph when I return. Poor Sister Mary Xavier! How little she knows her Mother's heart! She imagined I was pleased to leave my dear forest; that was an illusion. I was consoled at the prospect of seeing my other sheep, who are not of this fold, but it is always with regret that I leave Saint Mary's.

Be very fervent, my daughter, but do not imagine that for this end it is necessary to be in the chapel more frequently than your Sisters. I cannot make up my mind to give you permissions which are outside the Rule. Send your heart, if you will, a thousand times a day to Jesus in the Blessed Sacrament; but do not give your Sisters the pain of seeing you enjoy a favor which they could not share. It would be to their prejudice; or, at least, it would be a singularity, and singularities are always dangerous.

Goodbye, my dear little Sister. Love me as I love you, that is, very tenderly. Affectionate remembrance to all the Sisters, particularly to Sister Joachim. Just now I have not strength to write to her. . . .

TO SISTER MARIA, MADISON

January 13, 1853

You must not be uneasy, dear Sister, about the opinion of your confessor. It is not necessary to know whether he believes you or not. When you accuse yourself of your faults, you need only to be concerned about whether you accuse yourself of them in the right dispositions. Say with simplicity, and as if speaking to God Himself, whatever you know yourself to be guilty of. Repent of your sins and failings; take resolutions to do better and, after that, be quiet. The more we stir up a dung-hill the more it exhales bad odors. . . . How provoking you are! What a head you have! My poor child, it would be better for you to be obedient than to be guided by your own poor judgment. There is no common sense in such a way.

I am well pleased that you feel a little more at home at Madison. But, my child, a good Religious never asks herself whether she is pleased or not. She is always satisfied wherever God wishes her to be. Be careful not to give way to your tem-

per, which makes you insupportable. You would be a
thousand times happier in resisting it. Try your best to
make your pupils improve; this, you know, is a serious duty.
I recommend you to the Almighty, in whom I am always
your Mother Theodore.

TO MME. LE FER DE LA MOTTE, ST. SERVAN

January, 1853

Let me now, dear Madame le Fer, speak to you a little about
ourselves. Before the arrival of Elvire I thought it impossible
to love any one as much as my first daughter, my dear Sister
St. Francis, and lo! now I blend the two in my affection. I
might almost say that I feel something more tender and more
demonstrative for the former. There is no jealousy on the part
of the other.

Sister St. Francis says that Elvire [now Sister Mary
Joseph] and I resemble each other in disposition. I am proud
of it, for I find many good qualities in this dear soul; but I
feel that I do not resemble her. I wish you could see how
charming she is, how she advances in the path of virtue, and
how happy she is. From time to time, however, her pure
and serene countenance is slightly clouded, imperceptible to
others but perceptible to me. She has committed a little
fault, or has been guilty of an imperfection in the fulfillment of
her duty. I scold her a little, embrace her, encourage her, and
all is over.

How happy I am to have your daughters, my dear friend.
I am happy because they will do much for the glory of God.
What has not our dear Sister St. Francis done already! How
many souls now owe their salvation to her, and how many
will in the future! Elvire's time will come. She is preparing
herself by laying the foundation on which to raise the edifice

of her perfection. Her health is good. I find her looking plump and fresh, but always rather pale. I asked her yesterday if her face were not swollen. "No, indeed," she said, "it is good flesh." I beg of you, dear mother, not to be at all anxious about the food of your dear daughters. We have good bread. We use a beef every week, and have a good quantity of poultry. We have cured about five thousand pounds of excellent pork, so you see, meat is not wanting at Saint Mary's. Sometimes it is served three times a day, Friday of course excepted.

Besides this we have fifteen cows, which gives us plenty of good milk. We also have some red wine (Bordeaux), but only a small quantity; still, I have directed Sister Mary Joseph to take some occasionally. Yesterday she told me she did not wish for any more, but I did not allow her to discontinue taking it. I am sure the dear ones will get accustomed to the food of this country, as all our Sisters did who came from France. They could not now live as they did at Ruillé. Be very sure I see that this change is being made gradually.

I do not think that anyone, even you, Madame, her tender mother, could be more solicitous to preserve her precious health than I am. If you but knew how much I love her! If you but knew what are my hopes for the future in regard to this child of benediction! All here love and esteem her; it is impossible to know her and not to have these sentiments for her. Imagine, then, whether or not Sister St. Francis is happy to have her here. The latter has just had a nasal infection, which occasioned neuralgic pains in the head. Elvire wished to be chief infirmarian, after Sister Olympiade who yields her right to no one, but who was delighted to share it with Sister Mary Joseph. When the invalid was better they spent some happy moments together. They are now making flowers for the Bishop's chapel, and both of them are enjoying their tête-à-tête. . . .

Saint Mary-of-the-Woods, July 6, 1853

Beloved Sisters:

It is with the deepest sentiments of joy and gratitude that we call you once more to come to your beloved home after a year of labors and trials.

By the help of God and the union which reigns among you, a house is here to receive you. And yet it has only the walls and roof with scarcely any furniture, but such as it is you will love it, for it is the fruit of your labors and privations. How true it is that charity *edifieth!* Would to God that the Sisters of Saint Mary's would never forget this.

When we compare the little frame house in which we were received in charity twelve years ago with the splendid building erected here now, we clearly see the effects of those powerful words, "Increase and multiply." Indeed, my Sisters, we have increased and multiplied. Our exterior improvements are astonishing; but does our interior advancement correspond with the exterior? Have we increased in humility, mortification, self-denial, and all the other virtues which constitute a true Religious? It is in the silence of the retreat that we shall be able to answer these important questions. Come, then, my dear daughters, to refresh your souls alone with your God. Come to purify your hearts in order to work again at your perfection with more zeal and fervor. One thing however is wanting; that is, a Jesuit to give us our retreat. We were expecting one from St. Louis, but we received a letter informing us that he would not be here.

Our little chapel will be blessed by the Bishop on the 6th of August. I hope all will be here for the solemnity. Remember, dear Sisters, to be on your way home, models of reserve and

modesty. May your guardian angels preserve you from all evil;
this is the constant prayer of

Your truly devoted

SISTER ST. THEODORE,

Sup'r Gen'l.

TO MME. LE FER DE LA MOTTE, ST. SERVAN

Saint Mary-of-the-Woods, October 10, 1853

Madame and dear Friend:

For several weeks our beloved daughters have been busy
looking among our little nothings of Saint Mary's to find
something that might please their beloved mother. I was
also thinking about what I could put in the trunk. I could
find nothing, nothing. At length this happy thought, slightly
suggested by Sister Mary Joseph, struck me like a ray of
light—I shall send the daguerreotype of Sister St. Francis.
(I had promised this to myself a long time ago; now the time
has come.) The trouble was to get it from her. For many weeks
she was suffering from her summer smothering attacks. It
was not easy to take her to Terre Haute in that state. A
fine day presented itself. It was not too warm; we could go.
I had the horses put to the carriage. I invited Sister
St. Francis and Sister Mary Joseph to seat themselves in it,
and lo! we were all three en route, talking about the weather,
admiring the beauty of our forests, the progress of the railroad, etc., etc. Finally I spoke of the portrait. What a
shock! Imagine, if you can, all the objections made by our poor
little daughter and also the *eloquence* with which we opposed
them. We made fuss enough to deafen the horses. We had not
yet persuaded her, however, and we were already on the bridge
over the Wabash.

At last we found the vein of persuasion by painting in lively colors the pleasure you would have in contemplating those cherished features and in showing the picture to everybody. We represented the family assembled at the opening of the package; we heard their cries of joy, the conversation that ensued, etc. Then the tears flowed and the victory followed. Quickly Elvire puts the toilette in order, and behold us now in the studio—skylight above—determined to have the picture. Our dear little daughter was charming and lent herself with good grace to all we wanted. The trip, our little dispute, the walk from the carriage to the third story, had made her look beautiful. How I wish you could have seen her! The machine is brought near and put into operation. In a minute or two we were told it was over. They took out the plate and after the usual preparation brought it to us. I am ashamed to tell the rest. The shawl look burned. I wanted to remove the spot with my finger. I wanted to touch it. I touch nothing—all disappears! I remain confused at my stupidity. The operation has to be repeated. It takes more time than it did at first and our poor patient cannot stand it any longer. She thought that she was not allowed to breathe as long as the operation was going on; so her eyes were almost starting out. At last we had to leave without the picture, which did not quite please us. The next day, however, we returned and obtained what we wanted.

If Sister Mary Joseph had not left you her likeness, I should have sent hers also, but I shall send it in the religious dress when she will have taken her vows.

These two dear daughters are well. Sister St. Francis is really well for her. Her smothering spells are over and she has sick-headache less often. I think that the pure air she breathes in our new house will improve her health. Our dear Sister Mary Joseph had fever in September, but she is quite well now; both of them are my consolation and procure the glory of God, and will do so even more in the future. Sister Mary Joseph will speak English much better than Sister St. Francis does. I suppose these dear children give you all the news that can interest you. I got up from my bed to scribble you these lines. I have just had erysipelas, which caught me by the tip of the ear and spread and swelled up my head in the front and back, and added a new lustre to my beauty. Beg of our Lord to give me that beauty which is pleasing to Him, in order that I may love Him and cause others to love Him. . . .

TO SISTER MARY XAVIER, GIRLS' ORPHANAGE, VINCENNES

Saint Mary's, October 26, 1853

I am very much pleased, my dear Sister Mary Xavier, to receive a letter from you; indeed I was quite out of humor because you had not written a word sooner. But I had put myself in penance and I am already tired of it. I am especially happy to learn that you are more contented, and that you do your best to contribute to the happiness of your Sisters and of the children with whom you have to deal.

There is more than one kind of recollection, my daughter. When we are occupied for God we are sufficiently recollected. We are certainly more agreeable to the Divine Majesty when, in obedience, we are forming and teaching those poor little orphans than if, of our own will, we are praying all the day long on our knees before the Blessed Sacrament.

Endeavor to curb your temper with the children. Remember that you have not only to teach them how to sew, but also how to become meek, humble, patient, etc., and this kind of lesson is given much better by example than by precept. Be obedient, and above all, be patient. Never show temper with the children; but if you should do so, try to make amends by greater sweetness and condescension towards those poor little girls, who are not only children, but children bereft of their mothers. Poor little ones, how dear they should be to you! Never try to avoid the company of any of your Sisters, for that would be a source of trouble, temptation, and sin. Love all in God and for God, and all will be well.

I hope Bishop de Saint Palais is better; offer him my profound respects. Tell Father Benoit that I can send him the money, if he wishes me to do so, but that I would much prefer to see him. I want to speak of matters that concern him personally.

Father Corbe is well. I think he is going to become a hermit; for six weeks we have seen him but rarely. Poor Sister Olympiade has been sick all fall. She has frequent attacks of fever, and between times merely drags herself around. She wants me to put her name in this letter. She loves you tenderly; all the other Sisters also send you love.

On the feast of All Saints raise up your heart to God and ask Him to obtain for you a place among the blessed in heaven. How happy we shall be there. . . .

TO SISTER MARIA, MADISON

Saint Mary's, November 11, 1853

My dear Sister:

Sister Basilide having written to let me know the number of hours that each of you was occupied in teaching, I told her I thought you had too much to do and begged her to take something from you. This is the whole mystery.

It is an artifice of the enemy of our soul and of all good to make us think that we should perform well such and such an employment if it were given to us. He wants to turn us away from the real good that we can do at the present moment, and for this end he aids us in projecting an immense good for some future period, or under circumstances which will never be offered to us. Let us not allow ourselves to be caught by this father of lies. Give your music lessons, etc., to the best of your power, and do not think about what you might do if you were a lay Sister, or something else.

Continue to obey in regard to your Communions. Obedience is the best preparation that you can bring to Holy Communion.

TO THE REVEREND J. KUNDEK, JASPER

Saint Mary's, December 6, 1853

Reverend Sir and venerated Pastor:

If I had not depended on the visit of His Lordship to Jasper for the arrangement of things after the separation you have made of the boys and girls, I should have gratified myself with the pleasure of writing to you. The Bishop having told me that he had done nothing, I believe I ought to tell you that it is impossible to continue the establishment on the conditions that have existed until now. We have often been obliged to give money for the support of this mission, besides keeping the Sisters in clothing which, as you are aware, has always been gotten at St. Mary's. It is only by the strictest economy that the Sisters can extricate themselves at present from their debts.

I have always had a predilection for Jasper, and as long as the people were poor I never would speak about money. Moreover, in the first years you showed yourself so good and generous that I took care not to call upon you, thinking that

you had already too much to provide for. Your absence from
Jasper has proved to me that this house cannot support itself
if no assistance be given it. Your successor being there only
temporarily, I could make no arrangements with him. It is
therefore with you, my good Father Kundek, that some agreement must be made for this our first establishment. We are all
perfectly disposed to second your zeal for your dear mission; on
this account we are ready to continue to make sacrifices
in favor of it and to ask for less than we get in any other
establishment.

These are the conditions for our schools in all the establishments, except the German congregation of Fort Wayne. The
Catholics pay two dollars per quarter, of eleven weeks each.
Protestants, three, four, five and even six, according to the
studies they pursue. At Fort Wayne a school society pays two
hundred dollars a year, and supplies a house; and in both cases
the children provide the wood for winter. One Sister alone has
charge of the German school at Fort Wayne, and after school
hours she is free to use her time for the benefit of the establishment.

In order to show you our good will, we are very willing to
receive the children at half price, that is, at one dollar per
quarter, payable in advance, besides the one hundred dollars
that you have the kindness to give each year. Or, if you prefer
it, four hundred dollars per year, which you would have the
goodness to pay to the Sisters every three months by installments of one hundred dollars. These arrangements have the
approbation of the Bishop and of Father Corbe. His Lordship
says that if suitable arrangements are not made soon it is my
own fault, because you were always well disposed. I believe it,
for I know your liberality, and the interest you have borne
towards our Community, which looks upon you gratefully as
our first benefactor. The Bishop told me that you intend to

build a house for the Sisters in a short time. I thank you for it in advance and ask of you to continue your protection. Recommend, I beg of you, the wants of the Community to Our Lord, but in particular those of your ever devoted servant,

SISTER ST. THEODORE,

Sup'r Gen'l.

TO SISTER MARIA, MADISON

December 30, 1853

My dear Sister:

I have before me your last two letters. As you know the cause of my silence, illness, I shall not speak of it today. It is needless also for me to tell you that you have done wrong in listening to the follies of your imagination. You know this very well. You have the experience, moreover, of how unhappy you are when you yield to your caprices. This, it seems to me, should make you take once for all, and *keep*, the resolution to do better. Indeed, I truly believe that if you had been profoundly humble, very charitable, and very sincere, you would have made great progress in virtue. Even in that case, however, you might still feel movements of the passions; for, it is not *feeling* them that renders us more or less virtuous, but, rather, not consenting to them.

Try, my dear daughter, never to perform your actions with crooked intentions. What would it avail you to do better than someone else, if it is from the motive of being admired? God would say to you at the last day, You have already received your reward, you have not worked for Me, I owe you nothing. I trust that during the holy days just passed you have taken good resolutions at the feet of our Saviour in the Manger, and I ask for you, with all my heart, the grace to keep them. If I obtain this request, will it not be a good New Year's gift, which will compensate you for all your good wishes to me? I thank you cordially for your greetings; and, I may tell you, if you conduct yourself even better still than you have done since the retreat, you will contribute yet further to my happiness. So, now, my daughter, begin again with the new year. You are a thousand times happier when you are *ma bonne fille*. Be such, then, once for all, and your happiness is secured for this world and the next.

Our good Father Corbe is well and thanks you for your kind wishes and unites his with those of all the Community, who wish you every blessing.

Adieu, my dear child. Pray for the health of Sister Mary Cecilia. Pray also for another person who stands in great need of prayers, and who remains affectionately in our Divine Saviour yours devotedly. . . .

TO SISTER MARY XAVIER, VINCENNES

Saint Mary's, January 1, 1854

My dear Sister:

I intended writing to you yesterday to begin the new year and to wish you a good one; also to thank you for your kind wishes for a happy feast at Christmas and the New Year. Your kind thoughtfulness really gave me much pleasure. Were you not at Vincennes, Sister Theodore would not know whether we had daughters there or not. It seems something has made the atmosphere so cold that the ink is frozen.

I cannot tell you how happy I am to see you acting so sensibly; it is truly one of my greatest consolations and one fully appreciated. Continue, my dear Sister; you will be happy yourself in making others happy. May this year which we have just entered be a happy one for you, for all of us! May we profit by the years that yet remain for us to spend on earth, to prepare for eternity which will soon come and never end!

Give my love and greetings to all the Sisters, and say that I wish them every good thing which they themselves desire for time and eternity. . . . I suppose you have already given the knitted wear to Sister Mary Cecilia; if not, you must do so, and tell her that I wish her to use it, at least during her journey home.

Adieu, my dear Sister. I am called away. Cannot write to Sister M——but tell her that I wish her a "Happy New Year" and that I intended to write to her. My poor Taillard is dead. I am so sorry. . . .

Taillard was a scrawny little yellow dog, greatly prized by the Sisters because one night he saved their home from burning by barking fiercely. The house had caught on fire from live coals dumped into an ash-barrel which stood against the frame building. In a few minutes the stairs leading to the dormitory would have been ablaze, and escape for the Sisters impossible.

TO THE RIGHT REVEREND J. BOUVIER BISHOP OF LE MANS

Saint Mary-of-the-Woods, January 6, 1854

My Lord and venerated Father:

How long it is since we had the pleasure of receiving one of your good and paternal letters! Yet we stand in need of consolation from you in the midst of the trials we are undergoing at the present time.

The Protestant ministers continue to do their utmost to destroy our schools. They have obtained a new law which orders a general tax for the purpose of educating all the children in the same schools without distinction of sex or fortune.[30] These schools now in vogue throughout the Union have closed all the others, with very few exceptions. The Catholic schools are nearly the only ones remaining open, but the

---

[30] The Public School System had by this time been introduced into Indiana.

attendance is much smaller than in the preceding years, especially in some localities. We have always a fair number of Catholic children. The two new establishments at Evansville and North Madison are prospering. Between them they have over two hundred pupils.

Our house at Fort Wayne is not affected by this new movement. In that city there is a Methodist Seminary, a large boarding school, which prevents the establishment of these public schools. We have at Fort Wayne eighteen boarders and one hundred and fifty day pupils.

Our boarding school here at Saint Mary's is also well attended—seventy-eight pupils. But what most consoles us is the good that is being done here. Not only are there always several receiving instruction for Baptism, but there are many Catholics who are learning to know and serve God. The Catholics of this locality have for the past thirty years seen a priest only once a month, in passing, and some even only once a year. They are Christians, yet for the most part, very ignorant, scarcely knowing what is absolutely indispensable. Their daughters, brought up in our school where there is, I may say, a good spirit, return home like little apostles. They are listened to so much the more willingly because they are so greatly loved. You would be consoled could you see the fervor and piety of these young girls. At the great feasts they prepare themselves for the reception of the sacraments by a retreat which they make with as much regularity as the Sisters do. This year we have over thirty Catholic boarders, which shows you the prosperity of the country. Ten or twelve years ago there were not ten Catholics in Indiana who could pay for the board and tuition of their daughters, even for six months; at present a large number are able to give them a good education.

A Congregation of Benedictine Fathers has settled in the forests of Indiana; there are four here already. They will do a great deal of good here, especially among the Germans, who are very numerous and hard to manage. I believe they are more headstrong than the Bretons.

Our good Bishop has been very sick this year and has not yet quite recovered. We had the pleasure of seeing him last week. He was going to Cincinnati to pay his respects to the Apostolic Nuncio, who has been there for some weeks. We should be happy to see the Nuncio, but we fear the rigorous season will deprive us of the pleasure.

I send you a lithograph of our Saint Mary's; you will see that it differs much from the first. We are living in the new house, which is very cold this winter. Not one apartment is finished except the chapel. The men are making the doors now, but these cannot be placed immediately. The stairs have no balustrades. The furniture in the house consists of two beds and some tables for writing and for ironing. Instead of tables in the refectory there are planks on trestles; the rest of the furniture is at the Academy. Notwithstanding this poverty we are much better off than in the other house. Next year, if God spares us, we shall fare very well.

All the Sisters offer you, together with their profound respects, their best wishes for the New Year, begging as a New Year's gift your paternal blessing. Grant it especially to the one who is, my Lord, your very humble servant. . . .[31]

TO SISTER MARIA, MADISON

January 15, 1854

I have only time, my dear Sister, to thank you for your good wishes, and say I rejoice in what you tell me of your willingness to suffer for God. But you are still far, my daughter, from the dispositions in which I wish to see you. You would have

[31] Original in the archives of the Diocese of Le Mans

NEW PROVIDENCE CONVENT BUILT BY MOTHER THEODORE IN 1853

Old Convent shown in foreground. From drawing by Sister Esther Newport from an old lithograph

said nothing, you say, of the pain in your side, if you had not thought that some one else had told me about it. That is not right. It is not the proper disposition of a good daughter toward her mother. It is true that you do not complain for nothing, as you say. But I am very far from praising this conduct—you do not complain even when you *do* suffer. How little humility there is in that! Do not expect my admiration for virtues of that stamp; they are counterfeit. As to the rest, you know my opinion long ago.

If you show affection for Sister——she will appreciate it. Her disposition will change towards you—like for like—if you go about it nicely. Do this, my dear child, for the good of your soul. You know it has much to pay to the Almighty before it will be quiet; but God is ever ready to forgive and have mercy, if we are ready to receive His grace.

Sister Basilide writes that you take good care of my little Sister A——. I thank you and beg you to continue to do so. Father Corbe was pleased with your kind remembrance. He returns the compliment. . . .

TO THE RIGHT REVEREND AUGUSTINE MARTIN,
BISHOP OF NATCHITOCHES

Saint Mary-of-the-Woods, January 24, 1854
My Lord and venerated Father:

The letters you have received recently from Saint Mary's have told you with what holy joy we have learned of your elevation to the episcopacy, and with what fervor we have prayed God to bestow upon you His most precious gifts.

On the day of your consecration the Communions of the entire Community were for you, and very often since that day we have prayed for Your Lordship and for that favored portion of the Church whose chief shepherd you are.

How happy we should be, my Lord, were we able to second your ardent zeal and enkindle souls with the fire of your burning heart. How happy, could we reply affirmatively to the request Your Lordship has deigned to make us, and by which we are so highly honored—that of going to take care of the little girls that became ours, in a way, the moment you became their Father. But it seems to me we cannot go. Are you not too far away for an establishment? Are we not too young to make a foundation? In cutting off a good-sized branch from the little trunk, would we not kill both the one and the other? I am, my venerated Father, consulting you as if for another, and you answer, *"My child, you cannot do it."*

If we do not grant what you ask, it is assuredly because it is not possible to do so. You will see for yourself when we shall have once more the honor of receiving you into our solitude, a day that will be for every one of us a day of feast and happiness. Good Father Corbe says that we must give you all our reasons, and that if you are willing to wait, perhaps we could do something later. He said, "I would give to Bishop Martin the half of our Congregation; but," he added, "we cannot do it." You can form an idea of the pain it gives me to say No. I took up my pen twice before I could write the word. When you come to see us I shall impart to you a thought that has entered our minds—Sister St. Francis' and mine—which may be useful to you, and at the same time enable us to do something for Your Lordship. Father Corbe does not want me to write it.

I am sending you the lithograph of our present Saint Mary's. You will notice that we have built, I should better say, we are building, a fine large house. We are in it, but it is very cold, not yet having its doors and windows, and the winter is rigorous. One thing that is going to rejoice your paternal heart is that our little Community is doing well and giving us deep consolation.

All your daughters of Saint Mary's recommend themselves to your fervent prayers and ask your blessing. Give a very special one, please, to her who is Your Lordship's very humble servant. . . .

P. S. Father Corbe will write to you soon. My ink and my fingers are freezing.

TO THE REVEREND J. KUNDEK, JASPER

Saint Mary's, January 28, 1854

Good and dear Pastor:

While you were at Jasper we scarcely realized that we received so little. Your generosity knew how to supply; but when you had left for Europe, then we felt it. You wish that good may be done in your dear mission even when you will no longer be able to do it yourself. I also wish very ardently to see this first establishment of our Community in America well settled, well founded, before you give up the administration; hence with pleasure do I now speak about it.

The Bishop does not like the arrangements with the trustees; for this reason I much prefer to have each child pay, per quarter of eleven weeks, $1.50 for those who do not write, and $2.00 for those who do write, which is much less than what we require elsewhere. If this arrangement does not suit, I do not think we can take less than $300 per year, payable at the end of each quarter by the priest or by the trustees.

In either case, I think that if we want to do anything lasting, the Sisters ought to have a house and lot which would belong to them. If the house is not theirs the establishment will always be a temporary affair that will suffer from the caprices of men, and it may even be destroyed altogether. But if we had a house of our own, the Community will engage itself always to keep in the mission there three teachers on the conditions that shall have been agreed upon between us. If there were not a hundred girls, I would consent to take the little boys under ten years of age. Let me repeat: I much prefer that the pupils pay by the quarter, even should we receive less than three hundred dollars. And in that case, those who are poor would be received gratis upon your recommendation and treated like the others. See then, my good Father Kundek, if you can have this arrangement adopted by your parishioners; we should be more free on both sides. . . .

Your very humble and obedient servant,

SISTER ST. THEODORE,

Sup'r Gen'l.

TO SISTER MARIA, MADISON

February 25, 1854

My dear Sister:

If you think in conscience that you can fast without becoming exhausted, I permit you to do so; but if you perceive that you suffer too much from it, that you are weak and sick, you must not continue. I have only one word to say about your Communions, about the singing, and teaching the organ: Obey Sister Basilide. Do what she will tell you to do and omit what she will tell you to omit. Listen, my daughter: do not meddle with what does not concern you. If there is anything to be regulated, we shall see. about it when I go to Madison. In the meantime continue to go on your little round of duties; but peacefully. Believe me, my daughter, the best preparation for Holy Communion is obedience. Offer this preparation to Our Lord. . . .

Saint Mary's, Ash Wednesday, 1854

My dear Sister:

I am sorry to learn that you have fever so often. Try to avoid carefully whatever you think is the cause of it, for it is so wearing on a person. I think you ought not to fast.

It is not necessary for me to tell you to pray much for our good Bishop. You see him and have the opportunity of knowing how he is, and your heart will tell you what to do. I know not why, but I am quite uneasy about his health. He is not in danger, and yet I fear. We are always in fear about what we treasure.

Adieu, my daughter. It is for Him I leave you. Sister Cecilia is very sick. . . .

The death of Mlle. Marie le Fer de la Motte, Irma's aunt and godmother, calls for some words of condolence from Mother Theodore:

TO MME. LE FER DE LA MOTTE, ST. SERVAN

Saint Mary-of-the-Woods, Ind., March 26, 1854

Dear Friend:

It is with deep regret that we learned of the new loss you have sustained, which has not failed to reopen wounds that are still fresh and that will never more be closed. When we are condemned to pass a long life here below, we must also endure the pain of losing one by one all those who are dear to us, and often before dying we may cry out with Fenelon, "All my ties are broken." But for you, dear friend, it will not be thus: many of your dear ones will remain to weep over you. I hope and earnestly beg of God from the depth of my soul that you may be preserved yet a long time. Besides, if there are consolations for those who survive, there certainly must be for you and your family, which is a family of saints. Does it not seem to you, Madame, that you are only separated from these dear friends by a curtain, the corner of which is sometimes raised to let you glimpse their happiness?

When your letter arrived I was very ill of an inflammation of the lungs, from which I am recovering only slowly. Our dear daughters were admirable on this occasion, and they made sacrifices to obtain my cure; they are so very good.

You asked me in your last letter to speak to you with confidence of our affairs, and you showed the interest of a mother for us. I shall do so for your consolation, and in order that you may unite with us in thanking Almighty God for what He has vouchsafed to do for your friends of the Woods. We have, it is true, contracts to fulfill for our house; it will cost at least eighty thousand francs. Dear Madame, this is for yourself alone: I have paid more than sixty thousand francs, besides supplying the wants of the one hundred and thirty persons who compose our family. Now, are we not daughters of Providence? Do not, therefore, put yourself to any inconvenience in order to send us money; we are not in pressing need. Our Sisters are well fed, well clothed, and even well lodged; do you not think we ought to bless God? Nevertheless, we shall receive as coming from this dear Providence whatever you can dispose of in our favor, for we yet owe nearly thirty thousand francs; however, we hope that before two years our debts will have been paid. These, dear Madame, are the details of the temporal affairs of our Congregation, which I confide to you alone. These advantages are only a shadow, however, of the spiritual favors which the Almighty has bestowed upon us. Oh, how happy you would be if you could see all the good that your daughters of the Woods are doing, and the good spirit which animates them.

With deep veneration, tenderness, and affection, Madame and very dear mother, I am in the Heart of our Divine Saviour Jesus, ever yours. . . .

TO MME. CHOISNET [LE FER DE LA MOTTE], ST. SERVAN

Saint Mary's, March 27, 1854

Madame and beloved Cecile:

Yesterday I sent Sister St. Francis away and closed the door so that I might write a few lines to your excellent mother who is also ours (I am not allowed to write yet). Today I am a little stronger, and I seize the opportunity to give myself the satisfaction of talking awhile with you. If our dear Sister St. Francis and Mary Joseph caught me in the act, I should be scolded and perhaps punished; so I must make haste.

I wish I could tell you, my dear little friend, how much affection it has pleased God to put into my heart for you. Your name, and even the thought of you, makes it beat more quickly. I do not know why, for I am scarcely acquainted with you; nevertheless, it is true. It is one of those mysteries of the heart which cannot be accounted for.

No one wishes you well more than I do, nor more happiness in time and in eternity. Now that you may procure for yourself this good, my dear Cecile, never willingly dwell on thoughts about your happiness as a young lady to regret it. You have entered into your present state to accomplish God's will. Recognize and love this Divine will in the obligations of your state, and sanctify them in this Divine will. Do not stop to think of what is so painful, but look with satisfaction on the good that the Lord has bestowed upon you in giving you an excellent Christian as the guardian and companion of your life; this is a favor that you will appreciate fully only in eternity. Endeavor always to have a joyful and happy countenance, which becomes you so well, especially in the presence of your husband; you have no idea of the peace and comfort you will procure him by this constant amiability. The mistress of a home must be like the sun which warms and enlivens all that comes under her influence.

Why do I write thus to you, you who have always been a model of perfection in this respect? You will not be offended, and you will allow me to say, and repeat, that you ought not to give way to uneasiness about the future. Put yourself gently into the hands of Providence. Trusting all your affairs to Him and putting them also under the protection of Mary and Joseph, you will see that all will be well. Continue, while maintaining your rank in society, to practice a wise economy. Be sure that you will never be in want, I do not say of what is necessary but even of what is useful. We are happy to learn that your health is better; take good care of it. Do not let M. Choisnet occupy his mind so much with mathematics; at a certain age, that study fatigues the head terribly. Please offer him my profound respects but do not show him my letter—I should be too much ashamed. . . .

TO SISTER BASILIDE, MADISON

Saint Mary's, April 3, 1854

My dear Sister Basilide:

I am happy to have a letter from you. I was thinking you had remained too long without writing to me and I felt like getting *fachée*. Fortunately the Bishop arrived yesterday, as it were to take away my discontent and to bring me some news of you. This good Father is not at all well. Despite Sister Olympiade's remedies he suffers much. Though some better this morning, he is still in bed and it will soon be twelve o'clock. I just got up myself. I do not know if it is the prolongation of winter which keeps me so dragging, or whether I am, at last, at the illness that must be the last. As God wills! If it be, then I am greatly deceived, for I do not feel that I am dying, though I am very weak and miserable. When the fine weather comes I hope to gain a little life that I may be able to see you again after Easter. If I am not better soon I shall not go immediately after Easter.

The Bishop seems to look upon Father Dupontavice's plans as still very far from realization, or rather, as idle talk; at least, it seemed that way to me—I mean the few words that the good Bishop said in my presence yesterday, when he had the charity to come, notwithstanding his own indisposition, to pay me a little visit. First of all I wish they would think of our Sisters of North Madison. I do not believe they could live there another year, situated as they were last winter.

You must rebuke L——soundly and not let her take precedence of her Superior; she is, indeed, intolerable. I am always happy when hearing that your St. Ann's school is improving a little. I love that school which was started and organized by my dear Sister Liguori and which is now entrusted to my dear Sister Basilide. Having Catholic children in our classes is truly a great happiness, preferable, without any comparison, to having our schools filled with Protestants. Nevertheless, I like to have Protestants also, for it is the way to extend our holy religion. Where is the one educated in our schools who, if she is not a Catholic in reality does not become at least the friend of Catholics, the friend of the Sisters, and even their advocate in circles of the world. Well, my daughter, ours is a preparation for the generation that will succeed us, and eminent good will be done this way by us. You may not live to see it, but you will have sown the seed, and your Sisters will come to reap what will have been sown.

I do not wish you to think, my dear Sister Basilide, that when you lose me you will lose everything. No, my daughter, no. You will no longer have a Mother to love you as tenderly as I do—that, I concede—but you will have Sisters on whose affection you can rely; for, in truth, all love you dearly.

Everybody here finds the Bishop looking greatly changed. He is still coughing, which makes me quite uneasy. I am begging God the favor of sparing to us this true, this good Father. Please join with us in praying very much for him.

The unfortunate Lamennais has died in his obduracy—at least, so it seems. His body was conveyed in the common hearse, and six "bad subjects" who called themselves his friends were the only ones to accompany his remains to the cemetery of Père Lachaise, where he was thrown into the common grave with paupers without any distinction. What a reprobation!

Sister Mary Joseph is very grateful for your good letter. She loves you much. She also thanks Sister Ann Joseph for her note.

Good-bye, my dear Sister Basilide. Give my love to all, but keep a big share for yourself, and always pray for me. . . .

TO THE RIGHT REVEREND J. BOUVIER BISHOP OF LE MANS

Saint Mary-of-the-Woods, April 20, 1854

My Lord:

I cannot longer defer writing to you to express the gratitude of all your daughters of Saint Mary's, and my own in particular, for the precious gift you have had the kindness to promise us. Never have I received a present that has given me so much pleasure as this one will bring and everybody here has the same feeling. The day on which the dear portrait arrives will be a festive day at Saint Mary-of-the-

Woods. Your very good letter, so long awaited, came to hand only on Holy Thursday.

If it would be possible to enclose the portrait in a tin box it would be better preserved from accident and arrive in good condition. It is not necessary to prepay it. Have the kindness to address it to Mr. Edward Bayer, Brooklyn, New York. He is the son-in-law of Mrs. Parmentier and is our agent *gratis pro Deo*. He will forward it to us, but I beg of you do not send it by freight. If my niece, Sister Mary Theodore, should come to us from Ruillê, she could take charge of it. She would be certain then to be received here with open arms.

Must we now give up all hope of ever seeing you in our forest home, my good and beloved Father? Before saying No to our pleadings, let me call the attention of Your Lordship to the difference there is in travel now compared to the time when we came to America or when we returned. The first time we were sixty days crossing the ocean. Now a steamboat which has just been built at New York goes from that city to Havre in eight or ten days. Once we were three weeks coming from New York, now it takes only forty-six hours.

America is truly a wonderful country for "improvements," an English word which will soon be received into our language, if it has not been already. You will see from an oil painting which we intend sending you next summer, how much we have "improved" Saint Mary's where, fourteen years ago, we were received through charity into a small frame house, the picture of which you have. You perceive a great change already in the little sketch enclosed with this etter.

The exterior changes are not, however, the most important ones. When you sent your six daughters to Saint Mary-of-the-Woods, you thought they were going to lay the foundation of an establishment which, later on, would be of service to religion; but with the means you made use of—these persons, so poor in every respect, strangers to the country, the customs, and the language of the New World—you never expected to see the fruits of your zeal crowned with so much success. Today we are eighty persons in our Community, sixty-four, including twelve novices, wearing the religious habit, and sixteen postulants. There are nearly a thousand children in our schools, eighty-five boarders here at the Academy, thirty-seven of whom are Catholics.

Three converts received Baptism on Easter Sunday. On the same day eight pupils made their First Communion, and eighteen their Paschal Communion. They had been prepared long before, and prepared themselves more immediately by a retreat which they made during the last days of Holy Week. It is impossible to estimate what a Christian education does for these young people. Brought up among non-Catholics, they are ignorant of everything relating to our holy religion; they scarcely know how to kneel down when they come to us. But when they leave, they become little missionaries and do an incalculable amount of good to those around them.

The priest of Lafayette, a considerable town of Indiana, told me lately that the only school he had in his town was kept by two of our pupils, converts of last year, who are now fervent Catholics and show admirable zeal for instructing the little children of that congregation. Two others, converts of the preceding years, have entered the novitiate. One is full of piety and has an excellent disposition, but not marked ability; the other has strong feelings though she is a good child, and is endowed with a superior mind; both were a long time at the Academy and are well educated. There are among our young professed and novices able subjects who are being gradually formed for the more important services they will later on render to the Community. Until now God has made use of *nothing* with which to do His work, but it seems that for the future He wishes to make use of *something*.

I think you will soon have a visit from Bishop Martin, who was lately appointed to the See of Natchitoches in the north of Louisiana. At one time he was Vicar General in the diocese of Vincennes. We have told you about him as being a very devoted friend of our Congregation. This good Bishop was scarcely consecrated when he wrote a very pressing letter begging us to give him Sisters for his diocese. We reflected long on the proposal; finally, notwithstanding the pain it cost us to refuse good Bishop Martin, we decided not to send Sisters so far away. We are not certain whether His Lordship wanted Sisters to form a new Motherhouse or simply an establishment. The letter does not clearly say which; but it matters little, for in the first case, we are too young to cut off a branch from the tree, and in the second place, it would be very difficult in winter to have communication with our Sisters or to visit them. Besides, we do not think that an establishment depending on another Bishop would suit Bishop Martin. If he asks for Sisters from Ruillé, and you consent to give them, we could give him one or two Sisters to teach his Sisters English, and also music, since music must be taught in this country if we wish to have pupils.

Bishop Martin is very pious, full of zeal and ardor. Some people think that his ardor and zeal might better be tempered a little. I say this for yourself alone so you may know that with him matters must be treated in accordance with this disposition. I believe he likes our Rules very much and would leave our Sisters free to follow them. He is also very scholarly and considered an excellent writer and preacher.

Pardon me, my father, for entering into these details, which may be perfectly useless if Bishop Martin should not ask for Sisters. He was to have come this way, expecting to get our Sisters; but having received our letters, he wrote to Father Corbe that he would not come. I fear he is offended. This would cause us much pain. Still we do not think we can make any change in our decisions, unless you disapprove of them; in which case we should not adhere to them. The Bishop of Vincennes does not like us to go outside of his diocese; however, he has left us free to do as we wish for Bishop Martin.

At last they have finished painting our house. The painters are here in my room now, interrupting with their questions. I find the house too fine; it gives me great uneasiness about my vow of poverty. It looks more like a castle than the house of poor little Sisters of Providence. I think it might have been built cheaper and made less elegant. I wanted only simplicity, and I do not know how elegance has come in, in spite of myself. How unhappy I should be if, through my example, extravagance would be introduced among us. This thought takes away from me much of the pleasure I have in seeing my Sisters well lodged and their house finished. The last doors were hung on Holy Saturday, which tells you how much we have suffered this winter in this large open house. But next year we shall be better off. We have the consolation now of seeing Our Lord more suitably cared for in our chapel, which is pretty well ornamented for our Woods. The chapel does not give me scruples as the rest does. This house will cost between fifteen and sixteen thousand dollars—about eighty thousand francs, of which more than sixty thousand are paid. You see, my Father, your prayers for us to God have been heard.

All the Sisters are well at present. They have truly a good spirit. I beg of you pray for them always, and pray especially for this most miserable one who is, nevertheless, of Your Lordship, the most submissive daughter. . . .

Compared with the first poor little convent the new Motherhouse might have seemed to the Sisters "like a castle." It was, indeed, well and substantially built, yet it was

severely plain and had none of the present-day ordinary con-
veniences—electric light, steam heat, hot and cold water, or
hard polished floors. Coal oil lamps and candles furnished the
light; a few fireplaces and small stoves provided the heat. All
the water had to be brought into the house from outside wells
and cisterns and, even as the wood, carried to the third story.
The exterior of the building though plain, was attractive in
appearance, the dark green outside shutters contrasting pleas-
antly with the warm gray of the painted brick. The interior finish was void of ornament and the furnishings were scant and
of the simplest form, though of good quality. If there was elegance, it was the elegance of simplicity and good proportions.[32]

On a visitation tour from the south to the north of the state,
Mother Theodore spends a night at Indianapolis. From this
city she sends a few lines to the Sisters at home.

TO SISTER ST. FRANCIS, SAINT MARY-OF-THE-WOODS

Indianapolis, May 16, 1854

Dear Sister St. Francis:

My heart and mind are often with you. I suffer with you
and realize the agonies of your heart, though I mentally
reproach you for having them. I fear our poor child [Sister
Josephine Monaghan] is dead, or at least in her agony. How
painful it is for me to be only a few miles away from St. Mary's
and yet not able to be there. The fatigue, the expense, and the
time also, prevent me from satisfying my desire.

My health is better but I still cough. I have seen two doctors;
later you will hear what beautiful discoveries they have made.

Perhaps you will be surprised to see Sister M———return,
but more so to learn that I was on the point of sending
her back to her home. I never met any woman so completely

---

[32] This building erected by Mother Theodore was destroyed by fire
February 7, 1889. The front of the present Motherhouse, though a much more
extensive building, stands on the same site and on the same foundation.

useless. Besides, she is always so mysterious, and very obstinate. It is impossible to have her with children. Employ her at different things, wherever it may be necessary or advantageous, but do not permit her study of any kind, Catechism excepted.

To take the place of this unpromising novice, here is another postulant. While she is only a child, she belongs to a good family and appears to be in good health. She has, moreover, the consent of her parents, who are happy and proud to give their eldest daughter to God; and they hope to give Him others later on. She has little education, but she can learn, I think. We shall try her.

We are to leave tonight for Fort Wayne. We arrived here last night at eleven o'clock, and are at the Palmer House, so named in honor of Mr. Palmer. . . .

LETTER CIRCULAR

Saint Mary-of-the-Woods, July 2, 1854

My beloved Sisters:

It is with a heart full of joy that I call you once more to your dear home to have the happiness of making your retreat, a favor so much desired by all of you, and so loved by every one.

The retreat will begin the 8th of August, and will be given by a Jesuit of St. Louis. Try to be here before that time, in order to rest from the fatigue of your year's work and of your journey. Prepare yourselves to profit by this holy time to purify your heart from all the stains it may have contracted during a year of disturbing and laborious occupations, and to acquire new courage in order to do as perfectly as possible all the good that Our Lord still expects from you.

Let us with fervor ask also the light of the Holy Ghost for the elections which must take place at that time, and for which end you will recite fervently the prayers prescribed by our holy Rules, Chapter I.

Awaiting the pleasure of seeing you soon, I am always

Yours devotedly in Our Lord,

SISTER ST. THEODORE,

Sup'r Gen'l.

A new name now appears in the correspondence—that of Sister Mary James. A note of special interest attaches in that she was one of the witnesses in the diocesan process of the Cause for the beatification of Mother Theodore, and she also aided in the translation of some of the process writings.

Sister Mary James, Magdalena Stadelman, was born on May 22, 1834, at Fayetville, Ohio, of Swiss-German parentage. Her mother was Magdalena Eicher. Both father and mother belonged to old and distinguished families of Canton Lucerne.

Shortly after the child's birth her father was killed, being thrown from his horse one night; such, at least, was the supposition, as his frozen body was found the next day in the woods through which he was riding when returning from a visit to a neighboring farmer. His horse was a short distance away, and there was no evidence that he had been waylaid by evil-doers. The mother and child soon went to live with relatives in Cincinnati, where they remained about ten years. Then they moved to Indiana and settled at Ferdinand after spending a short time at Jasper. In the latter place Magdalena became acquainted with the Sisters of Providence. She is the little girl mentioned by Mother Theodore in the letter of "Easter Day, 1847," to Father Kundek. As a religious vocation seemed to be developing, this zealous priest kept a watchful eye over the child until he could consign her to the novitiate.

At the age of fifteen she lost her mother. Father Kundek then pleaded with Mother Theodore to receive her now into the Community, although she was a year younger than the usual age for admission. His request was granted. Four months after her mother's death, and still grieving deeply over her loss, Magdalena arrived at Saint Mary-of-the-Woods.

To turn her mind from her lonely thoughts, and because

of her youth, the little postulant was placed in the classes with the pupils of the Academy. She had a pretty voice for singing, talent for music, and facility for Latin and French. After two years of study and part-time novitiate, followed by two years full time, she received the holy habit and was sent out as a missionary. Her teaching career included many years at the Academy where her time was divided between music and the languages. Later she held the position of uperior in various places. When age and failing health entitled her to lighter duties, she remained at the Motherhouse, engaged with work connected with Mother Theodore's cause.

Sister Mary James developed into the type of the deeply ascetic religious. For a number of years she had charge of conducting the exercises of retreat for those who would be absent on account of their duties from the general annual retreat.

Her death occurred May 5, 1915, in her eighty-second year and the sixtieth of her religious profession. Two years previously she had the pleasure of hearing her cousin, the Reverend Michael Eicher, S. J., give the Spiritual Exercises of St. Ignatius to the Community. It was a never-to-be-forgotten retreat. This revered Father ranks among the special friends of the order, and his letters even to the present year (1936) are proofs of his unceasing paternal interest and friendly remembrance. The information concerning Sister's early life was furnished by him.

The letters of Mother Theodore to Sister Mary James are specially tender. This was probably due to the sorrowful circumstances of Sister's childhood, which excited Mother Theodore's deep compassion. Her Superior was "doubly her mother," as she says in one of her letters; and this double relationship was heartily reciprocated by the young Religious, who always found in the Mother-Foundress her ideal of holiness and every perfection.

A month after leaving the novitiate she received from Mother Theodore this her first letter:

TO SISTER MARY JAMES, VINCENNES

Saint Mary's, September 25, 1854

My very dear Child:

At last I am writing to you. Long ago I would have done so had it been possible. I am confident you know the heart of your Mother. To write requires time; but to *love*, to *cherish*, to *pray for*, through that desire we have for the happiness of our friends, time is not needed. And I may say that this kind of affection has not been wanting for you. Very often, even in my journeys, I have prayed for my dear little Sister Mary James. I have asked Our Lord to have her in His holy keeping, and so forth. I hope I have been heard. Oh, if you could understand the feelings of a mother's heart for a child which is not hers by nature but by grace—the feelings of the heart, I say for the temporal but more especially for the eternal happiness of her child—you would understand what I feel for you.

Try, do try hard to preserve the fruits of your retreat, by fidelity in keeping your heart pure and undefiled for Our Lord, by constant application to observe your Rule and to perform well all your spiritual exercises, and so on.

I am obliged to stop. I have so many letters to write and I am not well. I had to leave the chapel this morning during meditation and could not go back even for Mass. Ah, it is when we are young that we can do something for our salvation and for our neighbor's. When we are old we are good for nothing.

Write and tell me how you feel on mission. For my part, I miss you very much. . . .

TO SISTER MARIA, MADISON

Saint Mary's, November 24, 1854

I am sorry, my dear Sister, that you have yielded again to your caprices. You must make another copy of the pieces of music you destroyed. We shall see later what will be done with them. Think no more about these faults, now that you have acknowledged them. If they come back to your mind, humble yourself without falling into discouragement. Do not omit your Communions. As soon as you commit a fault be sorry, rise again and go on with confidence and love. When you do the contrary your imagination works and you go on from bad to worse.

Profit by the experiences of the past for the future. Accept the humiliation of losing your pupils in the spirit of penance. I have requested Sister Basilide to let you do the washing, without having told her that you asked to be permitted to do it. If you have time, I wish you would knit me, in your leisure moments, a woolen petticoat for winter. It should not be too wide. Do not make it too long either. You have nice yarn at Madison, and I know Sister Basilide will be willing to buy some for me. I know too that you will be pleased to work for your devoted old Mother. . . .

Accompanying Bishop Martin upon his return from Europe were two of Mother Theodore's nieces. Sister St. Francis had a letter awaiting him at New Orleans, to which Mother Theodore added a few lines.

TO THE RIGHT REVEREND A. MARTIN
BISHOP OF NATCHITOCHES

Saint Mary-of-the-Woods, December, 1854

My Lord:

I should like to be able to tell you how grateful I am for what you have done for the two young Sisters you brought with you. I should also like to say how deeply I share in the joy of your heart in being in the midst of the new family that Heaven has confided to your prayers and guardianship. As you are all happy together you will be still more so at your dear Natchitoches. Every day since your departure for

France we have prayed for you, and we shall continue to do so, asking God without ceasing to bless the shepherd and the flock.

Be so kind as to recommend our two Sisters to the good captain of the steamboat and send them as soon as possible to Evansville. If you have advanced any money to them we shall refund it at once. . . .

The unexpected nieces were Sister Mary Theodore (Le Touzé), a professed Religious from Ruillé-sur-Loir, and her sister Frances, who joined her at Ruillé but was to make her novitiate at Saint Mary-of-the-Woods. Having landed at New Orleans, they travelled by steamer up the Mississippi, the Ohio, and the Wabash to Terre Haute, arriving at Saint Mary's on Christmas Eve, 1854, a trip that took three weeks.

With a letter from Sister Mary Theodore to Bishop Martin, a few days after their arrival at Saint Mary's, Mother Theodore enclosed the following lines:

TO THE RIGHT REVEREND A. MARTIN
BISHOP OF NATCHITOCHES

January 2, 1855

At last our nieces have arrived thanks to God and to you. Thanks, yes, thanks a thousand times. The best and most delightful news they bring is that we may hope to see you here in our Woods. I cannot express what a happy day that will be for us. Good Father Corbe says that he will be more happy than we. I doubt it. Come, then, dear Father, come to bless your friends of Saint Mary's and to enjoy the happiness your presence will procure for them.

Pray that our dear Sister St. Francis may get well. This excellent Sister has been very sick for fifteen days; some better, however, the last two days. Oh, beg Our Lord to leave us this dear friend. I cannot bear the thought of losing her yet; still her health and constitution are most frail. She and all whose privilege it is to have known you offer you their profound respects. Accept mine also, with my heartiest wishes for a happy New Year, and give me in return your paternal benediction. . . .

TO SISTER MARY XAVIER, VINCENNES

Saint Mary's, January 8, 1855

My dear Sister:

I have received your good wishes with pleasure. I do not doubt of their sincerity any more than you doubt of mine. I earnestly beg of God that both you and I may become at last good Religious. It is indeed time for us to be what we ought to have been ever since we are in the house of God; but how far are we still from being so! You have asked this for me and I for you. I trust we shall be heard.

No doubt you have learned of the arrival of my nieces and that they passed by Vincennes without stopping. They would have been delighted to talk French with you. They had no chance of saying a word to anyone all the way from St. Louis. They were happy to arrive at last and we are happy to see them, for we were becoming uneasy about them. They send you much love. I thought of going to Vincennes, but could not leave on account of the illness of our poor Sister St. Francis. She is now a little better, but far from being well. Pray for this dear Sister that God may preserve her to us.

Our Superiors of Ruillé desire to be affectionately remembered to you, Bishop Bouvier says, but they have not written to anyone here, not even to me. They are so busy. They are well, and always fervent and devoted. How little, insignificant, are we compared to them, are we not? . . .

Saint Mary's, January 13, 1855

It is rather late to thank you, my dear Sister, for your good wishes for my feast, for the New Year, etc., but, *it is never too late to do well*. Be assured, then, of my gratitude and of the interest that I take in you. It was in great part on your account that I called Sister A————away, for I knew that you were not sufficiently busy, and I knew, too, that it is good for you to have rather more to do than less. In fact, I fear very much less a great number of employments than much free time. Thank God now with all your heart, seeing that He removes obstacles to your advancement and gives you opportunity of doing good works.

Never stop to ask yourself whether this or that pleases you, whether it is agreeable or not. Oh, no! But say to yourself: My God, you wish me to apply myself to this, or to that. I will do it for love of You with all the perfection of which I am capable. Then put yourself at the work whether you like it or not. In this way you will please Our Lord and you will fulfill your duty well, and your efforts will be blessed by Heaven. Be exact to renew your intention often and to purify it always more and more. For, my dear Sister, we do not know whether we have a long time to live or not. It might be that this year will be the last God will give us to work for Him and to prove to Him our love. What joy, if before the end of the year 1855 we are in heaven! There are many upon earth who suffer with us now in this land of exile, who will have paid all they owed to the Divine Justice and been admitted to behold and possess God this very year. I do not desire this for you (that is, that it be your last year), but what I pray earnestly for is that you will not commit one wilful sin, and that all your actions may be pleasing to God and tend to His glory. And, further, to be specific, that you may avoid these variations of humor which make you suffer so much and which also cause others to suffer so much from you. Please pray for the first two favors for me. . . .

Saint Mary's, January 20, 1855

My dear Sister:

I am not at all angry at you, I never was. But I am sorry or rather humiliated to see my name in all the newspapers, like a thief's. This proves that I am not very humble. I have at last received the letter of good Father Dupontavice, which is very charming and repays me for having waited for it for fifteen days. If I knew how to write a letter like that, I would be too proud. My letters are so poor that I dare not read them over after they are written.

Offer my profound respects and my thanks to that good pastor, and tell him that we all consider him already as one of the patrons of our Congregation. He will know what this means.

Bridget is, I believe, a little less unreasonable, but she is still bad enough. I hope her old mother will let her come. She has not yet answered me. Sister St. Francis is resuscitated enough to preach for the Jubilee. To see if she is dead, we shall have to take a little, or even a big, boy to her room and ask her about preparing him for Baptism or for Confession. If she opens neither her eyes nor her mouth, we may have the funeral in all safety.

You pay too much attention to the miseries of Sister Maria. Those are only miseries. Let her sleep. During that time she has no distractions. I wrote to the other person in question. I am glad that she is in better dispositions.

We are in the midst of the Jubilee. Father Chassé preaches twice a day in the village church and preaches well. Nearly all the "old foxes" have been converted. However, there are some yet who have not come; but very few. The church is full as an egg. Our Protestant pupils wished to be present at the sermons; of course we let them go.

I am in a great hurry today, as I leave tomorrow to take Sister Philomene to Evansville. I shall spend a day or two at Vincennes. The Bishop came to see us on his way to visit Father Bessonies. He told us that he wishes to put together his two asylums at St. Vincent's. I do not know whether this will succeed; we shall see. . . .

The Jubilee here referred to was published by Pope Pius IX in August, 1854, to procure prayers for the war-threatened countries of Europe, and to obtain guidance for the Council to be assembled in Rome in November to decide on the promulgation of the dogma of the Immaculate Conception of the Blessed Virgin Mary. This doctrine, which had been widely held by the faithful from the early ages of Christianity, was made an article of faith on December 8, 1854, by the decree of His Holiness Piux IX.

More than a month later Mother Theodore wrote in her diary: "January 14, 1855—Feast of the Holy Name of Jesus— Our Very Reverend Father Corbe announced publicly that the Conception of the Blessed Virgin, pure and immaculate, had been declared an article of faith by our Holy Father the Pope on December 8, in the presence of more than two hundred bishops. *O Mary, conceived without sin, pray for us who have recourse to thee. O Mary, without spot, protect thy House of the Woods!* On arriving from the church we assembled the Community to sing the *Te Deum* in the chapel. It will be sung again this evening. May God be praised!"

And in the evening the diary adds: "We have had Vespers and the *Te Deum*, with Benediction of the Blessed Sacrament, the chapel in its best."

The joy that this happy event had brought to Saint Mary-of-the-Woods was soon dimmed by sorrowful tidings. Death had claimed the revered Bishop of Le Mans, Jean-Baptiste Bouvier. Mother Theodore thus informs the Sisters on the missions of the loss the Community had sustained:

Saint Mary-of-the-Woods, Feb. 10, 1855

My very dear Sisters:

"We are the children of saints," said Tobias. We, also, my dear Sisters, are the children of saints. One of our dear Fathers has gone to a better life, braving, like a Christian hero, danger, sickness, death itself, to obey the call of the Vicar of Jesus Christ upon earth, and of the Blessed Virgin Mary.

He died in the Eternal City after having heard from the mouth of the successor of St. Peter the decree of the Immaculate Conception of our Blessed Mother—a decree which he had desired all his life. His heart was full of gratitude and consolation, but his happiness was a celestial joy. The world had now nothing worthy of his great soul. "It is good to die here," he said. Yes, it was good for you, dear Bishop, to pass from the arms of the Holy Father, the admirable Pius IX, to those of your God—that God whom you had so faithfully served during your long life. You are going to that heavenly home to which in your paternal letters you gave us a *rendezvous*.

O let us try, my dear Sisters, to imitate his faith, his rectitude of mind, his zeal, his devotedness to the glory of God, his forgetfulness of self; in fine, all his heroic virtues.

Our Community is indebted to him for its Rules and Constitutions. Saint Mary-of-the-Woods owes to him its very existence and preservation. This saintly and learned prelate was for us in our days of darkness what the cloud was for the Israelites in the desert—a shelter and a light. In our days of peace he was ever a father. Five weeks before starting on his great and last journey he sent us his portrait, expressing his regret at not being able to come himself to his "beloved daughters of the Woods."

We have a well-grounded hope that he is in heaven, increasing the long list of saints who have rendered illustrious the Church of Le Mans. Still, where is the traveler who has trod this dusty earth eighty years without tarnishing in the least the whiteness of his baptismal robe? You will, therefore, offer up for him the prayers prescribed by our holy Rules, Chapter 13, Art. 98. Moreover, for thirty days, five times the Our Father and Hail Mary will be said in each establishment at the conclusion of the morning and evening prayers for the same intention.

Your truly devoted,

SISTER ST. THEODORE,

Sup'r Gen'l.

Mother Theodore's statement that the Community is indebted to Bishop Bouvier for its Rules and Constitutions refers to the revised and enlarged edition, which had been prepared in 1835 under the direction of His Lordship and presented to the Pope for approval. The original Rule had been drawn up by the Abbé Jacques-François Dujarié, the venerated Founder of the Sisters of Providence of Ruillé-sur-Loir, assisted by the Abbé de la Chapelle, a member of the Society of Jesus then called Fathers of the Faith.

Some details that Mother Theodore did not know when she wrote her Circular may be added here. They are taken from a little book entitled *The Last Moments of Bishop Bouvier*, written by his Vicar General, the Abbé Chevereau.[33]

Preparatory to the Council proclaiming the dogma of the Immaculate Conception, the Abbé states, Pius IX had specially invited to Rome "from each nation one or two bishops

---

[33] *Les Derniers Instants de Mgr J. B. Bouvier, Évêque du Mans*, par un Ecclésiastique du Diocèse (2e édition; Au Mans: Chez Monnoyer, 1855).

from among those whose theological knowledge, piety, and authority seemed most eminent. For France the Bishop of Le Mans shared this honor with Cardinal Gousset, Archbishop of Rheims."

This call from the Sovereign Pontiff "went straight to the heart of Bishop Bouvier," says the Abbé. "Nothing could stop him, neither his age, nor his infirmities, nor the fatigues inseparable from a journey at all times painful. He heeded only the call of the Shepherd of the Shepherds, he heard only his voice, and he decided that his departure would take place Friday, October 15, 1854." He was to be accompanied only by his private secretary, the Abbé Sébaux.

Reaching Lyons, where he was the greatly desired guest of the Archbishop, Cardinal de Bonald, he fell sick of an intestinal disorder then epidemic in France. It was not until four weeks later that he was permitted, though still very feeble, to resume his travel. Exhausted and suffering, he reached Rome on the night of the sixth of December, and was carried at once to the Quirinal where, according to the Holy Father's orders, he was to be lodged. "Here we saw an elegant suite of seven rooms newly renovated, where everything had been provided to the least detail," wrote the Bishop's secretary. "The location was very beautiful and easy of access."

The Pope had appointed as special sponsor and guide to Bishop Bouvier, a bishop very close to His Holiness, Bishop Tizzani, then stationed at the Vatican. This devoted friend, knowing the ardent desire of the sick prelate to be present at least for the solemn reading of the decree, obtained a place for Bishop Bouvier near the throne of His Holiness. In the account sent to Le Mans, the Abbé Sébaux said," Mgr Tizzani arranged all with great care and exquisite delicacy; and when in the morning (December 8) our Bishop departed for St. Peter's, robed in his mantelletta, there was awaiting him, at one of the side entrances, the Holy Father's own chair with the four porters and their chief." That evening from his own apartments, Bishop Bouvier was able to view some of the magnificent illumination of St. Peter's.

The energy shown by the venerable invalid on the great day seemed almost a promise of recovery. But the promise was not to be fulfilled. Day by day the Bishop grew weaker, and on Christmas night the sacrament of Extreme Unction was administered to him by the Cardinal Archbishop of Lyons in the presence of two archbishops and eight bishops, a large number of the clergy, and all the laity from Le Mans who were then in Rome. The next morning the dying prelate received Holy Viaticum from the hands of the Bishop of Marseilles during the Mass said in the sick room.

In the afternoon of the same day a very special honor was to be his, a visit from the Holy Father—a favor the more precious as it was an exception to the usages of the Pontifical court. Pius IX remained twenty-five minutes alone with Bishop Bouvier. On leaving the room the Holy Father exclaimed amidst tears, "Oh, how good he is—this poor, dear sufferer!" and he expressed his astonishment at "the presence of mind and the clearness and rectitude of the ideas with which the Bishop of Le Mans had spoken."

Three days later the holy Bishop died surrounded by his household and several of the bishops. Conscious to the last moment, he kissed with loving devotion the medal of the Immaculate Conception given him by the Holy Father, and the crucifix blessed and indulgenced by His Holiness during his visit. "Finally, says the Abbé Chevereau, "he slept the sleep of the just, Friday, December 29, 1854, at three o'clock in the afternoon, the hour at which Our Saviour Jesus Christ willed to die for the salvation of the world." The next day the Abbé Sébaux, seated close beside the couch of death, wrote to Le Mans, "The Cathedral will have his body; the Seminary, his heart."

The writer of the sketch concludes: "One might say that our worthy Bishop died under the eyes and in the arms of the Episcopacy of the whole world, for the bishops of the foreign nations were around his couch of pain and bed of agony, as eager, as affectionate as the French prelates. Everybody recalled the words he had spoken in departing from the ceremony of the eighth of December: 'It is good to die at Rome. It will be sweet to die at Rome after what I have just seen.' "

On the morning after the Bishop's death the Holy Father offered Mass for the soul of the deceased and, to quote the Abbé Chevereau, "would himself take charge of the obsequies . . . declaring his intention of continuing through the funeral ceremonies the generous and devoted hospitality which he had tendered in the apostolic palace of the Quirinal." The French

Ambassador had proposed "to surround the illustrious prelate with the pomp worthy of him and of France in the French National Church of St. Louis, . . . but the Holy Father designated the Church of the Apostles, which was larger and nearer to the Quirinal." At the request of His Holiness one hundred Masses were offered for him in this same church during the solemnities. After the requiem Mass attended by hundreds of bishops and priests, state and court officials, members of the diplomatic corps and many other notables, the body of Bishop Bouvier was carried again across the Mediterranean to Marseilles in a vessel belonging to the papal government. All the expenses of the funeral and also of transportation were borne by Pope Pius IX.

The final funeral rites were celebrated with all possible splendor at Le Mans when, on January 23, 1855, the precious remains of the great Bishop were placed in the mortuary chapel of his own Cathedral.

The career of Bishop Bouvier was exceptional. Bishops were customarily chosen from other localities and from high stations in life. Bishop Bouvier was born in the Diocese of Le Mans and of poor parents. Without the advantages of wealth or family position, but with the careful training of virtuous parents, he rose to eminence through his own merits—his natural talents and profound learning, combined with the holiness of his life.

After his ordination in 1808 he was a professor of philosophy in the College for three years. In 1811 he was called to the chair of theology in the Major Seminary. In 1819 he was appointed Rector of the Seminary and, at the same time, Vicar General, positions he held until named Bishop in 1834. He was the author of a complete course in theology, which was widely used in the seminaries throughout France. He died in his seventy-second year and in the twenty-first of his episcopacy.

A subject with which Bishop Bouvier had recently been occupied before setting out for Rome, was the appeal made by Bishop Martin of Natchitoches for Sisters of Providence for his diocese. When Mother Theodore felt obliged to refuse Bishop Martin, she suggested that he apply to Ruillé. He did so; and the following letter refers to the arrangements that were being considered.

Saint Mary-of-the-Woods, February 16, 1855

My Lord and Father:

With great pleasure we shall give you two Sisters to teach English, if Mother Mary will give you Sisters from France capable of governing the house. I fear its administration would present some difficulties, which could be eliminated by our Congregation in France. I suppose it is immaterial to you whether this house be attached to Ruillé-sur-Loir or to Saint Mary-of-the-Woods. If there is sufficient property and a prospect that the institution will grow, it seems to me that it would be better for it to be independent, with powers to make establishments itself in Louisiana where there is so much good to be done.

A long time ago we had a proposal for an establishment in Thibodeaux, as you are aware. But the difficulty of transportation appeared an insurmountable obstacle. Our travelers [Mother Theodore's nieces] were three weeks coming from New Orleans to Terre Haute. Your last letter was a month, less two days, on the way. You see, dear Father, it would be very difficult, not to say impossible, for us to undertake the government of establishments so far from Saint Mary's, and they could be visited only rarely.

A letter from St. Servan tells us that you have procured some Sisters of Charity for your diocese. We rejoice as heartily as if the good that is going to be done were done by ourselves. God knows how we long to see your burning zeal crowned with success. Permit me to say with Breton frankness, my very dear Father, that, having in your diocese others who will accomplish better than we the two principal works of our Congregation, I do not quite see what we could do there, specially as we would be located so far from your episcopal city. This is simply an observation that I submit to Your Lordship. I do not intend hereby to withdraw my promise, if our Mother will send some Sisters from France. She has not yet said anything about it, I shall write to her today concerning the matter.

We have sustained a great loss in the death of Bishop Bouvier. That holy prelate was for us in our days of trial like a pillar in the desert, a light and a protection. But he will protect us from heaven where he now dwells, I hope, adding one saint more to the long list of holy prelates that have already rendered illustrious the Church of Le Mans. Some days before seeing you, this good Father wrote me that he was about to set out for Rome. He expressed his regret at not being able to come and see his daughters of the Woods, He announced his portrait, which he had had painted expressly for us, gave us his blessing, and predicted that soon we were going to accomplish greater good than we had done up to the present day. Could I have believed that that was the last letter to be written to me by that cherished friend, who had so often give me so much consolation! His death was so beautiful, so enviable! That helps to console us for the terrible blow. "It is good to die here," this holy prelate said in going out from the Assembly. He had seen enough, heard enough. Earth had nothing more to attract his heart. So it was that in a few days afterwards he passed from the arms of the Sovereign Pontiff into the arms of his God whom he had served so long and faithfully.

Father Corbe is always as kind and devoted as you knew him to be. He seems to be advancing rapidly in the way of the interior life—we seldom see him. Like ourselves, this good Father would be very happy to see you once more at Saint Mary's. That day would indeed be one of joy for everybody, even for yourself, my venerated Father. You would not view unmoved the Community you had so well protected, now so large and prosperous. You would share in its joy. Let us hope to see that happy day.

Sister St. Francis has been, and continues to be, in very feeble health this winter. Both of us together are not worth two cents. Sister has not been able to do any work for two months, but just now she is a little better. Sister Mary Joseph keeps up, though she is not very robust. She will be a very valuable daughter later on. These two dear Sisters, also Sister Mary Theodore and Frances, offer their profound respects to Your Lordship. The latter begins to stammer a few words in English. Sister Philomene is improving, Sister Augustine also. The brother of the latter has become a fervent Catholic. She will be glad I told this to you.

I have just read over my letter and I am ashamed to send it; but it would not be possible to re-write it. I have already exceeded the amount of work my head can bear. Have the goodness to excuse me, please, and give your blessing to all your daughters at Saint Mary's. . . .

TO SISTER BASILIDE, MADISON

Saint Mary's, February 17, 1855

You guessed very well, my dear Sister Basilide. I had made out the bills for the Academy. They were sent the day before yesterday. Before that, I had had my circulars, and since then I have had to send letters to high personages. This has taken all my time. I am truly tired, but I believe that I shall rest only in heaven, God giving me grace to get there. But I shall have to burn a long, long time before. No matter; if we get there somehow, all will be well.

For Lent, do as usual. I believe that all can at least try the American fasting. If you or your Sisters cannot continue

—well, you must cease. Make no remark on what they take, and let each one act according to her conscience.

All should go to Father d'Hope [d'Aube?] for confession. I wish I could go to him myself. That man is a saint. He suffers terribly and still he is always so cheerful, always edifying. He has done an amount of good to our Sisters at Lanesville. Offer my profound respects to him and tell him that I entreat him to pray for us, all in general and for *me* in particular. I need prayers very badly, I assure you. I cannot write to the Sisters today. I am scribbling these few lines during dinner. As to the little statues of the Blessed Virgin, I found them very pretty, at least those I saw; but I must tell you that I have not yet unpacked them. I have not had the time. I saw only those that are on top. You will do well to pay for them now.

When Sister Theodore has been well for one day, she spends three days repenting of her good behavior. She is incorrigible. I wish I could have written once more to your venerated pastor. It is not possible to do so at present. Present my profound respects to him. . . .

Mother Theodore now writes to the secretary and faithful attendant, privileged to be admitted into the confidence and intimacy of her departed Father in Christ. He later became Bishop of Angoulême.

TO M. L'ABBÉ SEBAUX, LE MANS

Saint Mary-of-the-Woods, Ind., March 2, 1855

Monsieur l'Abbé:

You have had both the affliction and the consolation of receiving the last sigh of a father. You will allow his daughters, while mingling their tears with yours, to congratulate you on being the chosen one among many devoted priests to accompany him in that journey, which was to be his last. Our hearts were relieved when we learned that you were near him in his last moments, you whom he loved so much and by whom he was likewise so tenderly loved. Your filial devotedness must have been consoling to this holy prelate when he saw himself at the point of death—I was going to say in a strange land, but no, Rome was not a strange land for him; on the contrary, it was consoling for this faithful son of the illustrious Pope Pius IX to pass from the arms of the great pontiff to those of the Almighty, whom he had served so long and so faithfully. We thank God, however, for having inspired you to take his mortal remains to his dear Church of Le Mans. There will then be another protector for that city, which is already renowned for the great number of holy prelates who have adorned it previous to Monseigneur Bouvier. It will also be a compensation for his numerous children to have him again in their midst.

We are the only ones who possess nothing to remind those who will come after us of what we owe to this venerated Father. And who owes as much as we do? His generous heart knew not that forgetfulness which distance causes. The portrait of this devoted Father, whose loss we feel so sensibly, this portrait, I say, which we await with love and respect, has not arrived. If you could have another copied for us, how grateful we should be! We would willingly impose on ourselves the greatest sacrifices to obtain this treasure for our Community.

If you have any engravings of the holy prelate, or other things that belonged to him which you could dispose of in our favor, it would be a great kindness to send them to us. What encourages me to make this request is the kind welcome I received from you and your family the last time I was in France. I have not forgotten it, and since that time you have had a share in the prayers which we do not fail a single day to offer up for our benefactors. . . .

TO SISTER BASILIDE, MADISON

Saint Mary's, March 22, 1855

My dear Sister Basilide:

Though my health is still very miserable, I wish to tell you that I truly share greatly in your sorrow. It is indeed very painful to see the number of your pupils decreasing every day. You have seen your Protestant pupils disappear one after another; but that was not all. Now you must see your dear Catholic children also abandoning you, and go to get the liberty which is allowed them in your too culpable city of Madison. God will punish it, I fear, in a way still more severe.

Have courage. Pray, pray much for yourself, for your mission, for that erring city, but resign yourself to what it will please God to order, and try not to let these contradictions have any influence on your dealings with your companions. This is not asking little. Indeed it is very difficult, and it requires an uncommon virtue, not to make others suffer when we suffer.

I do not yet find in my Sister Basilide that wisdom which asks of each one only what she can give. Remember the fable of Lafontaine, which tells of the animals going to war; how their king knew how to use advantageously the talents of each one and give to each a post according to its instinct. The talent of a good Superior is to do the same—to require of each one only what she can give. Up to this time you have not known *how to deal with a person who is in the wrong*. Perhaps you are not able to do so. I must not myself require from you more than you can give. I only wish you to renounce all feelings of humor and, directing yourself by the spirit of faith, of reason, and of *self-denial*, to use all the means that prudence suggests that your Sisters may be happy and satisfied. If one way does not succeed try another. Believe me, dear Sister, always and everywhere you will find people who will try your patience, and you yourself will try theirs—except in heaven.

It is useless to expect me with the hope that I shall permit you to have a school of boys and girls together in the town of Madison. I shall never permit it. Sister St. Francis intended writing to you, but since St. Joseph's day she has been in bed. Sister Mary Joseph has inflammation of the lungs. We are all very miserable. As I expect to go to see you after Easter I say nothing further. Here winter ends only towards noon and begins again in the evening.

Several weeks passed before Mother Theodore was able to make her promised visit to Madison. Continual bad health and frequent long illnesses had marked her years ever since her arrival in America. Yet, with almost superhuman courage she had gone on with her laborious work, and undertaken long and wearisome journeys filled with the discomforts and hardships incident to the primitive modes of travel. She was now evidently growing weaker, and her young companion on this trip, Sister Mary Joseph, was faithful in keeping the Sisters informed of her condition. The letter that follows, however, is from Mother Theodore herself.

TO THE SISTERS AT SAINT MARY'S

Madison, May 6, 1855

Good day, my dear Sisters. In spirit I am with you all, but in particular in the room of my poor little Sister Josephine. I saw her this morning receive Our Lord. I united with her and thanked Our Lord for her. Give her my best love. The dear child! How much I am occupied about her.

I suppose Sister Mary Joseph gives you news of me, but you will be glad to know from my own self that I am a little better. I slept tolerably well last night and feel some stronger this morning. Good Father Dupontavice came to give us Holy Communion and sent a carriage to take us to High Mass, and again to Vespers. I have just come back this moment and feel a little tired.

I offer my profound respects to good Father Corbe, while waiting for him to come here. They scarcely knew whether they should receive us here without him. I shall write to Sister Mary Cecilia before leaving Madison, to let her know exactly when I expect to be at Indianapolis. At present I think it will be Tuesday of next week. The two little girls should take the cars on that day at Terre Haute; but I shall write again Tuesday or Wednesday.

A letter comes from our dear Mother Mary. She is desolate because her little Sister Elise [her secretary] is dying. This dear Mother sends much love to you all.

I am sure poor Sister Olympiade is quite sad not to have me on her hands. I miss her too. And you, Sister St. Francis, you are doing fine, are you not? Whatever you do, do not get sick, and do not let my dear Sister Josephine die without me. Pray for me. . . .

But not all their care nor their prayers could save Sister Josephine. Mother Theodore then wrote to the missions from the convent in Madison.

LETTER CIRCULAR

Madison, May 20, 1855

My beloved Sisters:

Our Lord has again plucked a flower from his garden at St. Mary's. On the 13th instant He took our dear Sister

Josephine Monaghan. Like another Joas, this privileged soul was sheltered under the wings of the Lord from her infancy; but, happier than the ungrateful prince, she died in the house of the Lord. The wickedness of the world had never corrupted her heart. It did not even trouble the serenity of her beautiful mind, which never suspected evil in others.

We have the greatest confidence that she took to her Divine Spouse her baptismal innocence, embellished by all the virtues which she practiced during her too short life. Many of you knew her in her childhood and in her youth as a pupil. In both stages she was a model. You admired her virtues in the novitiate, but especially in our Academy where her precious wisdom and the amiable dignity of her manners and conduct ever deserved, and obtained, the respect and even the veneration of the pupils and of all the strangers who had intercourse with her. But, like gold in the crucible, her precious qualities shone more brightly in her long and painful sickness, during which she practiced all the virtues of a good Religious.

Her faith was immovable, her confidence in God unbounded, her love for her Beloved, most ardent and strong. Oh! what a happiness it was for her to be permitted to take her vows, and with what fervor she pronounced them! As for charity toward her neighbor, which was her favorite virtue and which she had so well practiced all her life, it was more remarkable during those days of suffering, in which it is so difficult to maintain evenness of mind when poor nature is so reduced. She had always a pleasant smile and an amiable word for those who approached her. Forgetful of self, she was occupied only with the sufferings of others. During the last weeks of her life she bore the most excruciating pains without the least complaint, saying simply where she suffered. She had constantly the greatest desire to go to Our Lord, the most tender devotion to the

Blessed Virgin Mary, and to her holy patron, St. Joseph. So, my dear Sisters, we have the well-grounded hope that her death was most precious in the sight of God, and that she is, or soon will be, enjoying the happiness of heaven. You are so well convinced of this that nearly all of you are envious of her lot. But I should be sorry, my dear children, were you to indulge in such a feeling; it would not be according to the spirit of your vocation.

My dear Sister Josephine did not take sufficient care of her health; she acknowledged it when it was too late. That is the only cause of pain she ever gave me. You must not imitate her in this. You ought to take a reasonable care of yourselves, so as to preserve a life which is entirely devoted to God and to the souls He loves so much. After a long and painful career, though you may not have her innocence, you probably will have procured more glory to God; you will have been instrumental in the salvation of a greater number of souls with whom you will love, praise, and enjoy your beloved Spouse during all eternity.

Though the death of our Sister was most consoling, we know that He who found spots in the angels themselves will not admit the smallest blemish into His blessed abode; therefore, you will offer for the repose of her soul the prayers prescribed by our holy Rules. Also pray for one who needs prayers very much and who will always remain in Our Lord,

Your truly devoted

SISTER ST. THEODORE,

Sup'r Gen'l.

A few weeks later Mother Theodore is again at home and issuing another call to the Sisters on the missions.

LETTER CIRCULAR

Saint Mary's, July 5, 1855

My beloved Sisters:

The longed-for time of our annual retreat has come once

more. The voice of the Lord calls you to your dear solitude of Saint Mary's not only that you may rest after a year of painful labors, but especially that you may purify your hearts more and more in communion with God and acquire new strength and fervor for the time to come.

Put everything in good order in your establishment and in your employments, and come as soon as possible to give me the consolation of seeing you all, fervent and united, which is the greatest happiness that I can have in this world.

Your truly devoted

SISTER ST. THEODORE,

Sup'r Gen'l.

The brevity of this Circular must be attributed to another severe illness from which Mother Theodore had not yet recovered. On June 13, 1855, she had written in her diary: "We leave with the Bishop for Vincennes. I cough all the time and go to consult the doctor." And later: "I return on the 2nd of July very feeble. A novena was made for me to the Blessed Virgin, Mary Immaculate, and Father Chassé said Mass for me every day of the novena. The Sisters and children united and said special prayers. It is to the favor of the Virgin Immaculate that I owe my improvement. O my Mother, obtain for me the grace to profit by my state of suffering, and to draw from it all the benefit that your divine Son expects from it for His glory and the good of your little Community of the Woods!"

In August she wrote: "On the morning of the 6th Father Boudreaux, a Jesuit, arrived to give our retreat. My God! Grant that I may be the victim for all my dear daughters, since I am the only one deprived of the happiness of making the retreat. Have pity on them and on me." Two weeks later she wrote: "On the 14th a terrible fever reduced me in a little while to an almost hopeless state."

The letter of July was Mother Theodore's last "Letter Circular" calling the Sisters to the retreat. In so weak a condition was she at the end of the retreat that the Sisters had to leave for their missions without saying good-by to her. They never saw her again. She rallied sufficiently, however, to write a few more letters. The one that follows is another to her first postulant of 1841, the "good little Easterner."

TO SISTER GABRIELLA, FORT WAYNE

Saint Mary's, September 23, 1855

My dear Sister Gabriella:

It is with pleasure that I can satisfy your desire of receiving some lines from me. They may be the last, for my health is far from being good. I look better, as my face and left side are much swollen; but in reality, *all* my better is to feel a little stronger than I did. I am very grateful to Our Lord for this, for I can go to Mass, and after that I am more courageous to carry the cross that Our Lord has sent me in His mercy. Had He taken me sooner I do not think I would have loved Him so much; or at least I would not have appreciated enough the happiness of suffering for Him who has suffered so much for us. I do not think that I yet esteem enough that inestimable favor, but I may say that I do value it more than I did. I would not change my cross for any consolation that Our Lord might give me instead, though I must say that it is painful to be in the state in which I am. But, dear Sister, I must stop—I have already spoken too much about myself. You will excuse me, and you will continue to pray for your old Mother and to offer some of your good works for her particular necessities. I am happy to know that you have the prospect of a good school this year; thus to be afforded more means for doing the work of your holy vocation.

Give my love to all our dear Sisters at Fort Wayne, and my best respects to Father Benoit. Good-by, my very dear Sister Gabriella. Believe me always, in the Heart of Our Lord, your very truly devoted Mother.

The next letter was to a young Sister who was having her first experience in charge of a mission kitchen. Sister Veronica Smith lived to a ripe old age, dying only in 1917. In July, 1910, she had the privilege of testifying in the cause of Mother Theodore.

TO SISTER VERONICA, FORT WAYNE

Saint Mary's, Sept. 29, 1855

My dear Sister:

As I can hardly write at all, I am taking only a little scrap of paper, just to tell you that I am very glad you are pleased at Fort Wayne and that you are trying to correct yourself. Try for your Particular Examen not to taste anything between meals without necessity; and as a help towards your amendment impose upon yourself the penance of eating your bread dry in the evening when you have thus indulged sensuality during the day. Hence, you will punish yourself in the way you have transgressed. When you will have overcome this inclination, make your examination upon gentleness, taking for your models Our Lord and the Blessed Virgin. Work hard to acquire these two virtues—abstemiousness and kindness. If you acquire these two this year you will have taken a long step forward. I have written to Sister Agnes to receive your sisters if they apply to her. Everybody sends you a thousand good wishes. Offer mine to all our Sisters, in particular to Sister Rose Ann. . . .

Sister Agnes (Genevieve Dukent), mentioned above, was the first American postulant. Her home was in the neighborhood of Vincennes. As stated earlier, she was one of the four subjects awaiting the Sisters at Saint Mary-of-the Woods in 1840. When in 1842 a school was opened for the village children, Sister Agnes was the teacher. Though her pupils numbered only a dozen at the beginning, and a little log hut was their school, she was most enthusiastic about her work.

On Christmas day of the ensuing year took place the First Communion of the village children. Nine boys and five girls made up this first class. The touching ceremony marked the formal opening of the new village church. For nearly four years the parishioners had been without a church, the one built in 1838 having been destroyed by fire in February 1840.

In 1845 Sister Agnes was assigned to Jasper. In 1849 she was one of the corps of teachers that began St. Joseph's, Terre Haute. The next twenty-five years she labored at the orphanages in Vincennes, or again at Jasper as Superior. Her latter years were passed at the Motherhouse, filled with zealous offices, especially those of the apostolate of prayer and suffering. She went to her reward October 30, 1894, aged ninety years.

On Wednesday, October 17, Mother Theodore wrote a grave and important letter to Sister Basilide pertaining to France. After her signature she even added the official "Sup'r Gen'l." Then on the third page she wrote the following without any formal address:

You will find the first part of my letter very serious, but I wanted to write it to you that you may make use of it, before or after my death, according to your wishes.

Concerning your trip to Columbus, say nothing more about it. It pleases me much to know that our Sisters of North Madison will move to their beautiful home before winter. I do not think it will be permitted me to see them this winter. Poor "Mater Dolorosa"! What is the matter with her now? Elizabeth is "matée" as Father Lalumière would say. It will do her good. Have Mr. H——paid entirely; he is too annoying. Mary should ask a receipt from the merchant, or dressmaker, that they may not come to importune us every day.

Poor Margaret has been very sick; for the last two weeks she has not left her bed. When she gets better we intend sending her home to see whether she will recover entirely. She has been sick ever since she came here; her mother will see just how she is. At present she is better and might leave next week, I think, if there is no relapse. She is a good child and we are all very sorry that her health is so poor.

Our good Father Corbe and all the Sisters send you their regards. My best love, please, to all your companions. . . .

Mother Theodore then evidently thought it better to withhold the main part of the letter, for she tore off the first leaf from the large double sheet and to the preceding note added these lines:

Saint Mary's, Thursday morning.

I have decided not to send you the first part of my letter; you will get it some other time, if you desire it. It concerns France. Are you still desirous of going back? But that is not the question this morning. Our dear Margaret is much worse; her head is very bad. I have sent for the doctor and I think she is very sick. Tell her mother that she is sick and that I should be pleased to see her here if she would like to come. She must not delay, for her daughter is much worse than she was yesterday, though she is not dying; those brain fevers are no trifles.

I shall soon see you, dear Sister Basilide. Adieu. They are leaving just now for Terre Haute. *Votre amie*, Sr. St. T.

Sister Basilide must have replied at once, for four days later Mother Theodore wrote again:

TO SISTER BASILIDE, MADISON

Saint Mary's, October 21, 1855

My dear Sister:

You wish to have the first part of my letter. Well, here it is. I wrote it that you might read it, if necessary, when I shall have closed my eyes and if you still have the desire then to go back to France. If you have, I think you would very soon repent going. You would desire to be back at Saint Mary's and could not be here. However, if you think the contrary, if in the depths of your heart you are persuaded that on the day of your death you will congratulate yourself for having abandoned your beautiful mission, leave it so. But before determining, I repeat it, reflect well and consult your confessor. It seems to me that you ought to do this. If you decide to remain, then take the firm resolution not to talk anymore about your desire to go back to Ruillé, a desire you should no longer have, and never write about it to anyone whomsoever. . . .

With these lines Mother Theodore enclosed the "first part" of the letter mentioned. As to the letter of the "9th instant," referred to in the following, it has not been found.

Saint Mary's, October 17, 1855

. . . My dear Sister Basilide, as usual I shall speak to you without reserve. When I wrote on the 9th instant that my heart was turned towards France, I did not intend to insinuate that I desired to go back. No! On the eighth of September fifteen years ago, the day when for the first time we received Our Divine Saviour in this land of America, at that very moment America ceased to be for me a stranger-land. It became the land of my adoption; and there, under your own eyes, in the church of Brooklyn, I took the vow of living and dying here, unless Obedience should direct me elsewhere. Since that day not a thought, still less a desire, of seeing France again, to remain there, has ever come to trouble my soul, even in our stormiest days.

It has not been the same with you; you have always looked back at that dear country with regret for having left it. I did what I could to persuade you not to look back, and to make a great and generous sacrifice to God. You have done and undone it many times. Poor Basilide! You are so wanting in constancy and firmness. The reason, it seems to me, of this inconstancy in your character is, partly, that you permit yourself to listen to nature's voice; you are not dependent enough on the spirit of God. Age does not change us much in this particular; only the habit of recollection and the spirit of faith in all our actions will effect this change. Be that as it may, you still have the desire of returning to France? Well, my daughter, I shall keep my promise—you may return if you wish. I promised the same to all the others before we embarked.

I feel now that my life is very near its end, and before I die I want to say again what I said to you fifteen years ago: If you wish to return to France you may do so. I only repeat what our good Mothers told us when they bade us depart. The four of us who remain of that number have the same privilege; consequently, you are entirely free. Reflect seriously on what you desire to do; above all pray much that our dear Lord may make known to you what He wishes you to do. If you decide to go, the money will not be wanting.

Good-by, my dear Sister Basilide. I am going to offer my prayers, or rather my languors, for you that the Holy Ghost may inspire and lead you, and the Blessed Virgin protect you.

Your sincere and devoted friend,
SISTER ST. THEODORE,
Sup'r Gen'l.

The prayers and languors of the beloved Foundress were not offered in vain. Sister Basilide came through her trials of homesickness victoriously; and when, ten years later, she did return to France in company with Sister Mary Joseph (le Fer de la Motte) on business for the Community, Ruillé could not hold her—her heart was at Saint Mary's. Four months away from her "dear woods" cured her forever if, until that time, she still looked back with longing.

TO SISTER MARY XAVIER, VINCENNES

Saint Mary's, October 21, 1855

I am very much pleased, my dear Sister, to see you once more determined on endeavoring to correct whatever displeases God in you and to acquire the virtues which are wanting in you, especially those mentioned: they are the characteristic virtues of our Divine Spouse who said, "Learn of me who am meek and humble of heart," as though these two virtues were inseparable. Later on He says that His disciples will be known by their love for one another. Hence, my daughter, love of the neighbor. Bear with the defects of others. Endeavor not to cause others to suffer, and you yourself try to endure the little annoyances which are unavoidable in the necessary relations with others. We often cause pain to one another on account of the differences of our dispositions and natural inclinations.

The other day I was reading in St. Francis de Sales that a person of a melancholy turn of mind, of a cold and disagreeable disposition, might love God as much as another born with better inclinations, but he would not have as much joy and satisfaction, although he would have the same merit. Then I thought of my poor "fagot of thorns," and I prayed our good God to make her love Him as much as she is capable of loving Him. I shall be heard, if you are willing.

A little impatience with the children who are around you is not a fault that removes you from God, when it escapes without your will sharing therein. As soon as you see that you have failed in meekness, try to regain it quickly. Speak to the child with kindness, lower your voice which was getting too high, and show her again that gentleness and sweetness of manner which she should always meet with from you. In short, when you have committed a fault disavow it before God; ask His pardon, promise to do better in the future. Make a good act of love, and after that, go your way as though nothing had happened. Think no more about it, except when you go to confession.

It is not necessary that you should have a feeling sense of the Divine Presence during your daily occupations; that is not practicable in our vocation of an active life. Make a good offering of all your actions to God in the morning, and then from time to time during the day; for instance, when the clock strikes, at the "Reunion," etc. Know that in sewing for the children, you are doing the will of God and that, consequently, you merit as much as if you were in prayer from morning until night, nay more if it were from your own will.

Well now, my dear Sister, this is a long letter, written at different intervals. As I shall not be able to write often, you can read this over sometimes; it will bring before you all I should have to say. Continue to pray for me. I am not worse than usual.

October 22! Fifteen years ago today we arrived in our forest. How many graces since then!

TO SISTER MARIA, MADISON

October 25, 1855

I am truly grateful, my dear Sister, for your kindness in praying for me—for my cure. I also ask it of God if it be for His glory and for the good of my dear daughters, whom I love as my own soul. May God's holy will be done! This is what we must come back to under all circumstances, and this is what we must start out with—"Thy will be done on earth as it is in heaven!"

Call to mind this beautiful petition of the Pater Noster when you feel discouraged, seeing the little success you have with your classes; when you feel that you do not inspire others with the feelings you think they ought to have for you. All this will be very meritorious if borne with love and resignation. Then, too, you might draw profit from these contradictions by accepting them in a spirit of penance. A soul which has deserved the justice of God should not find it amiss if some persons, without willing it, or even with a determined purpose, take in hands the interests of our Heavenly Father by making it suffer. For, what could it suffer in this life compared to what it deserves to suffer in the next?

What I would now say to a certain person who is endowed with fine natural qualities, who could make herself loved by everybody, is this: *Try to bear everything from others without making them bear anything from you.* I do not say this to cause you pain, or to discourage you. No, no, but to show you that you yourself are often the cause of what you suffer. And I say it also in order that you may endeavor to become more amiable and loving, more united to Our Lord, more docile, more yielding to your companions; in a word, more religious. You would then see, dear Sister Maria, that everything would change around you. You would be loved because you would be amiable. You would please without seeking to do so, for when we seek only God He generally arranges things so that all good is found with Him. Try this and see for yourself, my dear daughter.

As for your Communions of Rule, never miss them without good cause. It would not be sufficient cause to think that someone has something against you when you feel that you have not given her occasion for it. Have humility enough to ask, and then go peacefully to receive your God, your Support, your Sustenance. He will give you all that she can only wish you, she who, notwithstanding all your defects, loves you and is, in His Divine Heart, your Mother Theodore.

TO SISTER GABRIELLA, FORT WAYNE

October 25, 1855

I write only a few lines today, my dear Sister Gabriella, to tell you that your truly filial and affectionate letter, just received, has given me a great deal of deep joy, for I do not doubt of the sincerity of the feelings you express. But, my poor Sister, you are in error if you think that I am cured. I am far from it. But the One who has kept me alive until this day can continue to do so, if He so wills. He will not take me away until He no longer wishes to use this poor instrument any more. Another will be much more useful in His holy hands than myself. Do not fear for our dear Congregation. Our Lord loves it too much to abandon it.

I am happy to know that good Father Benoit escaped so well from his accident. Offer him my congratulations with best respects, and ask him if he has received a letter from me with a check for one hundred dollars, that I took the liberty to address to him for Mr. Rudisile. I should be glad to know whether he has received it.

I am sorry your class is no larger; we must hope for better times. My love to all the Sisters. I am happy to know that all are well. Please distribute the enclosed and all continue to pray much for me.

TO SISTER MARY XAVIER, FORT WAYNE

Saint Mary's, Feast of All Saints, 1855

Here I am about to contradict myself. Only a few days ago I told you, my dear Sister Mary Xavier, that you would hear from me but rarely, and lo! already I have my pen in hand to converse with you; but I shall say only a word. Be very submissive to the will of God. Will only what He wills. Remember your resolutions of the retreat, especially this one: "To suffer everything from others, and not make others suffer." If you would be faithful to this little practice, soon after your death your feast would be celebrated with those of the saints. You would be in heaven. Do you think of this, my daughter? In heaven! You would be a saint! From your throne, reigning above, how you would look down upon the trifling sacrifices which cost you so much at present. . . .

After the death of Bishop Bouvier, Mother Theodore begged his secretary for some souvenirs of their departed friend. She now writes acknowledgements.

TO M. L'ABBÉ SEBAUX, LE MANS

Saint Mary's, Feast of the Presentation,
November 21, 1855

Monsieur l'Abbé:

Only yesterday did we receive the dear mementoes which we owe to your kindness. I cannot describe all the various emotions which filled our hearts when we opened the precious package, dearer to us than all the gold of California. I can assure you, dear friend, that gratitude was not the least among those sentiments. I myself have the ardent desire of becoming better in order to have more power with God for obtaining everything that may render you happy in time and in eternity. But alas! In my profound misery what can I do?

I have just inscribed your name on the register of benefactors of the house after that of our venerated Father whose loss we so deeply lament. As the Community will never forget Bishop Bouvier to whom, after God, it owes everything, neither will it forget you; and long after you will have left this world you will be prayed for at Saint Mary-of-the-Woods. There was a general Communion today for all our benefactors. I offered mine for you—indeed you deserve it—as your choice of the objects you sent to us could not have been better, nor made with more delicacy by a father for his beloved children. It is evident that Bishop Bouvier trained you well. Loving you as his son he bequeathed his spirit and his heart to you. Oh, the dear good Bishop! He will not forget you, and from heaven he will protect you. He will protect us also. He seems to be doing so already. When passing before his portrait I feel the veneration one has for a saint and, while praying for the repose of his soul, I invoke him with great confidence.

From these last lines you will perceive, dear Reverend Abbé, that we have finally had the consolation of receiving the dear portrait. It had been detained at New York, but it is not injured in the least. We are awaiting a frame for it, ordered in the same city. The portrait will be placed in the Community room, and the precious medallion will hang below it. The alb, which would be dear to us even were it not so handsome, will be used on the four great feasts of the year and at the end of the retreat. The ten photographs, including the one in the little pamphlet, will be distributed among our ten missions, where they will draw down the blessings of God and remind the Sisters that they are the children of saints. . . .

TO SISTER MARY JAMES, EVANSVILLE

Saint Mary's, November 25, 1855

My truly dear, dear Child:

I have your two letters under my eye, from which I see that the old tempter has not let you alone, even after you

have so positively renounced by your vows all that belongs to
him. I see also that Our Lord has permitted that your confessor does not give you the consolation you expected from the
minister of God. Well, now, my dear Sister Mary James, what
shall I say? You know that I love you, do you not? Very well,
then, I will say *I am glad* at what you tell me—glad that you
have had to *suffer*. Yes, I am glad, for in passing afflictions I
see a mark of the love of preference Our Lord has for my
beloved child. I see it more clearly still by the progress you
have made. Yes, my dear Sister, you are entering the true
way of serving God, your dear Spouse, your dearly Beloved,
your All. I say you are *entering* the way of loving God and trying to keep close to Him, no matter who or what may rise
against you.

Continue, my dear and truly *chère fille*, to walk in the
presence of God, to do your actions solely to please Him, and
to bear courageously all the trials which He may permit
you to have. Let the evil one make all the noise he wishes
around you. Do not mind him, but put yourself entirely beyond the reach of his malice by keeping close to Our Lord.
Tell your Divine Spouse a hundred times a day that you love
Him, that you are happy to be His spouse. Tell Him that if
you had a hundred souls, a hundred lives, they would all be
employed in loving Him alone, in serving Him alone, and
none would be given to the world. In the morning say in
your heart: O my God, here is another day given me to love
and serve You. Be glad of it. Offer Him all your actions,
your temptations, you little humiliations—everything, and
then go to your duties with cheerfulness. Sadness is very
hurtful for soul and body; do not indulge in it. On the contrary, be strong, manly. If you do what I tell you, if you fight
valiantly in union with your God, if you cultivate more and
more that disposition of loving Him which He has put into

your heart, and if you put your confidence in Mary Immaculate, you will come out of your trials as gold that has been
purified in the crucible.

I am happy to know you feel so well pleased at Evansville. We have no thought of changing you. Good-by, my
dear child. I have written more than I thought I would, but
I feel confident I have written under the inspiration of the
Holy Ghost. . . .

TO THE SAME

Saint Mary's, December 19, 1855

My dear Sister:

Your two letters lately received, my dear child, are before
me. I am truly much grieved not to be able to grant the request
you make—that of coming home to spend the Christmas holi-
days. Could I but follow my own inclinations I would grant it
immediately. I would be very happy to see many of my dear
Sisters together during these holy days; but after serious
reflection I see clearly that I cannot give you this permission,
for various reasons which I shall tell you when you see your
old Mother again.

I do not consider that what you feel for your Superior is
a particular friendship; at least it has not all the properties
of such. It seems to me that in avoiding whatever is forbidden by the Rule you need have no further uneasiness
about your affections. I do not think your feelings would be
displeasing to Our Lord in any way whatever. You attach
too much importance altogether to the subject. Be simple. Love
your Superior and your Sisters with singleness of
heart. Turn that heart towards God when you perceive that
it leads you to run too fast towards creatures. What you
feel is probably more the effect of your imagination. I

would much rather see you loving any one of your Sisters very much than loving persons of the world. Do not let yourself be guided by the imagination, which is *la folle de la maison*.

As for going to confession twice a week habitually, that cannot be. If occasionally, well, that can be; but habitually, no. The best means to overcome temptations and to break off our bad habits in religion, is to follow the Rule and to live gently like everyone else, without any singularity, which always gives some room to pride and vanity.

I am grateful for all your good wishes, dear Sister. Be sure that I desire for you as much good as you want or need, in order to be a great saint some day. Give my love to all the Sisters and pray for me. I cannot write any more today.

TO THE SAME

Saint Mary's, January 8, 1856

Dear Child:

May Our Lord direct my pen, that I may say to you all that He wishes me to say for your good. Our holy faith is so clear and so sure that the mind cannot help believing unless the heart is not right. The greatness of the mysteries of our holy religion is the very proof of their being a divine institution. Where is the man that could have imagined them? When you consider creatures, and even yourself, you cannot help knowing that they have not made themselves; therefore, they have been made by another, more grand, more powerful. That Being is the God we adore, who has manifested Himself sufficiently as to convince, not only some ignorant *filles* like you and me, but millions of learned men who have been faithful to Him from the beginning of the world, and even now are serving Him with their whole heart and soul.

When you are saying your Office, pay no attention to the storm that might be raised in your mind at that time. You pay too much attention—a great deal too much—to what the tempter suggests. If you only laugh at what he says, he will not stay near you, for he is too proud; but if you pay attention to him he always has the hope that some time or other he will succeed in making you fall. O my dear Sister, be faithful to your Rule! Follow the inspirations of your God, who is so greatly occupied with you, who loves you so much as to interest Himself in your true happiness as if He had no one else in the world to take care of but you. Oh, when will you really love Him? He wants you to move rapidly in the way of perfection: are you not willing?

Good-by, my dear Sister, I have no time to read over my letter, written while there is talking all around me. Believe this, my dear Sister Mary James: nobody loves you as does your Mother Theodore. . . .

TO SISTER MARIA, MADISON

Saint Mary's, January 18, 1856

My dear Sister:

It is not enough to acknowledge our faults; we must correct them. Learn, then, to practice simplicity, which makes us pleasing in the eyes of angels and of men, and which is especially pleasing to God. It is not a fault to try to please your Superior for the sake of peace; it is rather a perfection than a fault. I am sorry Sister A——'s health does not continue to improve. The weather is so severe I am even surprised that poor weak lungs are not frozen.

You do well not to miss your Communion any more. When we are cold is not the time to keep away from the fire. Humble yourself—that is very good—but do not yield to discouragement. We are never hypocrites when we do not intend to be; hence, you must not exaggerate anything. You are bad enough without making yourself worse than you are.

It is not always a sign of greediness to be thinking of eating; it is sometimes a want of health. Eat what is served, without ceremony. When it is agreeable to your taste, thank God for it; when, on the contrary, you do not like it, still thank God who gives you an occasion of mortifying yourself. Thus will you draw profit from everything. Since in the preceding years you were able to keep the fast as it is kept in America, you may try it again this year, at least for the first weeks. We shall see later on about it. We must work as diligently as we can and endeavor to keep recollected while working. If we raise our heart to God from time to time during an action which has been offered to Him, that is enough, at least for a person of your character. We must always correspond to the grace of God to the best of our power, not through fear of sin, but from a sentiment of love.

I thank you very much for my woolen skirt. I think it will fit very well. Confidence in God, peace in His arms, no fretting nor *fantastiques*, and you will find happiness.

On the last day of January occurred the greatest personal loss that had yet befallen the Community—the death of Sister St. Francis Xavier, Second Assistant and acting Mistress of Novices. This sad event is now announced by Mother Theodore.

LETTER CIRCULAR

Saint Mary-of-the-Woods, February 3, 1856

My very dear Sisters:

You will share the deep sorrow in which we are plunged at Saint Mary's when you read this letter, announcing the immense loss we have just sustained in the death of our dear

Sister St. Francis Xavier, whom Our Lord has called to Himself. She departed this life towards two o'clock in the afternoon of January thirty-first, after eight days of severe convulsions which from the beginning left us very little hope.

You do not expect me, my dear daughters, to write a eulogy of her whom we have so many reasons to regret, of her whose absence leaves such a void in the Community. Her name alone suffices to bring to mind all that is sweetest, purest, and most attractive in virtue. She was for those who knew her the ideal of religious perfection. Not only have we unanimously considered her the saint of our Congregation, but persons of the world, even those of a different faith, could not behold her angelic exterior without being led to the thought of God.

Her death was the echo of her life; or rather it was the bursting forth of a volcano of love. The divine fire with which her soul burned sent forth only sparks during her lifetime. But when the near prospect of heaven had taken away that reserve which caused this humble soul to hide its treasure; or rather, when her heart was no longer able to contain its ardent love, a torrent of burning aspirations escaped from her lips with such vehemence that it would seem enough to break the feeble bonds that united her soul to her body. In calling upon Jesus in the Holy Eucharist, her voice was so full of love and her countenance so heavenly that she appeared to belong no more to earth. She was already in heaven.

I understood that this fruit of the garden of the Spouse had reached full maturity and that He wished to gather it in. I saw that I must immolate my Isaac and consent to be separated from her who, firm as a rock, had always supported me in my trials; from her who, notwithstanding the infinite distance which separated us (for she was saint) had almost blended her existence with mine. I made the sacrifice of her, O my God! without a moment's hesitation; for who am I to resist Thee? But Thou knowest that the deep wound it has made in my heart will be healed only when I shall be reunited to her in that heaven which she beheld so beautiful in dying.

We shall all have the happiness of rejoining her, my dear Sisters, if we are faithful to follow her example; if we fulfil perfectly our holy obligations, which are the same as hers were. We are devoted to the same Spouse, we expect the same recompense; let the remembrance of our cherished Sister St. Francis encourage us in the combat. As for her, so for us. The day of triumph will come very soon.

Although we have the sweet hope that our dear Sister is in heaven, we must nevertheless conform to the spirit of Holy Church and to our Constitutions; therefore, do not fail to fulfill punctually for our departed one what is prescribed by our Rules for the deceased Sisters.

You will also recite for nine days the *Veni Creator* and the *Ave Maris Stella*, to beg the light and grace which we need in order to make the necessary changes under these sad circumstances.

I am in the Heart of Our Lord, my dear Sisters,

Your truly devoted

SISTER ST. THEODORE,

Sup'r Gen'l.

In the second summer before the death of Sister St. Francis, the annual retreat was given by the Reverend John L. Gleizal, S.J., at that time Master of Novices at Florissant, Missouri. Father Gleizal became greatly interested in the Community at Saint Mary-of-the-Woods, and continued to render spiritual aid by correspondence with the Mistress of Novices, first with Sister St. Francis and after her death with Sister Mary Joseph. This intercourse continued almost until his own death five years later. He aroused in the Community a deep devotion to the Sacred Heart, and he gave to Mother Theodore the first "Manual of Devotions to the Heart of Jesus" possessed by the Sisters. In after years the Reverend Walter Hill, S.J., who had been one of his novices, gave to the writer this tribute: "He was an impressive, earnest, eloquent preacher, and converted many to the faith. He was a man of deep piety, and was especially successful in conducting the Spiritual Exercises in religious communities. From 1849 to 1857 he occupied the position of Master of Novices. His devout and holy life gave him the confidence of the people, who regarded him as a saint."

To this esteemed and holy director Mother Theodore wrote a few days after the death of Sister St. Francis, giving him the intimate details of Sister's last days on earth.

TO THE REVEREND JOHN L. GLEIZAL, S.J., FLORISSANT

Saint Mary-of-the-Woods, February 4, 1856

It costs a great deal, my venerated Father, to say "My God, Thy will be done." Yes, it costs much to lose a subject like Sister St. Francis Xavier. I know you yourself feel it, my Father, in reading these words. Your eyes are suffused with tears also, for you loved that dear child of the Lord. You knew that heart all on fire with love of God. You knew with what zeal she labored to form Jesus in the hearts of others. If you thought you found a good spirit in the Community, it was hers. For upwards of fifteen years she formed the subjects of the Congregation, and sustained them after they left the novitiate by her letters, her exhortations, and her prayers. Well, good Father, she is no longer on this earth of sorrows and miseries. She was taken from us last Thursday by a painful illness, a sort of tetanus.

During her years at Saint Mary's, we have seen her walk with a firm step in the constant practice of the religious virtues, without ever relaxing or showing those vicissitudes of good and bad days so common among persons like us. She was always a fervent Religious and, I dare say it to you, Father, the most perfect I have ever known. We were always obliged to hold her back with the curb of obedience, to which she was perfectly docile.

You know, Father, how fervent she was, how she loved Our Lord in the Blessed Sacrament. When fever took away from her the fear of being remarked, the divine fire hidden in her soul broke forth like a volcano of love, pouring itself out in a torrent of flaming words. Her exclamations could be heard almost incessantly for three days. After repeating twenty times without taking breath the words "Jesus in the Blessed Sacrament," she would add all that the most passionate love in others has been able to invent, the most tender and affectionate words to her Beloved; and when her memory was exhausted, she supplied by her own invention.

And she was beautiful—with an angelic beauty. She belonged no longer to this earth; it was unworthy of her. I understood that the Divine Master wished to gather this ripe fruit and I made the sacrifice. You, Father, know whether it was a sacrifice!

Now I am going to confide to your Paternity what this dear child told me in secret two days before she died. On Monday night, eve of the feast of St. Francis de Sales, she thought she was cured by water of La Salette which we had given her. Thinking that perhaps she was delirious I left her alone with her attendant. Scarcely had we withdrawn than she began again to speak to Our Lord with great vehemence. The little watcher approached and called her, but she could not get her attention, so she came in haste for me. Going as quickly as possible, I heard her voice afar without however understanding what she said. I arrived all trembling beside her. She did not see me and continued to speak to God with such energy that I thought she would kill herself. I said in a firm tone, "Be quiet, Sister St. Francis!" She did not hear me and kept on repeating: "O Love! O Justice! O Heaven! Forever! Forever!" and so forth. Finally I succeeded in making her hear me. I bade her keep still and lie down (she was sitting up in her bed).

She was quite surprised to see us, in particular Father Corbe, for whom we had sent. This was between ten and eleven o'clock. She now became calmer, so, leaving an additional watcher, we withdrew to take a little rest. In the morning, I found her so absorbed in God that I thought it my duty to forbid her to speak even to me. She obeyed. An hour later she sent for me and said she needed ray advice. She had then the full use of her reason. "Last evening," she said, "I had a real ecstasy." (I repeat just what she said to me.) "Our Lord called me by my name and showed me heaven. O Mother, how beautiful it was, how delightful, how ineffable I saw God, the Blessed Virgin—oh, what beauty, what—" Here I interrupted her narrative. "That is very well, my daughter," I said, "I can believe very readily that Our Lord has consoled and strengthened you. You must thank Him very gently, and be quiet."

"How would you have me quiet and silent when I see my God, Jesus, my—" "Enough," I said to her again, "the doctor wishes you to sleep. It is to please Jesus that you must be silent. Now, my dear daughter, lie down and remain very peacefully with your Spouse Jesus, who visited you this morning in the sacrament of His love." (She received Holy Communion that day as viaticum.)

She was silent for some minutes, then began again with redoubled force those loving colloquies with Our Lord. Heaven was engraved on her mind and in her heart. Her night was very bad. She had her senses and spoke now and then like a flash. I left her towards three o'clock to rest a little. At five she sent for me, and having asked all the others to leave the room she told me that she wished to know what to do. Fearing another crisis I told her she had absolutely nothing to do but to place herself in the hands of God and let Him do with her what He pleased. "I know that," she said, "but I must speak to you. I had something to tell you and I fear it is too late; my thoughts are getting confused." Then, Father, I prayed with all the strength of my soul that she would be able to talk to me.

"Is it for your postulants, my daughter?" "No." "Is it for the Community?" "No, Mother." "Is it for myself? Dear child, you have always told me your thoughts—you will do it again?"

A smile was the answer. "Oh, now I have it," she said, "I did not finish what I was saying to you yesterday. Our Lord called me by my name, Irma, and in opening my eyes I found myself in heaven." Then repeating what she told me in the evening she added, "Our Lord said to me, 'All this is for thee—for thee forever.' I thought I was dead, but Our Lord said, 'It shall not be just yet.' "

Here, Father, I embraced her and a ray of hope shone before me. I said to her, "So He leaves you with us yet awhile?" "Yes, Mother, for a day or two in the state in which I am, and after that—heaven! O my cherished Mother," she said, "and you are to come there also with me. You, too, will be saved." Her sister having entered during this time, she looked at her saying, "Elvire, you also will be with us during all eternity."

She told me the vision lasted seemingly only a moment but that the impression was ineffaceable. Sister Mary Joseph [Elvire], having reached her room before I did the night of which Sister St. Francis spoke, found her in exactly the state in which she told me she had been. Soon after this conversation she lapsed into unconsciousness, having occasional moments, however, when she was rational. In those lucid intervals she always expressed the strongest and most ardent love.

Excuse, Reverend Father, this long and poor letter. My head feels so weak since the loss we have suffered that I scarcely know how to write. But I feel the need of pouring my heart out into yours, of asking your prayers for a Community in desolation, and of telling you that you will ever find at Saint Mary's a devoted daughter in your very humble servant,

SISTER ST. THEODORE.

Ask Our Lord to send us another Sister St. Francis Xavier.

Replies to letters of sympathy now claim Mother Theodore's pen. The first here given is to one of the Community's most devoted friends of the early days, and always, the Reverend Julian Benoit. Father Benoit came over from France in 1836, as a young deacon with Bishop Bruté. After his ordination the following year he labored in southern Indiana near Evansville; then at Chicago and other towns in the Lake region. In 1840, he was appointed to Fort Wayne, where he remained until his death, which occurred January 25, 1885, excepting for about ten months that he spent in the South in 1853, collecting funds for a new church to replace his old St. Augustine's, built in 1837 by his predecessor.

In 1846 Father Benoit secured Sisters of Providence for his school. He had erected a large brick building for them for both school and dwelling and furnished it completely. This was the first foundation made by the Community in which difficulties about the financial support of the house did not give a precarious tenure. The first teachers were: Sister Mary Magdalen (Linck), Superior; Sister Catherine (Eisen), and Sister Caroline (O'Dell). They were accompanied to Fort Wayne by Mother Theodore with Sister Basilide as her companion. It was a pleasing coincidence for them all that they arrived on the eve of the feast of St. Augustine (August 28), the patron of their little frame church. The school was named St. Augustine's Academy. Classes opened the first week of September with sixty day and fifteen boarders.

This pioneer boarding school furnished to the Sisterhood such worthy members as the four Buchanans, Sisters Mary

Antoinette, St. Felix, Agatha, and Mary Bernard, from Huntington, and the two O'Donalds, Sisters Mary Ambrose and Mary Angele, from Peru; all of whom entered the novitiate between 1849 and 1857. They have been followed from year to year by many others from this still flourishing academy.

In later years, when the Sisters had to enlarge the building to meet the needs of the growing parish, Father Benoit contributed five thousand dollars from his own resources. His constant generosity and kind consideration continued up to the time of his death, and have placed his name on the Community's register of benefactors, assuring for him daily remembrance in prayer.

When in 1857, at the solicitation of Bishop de St. Palais, the Holy See formed the diocese of Fort Wayne out of the northern half of the diocese of Vincennes, Father Benoit remained in the new episcopal city. During the ensuing years many honors were conferred upon him. Quoting from Bishop Alerding's history of the diocese, Father Benoit "was made Vicar General of Fort Wayne in 1858. During Bishop Luers' visit to Rome in 1865 Father Benoit was Administrator of the diocese. At the Second Plenary Council of Baltimore, 1866, he was the theologian of Bishop Luers. After the death of Bishop Luers he was again Administrator of the diocese, from June 1871 to April 1872. He attended the four Provincial Councils at Cincinnati, as theologian to the Bishop. In 1883 he was again Administrator of the diocese during Bishop Dwenger's absence in Rome. A papal brief of Leo XIII, bearing date of June 12, 1883, conferred upon Father Benoit the honors and title of Domestic Prelate of His Holiness. The investiture took place in the Cathedral on August sixteenth of the same year."[34]

To this it may be added that in 1874 Father Benoit was a member of the first American pilgrimage to Lourdes and Rome—led by Bishop Dwenger—and that in the fall of 1879, after the death of Father Chassé, he was temporary chaplain for three months at Saint Mary-of-the-Woods.

The diary shows that many letters were addressed to Father Benoit by Mother Theodore. The only one surviving, however, is the following, written two weeks after the death of Sister St. Francis Xavier.

[34] Alerding, The Rt. Rev. H. J.: *The Diocese of Fort Wayne* (1907), p. 61.

Saint Mary-of-the-Woods, February 15, 1856

My dear Father Benoit:

I must thank you for your very true, very heartfelt sympathy. Yes, I believe you share in the sorrows and consolation of my heart. I feel it. A victim was indeed required to be immolated at Saint Mary's. One was brought to the altar.[35] The Angel of Death had his arm raised. He was about to strike, but the victim was rejected. For a very short time, however; a little more time is still given to her in mercy to prepare herself. Pray, oh, pray that she may profit by it.

Another, always ready, was found. I do not think she offered herself; she would not have done so without my permission, and she knew that she would not obtain it. She knew that she was necessary to my existence, and for nothing in the world would she have given me the sorrow of seeing her die. And the sacrifice of accepting to live for the glory of God and the good of those whom she loved in Him cost her much more than dying. To live far from her God was for her the greatest of her sacrifices. To die would have been her greatest happiness, and not to ask that favor of God was her supreme sacrifice. But she was too generous, and she thought too little of herself to ask it. During one of the crises to which we could well give the name of ecstacies, she believed herself in heaven. She enjoyed the ineffable happiness of the celestial abode. This showed on her countenance. She looked like an angel. She said to Our Lord, "No, my Jesus, not yet? Then let me make You known on earth, let me suffer for You. You know it—I am ready for the love of You even to go to hell, provided I could there love You."

We heard these words falling from her lips, but we did

---

[35] Mother Theodore here refers to herself and her late illness.

not hear what her Beloved answered her. Thirty-eight hours before she died she told me that Our Lord had said to her: "Thou wilt remain to suffer a day or two longer, and then thou shalt come and be with Me *forever*." These words—"Jesus! Forever!"—were so deeply engraved in her soul with the thought of heaven, that she repeated them twenty and thirty times in succession and this with so much force that she was heard from one end of the house to the other. What she said to me, and this I confide to you in secret, is, that I am to follow her soon. Oh! no matter when, if I could but follow her, as she said. But, no. I shall never have her virtues, I shall never love as she loved. Obtain for me, my Father, the grace to do penance and bear with joy and love the loss of my cherished daughter so that I may be less unworthy of her. . . .

P.S.—At this moment I am in receipt of your letter of the 14th. How kind you are! How much good you do me when speaking of heaven! I do not ask to go there soon, I am willing to remain here, if it be the will of God. Be sure now that I shall remain, if it is for the good of the Community. I have in heaven a daughter who will obtain for us what is best. Then, if I die, it will be for the good of all; so let us be resigned to the Will of God, but never say that my life is the price of my Sister's. Except it were the will of God, that thought would be unbearable to me.

Little by little I shall tell you all that I know about my dear Sister St. Francis. But you must give me time. Good-by, my Father. I feel stronger today.

Yes, Sister St. Francis is in heaven, I believe. I find you too humble. Why put yourself so low? Sister St. Francis feared that her last letter would not be pleasing to you. I am glad she was mistaken. . . .

Saint Mary's, February 16, 1856

My dear Sister:

It will indeed be good to die like Sister St. Francis, but for that we shall have to live as she did. She did not even once think that she had to be judged. She heard her Jesus, her chaste and beloved Spouse, calling her by name, and she ran towards Him with the greatest love and without a particle of fear. Oh, if you would only love Our Lord, very soon all your fears would vanish and give place to unbounded confidence.

I thank you for praying for me. Continue to do so, for I need God's help very much. The half of myself is gone, but gone to heaven. . . .

TO THE SAME

February 22, 1856

Yes, our beloved Sister St. Francis has gone to heaven. I feel as sure of it as if I had seen her going thither. All the elect die in the love of God, but it is the privilege of few to die *of* the love of God. Love for Jesus in the Blessed Sacrament was so strong in our dear Sister that it broke the bonds that united her soul with her delicate body. And to die of the love of God is the surest way of going to Him at once. It is true, my dear Sister, that I feel deeply the loss I have sustained. I could not present to Our Lord anybody so dear to me as was my beloved Sister St. Francis. But she was too pure, too holy, too much inflamed with the love of God to remain with us any longer. I did not ask her from Our Lord. As soon as I perceived that she had advanced so much in a few days I gave her to my God and hers. It was the greatest offering I could make to Him. Oh, how little, how small I feel in thinking of our dear and beloved Sister St. Francis.

You know, my dear Sister Mary James, that I love you much. I have had constantly a deep affection for your soul since the time you became doubly my daughter. Well, if you were as well prepared as Sister was, I could see you die—yes— and say for you, as I did for her, the prayers of the agonizing and the *De Profundis*. But no, my child, you are not ready yet. You have scarcely entered into that beautiful way of per- fection, which is a way of self-sacrifice, self-immolation in every respect; the one in which Sister St. Francis entered so perfectly when she gave herself to God.

My poor child, do try to enter in good earnest into the way of perfection. You will find it much easier than you think. You have, and have had, a great many good impulses; but the world still has some claims on your affections. You cannot say, with St. Paul, "The world is crucified to me, and I to the world."

I am glad that you have written to poor Sister Mary Joseph. She has been admirable in her sacrifice. I can tell you she has a strong and great soul.

Positively you must not make the whole fast on school days. But you can mortify yourself on a thousand occasions, which occur daily and even hourly.

Good-by, my dear child. I pray Our Lord to give you the spirit of Sister St. Francis. This will be the best way for you to console the heart of your truly devoted and afflicted Mother. . . .

Immediately after the death of Sister St. Francis, Sister Mary Joseph gave her mother the details of Irma's last hours. The death could not have been unexpected, as Sister's health had always been very delicate, and her fifteen years in America seemed to her family to be almost a miracle.

A month later Mother Theodore wrote to the bereaved mother.

TO MME. LE FER DE LA MOTTE, ST. SERVAN

March 5, 1856

Esteemed and cherished Friend:

Allow me to thank you for the great kindness in making a visit for me to St. Anne's shrine. I do not think that I presumed upon your goodness in asking this favor of you, for your dearly beloved daughters have taught me to consider you as my mother, since you are theirs. I have no other excuse. Thank you, then, dear Madame, thank you. In order to give you a stronger proof of my gratitude, I offered my Holy Communion for your intention this morning. The Mass and general Communion were for poor Joseph, but I shall think of him at another time; besides I have prayed for him and have had others do the same. We are praying a great deal for the repose of the soul of this good Christian who, however, for the last two years, has known how to try those with whom he lived. I hope there was no malice in what he did, but still I feel that he will have something to atone for before he enjoys the vision of God.

It is not thus with the angel who has left our forest and taken her flight to heaven. All who knew her intimately, or otherwise, have almost reproached themselves for praying for her. To pray for one who was so devoted to Our Lord, whose whole life—at least for the last sixteen years—was one continual act of love, seemed almost an injury to Him. As I said before, love caused her death. Love broke the bonds that held her soul captive. What a death! Oh, no, not death, but rather the beginning of life—and of what a life!

What glory for you, Madame, to be the mother of a saint, of

a saint of the first order, for she is, I am sure, very high in heaven. She prays for you there, and God knows how much she loves you.

It is said in the world that Religious do not know any longer how to love. This is a great mistake. I am sure that among all your good and devoted children, there is not one heart more devoted than was your dear Irma's. Is there another that possesses the same power of loving? I doubt it very much. During the thirty-one years that I have been a superior, I have seen many sorts, if I may use the expression, but I have not found another heart like that of my dear Irma, my well-beloved sister, my first daughter, Sister St. Francis Xavier. Judging from Cecile's letters she, too, must have a very remarkable heart. Poor heart! How it has been bruised, broken, crushed! May it find now the peace and repose that we are asking for this dear child and for your entire family with all the fervor of which we are capable. Have the kindness to remember me to her, also to all your daughters, *our* sisters. I wish to thank Clementine for her kindness in praying for me at the shrine of St. Anne.

Do not be surprised that I have talked of naught else in this letter but of my dear Sister St. Francis. Ever since I lost her it seems impossible to treat of any other subject. I apply myself to business matters with the greatest repugnance and only because duty demands it. Our religious instructions, and even our recreations have this dear daughter for subject. The thought of her is like an angel guardian to the Indiana priests. What a veneration they have for her! All our Sisters are animated with renewed zeal to continue the work that this dear Sister was so eager to see prosper, and to labor for which she was willing to postpone her entrance into heaven which Jesus had show her to be so beautiful.

No one is a better imitator of our blessed Sister than our dear Sister Mary Joseph. She does not possess the same tenderness of feeling, but hers is a soul of great strength that will accomplish untold good in the house of God. She is my great solace and I try to be hers.

Sister Mary Cecilia has been home since Sunday. She will have charge of the postulants until the retreat, when we shall elect a mistress of novices.

Good-by, my esteemed and cherished friend. Be assured of the filial devotedness of your friend of the Woods. . . .

To the foregoing Mother Theodore adds:

You could never imagine what a void the death of Sister St. Francis has left in our house. I not only miss her, but it seems to me I have lost a part of my life. Day and night she is present in my mind. But the thought of her is not distracting; on the contrary, it raises me above the things of this earth, which never before appeared so insignificant, so unworthy of a heart made for God alone. The effect that her saintly death has produced is remarkable. She still causes Our Lord to be loved although she is no longer of this world. I only wish I could send you some of the letters I have received during the last three weeks. Even zealous Jesuits have experienced a renewal of fervor. You, too, dear friend, have received many favors from Heaven through her intercession. I am writing these lines while talking to my dear Sister Mary Joseph, who is drawing at the table where I am sitting. We embrace each other for you. Again good-by from your children of the Woods and Mother T.

Mother Theodore's hopes and expectations that Sister Mary Joseph would accomplish "untold good in the house of God" were fully realized by the Community in after years.

In the opinion of her contemporaries, she ranks next to the holy Foundress herself for the good she achieved. From 1856 until 1868 she was Mistress of Novices, and from 1868 until her death on December 12, 1881, she held the office of First Assistant. Thus for twenty-five years she had the chief care in the training and guiding of the Sisters.

Sister Mary Joseph's entire religious life was passed at the Motherhouse. When she entered in 1852, at the age of twenty-six, she was a valuable acquisition, as well for her talents, accomplishments, advanced education, and experience, as for her superior judgment and deep piety. During her first years she taught music and French at the Academy and in the novitiate. Her beautiful voice had been trained in Paris, and she brought her harp and guitar with her; yet, these things interested her less than the domestic service she could render. It seemed there was nothing she could not do, and her generosity was unflagging. Particularly was she efficient in the care of the sick Sisters, a work she never entirely relinquished until her own health failed late in life.

She was noted for a remarkable personal power. To cite an instance: it was due to her persuasion that Bishop de Saint Palais consecrated the Diocese of Vincennes to the Sacred Heart of Jesus. The solemn ceremony took place throughout the diocese on New Year's Day, 1874.

From the time Sister was made Mistress of Novices, on the death of Sister St. Francis, she exerted all her energies to the transmitting and the establishing of the ideals that had been given to her. When she departed this life after twenty-nine years in religion, she was reputed a person of rare distinction and great holiness of life.

The following fragment of a letter, a postscript, and all that remains of the ninety letters written to Sister Anastasie by Mother Theodore, as recorded in her diary, has a special interest as it is the last on hand from the pen of the venerated Foundress.

TO SISTER ANASTASIE, EVANSVILLE

March 15, 1856

P.S. Sister Mary Theodore is writing to you and will tell you that I am sick again, which is true. I was in bed all day yesterday, except for a few hours. Today, however, I am a little stronger.

About that affair, if I were in your place I would speak to the person with charity and firmness, and would tell her what I think, and would advise her to reflect on it before God; for it is not by pride and selfishness that we can please Him.

If there are four girls to come together to be brought up in the principles of our holy religion, we will take them for their board and tuition in all the common branches of education, with all kinds of needlework, for eighty dollars ($80) each, the scholastic year, and will prepare them to do for themselves when they leave school, if they remain a reasonable time with us; of course, their clothing and stationery will be extra.

I am glad Sister Mary James is getting better—she must not fast—and that Sister Felicitie is well again. My love to all from your poor sick Mother. Pray for her.

Two days after the foregoing letter—or, rather, the P.S.—addressed to Sister Anastasie, Mother Theodore wrote in her diary: "March 17—I am obliged to remain in bed. What a beautiful week [Holy Week] to be upon the cross! *O good cross, I will love thee with all my heart!*"

These were the last words written by Mother Theodore.

EPILOGUE

SCARCELY two months after the final words written by the Foundress, another hand wrote in her diary: "May 14—Mother dies at a quarter past three A.M., the life, the all of the Community!" The Sisters meant, of course, that humanly speaking they had lost their "all" in losing Mother Theodore. So implicit was their trust in her superior guidance and guardianship, spiritual and temporal, that no other words could express their sense of loss.

The general sentiment was described by Sister Mary Joseph when she wrote to friends in France:

"God has struck us a second time, more severely and more painfully than the first. Is it because it is a second blow? Or is it because the object taken from us was dearer to us? Our hearts in their bitter anguish cannot answer, except to say that in three months they have lost all—their dear Sister St. Francis and their beloved Mother Theodore.

"This 'gift of God,' our good Mother Theodore, united in her person the most precious qualities that can be given on this earth. Her heart contained them all. She alone was unconscious of it. But God who is pleased to exalt the humble formed around her an aureole of glory, so to speak, by the love of her children and the esteem of her numerous friends; however, this was only a reflection of that which He had prepared for her in heaven.

"On the 14th [May, 1856], about a quarter past three in the morning, this cherished Mother departed from her desolate daughters, from this land of exile, to enter on the road to her true country, after having spent thirty-two years in the religious life. Charged for the last sixteen years with the most important functions that it is given a woman to fulfil, she ever showed herself superior to her task.

"A willing exile from her beautiful country, full of zeal for the salvation of her fellow-beings, the charms of her mind drew them towards her, while the goodness of her heart attached them to her; then, the rectitude of her judgment, the power of her words, finished the conquest, and no one left her without praising her and feeling grateful to her.

"When she arrived in this forest, where a part of a poor farm house was all that she found as a shelter for herself and her daughters, she knew so well how to inspire the latter with the love of the cross and mortification, that they have said since then that they were never happier than in that humble abode. Later on when, thanks to her care and talents, Mother could offer us a large and substantial brick building, the gaiety of her conversation enlivened all her children, and the tenderness of heart was such that all the Sisters on our ten missions longed for the moment when they could come home and gather around their cherished Mother. Now they will find her no more. Two rooms are vacant, two graves are filled. She sleeps near her beloved Sister St. Francis. But, oh, how happy will be their awakening!"

Ten years later, at the Commencement exercises, June 27, 1866, the Honorable Bayless Hanna of Terre Haute, United States Senator from Indiana, concluded his address by saying: "The unostentatious tomb of Mother Theodore over yonder in the little village of the dead is unembellished with monumental significance, but the narrow path that winds its way there will every year become furrowed deeper and deeper, by the footprints of the grateful pilgrims who will go there to do homage to the memory of the Foundress of Saint Mary-of-the-Woods."

For over fifty-one years the remains of Mother Theodore rested in the convent cemetery; then, on December 3, 1907, they were transferred to the vault under the sanctuary of the conventual church. A small portion, however, was left in the grave of the cemetery circle. The only monument that marked the hallowed spot was the original wooden cross bearing the inscription: *Ego dormio sed cor meum vigilat super hanc domum quam aedificavi.*[1] The remains of Sister St. Francis Xavier and Sister Mary Joseph were also removed to the vault and placed on either side of Mother Theodore.

During a visit to Saint Mary's in December 1917, the Reverend T. Gavan Duffy, Missionary Apostolic of Pondicherry,

---

[1] Replaced in 1940 by a Celtic cross of white stone.

went to the cemetery on the feast of the Immaculate
Conception. While at the grave of Mother Theodore he composed the following lines:

> Daughter of Brittany, behold I kneel
> Among the crosses borne and left behind,
> And met as crowns of everlasting weal
> By thee, gone into life.
>   The busy wind
> Tempers unfathomable silences
> And is the heart of them. The virgin snow
> Throbs with eternal, blank analogies
> And the vague voices of the dead below.
> Hardly dare I, with traces of this flesh,
> Defile the utter whiteness; but the breeze
> (Or the quick praying of thee, dead) comes fresh
> And drifts the snow where rested now my knees.
>
> Daughter of Brittany, be still and rest,
> Yet with a peace akin to the divine,
> To the All-Mover's peace, who motherest
> Enough for even such a zeal as thine;
> The while thou slumberest thy daughters still
> Do feed the world-wide hunger of thy heart,
> And, by a gentle Providence's will,
> Give thee, in all that is, a mother's part.
> Behold the splendor which thy tears begot;
> And have no fear lest thought of them be dead,
> Or lest, perchance, thy children have forgot
> Their Mother begged her missionary bread.
> No, I have proof, the infant Child's sad wail
> Doth stir their mother-heart, as thine, to give
> Rather of their own hungering than fail.
>
> And I, the passing beggar, at thy grave
> Do for their charity give thanks to thee,
> And make petition that the Lord who gave
> And proved, may now proclaim thy sanctity.
> This too I ask of the Immaculate
> Upon her festival, amid the vivid snow
> That doth proclaim her; and I celebrate
> The coming of thy kingdom. Be it so.

GRAVE OF MOTHER THEODORE
In the Convent Cemetery
Shifting clouds produced this unusual
effect of light in the photograph

CONVENTUAL CHURCH
Saint Mary-of-the-Woods

TOMB OF
MOTHER THEODORE
In the crypt of the Church
Translation of remains in 1907

A deep impression of the holiness of Mother Theodore remained in all who knew her. At her death, seculars and Religious alike pressed around her bier to touch their devotional objects to her precious remains. Many at once invoked her, and favors were obtained that were attributed to her power with Almighty God.

Later generations have imbibed the same spirit of confidence in her and, finally her cause has been introduced at Rome. Hundreds of favors and some alleged miracles are recorded as having been granted through her intercession, and devotion to her is ever on the increase. This is affirmed by the testimony of witnesses, and by statements in "Positions and Articles Proposed for the Beatification and Canonization of the Servant of God, Mother Theodore Guérin" by the postulator of the cause in the diocesan process, the Most Reverend Alphonse J. Smith, late Bishop of Nashville.

The work begun by Mother Mary Cleophas, of cherished memory, to obtain the Church's recognition of the heroicity of virtue in the venerated Foundress, has been zealously pursued since her death by her successors in office, Mother Mary Raphael, lately deceased, and the present Superior-General, the Reverend Mother Mary Bernard.

As previously stated, the writings of Mother Theodore have been approved by the Sacred Congregation of Rites. The various Apostolic processes are under way, and the Sisters of Providence of Saint Mary-of-the-Woods now prayerfully await the crowning joy when, if so it be the Divine good pleasure, the honors of the Altar shall be conferred upon their revered and beloved Mother-Foundress.

INDEX

Academy, Saint Mary-of-the-Woods, under construction. 63; 65, 70, 72, 95; directress of. 104; enlarging of, 196, 201. 207; 282; benefit of Catholic education at, 363, 376
Adelaide, Mme, 119, 120, 131
Agatha, see Sister
Agnes, see Sister
Alerding, Rev. H. J., 75, 78; 173. 182, 209; Rt. Rev. H. J., Bishop of Fort Wayne, 430
Alleghany Mountains, 44, 45
Alsace, 62, 197, 313, 314
Amelia, Queen of the French. audience with, 118, 119, 122: benefaction from, 120, 122: letter to, 130; portrait of, 130. 131, 146
America, country of "improvements," 375; 410, 442
Americans, 9, 25, 26, 30, 40, 42. 45, 46, 47, 51, 60, 64, 288
Anastasie, Mother, 225, see Sister Anastasie
Angelina, see Sister
Angers, Sisters of Charity of, 266; University of France. xix; 3, 266
Ann, see Sister
Annals, quotations from, 95, 126. 196, 197, 213, 216, 217, 221, 222. 251
Anne d'Auray, Ste, 145; vow in honor of, 154; Shrine of, 155
Apostolic Nuncio, 364
Astor, John Jacob, 103
Athanasius, see Sister
Aubain du Cormier, 305
Aubineau, Leon, 139–145
Audran, Rev. Ernest, 251, 252, 255
Augustine, see Sister

Badin, Rev. Stephen, 50, 51
Bagot, 7
Bahamas, 124, 156
Bailly, Éleanor, "The Belle of Detroit," 104, see Sister Mary Cecilia; Joseph, 103
Baltimore, 40, 41; Sixth Council of, 174; 208; letter to Archbishop of, 213; Second Plenary Council of, 430
Barclay Street, St. Peter's Church, 29

Barston, Capt., 9, 10, 20, 22, 23, 25, 26, 27, 31, 32
Basilide, see Sister
Baty, Dr., 248, 252
Baton Rouge, 72
Bayer, Adele, 67; "The Angel of the Navy," 68; Edward, 375
Bazin, Rt. Rev. John Stephen, third Bishop of Vincennes, 209, 217, 218; consecration of, 219; letters of, 219, 220; visits Saint Mary-of-the-Woods, 221; 246, 250, 251, 252, 253; purchases St. Gabriel College, 246, 267; transfers orphans to old college, 278, 279, 318; confirms title of Sup. Gen'l on Mother Theodore, 258; characteristics of 250; illness of, 246, 250, 251, 252, 253; death of 256–260
Beauty of Indiana Scenery, 176, see Indiana
Bellier, S. E., Rev. J., 209, 246, 248
Benbridge, Mrs. 270, 283, 284, 285
Benedictine Fathers, 78, 225, 363
Benoit, Rev. Julian, 216, 406, 429–431
Benziger Brothers, xiii
Berille, xxiii
Bernard, Mlle, 83, 91
Bernard, Reverend Mother Mary, 443
Bertaudière, M. Perrault de la, 7, 115
Bessonies, Rev. Aug., 334, 389
Blanc, Rt. Rev. Anthony, Bishop of New Orleans, 72, 163, 199, 205
Bodin, Jeanne-Marie, 260, see Sister Joachim
Bonaparte, 142, see Napoleon
Boston, Archdiocese of, St. Augustine Cemetery in, 95
Bouvier, Rt. Rev. J. B., Bishop of Le Mans, 80, 84, 89, 110, 111; gives permission to the Sisters to leave diocese of Vincennes, 184–185; letter from Bishop de la Hailandière to, 100; letter to Bishop de la Hailandière, 128; letter to Sister Councilors, 186; letters from Mother Theodore to, 81,

445

90, 109, 123, 206, 220, 248, 256, 266, 274, 287, 295, 301, 324; visit of Bishop de St. Palais to, 328; attendance at Council in Rome, 391, 392; death of, 393, burial of, 394
Bowers, John O., 104, *see* Bailly
Bradley, Mrs., 284
Brassier, Thomas, 17, 40, 64
Brétons, 17, 155, 364
Bright, Michael Graham, 295
Brissac, Castle of, 117
Brittany, 2, 6, 75, 225, 442
Brooklyn, 28, 29, 32, 67, 375, 410; Navy Yard, 68; *Tablet, The*, 68
Brothers of Holy Cross, The, 175, 202
Brown, Jane, 173, *see* Sister Anastasie
Bruté, Rt. Rev. S. G., first Bishop of Vincennes, xix, 54, 75, 94, 168, 170, 223, 272
Buchanan, 429, *see* Sisters Agatha, Mary Antoinette, Mary Bernard, St. Felix
Buffalo, 75, 200
Buteux, S. E., Rev. Stanislaus, 56, 59, 60, 63, 65, 93–95
Byerley, Samuel, 28, 29, 31, 32, 40, 62, 68, 91, 105

Calumet, 104
Canal, 34; in Ohio River, 52, 277, 283
Carmelites, xvii, 121, 148
Carroll, Eliza, 240, *see* Sister Seraphine
Cathedral, of Baltimore, 41; Cincinnati, 48; Le Mans, 2; New York, 30; New Orleans, 165; Philadelphia, 36; Séez, 3; Vincennes, 55
Catholic Builders of the Nation, 7
Catholic Encyclopedia, 142, 155
Catholic Historical Review, 24
Cause for beatification and canonization of Mother Theodore Guérin, vii, xiii, 342, 381, 382, 442, 443
Celeste, *see* Sister
Chapelle, S. J., Father, xvii, 391
Charity (Angers), Sisters of, 266; (Emmitsburg), at Baltimore, 39; Cincinnati, 41, 42, 47; Frederick, 42; Philadelphia, 35, 37; Vincennes, xxi,

126, 321; (Nazareth), Sisters of, at Louisville, 48, 49, 126; Vincennes, xxi, 55; (Order of St. Joseph), Sisters of, at New Orleans, 165
Chartier, Rev. Wm., 39, 41, 44, 47–49, 54, 55, 187
Chassé, Rev. J. B., 94, 95, 96, 209, 248, 256, 389, 405, 430
Chateaubriand, 178
Chateaudun, xxi, 179
Chatard, Rt. Rev. F. S., fifth Bishop of Vincennes, 251, 279, (transferred the See to Indianapolis)
Cheminant, 129, *see* Sister Laurence
Chesapeake Bay, 41
Chesterton, 104
Chevcreux, Abbé, 391
Chicago, Diocese of, 126
Chili, 315
Choiselet, M., 126
Choisnet, Mme. Cecile, 331, 371
Cholera at: Cincinnati, 276; Indianapolis, 287; Lafayette, 285; Louisville, 276; Madison, 280, 281; New Orleans, 275, 276; St. Louis, 276; Saint Mary-of-the-Woods, 287; Terre Haute, 287; Vincennes, 279; Washington (Indiana), 287
Church, Log Chapel, Saint Mary-of-the-Woods, 61; St. Augustine's, Fort Wayne, 429; St. Augustine's, New Orleans, 165; St. Joseph's, Terre Haute, 94, 96, 287; St. Mary's (village), 95, 407; St. Peter's, Barclay St., N. Y., 29
Cincinnati, Bishop of, 48; city of, 46, 47; epidemic, 276, 277
Cincinnati, The, sailing ship, 5, 10, 24, 31, 33, 161
Cleophas, Mother Mary, 273
Coffeetown, 94
Coliche, 105
College, St. Gabriel's, Vincennes, 95, 96, 209, 246, 278, 279; Saint Mary-of-the-Woods, ix, 70; St. Mary's, Lebanon, Ky., 75; of Rennes, 72
Columbus, Remains of, 154, 157
Combourg, 251
Conference of St. Vincent de Paul, 131
Connery, 321, *see* Sister Angelina
Consecration of the Diocese to the